LOVE AND LUST,
LAUGHTER
AND
LOSS

Love and Lust, Laughter and Loss:
The Life of
Juliet
"Aunt Peg"
Anderson

Marian Rhys

Cover design by Lisa Yagoda, Corvallis, Oregon and Giovanna Carpentieri, Portland, Oregon.

Interior design and typography by Marian Rhys, Portland, Oregon.

Cover photographs: full-color foreground photo on front cover by Paul Johnson; black-and-white background photo on front cover by David Steinberg; back-cover photo by Frank McGrath. All used with permission.

Family photographs, and excerpts from Juliet's personal writing, ©2010 by Christine Carr Pettit; used with permission.

Published by Marian Rhys, Portland, Oregon.

Printed in the United States of America.
ISBN 978-0-9637672-4-0

Skin Dance

I brush my skin across your chest, arms, back — a
*   butterfly caressing you*

with my skin I inhale your scent — breathe in the
*   dampness of your strong neck*

with my skin against yours, the hairs rising in shivers
*   of delight*

with my skin I trace memories of dreams across your
*   brow — lick the tears on your cheeks.*

with my skin I smell lilac blossoms after the rain

with my skin I taste the early morning breeze across the
*   bed*

a dance of skin on skin — touching, flowing — limbs
*   intertwined — my skin sighs — yours smiles*

with my skin I hear the song your body hums in the
*   pale afternoon light.*

— Juliet Anderson

A Note to Readers

There is no law stating that a reader must start at the beginning of a book and read straight through to the end, without skipping any pages.

Feel free to start with the sections that interest you most, returning to the more mundane parts later, or not at all. No law enforcement officer will show up on your doorstep to arrest you for such an action, nor will you be prosecuted in any court of law.

This writer accepts no responsibility for any lack of reader initiative in this regard.

— Marian Rhys

CONTENTS

LIST OF PHOTOGRAPHS

A FEW CLARIFYING NOTES

Opening chapter: The opening scenario in the first chapter, a "typical" film scene, is a fictional composite, taken from a number of Juliet's films and still photographs. Readers will not find this exact scenario anywhere on film.

"Supplementary" chapters: Three of the chapters in this book are focused more on background material, rather than specifically on Juliet and her life, although they do relate to Juliet. "The Not-So-Golden Age" is a brief history of the pornographic film industry in the United States; "Some Mistakes Are Expensive" tells the story of Juliet's ex-husband Bob Watt's criminal conviction; and "A Gathering of Whores" is primarily a report on the 1997 International Conference on Prostitution held in Van Nuys, California. Readers can, if they wish, skim through these chapters, noting only the references to Juliet, without losing any information critical to her life story.

Dollar amounts / Inflation: Because so much of Juliet's story involves financial transactions, and because inflation has been so rampant during the last hundred years, I have included, in square brackets, most dollar amounts adjusted to 2015 dollars. These figures were calculated based on the federal Bureau of Labor Statistics inflation calculator (http://www.bls.gov/bls/inflation.htm). This will give readers a better idea of the real value of Juliet's income and expenses. Readers in future years will of course have to make further adjustments.

It should also be remembered that inflation is irregular over the various categories of living expenses. Housing, transportation and health care costs have increased more than the general rate of inflation; food, on the other hand, has gone up less. This may be obvious from the numbers, but it should be kept in mind.

Author's work in the sex industry: My primary work in the sex industry has been as a phone-sex operator. I only did three in-person, physical "calls" in my career, all of them doubles with women whom I knew through the sex-worker network. One of these was with Juliet. Also, I never performed sex work "under the table"; I have always reported and paid taxes on my earnings, as did Juliet, so far as I have been able to determine. Many sex workers, though, do work under the table, a strategy that increases one's income up front but may exact a heavy price later in life.

Personal observations/opinions: Any direct comments on character or personality traits of persons other than Juliet herself are Juliet's observations, as expressed in her private writings, and do not necessarily reflect the views of the author. It should also be remembered that Juliet often used her journals to vent her anger and frustration, and that her comments often reveal more about herself than about her subjects.

ACKNOWLEDGMENTS

My first thanks go to Juliet herself, for inspiring me to tell her story, and for writing such prolific journals and letters, and saving them, along with photographs and other memorabilia, for so many years. While I was at first overwhelmed with the amount of material I had to go through, I was amazed over and over again at the details Juliet had saved. Many a time, after I had despaired of finding a missing piece of her story, I stumbled upon exactly the right material —another journal, a newsletter, a postcard, a legal document, a news article, even a photograph—that answered a question or filled in a blank. It was like working on a jigsaw puzzle: coming across an elusive piece just when I was sure it had been lost, and seeing a cohesive picture emerge from the details. The only exception was Juliet's time in Greece, which still has many missing pieces, but even there I found some factual evidence, and enough hints to allow me to reconstruct a plausible sequence of events.

I also thank Juliet for being so honest and vulnerable in her private writings, which I am sure she never intended for anyone else to see. Even after it became clear that she would never write her autobiography, she kept this private material, trusting, perhaps, that it would not fall into antagonistic hands.

I was surprised that, during the two years that passed between Juliet's death and my initial meeting with her sister Chris, no one else stepped forward to write Juliet's biography. That no one did, I count myself fortunate. Perhaps this is the way it was supposed to turn out; perhaps this is the way Juliet would have wanted it. We will never know, of course, but I sometimes wonder if she had any premonition that someone would write her story, or that I would be the one, in those last months of her life, when she was experiencing more frequent illnesses and feeling more miserable more of the time.

I was also surprised when Chris welcomed me into her home and entrusted me with that first box of memorabilia. She said that she felt that she was a fairly good judge of character and that her instincts told her I was trustworthy. For this trust, and for her unfailing help, my second thanks go to her. Chris was invariably friendly and patient, taking time out of her busy life to continue to search for old letters and photographs, and to review my writings—several times in some cases—for factual accuracy. This book would never have come to fruition without her help and support.

Chris's daughter Monica filled in some important details, and her point of view was especially helpful, as she experienced Juliet from a child's perspective as well as an adult's. Juliet's cousin Pam Saunders's assistance was also invaluable, as she shared many amusing anecdotes and insights about Juliet and the family dynamics, as she perceived them. With her vibrant sense of humor and easy-going personality, Pam enjoyed the right balance of closeness to and distance from Juliet: she was able to love her cousin without high expectations or ambiguous entanglements.

Another person I contacted early on in the project was Juliet's ex-husband Bob Watt; he provided me with many details of Juliet's young adult life, identifying people and places in photographs and supplementing her written material with his own recollections. The year I started writing the book was also the year he first came up for parole, and I have shared in his disappointments over the continued refusals. I hope that he will soon be a free man again.

For information about Juliet's life after she entered the sex business, Paul Johnson was the most helpful overall. He is a walking encyclopedia about the porn industry; his life has spanned its beginnings in the 1960s right up to the present day. He also shared much of his personal life as it related to Juliet, and invariably answered my questions promptly and comprehensively. He has allowed me the use of several of his photographs, including the superb full-color picture on the book cover, which so captures Juliet's spirit. He also lent me his copies of several of Juliet's films.

David Steinberg has my gratitude for allowing me to use his wonderful black-and-white photograph of Juliet on the front cover—which inspired part of the title: "Laughter and Loss"—as well as giving me contact information for many critical people in Juliet's life. David seems to know everyone who is anyone in the professional pornography industry, and to keep in touch with them all.

Videographer Graham Hill was also very helpful in the early stages of the project; he kindly sent me copies of his collections of clips from Juliet's films (*Sex is No Act*), giving me my first preview of Juliet's film work. Graham is one of Juliet's most loyal and articulate fans, and he has collected a wealth of information on her professional life.

One of my earliest supporters was my friend Mitch Gould. The format of the opening chapter, "Juliet, Wicked Temptress of the Silver Screen," was his idea, and I thank him not only for the idea but also for re-writing portions of the sex scene in a more vibrant style. His help was also invaluable in other ways: lending me the Sam Steward book as well as a book about privacy rights and copyrights, and coaching me in the use of Adobe Illustrator for touching up the cover design. A Walt Whitman scholar, Mitch also directed me to the Whitman poem, "Truth."

A number of people read drafts of chapters and gave me valuable feedback. The most thorough and useful of these critiques was from my sister Nancy Dollahite, a published writer herself. Nancy also scanned through Juliet's radio scripts and picked out some of the more interesting topics from them. My editor, Tanya Jarvik, thoroughly critiqued the entire manuscript, tightening up the writing and improving its flow and style, making helpful suggestions about organization and content, and finding typos I would never have been able to catch myself.

Two of my colleagues from the Pacific Northwest chapter of the American Society for Indexing, Scott Smiley and Maria Sosnowski, along with my friend and professional indexer Marcia Carlson, gave me valuable feedback on the index. Marcia also introduced me to Tanya, my editor, and the three of us watched several of Juliet's movies together. Their perspectives on Juliet's acting style and personality were extremely helpful. Through a fortuitous chain of events, Marcia also discovered Tom Tilton's connection with Juliet and put me in touch with him.

Annie Sprinkle, one of Juliet's longest-term friends and colleagues, provided me with recollections of Juliet's warmth and vitality—two qualities she and Juliet shared—and also permitted me the use of several of her photographs of Juliet.

Nina Hartley and Karen Summer filled in important details about the production of *Educating Nina*. Howie Gordon (Richard Pacheco) contributed helpful insights about the porn film business in general, both in my phone interview with him and in his memoirs, *Hindsight*. Kay Taylor (Parker) was a wonderful connection as well, not only helping with factual information, but also providing her unique perspective on Juliet; she was one of the few people who knew Juliet both professionally and personally. Both Howie and Kay also kindly critiqued the book and wrote endorsements for it.

Layne Winklebeck and Kat Sunlove, publishers of *Spectator*, also knew Juliet both personally and professionally, and shared useful information from both points of view. Juliet's longtime friend Carolyn Elderberry was extremely helpful in relating her insights about Juliet and in clarifying factual details. Greg Franke, Juliet's hair stylist and friend since 1982, also gave me information and insights, as well as reading and critiquing the final manuscript, and writing an endorsement. Frank McGrath, Juliet's partner for two years during the height of her fame, shared his memories and several photographs, including the one on the back cover. He also recovered Paul Johnson's iconic photograph, which graces the front cover of the book; Paul had misplaced the negative, and some highly technical photographic work was needed to reproduce a usable copy. Tom Tilton, Juliet's first webkeeper and casual friend, filled in some details from Juliet's life in the late 1990s, a time that was difficult to reconstruct because she stopped keeping journals in 1994. Jim Riggs, one of Juliet's companions on her theater and opera outings, provided helpful information about her final years. Finally, several of my own phone-sex clients who were also Juliet fans and/or customers related anecdotes and incidents that gave me a perspective I could never have obtained otherwise.

Maggie Rubenstein, while not able to participate in this project due to circumstances in her own life, gave me her wholehearted support and encouragement. I also honor her as one of the seminal people who brought professionalism and integrity to the sexual liberation movement of the late twentieth century.

Last of all, my thanks to: the unnamed people who helped me contact Nikolas, Juliet's lover in Greece; Nikolas himself for calling me from Greece; the unnamed people in Placerville who helped me research the address of Juliet's house in Pollock Pines; El Dorado Transit for providing me with the means to travel to the house and photograph it without having to get into an infernal automobile; and Bob Dylan for two clever chapter titles.

AUTHOR'S INTRODUCTION

Juliet always stood out in a crowd. Her warmth, high energy and sense of humor filled the living room of the small apartment in Oakland where the Cyprian Guild, our sex-worker support group, was holding its monthly meeting. Juliet was optimistic and ebullient, a vibrant contrast to the group of about half a dozen women and one man, most of whom were at least mildly depressed.

It was the spring of 2002, and the post-9/11 recession had hit the sex-work business hard. Most of us were struggling just to find enough work to hold it together. And there was the usual litany of problems: one of the women had recently been arrested on a working trip to Las Vegas; another had been stiffed for payment by a john who figured he deserved to get it for free.

At that first meeting, I had no idea who Juliet was. She introduced herself simply as an erotic massage therapist who did in-calls, and did not mention her past accomplishments. I'm sure that at least some of the women there already knew her, even though I did not.

She seemed happy, relaxed, self-assured. She brought light and levity into that small room, as we sipped tea, ate cookies and discussed the Dirty Tricks List, the pros and cons of lowering our rates to attract more economically stressed customers, and how to advertise effectively without getting busted.

This was actually the only meeting of the Cyprian Guild that Juliet ever attended, at least during the time I was active in it. She would not travel across the bay to San Francisco for our meetings, and had only come to this one because it was in the East Bay. So I was in luck that day, and I will always be grateful for that, for otherwise I don't know that I would ever have met her.

Actually, I had encountered Juliet briefly about five years earlier, at the March 1997 International Conference on Prostitution in Van Nuys, California, where I attended a panel on sexual healing. She was one of the presenters, but she did not particularly draw my attention at that time, and I did not realize, until I started on her biography, that she had been one of the speakers I had heard.

So it was really on that overcast day in Oakland that I first saw Juliet. She was sixty-three at the time. She wore her gray hair in her signature short swept-back style, was neatly but comfortably

dressed, and had on a moderate amount of make-up—nothing overdone. Lively, with sparkling eyes and a ready smile. Trying to sit still in that small room, but obviously not wanting to.

Juliet loved sex work. You could tell from the way she talked about it. The warmth and enthusiasm in her tone of voice, her energy, her laughter—all bespoke a love of life and of sensuality. She talked about her "tender loving touch" technique and about how she sometimes helped her clients improve their home sex lives.

When the conversation turned to how to get more business, she told us what her current ad read, and had read for years: "Sensuous massage with lovely silver-haired mature lady. Experience my tender loving touch. In-calls only." followed by her phone number. At $160 per visit, she was undercharging for her services, as she did until the day she died.

Our being the two oldest women there gave me an excuse to talk with her after the meeting. She was very approachable, and I was very interested in connecting with her. We chatted, and gave some thought to doing a call together but made no definite plans.

After this initial meeting, I kept up with Juliet irregularly. She never came to another guild meeting. At my urging, she did come to a Christmas party of the guild in 2002, even though it meant making the trip to San Francisco. I still have a photo of that gang, with Juliet in the middle, smiling broadly, her vest open to showcase her lovely breasts.

Starting in 2003, the year I moved to Portland, Oregon, Juliet and I began to keep up with each other more regularly, primarily by phone but occasionally through letters and cards. I liked talking with her on the phone, partly because she had good boundaries around phone conversations, keeping them to about twenty minutes or so: long enough to have a decent conversation without turning it into a marathon session.

Over the next several years, we became somewhat closer friends. She was becoming more isolated, partly because of her health problems and partly because she really had not built a foundation of long-term intimate friends in her life. There were long spells, sometimes six or eight weeks, when I would not hear from her or be able to get hold of her, and then, when we did talk, she would often tell me that she had been very sick.

In 2005, she seemed really energized about writing her auto-biography. I offered to help her, more or less as a ghost writer. Juliet was a good writer, but she could never stay focused on anything for very long. I hoped to be able to keep her organized and on track. Yet she was not able to stick with this project, and I did not push her.

The last time I saw Juliet was in September 2008, on a visit back to the Bay Area. We took that opportunity to do the double session we had first considered six years earlier. The client was one of her regulars and not particularly memorable. Working with Juliet, though, was definitely memorable. It was clear to me that day, as never before, how much she loved sex and sensuality. As we were putting on our makeup together in front of the bathroom mirror, she exclaimed, "Oh, this is going to be so much fun!" like a kid embarking on a long-anticipated trip to summer camp.

Her energy was high during the session, too, and it *was* fun to be with her: bouncing around on that big bed in her pleasant, sunny bedroom, with a woman who was full of life, doing one of the things she loved best. At the same time, Juliet could be very business-like when the occasion called for it. "All right, it's lunch time," she announced to the john as the session was nearing its end. "You have two minutes to come." And then she very efficiently jacked him off.

That bed we romped on was the same one she died in, less than a year and a half later.

I found out about Juliet's passing about three months after she died, from a phone-sex customer. "So Aunt Peg died," he mentioned to me casually, knowing that I had known her. "What?!" I exclaimed, not having been informed by my one remaining connection who usually kept me up to date with the sex-worker grapevine. It dawned on me then that I had not received any humorous emails from her—one of her few remaining regular social activities—for months. By the time I got the news, her memorial service had already long passed.

I felt, after her death, that I needed to follow through on her dream of telling her life story. I was as logical a candidate for that job as anyone. Through her webkeeper, with whom I had been in touch for some years, I was able to contact her sister Chris, although circumstances in both our lives prevented our getting together until April 2012. Chris loaded me up with journals, letters, and photographs, as well as Juliet's passports from 1966 through 1991, and several address books. I took a box full of all this stuff back to Portland with me, and started sorting through it, getting to know this fascinating woman better than I ever had while she was still with us. It has been an amazing journey and a labor of love.

Writing Juliet's story has also provided me the opportunity to offer some of my own insights and commentary, not only on her life, but also on the subculture that she lived in for so many years: the professional sex industry. While I was not as deeply immersed in this subculture as Juliet was, I was an insider in my own way, and I got to know some of the other workers, not just the high-profile crowd but many of the less glamorous players on the sex-work stage. For example, I worked for a while as a professional organizer (someone who helps people clear out their clutter and get better organized) for a woman who ran an escort service (a "madam"), and in the course of this work I met most of her call girls. None of these women, including the madam herself, were particularly sterling characters. Yet I also met some wonderful people in the business—highly intelligent, self-aware, thoughtful, creative people who were truly striving to lead lives of integrity. As nineteenth-century sex worker Nell Kimball once commented, "...some of the best people I ever knew came out of this way of living (some of the worst ones, too.)"[1] Juliet was in some ways representative of this crowd and in other ways different, unique.

Juliet started life as Judith Carr, a name she returned to using after she withdrew from her film career in 1985. In writing about her, I have chosen to refer to her as "Judy" up until the beginning of her porn career, in 1978. Thereafter, she appears as "Juliet," because once she took on that persona, it became who she was, even if she did not always officially, or even informally, use the name.

One of the first things I found out, as I delved into Juliet's papers, was that she liked to enhance the autobiographical stories she told in public, sometimes adding more drama than had actually occurred, or making it appear that she was more in control of the people and events in her life than she really was. She was actually much more human than she let on. At the same time, her life did indeed include

---

[1] Stephen Longstreet, ed. *Nell Kimball: Her Life as an American Madam* (New York: Macmillan. 1970), 285.

plenty of real drama and adventure. She was like many of us, only more so.

I have tried to tell her story with truth and compassion. I hope I have succeeded.

1

Juliet, Wicked Temptress of the Silver Screen

The woman at the window turns and gazes directly into the camera with a knowing, seductive look. "Watch me!" her deep blue eyes seem to command us. She is beautiful: high, wide forehead, gracefully arching eyebrows, strong but finely shaped nose, high cheekbones that bespeak a Nordic ancestry. Her short blonde hair, swept back and upward, flows in soft waves toward the top and back of her head.

There is a lazy warmth to this intimate living room scene: deep rust-orange sofa, dark wood trim, plush gold carpeting. Filmy beige drapes at the large picture windows billow in the soft breeze, framing a view of the blue-green ocean, which sparkles as the mid-afternoon sunlight dances on the water. Far across the wide bay, beyond the whitened buildings marching up the hills of the city and shrouded in the approaching fog, is the ghost of the Golden Gate Bridge.

Juliet's white blouse falls in soft folds over her shoulders. The open neckline tapers down to the cleavage between her breasts, and a little red scarf encircles her neck like a choker. Her long dark blue skirt fits snugly over her hips, but flares out below them, falling to well below her knees. We can barely see her black-tinged see-through stockings and the glossy black stilettos that elevate her already tall frame.

She turns on a wicked smile, her teeth flashing, as the camera pans over to John, the broad-shouldered curly-haired young man lounging on the sofa, his unbuttoned white shirt and tan slacks with unfastened waistband and partly unzipped fly showing the dark brown hair covering his chest and belly. As Juliet turns toward him, she reaches between her breasts and starts to unbutton her blouse.

She takes her time. Her long-fingered hands with their red-painted nails move slowly but deliberately down to her waist, then pull the blouse open to reveal her black lace bra and the soft skin of her midriff. She shrugs each shoulder slightly as she slips it out of the blouse, and lets the white cloth shimmer down to her wrists and off her hands, then drapes it delicately over a chair.

Her gaze now meets John's, boldly. Tilting her head back, she opens her mouth and curves her tongue up to touch her upper lip while she reaches behind her back to unzip the skirt. Lowering her head and pursing her lips, she watches the skirt fall to the floor around her, the whiteness of her pelvis setting off her black lingerie. He, meanwhile, fixates almost in disbelief on her lacy garter belt with its long black straps and the high-cut lacy panties that barely cover her crotch.

With a swift but graceful movement, she picks up the skirt and tosses it over the blouse on the chair. She spreads her long shapely legs as her right hand moves between them, stroking her pussy through the panties, as she gently lolls her head back and slightly to the side, eyes closed and mouth open, the tip of her tongue protruding between her startlingly red lips.

Now the camera finds John, wide-eyed and with an ominous bulge in his slacks. Juliet approaches him, hips swaying as she walks, but she pauses just beyond his reach. He thrusts his hand into his pants. She is slipping each bra strap over her shoulder—first the right, then the left—her firm breasts swaying ever so slightly as each is freed from confinement. She cups her breasts in her hands, then licks her fingers and traces circles around each pink nipple, tugging it erect. At last she unhooks the clasp holding the bra together in front, pulls it open, and, as she straightens her arms behind her, it glides to the floor.

Turning slightly away from John, Juliet lifts one shoulder, and from behind that high vantage, looks coyly down at him. She turns toward him then, placing her right hand on her right shoulder, running it down over her breast, across her chest and belly, down to her crotch, stroking herself between her legs, closing her eyes and pursing her lips, then running her hand back up over the other breast. As she massages both breasts, she studies the man's reaction, moving her gaze voraciously over his partly clothed body.

She turns on her wicked smile again, slips her fingers under the waistband of her panties and pushes them slowly down, her short light brown pubic hair a triangle between the creases of her groin.

She shimmies out of the panties, drops them and steps out of them, one leg at a time, finally tossing them aside with one foot.

As the camera zooms in on her pussy, she spreads her legs, sliding a finger inside her vagina to lubricate it, stroking first her clit, then her vaginal opening. She spreads open the inner lips, strokes and plays with these, folding and unfolding them, running her fingers sometimes between them and sometimes over the outer lips. As the camera pans back to her face, we see her smiles and grimaces of pleasure.

Finally she reaches for her lover, helping him up from the sofa and out of his shirt, then tugging down his pants. As he has arrived at her place commando, his stiff cock springs out the instant the pants clear his crotch. In obvious delight, she grabs it with both hands, gives him a sidelong upward glance, opens her mouth wide and starts sucking him hungrily. She is squatting now, her legs wide apart, dressed only in stockings, garter belt and neck scarf.

"No, don't touch your cock," she admonishes John as he reaches for it. "Let me do it. Just pinch it hard at the base; that will keep you from coming." Her voice, despite her commanding words, is soft and mellifluous. She continues to lick and suck his now steely cock, sometimes running her tongue up and down along the shaft, sometimes flicking it over the bulging head, sometimes taking the cock deep into her capacious mouth, meanwhile circling her head around briskly, moaning with pleasure. Her breasts, with their erect pink nipples, sway slightly as she moves. Sometimes she uses a free hand to stroke her now wide-open pussy or to squeeze or massage one of her breasts or lightly twist a nipple. The red scarf still tied around her neck emphasizes her bright red lips as she flicks her tongue out from between them, then stretches them over John's cock, seeming to almost devour it.

Finally, perhaps sensing that John is about to lose his load, she detaches completely and leads him to lie down on the sofa. She mounts him then, her wide-open legs revealing the slight pinkish brown of her vaginal lips surrounded by the darker pubic hair. She helps guide his stiff ruddy cock into her well-lubricated pussy, and slides down it, taking it deep inside her, gasping with pleasure as he enters her. She rides up and down, slowly at first but then faster, with staccato moaning.

"Can you feel me squeezing your cock?" she asks breathlessly. "You like that?"

Her own excitement is clear, between open-mouthed smiles of immense pleasure and grimaces of intensity. Juliet asks John to grab her ass in both hands as she rides. She leans forward and grips the sofa cushion under his head, as she loses control, tossing her head and uttering cries and moans of pleasure, surfing the orgasmic waves.

Eventually she quiets down, opens her eyes, still panting, and slides off John's cock to kneel on the gold carpet next to him, taking his cock in her slender hand and stroking it rapidly until the white jizz squirts out. In delight, she licks some of it, then dips her fingers in it, rubs some around the edge of her lips, and circles her tongue around her mouth. She licks his cock completely clean, then runs her tongue along John's belly and chest up to his face. Finally, she lies down by his side, limp with relaxation. She starts to laugh. He joins her, and the scene ends, with their heads thrown back together in joyous laughter.

.   .   .   .

From the spring of 1978 through the summer of 1985, Juliet Anderson was one of the icons of the so-called Golden Age of Porn. Entering the business at the then-unheard-of age of thirty-nine, with a minor role in director Alex de Renzy's film *Pretty Peaches*, she went on to star in more than seventy films and loops (twelve-minute films than ran in porn stores, priced at a quarter for each two-minute segment). Before long, she had acquired a group of devoted followers—men from their teens on up, many of them intelligent and well educated, who had the capacity to appreciate truly fine performances. In 1979, in a film in the *Swedish Erotica* series, she developed the character that became her alter ego: Aunt Peg, a lusty older woman who knows her way around and isn't ashamed to show it.

For many young straight men, Juliet was their introduction to sex. For all of her fans, she was a breath of fresh air—not only beautiful and sensuous, but full of life and fun, creative, and with a wicked sense of humor. She had fans from all over the world, and many of them wrote to her. She always signed her return letters "Love and Lust—Juliet."

- I first saw you in a movie when I was about 16... You painted a picture in my mind of what an intelligent, sexy, mature woman should be, and it stays with me today. Thank you for helping to shape me sexually, and for remaining in my dreams!
- I am a true fan of yours since I had the pleasure of seeing you in *Coed Fever*. I also had the extreme pleasure of seeing you perform at the Mitchell Brothers theatre in San Francisco several years ago and came for every show. Or should I say I came at every show.
- I'm probably like thousands of other young men who literally came of age watching you and your wonderful movies. I'm thanking you because in your films you convey just how sexy an independent, classy, mature woman conducts herself. There's nothing sexier than a woman who know what she wants, and goes and gets it.
- I would have to say that the scene with the handyman is my favorite. You look incredibly sexy, but you also give off such an air of class and sophistication, which is rare especially when a woman is performing oral sex!
- My wife and I are both turned on by you. Watching you in action has led us into some hot times... My wife says watching your movies has turned her into a total slut.
- [from Mexico] When I see that scene I feel fire in my brain! When I saw that scene in the cinema too much guys move in his seats. I can assert you the latins are very ardents! Good, Queen of Porno, please write me.
- [from Japan] You are the admiration lady of myself forever. Your activities are a source of inspiration for me. I will cheer you all the time and forever.
- [from a woman] I just wanted to say thank you for being a role model for me, and proving that "older" women can be just as hot as or hotter than those younger folks.

Juliet Anderson died in her sleep sometime during the night of the 10th to the 11th of January 2010. She was seventy-one years old.

The following weekend, her sister Chris, along with her daughter, Juliet's niece Monica, arrived to collect her belongings and clean out her Berkeley apartment. As they stood at the door, looking around the room, saddled with grief, it seemed as though Juliet had just stepped out and would be returning soon. A bowl of grapes sat on the kitchen counter, the cats were curled up waiting for some snuggles, her voice mailbox was blinking '22', there were post-it notes everywhere reminding her of various things, and her table was covered with half-written letters and things to attend to.

"What happened?" Chris and Monica wondered, still not able to fully grasp the fact that this energetic woman, so full of joy and determination, would never again be a part of their lives.

"My aunt," Monica writes, "was, as we all know, like no one [else] on this planet. She lived life on her terms and fought for her right to do whatever the hell she wanted. She was kind, passionate, a free spirit.

"Though I took a more conventional life path with a husband, kids, dogs, cats, fish, etc., my aunt always inspired me to be true to myself. [When I was] a young woman she taught me life lessons I [would] carry with me always: how to be a Wild Woman, how to apply make-up so I don't look like a trollop, how not to use products on my face with mineral oil (oh the horror!), how when applying face lotion to always pat or move in the 'up' direction to prevent wrinkles, and how it is humanly possible to love someone and not like them at the same time."

Juliet had long wanted to write her autobiography. But with her increasing memory lapses ("I suffer from CRS disorder," she often joked. "Can't remember shit.") and her inability to persist in long-term tasks, that project never got further than an outline and short proposal, found among the papers she left behind.

"I have led a life of creativity and adventure," she wrote, "overcoming serious childhood illnesses, social stigma and other limitations to become, in the late 1970s, an internationally recognized name in the sex industry... I am a personification of the American Dream, overcoming difficulties, blazing my own trail and achieving world renown on the strength of my talents, creativity and perseverance. My story is not just about the sex business but also one of personal struggle and a history of the changing times and diverse cultures in which I have lived."

Her erstwhile co-star Richard Pacheco said of her, "Juliet brought a European sensibility to the sex business. She was a woman among girls. It was fun to watch her because *she* was having fun. She came alive for you."

"Juliet was at home in front of the camera," her longtime friend, erotic photographer Paul Johnson adds. "She could get in front of a camera and turn it on for you."

"Whether billed as Juliet Anderson or her often-used screen persona Aunt Peg," wrote her fan, videographer Graham Hill, "with her short, swept-back blonde hair and her trademark black stockings, garter belt and neck scarf, Juliet was the most seductive, teasing temptress to ever grace the adult screen."

Yes, Juliet was one of a kind. She brought her love of sex, sensuality and life itself to a business that, even during its "golden age," was for the most part sordid and peopled with shiftless opportunists and organized crime moguls. She was a misfit in that world—too principled, too ebullient, too trusting in some ways, which is perhaps why she ultimately had to withdraw from it, seeking other avenues to express her love of life and other ways to share her sensuality with those adventurous enough to seek her out. Tragically, along with that joyousness, pain and suffering, both physical and emotional, followed her all of her days.

This book is the story of that remarkable life. It is *not* the memoir that Juliet left unfinished, for no one can write that now. Yet much of the story is in her own words, drawn from her voluminous although intermittent journals and other creative writings, and from letters both from and to her. It is also the story of her life as seen from the vantage point of those who knew her best, a story that informs and is informed by the history of the times and the cultures in which she lived and loved, and of her part in some of that history.

2
Love, Laughter, and Loss: Growing Up

Judith Cathleen Carr, the first child of Dorothy and Fred Carr, was born on 23 July 1938[2], in Palmdale, California. At the time of Judy's birth, the Carrs were living in a small house behind Fred's parents' home. Fred made his living as a jazz trumpeter in the Pinky Tomlin Band, and his income was somewhat irregular, as were his working hours and locations. Gigs included providing entertainment in the casino on Catalina Island, and on the ferry boats to and from the island. Other engagements took Fred even farther afield, traveling to distant cities by train, with Dorothy and toddler Judy often along for the ride. This traveling lifestyle was part of Judy's first experience of the world, and may have contributed to her later tolerance (and perhaps even craving) for irregularity and frequent changes of scenery.

In those days, people dressed up for travel, and Dorothy spared no effort to make both herself and her daughter presentable: picture a petite, vivacious young woman, her rich auburn tresses stylishly coifed, wearing a smartly tailored dress designed to show off her ample bosom and curvy legs, accompanied by her blonde, blue-eyed doll-child arrayed in a frilly dress, ruffled socks and patent leather shoes. Judy was cooed over, and offered sweets and treats by bored adult passengers.

On a particularly memorable trip to New Orleans in 1941—a three-day journey that must have seemed interminable to a three-year-old—Judy was getting cantankerous and unmanageable in their small train compartment, and Dorothy's nerves were beginning to fray. To their rescue came the Pullman porter, resplendent in his blue uniform with brass buttons and gold braided shoulder epaulets, bearing a special gift: a pair of handmade Raggedy Ann and Raggedy Andy dolls. The little girl, overawed both by this imposing

---

[2] Juliet variously listed herself, later, as either a double Leo, moon in Gemini; or a Leo, Gemini rising, moon in Cancer.

personage and by his show of kindness, could only manage a whispered "thank you" as she clutched these treasures to her heart.

Judy, not quite two years old, with her mother, on a trip to St. Louis, Missouri, 1940. Photo: Carr/Pettit family collection.

Upon their arrival in New Orleans the special attention continued, as they joined up with the other band members, all of them male. After the gig, the musicians gathered at their shabby hotel for late-night drinks and poker games in the Carrs' room, where the decrepit bed sagged so much that Dorothy decided to remove the blankets and put them into the sturdier bathtub as a bed for Judy. As little Judy lay there drifting in and out of sleep to the sound of tipsy laughter and clinking ice cubes, one of the musicians came in to use the toilet, and couldn't keep his hands off the pretty toddler. So soft and innocent, compared to his usual fare, the hardened whores dragging along the deserted streets. The little girl's thighs and butt felt so good against his hardening cock. He must have wondered why his picking her up hadn't awakened her.[3]

Judy was not really asleep, however, only responding as many molested children do, partly paralyzed with fear and partly hoping that "If I don't respond, maybe he'll stop and leave me alone." That

_____

[3] These speculations about what the molester was feeling are entirely Juliet's conjectures, as recorded in her later journals.

technique never works, of course, but a child has few options in the situation. Even after the incident, there was no point in telling anyone about it. As young as she was at the time, Judy assumed that all adults, including her parents, knew about and approved of everything that went on. No need to speak of it, then; she was too ashamed, anyway. She simply endured it and hoped it would not last long or happen again. Yet... to be safe, she had to be on guard. Always. That necessity leads one to hyper-vigilance and bestows an ability to "read" people. Helpful survival skills but often leading to an inability to access genuine intimacy, qualities that Juliet demonstrated throughout her life.[4]

Judy at age one and a half, and three. Photos: Carr/Pettit family collection.

From these early experiences in the entertainment world, Judy came to understand both the ego boost and the pitfalls inherent in getting lots of attention. Writing later in *Women of the Light*, she publicly mentioned only the up side: "I was a born ham, ... singing and dancing—a natural performer." Yet, along with the dangers of being exposed to a seamier side of life, another down side of her parents' lifestyle was that Judy developed an overblown sense of her

---

[4] How much influence this incident had on Judy's later decision to enter the sex business is debatable. Most likely it was one of the influences in that decision, but certainly not the only one. While there is a correlation between childhood sexual abuse and adult sex work, the relationship is (in the terminology of Aristotelian logic) neither necessary nor sufficient.

own importance and had her natural dramatic tendencies reinforced, leading to major crashes whenever real life caught up with her.

The next trauma in Judy's life, and one from which she did not recover for decades, was the birth of her sister Christine in 1942. Not only did Chris's arrival signal the end of Judy's monopoly on her parents' attention, but it also brought an end to traveling along on the band's gigs, and to Judy's special place as the "band baby."

Judy's resentment knew no bounds. One day, as Chris lay gurgling in the baby buggy, their mother in the kitchen fixing lunch, Judy took the pillow from under the baby's head and pressed it over her face, determined to stifle this little usurper. Fortunately, like all parents, Dorothy knew that sudden silence between the children spelled trouble. "Judy," she called, "What are you doing? Why is Chris so quiet?" Judy, struck by fear and guilt, slunk under the sofa, flinging the pillow away in hatred and knocking over a floor lamp, as her mother rushed into the room, the rapid tapping of her high heels against the linoleum floor signaling her trepidation. Judy forced herself to put on her sweet face, as baby Chris choked and then howled, gasping for breath.

Judy at age four with her father. Note on back of picture reads: "She does love for him to play with her, and he does, all his spare moments." Photo: Carr/Pettit family collection.

"Judy, have you been teasing your little sister?"

"I'm sorry, Mommy, I was just playing pillow games. Want me to walk Chris around the block in the buggy, and maybe she'll stop crying?"

"Good idea, Judy. Just around the block. When you get back, I'll have lunch ready. Your favorite, peanut butter and banana sandwiches."

A close call for both Judy and Chris. Judy couldn't suffocate her rival on a public street.

Realizing the futility of such direct tactics, Judy soon developed other methods of regaining attention. Throwing temper tantrums was one; another was being sick. One evening, as her parents prepared to go out, five-year-old Judy was ill, doubled up on the living room couch, moaning in pain, legs aching, face flushed with fever, while her parents hovered over her, their faces strained with worry, anxious yet also irritated that, as Judy later described it, "again their cherished darling was sick and they couldn't go out that evening. The pain made me breathless and yet I secretly enjoyed their doting. Yes, I'd get even with them for her—that smiling happy baby I'm told was my sister. How dare they take me from the center of their universe! Age five was the fatal year when I learned to use sickness to get attention."

When not engaging in high drama, though, Judy led a fairly conventional life, for the Carr family was in many ways a typical American family of the 1940s and 1950s, upwardly mobile, taking advantage of the postwar prosperity that lifted many white Americans out of the working class and solidly into the middle class. After Chris was born, Dorothy worked at various secretarial jobs to help support the family, and in 1947 they were able to afford a house of their own, in one of the ubiquitous new post-World-War-II developments, in Burbank, California. The area was still transitioning from orange groves to suburbia, and the neighborhood was quiet and well-kept, with newly planted trees, and nearby parks and schools. The Carr house, like others in the neighborhood, was a boxy pastel stucco affair, with a garage and small front and back yards, the latter containing that then-essential commodity, a clothesline. The girls had a pet rat named Josie, whom they trained to run along the top of this clothesline, to their immense entertainment. It was here in this new neighborhood that Judy found a best friend—Gail Heisler, a girl who lived across the street; they remained close for many decades.

In 1948, about a year after the move to Burbank, a tragedy befell the young family. A younger brother arrived, but was stillborn. Unnamed, he was buried quietly at Forest Lawn Cemetery. Although little was spoken about this event in the Carr household, it did leave its mark on the girls as well as on their parents, as Juliet mentioned it many years later in a list of significant losses in her life.

Putting this sad event behind them as much as possible, the Carrs continued to settle into their new environment. Dorothy loved gardening, and planted rose bushes and sweet peas that trailed over trellises. Perhaps nourishing and tending the plants provided her some catharsis in dealing with the loss of her son. She was a hard worker inside the house as well, sewing most of the children's clothes, and making meals from scratch. In those days when cooking was more labor-intensive, Judy and Chris helped with tedious tasks like shelling peas, stringing beans, and cracking walnuts, and learned to sew their own clothes as they grew older. The girls took to these domestic arts with at least willingness if not enthusiasm. Judy always loved to cook (and eat!), and she later put her dressmaking skills to work as a costumer designer in college, as well as in her porn career (yes, porn actors do wear costumes, if only to take them off).

The house in Burbank, where Judy spent the second half of her childhood.
Photo: Carr / Pettit family collection.

Much of this domestic work was done to save money—never a plentiful commodity in the Carr household. Dorothy even made laundry soap by hand, pouring saved bacon grease into a large porcelain basin, stirring in lye, and mixing it with a large metal spoon, then scraping the thick mixture into a shallow pan and setting it onto the back porch to cool for a week, finally cutting it up into rectangles she set out to dry in the driveway.

As Judy grew older, she felt deprived by this frugal lifestyle. She longed for store-bought clothes, but it was not until she was in college, out on her own, that she could acquire these treasures. She made up for this lost time, though, and throughout her life, buying new clothes was a comfort activity for her, whether she could afford them or not.

By the time Chris was past toddlerhood, the personalities of the four family members were clear, and the family dynamics established. Tall, slender Fred was quiet and artistic, preferring to withdraw from conflicts. Dorothy was a contrast to her husband in many ways: petite and lively, with a stronger personality; she was the glue that held the family together. Judy was the family trouble-maker, the identified problem, strong-willed like her mother; the two developed conflicts as Judy grew older. Judy was always more drawn to her father, and his quiet warmth was a calming influence. Chris was the family peacemaker. "I always try to look for the good in everything," she told Juliet many years later. Her amiable and easy-going nature often gained Chris more positive attention from adults, and later from boys, adding to Judy's resentment.

Still, this blend of personalities allowed the family system to bumble along as well as any other, and, aside from Judy's ongoing jealousy of Chris, the Carrs were generally warm, loving and demonstrative, free in expressing physical affection for each other. One form this expression took, at least among Dorothy, Judy and Chris, was scratching each other's backs, or running their fingers lightly over them—a technique Juliet used later as part of her "Tender Loving Touch" services.

As for the more delicate subject of sex education, the Carr family was probably about average in its approach. Judy, like most children lacking an opposite-sex sibling, was not aware of anatomical differences between the sexes until well past pre-school age. She wrote later about her first glimpse of a penis—catching sight of a neighbor man urinating—although whether this was at the Carr house or the neighbor's is not certain. Neither did Juliet elaborate, in her recollections, on whom she approached with her questions—whether it was her parents, the neighbor (not likely) or someone else. (That

Juliet identified this incident as her introduction to male anatomy, rather than the molestation she experienced at age three, does not discredit the latter story. The molester may well not have exposed himself to her, limiting his activities to fondling her, and she may have suppressed the memory of the molestation throughout the rest of her childhood, recalling it only later, in the safety of middle age.)

Judy at age ten (left) and twelve (right, with Chris, aged eight). Even at this young age, Judy knew how to pose for the camera. Photo: Carr/Pettit family collection.

It is not clear at exactly what age Judy experienced her third major life trauma—being diagnosed with childhood arthritis. She sometimes mentioned being as young as four or five; other times, she put her age at ten. Whenever it happened, though, it was severe enough to require hospitalization, and she was sent to Children's Hospital in Hollywood. She returned there several times, into her high-school years, sometimes under emergency circumstances, being transported by ambulance. These hospital experiences and their aftermath had a profound effect on Judy; indeed, they constituted the signature events of her early life, even more than the early molestation or her jealousy of Chris.

In those days, when medical technology was just beginning to develop into a highly sophisticated science, meeting patients' psychological needs was not high on the agenda. While there were no doubt kind and caring nurses and doctors, children were given virtually no information about what was going on, or told what discomfort or benefits they could expect from medical procedures, it being assumed that such information was beyond their capacity to grasp, or, worse, that they might panic and resist, requiring restraint. Parents were not allowed to stay with their children, the environment was cold and sterile, and cases were discussed in front of patients as if they were not even present, treating them as if they were objects rather than persons. Indeed, in *Women of the Light*, Juliet related her experience of hearing the doctors discuss her potential fate as a lifelong invalid.

Given this stressful environment, many children, Judy included, suffered what amounted to emotional abandonment, albeit unintended. Hospitalization was frightening indeed for a child, who had no way of knowing what to expect or how long she would be there. This lack of information required her to be constantly on alert for the worst. She never knew who was going to come into her room, when, or what they were going to do to her. The consequent feelings of helpless rage had a profound influence on Judy's emotional health, leading to a lifelong compulsion to be in control—of her own body, her environment, and other people.

Reflecting on her hospital experiences in her journals many years later, she wrote about her ordeals:

> Wheeling me down a long green corridor strapped to a gurney, too-bright lights burning my eyes, shrieking. Their incandescent probe beyond my closed lids, the smells of death, antiseptic and fear surround me, pulling on my clammy skin. We stop. I open my eyes to instruments of torture—tubes, needles, machines being clamped, rammed, stabbed onto, into me by alien creatures shrouded in white ceremonial gowns, only eyes leering at their sacrificial victim.
>
> A huge blinding overhead disk exposes my every pore, nerves, probing all my secret places; lights, the alter with unholy light. I can't move. I struggle, [but] no escape, mouth held open, tube jammed down my throat, the whirr of a suction, the bottle at my right side fills with blood, the bottle at my left drains into my skinny outstretched arm strapped onto a board,

needle in vein at inside elbow. I can't breathe, I can't
swallow, I'm going to die. I don't care, I want to go
away to someplace quiet, peaceful, with soft light and
soft people, to be held, caressed and listened to, to tell
someone how much my heart hurts, my body aches,
how sad and scared I am, someplace where it's OK to
be a scared little girl, not have to pretend 'everything is
fine.' No one tells me the truth. I want a place where I
can run and skip thru the grass in the sun, play with
animals, play games with my friends, where I belong,
am not a crippled outcast, where love is not enough,
truth and compassion keep love real and honest. Not
one doc or nurse treated me like a human, only a body,
a machine that malfunctioned and needed repair; not
one caring stroke or hand held, no soft voice in my ear
to relieve my terror. Monsters in white stalking the
corridors, seeking victims to experiment on, practice.
Knowledge they've crammed into their heads is
straining to be unleashed thru their hands, beasts who
have lost touch with their hearts, their humanity,
whose insensitivity dooms one small blood-streaked
blond-haired girl to a lifetime of demons to haunt her
[for] 40 years, to forgive them their brutality yet
bearing scars that will never heal.

   Poor, lonely, scared little Judy, asking 'What have
I done to deserve such pain? Why am I being
punished? I must be bad... if I'm bad I'm unlovable... if
I'm unlovable, my family will abandon me (withhold
love).'

The physical intrusions Judy suffered in the hospital had their
effect on her as well. Sometimes they triggered the feelings, if not the
memory, of her earlier molestation. When she was old enough to
start keeping a diary, she started repeatedly drawing pictures of
hands pulling down panties on a female body.

Whatever trauma Judy may have suffered during this hospitalization, though, there was an up side to it as well. Whether triggered
by anger at being degraded or simply because of her naturally strong
will and independent mind, Judy rejected the doctors' assessment of
her as a potential invalid and became determined to prove them
wrong. This may have been the beginning of her awareness that she
needed to define her own path in life, to step outside the accepted

norms and draw on her inner strength to survive. Her illnesses became both a nemesis and a catalyst.

In the meantime, however, there were crosses to bear. The cortisone shots she was given to treat the arthritis made her bloated and gave her an appearance of being overweight, and she had to wear ugly corrective shoes, which she hated and which made her gait awkward. Judy suffered teasing and isolation from her peers, and developed a self-image as an ugly duckling and an outcast. Her illnesses also kept her out of school for extended periods, and at times she was hospitalized again for tests and surgeries. She described the years from age ten to eighteen as a time of "constant, often excruciating pain."

The low self esteem she felt during these years no doubt contributed as well to her compulsive need, later in life, to prove her attractiveness, long after the period of "ugliness" had in fact passed. It also ratcheted up her jealousy of Chris, who was perfectly healthy and had no such trauma to deal with.

Not that Judy was an easy-going or friendly child, even under the best of circumstances. She was self-absorbed, given to temper tantrums and drama. And her illnesses gave her an opportunity to draw attention to herself, exaggerate her problems, and manipulate people. Sometimes it was hard to tell when her ailments were real and when they were an act she put on to gain sympathy.

Illness was a double-edged sword for Judy, and it was not until middle age that she began to acknowledge it and deal with it without letting it take over her life. It is surprising that Juliet, unlike many people who suffer chronic pain, actually lived in her body, rather than shutting down and numbing out. Indeed, her capacity to be alive in her body was one of her most defining characteristics, one of the things that made her unique in a culture in which very few people are truly in touch with their bodies. And it was this very capacity that ultimately became her real gift to the world.

In between these traumatic hospital stays, Judy led as normal a life as she could. A quick study, she managed to keep up with her school work enough to stay caught up with her classmates, even though she felt like a social outcast. And her family, despite Judy's fears of rejection and abandonment in the hospital, did stand by her. Dorothy worked hard for her children, loving them fiercely, and Fred was tender and loving despite his shyness. Judy identified more with him than with her mother because she shared his passion for art and creativity, even while she had inherited her mother's strong-minded personality.

The family spent much of their leisure time together, playing cards, board games (including chess), and ping pong (they had a table set up in the garage), and taking vacations around California. Like all children, Judy and Chris loved drama, whether listening to cliff-hanging radio serials or putting on short skits of their own creation, charging five or ten cents to whomever they could induce to attend. Judy even started a drama club that met in her backyard. With her active imagination, in fact, everyday life was sometimes a drama for her. In their first house, the bed she and Chris shared was a high old-fashioned one, and Judy fantasized each night that she was a princess climbing onto her throne.

Living in Burbank, the Carrs could hardly fail to be aware of the presence of the professional film industry, and at one point, when she was eleven, Judy somehow managed to get the opportunity to do a screen test, the first step toward a professional acting career. She was thrilled, of course, but her parents were appalled, and would not permit her to go through with it. Judy was devastated, beset with the same feelings of helpless rage that her hospital experiences had evoked. Powerful and malevolent authority figures were again in control—not just of her body, but of her dreams, her identity, her very essence. She must reach out to grasp this opportunity, whatever it took. Running away from home seemed her only option. One night, after she was sure Chris was asleep, she packed her things, including a little food and her medications, and dressed, carefully selecting her clothes even at that age: grey slacks, blue blouse, wool sweater. She would live on the hill behind the film studio, sneaking into it at night to pilfer food.

She fantasized about how distraught her parents would be when they discovered her absence, how even Chris would miss her. Served her right, though, for not taking Judy's side and advocating for her. Ultimately, Judy's courage failed her and she undressed and went back to bed. She never got over the devastation of being deprived of this momentous opportunity, though, mentioning it often in her later writings, both public and private.

I Long to See My Mother

*I long to see my mother in the doorway, bringing
homemade soup and bread to my sickbed, her auburn
hair curled around her face, her print dress crisp and
neat.*

*I long to see my mother in the doorway, hugging my
father, kissing and laughing together, he lifting her off
the floor, the rich aroma of roast beef hash filling the
kitchen.*

*I long to see my mother in the doorway, holding a rare
invitation to a party, excited that she would be able to
escape the prison of housework, needy, passive
husband and a demanding, sick child, escape for a few
hours of glamour of drinks and cigarettes with her old
sorority friends.*

*I long to see my mother hanging sheets, clean, wet,
fresh, on the clothesline, billowing in the breeze.*

*I long to see my mother standing over my bed, tucking
me in with a kiss, saying "Don't let the bed bugs bite."*

-- Juliet Carr

Life went on, however, and Judy alleviated her pain with the
family warmth that did exist. Music was of course an everyday
presence in the house, and the girls sometimes sang in harmony
while they washed and dried the dishes together. Family friends and
neighbors commented that they sounded like the Andrews Sisters, a
popular singing group of the 1950s. Laughter often filled the house,

too, as both Fred and Dorothy had a great sense of humor. Joking and cutting up were a frequent part of family interactions.

Dinner was always a sit-down affair at the dining table, a time for the family to gather together after the activities of the day. Holidays were a big deal, too, with Christmas caroling and decorating the house, and Dorothy sewed the girls' Easter dresses and Halloween costumes, the girls assisting as they got older. While sports and outdoor activities were not high on their priority list, Fred encouraged the family to keep physically active. He had played football in high school, and he loved tennis. He taught both the girls to play, although neither took to it as passionately as he did. Judy and Chris also wandered far and wide through their Burbank neighborhood, hiking the nearby hills and playing the usual childhood games. Neighborhoods were safer back then, and Judy and Chris would stay out late in the summer evenings, until they heard their mother whistle for them to come home. Sometimes, on warm summer nights, they camped out in the backyard, making a tent out of sheets hung on the clothesline. They slept under the stars, the subtle scent of orange blossoms from the nearby groves drifting over them.

Extended family also played an important role in the Carrs' lives, although while Fred's mother lived, their relationship to the paternal grandparents was more formal than affectionate. After she died, however (about the same time as the Carrs' move to Burbank), his father, known to the girls as Grandpa Carr, took the initiative to develop a somewhat closer relationship with the family. He would come over a couple of times a month and take them out to dinner, usually at the Pump House in Burbank, and helped them out in other small ways. Judy mentioned staying with him briefly during a college vacation.

The Carrs maintained closer ties to the maternal grandparents, Clarence and Grace Skeen, as well as to Dorothy's sister Barbara and her brother Lynn. Grace was a warm, outgoing person, fun to be around and much loved. The Skeens owned a cabin in Wrightwood, in the San Gabriel Mountains northwest of San Bernadino, and the Carrs spent time there almost every summer, along with Aunt Barbara and Uncle Bob and their children Pam, Andy and Dan. Although Pam was ten years Judy's junior, she greatly admired her, and years later was intrigued by Judy's sex-work career; the cousins remained close for the rest of Judy's life.

Other vacation spots included Palm Springs, Warner Hot Springs, and Yosemite National Park. Although Fred Carr disliked the mountains himself, he felt that it was a good environment for the children, and they made three family trips there, staying in cabins at Camp Curry; Judy and Chris bicycled around Yosemite Valley and hiked some of the nearby trails.

Sometimes the family went south to Venice, where they would stay in a cottage-style motel and spend long days on Venice Beach, known at that time as Muscle Beach, where attractive young men hung out, surfed, and generally showed off. (It obviously also functioned as a gay male pick-up place, although that activity was more discreet back then than it is now.)

When the girls were older, the family starting taking trips to Las Vegas. Fred liked to play keno, Dorothy, craps. Judy and Chris hung out at the motel pool, or wandered down the streets on the strip, window shopping. While this venue was a reflection of the family's moving up in the world, 1950s Las Vegas was not the flashy tourist trap that it now is; it was a place a normal middle-class family might go for a little more excitement than, say, camping. A city vacation rather than a rural one.

Contrary to Juliet's claims that her family was non-religious, they were in fact reasonably active in the Presbyterian church, attending services regularly, with the girls staying on for Sunday school while their parents returned home (probably to have some private time together). Judy was more drawn to religion than were either her parents or Chris, especially as she grew into her teens. She became deeply involved in the church, singing in the choir, helping teach Sunday School and participating in the youth group, and at age sixteen she chose to be baptized. Like many young people, Judy may have been drawn to the drama and intensity of religion, as well as to the opportunity it offered to begin separating from her family, to form social bonds of her own choosing. She stuck with it for some time, continuing her church-going into her college years and her early married life.

As Judy grew into adolescence her bouts of illness lessened and she was able to attend school regularly enough to excel in her schoolwork. She loved art, and surprisingly, one of her favorite subjects was Latin—at that time an absolute requirement for college entrance. She began to overcome some of her social awkwardness, as she realized that she was developing into an attractive young woman. Leaving high school early one day to go to a medical appointment, she heard an appreciative whistle as she passed by a classroom window. Later, running for queen of the Latin Banquet, she was savvy enough to realize that she had all the boys' votes because she was prettier than her rival, and she managed to tip the balance enough to win by cheating, voting for herself twice. This was Judy's first real social recognition, and she took the opportunity to revel in the attention and power it briefly gave her. She and her king led the formal procession to the "palace" (the impressively decorated school cafeteria), accompanied by their slaves. Mounting the dais, they took their places reclining on their "regal couches" (iron bedsteads from the nurse's office), where they were hand-fed fresh fruit and fanned by the obsequious slaves: "... a moment of glory," Judy reflected years later. "[I am] still remembering the power of a lie." Feeling guilty but not regretful.

This realization that she could use her physical beauty to get what she wanted was Judy's first awakening to the power of sexuality, and it led her in a new direction. On family vacations, her activities now began to include looking for male attention. Visits to the Skeens' cabin included walks to the lake, where teenagers hung out and hooked up. Chris, more easy-going and confident than Judy, was usually more successful in these pursuits, adding to Judy's jealously.

Judy did find her first true love, however, during a trip to Yosemite, where she met Jerry Stamm. They kept in touch for several years, although he lived in Santa Rosa. She carried a torch for him into her college years, even after their correspondence had ended.

Judy graduated from Burbank High School, with honors, in June 1956, just before she turned eighteen. She then worked for a year as an information operator with the phone company (probably Pacific Bell) to earn money for college. She entered Long Beach State College in the fall of 1957, planning to major in art.

Around the same time as Judy's graduation from high school, both the world and the Carr family began to change in significant ways. In the early years of the Carrs' residency in Burbank, it was still possible to climb the hills east of town and look out over the orange groves and observe the gradual shift from agricultural to residential development. It was when the smog became so thick that it blocked this view that the Carrs decided it was time to move.

Family finances were becoming more stressed, too. The big band era had faded away, replaced by rock-and-roll and more recorded music, and it was no longer possible for Fred Carr to support the family on a musician's income, even with Dorothy's supplemental wages. Judy's illnesses had stressed the family finances as well, for there was no such thing as health insurance in the United States at that time. The high medical expenses prevented Fred and Dorothy from building any substantial savings, even with their two (albeit modest) incomes. Clearly, something needed to change. Fred first took a job managing a Standard Oil gas station, but he hated the work, and after about a year he and Dorothy decided to buy a franchise doughnut shop, Heavenly Donuts.

The family sold the Burbank house and lived for a short time in an apartment in Burbank, so that Chris could finish out the school year, then moved to an apartment in Lynwood, a suburb of Los Angeles near Compton—a run-down area even then. There, Fred and Dorothy attended a training program and started operating the doughnut shop in Huntington Park. Both Judy and Chris helped out in the shop after school, until Judy left for college that fall. In 1958 the Carrs took over an independent doughnut shop in San Diego, renaming it "Dottie's Donut House." Chris finished high school in San Diego, and Fred and Dorothy continued to live there for many more years, although always in rented housing; they never owned a house again.

It was during their time in Lynwood that Judy experienced her first attack of Crohn's disease, an inflammatory bowel disorder. She had come home from college for a few days to stay with Chris while their parents took a short vacation to Las Vegas. Fifteen-year-old Chris had to call an ambulance (this was before the advent of the 9-1-1 system, and was generally done by calling the telephone operator and asking for the hospital). With Judy's tendency for drama, Chris was not even sure at first whether Judy was faking it, but it was a scary incident for both girls. Thankfully, though, Judy was transported to the hospital and stabilized. This was the beginning of her awareness that she had not one, but two serious diseases, neither curable. It must have been a daunting blow at a time when life seemed to be just taking off for her.

Although the family finances stabilized with the acquisition of the doughnut business, the stress of running the business started to wear on Dorothy, and she began a long battle with alcoholism. While there had always been a lot of social drinking in the Carr home— beer at first, then cocktails when finances improved—it had been kept to an acceptable level. Now, though, Dorothy would start drinking as soon as she got home from work, and continue until bedtime.

Alcohol seemed to act as somewhat of a social lubricant for Dorothy, who was actually a rather retiring person when sober; she could become lively with a few drinks. Her drinking may also have been a form of self-medication, as she was eventually diagnosed as bipolar.

Dorothy's alcoholism was a disruption to the family for many years; it was behind Chris's decision to get away from home as soon as possible; she got a job and an apartment of her own right after graduating from high school. Judy, thankfully, had already escaped to college before Dorothy's alcoholism manifested itself, although it affected Judy's relationship with her family for years to come.

In the fall of 1957, though, Judy was simply glad to get away from this turmoil and start building a life of her own.

3
Sex 101

It was upon entering Long Beach State College that Judy began to separate from her family and try her own wings. Her freshman and sophomore years were times of self discovery—what intrigued her, what inspired her, what put her off—years of exploration, but also of confusion. Most of all, these early adult years were Judy's awakening to sexuality—its excitement, its power, its promise of a magical world beyond pain and sorrow.

Although she claimed, in later writings and interviews, to have been too busy for much social life in college, her diary from 1958 shows otherwise. While the year seems to have begun badly—her only diary entry for January 1 (Happy New Year!) reads "*WHAT IS SO HAPPY ABOUT IT?*"—she made up for this unhappy start as the year went on. Beautiful, lively and outgoing, Judy attracted attention from many young men, and spent a great deal of her free time attending parties, including a few all-nighters, as well as going out to restaurants, movies and concerts. She also took two trips during this year, both in February: one to go skiing in Snow Valley with one of her boyfriends, and another, with two girlfriends, north to the Monterey Bay.

Judy started the school year living at home with her parents in Lynwood, but in early March 1958 she moved in with some family friends, the Briggs, and this change seemed to help stabilize her a little, as Mrs. Briggs was a motherly type who provided some much-needed nurturing. In mid-June Judy moved back to her parents' house for the summer. Then, in September, she and her friend Sheila secured an apartment half a block from the beach, in Belmont Shore, a sort of bohemian area of Long Beach.

Unlike most college students in those days, Judy owned a car, and was therefore able to get around to many more places than most of her friends could; in fact, she often provided transportation for her car-less friends.

Judy was in many ways a typical young woman of the fifties: focused on clothes, makeup, partying, and cavorting with young men, but also determined to be a "good girl" and not "go all the way." Only a slut would have done such a thing in those days, and Judy saw herself as a respectable woman, even if she did long to be a free spirit.

Judy did not, however, feel drawn to the Beat subculture. Her one foray into that underworld was a party she attended on Long Beach's Naples Island in October: "I really dressed up and played the part, complete with black stockings, no lipstick, etc." But that was enough. It was a game, an act; amusing but not a serious lifestyle choice.

Presumably, Judy spent some time and energy studying, because she was able to remain in school, but her primary activities seemed to be partying and pursuing men. These activities were the focus of her 1958 diary entries, at any rate. By one young man after another, she was swept off her feet. Although these activities were limited to kissing and heavy petting, with apparently only one exception, it did not take much to convince Judy that she was in love, which at that time in her life she saw as a prerequisite to being sexual with a man. It is sad that she had little guidance from any mature adult who could have helped her put her feelings in perspective. It was a con-fusing time for anyone coming of age: societal sexual standards were loosening somewhat during the fifties, but they had not yet reached the liberating level of the late sixties, and Judy's generation was caught in the middle.

Although young people had a great deal of freedom—to travel, to drink, to attend late-night parties, without the chaperones required in an earlier generation—they were still expected to rein in their sexual drives. Those who never experienced these ambiguous societal messages can only imagine the extreme frustration they aroused in young men, and the equally extreme pressure they put on young women. As for Judy, although she was actually awakening not just to sex but to sensuality, her primary focus, at nineteen, was sex, pure and simple.

At this point in her life, Judy had lost touch with her first real love, Jerry Stamm, the young man she had met at Yosemite, and she tried for several months to get news of him from mutual friends. Near the end of April, someone finally told her that he had married, badly, and was unhappy.

Judy was devastated by this news, and wrote in her diary, in a typical teenage (and Judy) overstatement, "Life is here and will be for many years, but true happiness—the ability to love—shall avoid me the rest of my life. And if...I do find a small place in my heart for someone else, one of these days, he will only fill my lonely days, not my lonely heart."

The next day, though: "It has happened. I finally found a guy that makes my heart do flip-flops." But "this is just physical attraction, not emotional love." She stayed at the party where she met him, though, until three a.m., and could think of nothing else the following day.

Bob was a classic womanizer, sometimes showering her with attention and sometimes ignoring her, and he was dating a number of other women. Her moods fluctuated along with his behavior. During one of her down spells, she pulled out an old letter from Jerry and sobbed as she read it: "Cross off the days, my darling; only 8 more months and I'll be in your arms!"

This kind of vacillation was par for the course for Judy during that year. Almost every young man who met her—at parties or through other friends—seemed to ask her out, and the word "no" was apparently not in her vocabulary, unless the man in question was a real nerd or was pressuring her to "go all the way." She was thrilled with every one of them, at least until the next one came along. Her need for attention and validation was inordinate, and being the object of male sexual desire fulfilled that need.

Judy did have two ongoing relationships during this year, with a Jekyl-and-Hyde pair. Don Tredway was a profligate and could probably be categorized as a batterer: extremely possessive and demanding, but also given to spells of contrition. He had a drinking problem as well. Walt Houseman, on the other hand, was "a gentleman to the letter...never got fresh." Walt always treated her with respect, and they had long talks together—intimate but not provocative.

Judy's relationship with Don was in full swing by the beginning of 1958. Times with him were always wild in one way or another—partying, drinking, and of course, heavy petting. He was constantly pressuring her to have sex. "[Don] really got out of hand and had me scared. His hands were all over and he held me down so I couldn't move while he just continued to fool around. I really had to get mad to bring him to his senses." But she was also learning how much her body responded: "A strange feeling came over me today and it is almost frightening... when [Don] starts fooling around I really get hot and still I have to put a halt to it... Biology will get the best of us."

As for Walt, Judy met him on June 14th, at the beach. He was in the Navy, stationed at Miramar. It was summer vacation, and she had just arrived in Pacific Beach to spend a few days with her grandfather before returning to live with her parents for the summer.

Walt was "a most charming and handsome young man," just seventeen days her junior. At first, Judy kept her relationship with Walt secret from her family: "Being picked up by a sailor doesn't look too good." She was disappointed that he did not attempt to kiss her goodnight on their first date, or even touch her, "but now as I look back it is better he didn't." This reticence continued until October, when Walt finally started becoming more physical: "The tiger is no longer sleeping."

Judy moved back to her parents' house the day after her first meeting with Walt, and started working swing shift as a restaurant hostess. Despite this step toward responsibility, however, she lost no time in resuming her dating and partying schedule. She enjoyed flirting with the customers, and soon took up with two new men: Rob, "a nice guy but it sure doesn't take much to excite him," and Lindy, a real wooer, who "could charm you into standing in front of an onrushing train before you realized what you were doing." Lindy was highly intelligent as well, and Judy enjoyed long philosophical conversations with him, although he certainly had his sensual side: "That boy is dynamite!"

Don, however, was always in the picture, and her feelings about him fluctuated constantly. There were times when she was busy with other guys and paid him little heed; at other times she felt she was madly in love with him and had fantasies of marrying him.

It was Don with whom she lost her virginity, and probably also had her first try at oral sex, but the process was nowhere close to the story she gave out later. Far from a respectful, caring relationship, with a summer spent in exploration and gradual buildup to intercourse, her interactions with Don were contentious. He pressured her more and more for intercourse, and she continued to feel ambivalent —loving the physical sensations of petting and drawn to the excitement, but fearful of both social disapprobation and pregnancy. In fact, it is clear that she did not, as she later claimed, prepare for intercourse by getting fitted with a diaphragm. In 1958 it was actually not possible for an unmarried woman under the age of twenty-one to obtain any kind of contraception without her parents' permission, and that would clearly not have been forthcoming. While it is true that Judy did pay a visit to her family doctor a few days before her deflowering, it was not to procure contraceptives, but to get her hymen cut.[5] "Now I can wear Tampax... It is great."

The final breakdown of Judy's barriers occurred in September. On the 8th, Judy and Don spent the night together, sleeping on a friend's couch, and came close to actually having intercourse. "Good thing it was my period or I might have given in." Exactly what they did do is not entirely clear, but it was probably oral sex. "I will never forget this night, and the substitute was delicious. Mom would disown me if she knew even though I didn't go all the way... I am deliriously happy!"

It was on September 14th that Judy and Don did "go all the way." The date is circled in red in her diary, and she wrote, "I really have no regrets about last night; I just have one big fear now. Dear God I hope not!!!" She had an agonizing month until her period started on October 10th. She also suffered fears that Don would dump her—another detraction from her later claims that Don was simply the agent of her deflowering and not someone she was particularly attached to. Furthermore, Juliet's claim that Don went off to "a distant college" is certainly stretching the meaning of "distant"—he attended USC in Los Angeles.[6]

Sex workers always have been outrageous liars, especially about their sex lives. It's part of their job, after all.

Judy's diary entries about both the "substitute" for intercourse and the deflowering itself show a surprising degree of self-censorship. She made only oblique references to the activities she engaged in, evidently uncomfortable—even with herself, in this very private

---

[5] Why she had her hymen cut is not clear. Perhaps it was standard procedure in those days, but it is practically unheard of now. Fortunately, this custom has fallen out of favor, like the prevalent tonsillectomies practiced on children in the 1940s and 1950s.

[6] For details about Judy's public version of losing her virginity, see Appendix D.

venue—with explicit language, although her limited vocabulary for sexual activities may have contributed to this reticence as well.

Judy's diary entries about her deflowering. September 14: "Don took me to dinner - a Swedish smorgishberg [sic], then bought some T-bird wine and then ... I can say no more!!!" September 15: "It is terrible but I really have no regrets about last night. I just have one big fear now. Dear God I hope not!!! He was suppose [sic] to come over tonite but didn't show. I am constantly afraid that he is going to drop me & I'm afraid another heartbreak would really undo me."

Despite her alleged elation—in her later public pronouncements —at losing her virginity, Juliet reminisced about this experience in her journal in 1991 in a way that puts it into a very different light. While Don slept, Judy was wakeful, and crept into the bathroom to gaze at her naked body in the mirror.

> Shouldn't it look different now that I was no longer a virgin? In the dim glow of the bulb over the bathroom sink I could see small firm breasts and a slender neck, long fine blond hair down my back, sleepy eyes startled from slumber. The shock of having his cock inside me didn't show. What were the signs? I couldn't see below my navel, the cold white sink hiding my curved belly so recently beneath his thrusting, my damp thighs and burning pussy radiating heat down my legs to my bare feet on a dirty linoleum floor.

> So this is it? There has to be more. I ran my hand over
> my chest and abdomen as I peered closely into the mirror
> and gazed at a woman's face.

It is also noteworthy that Juliet made no mention, in either her 1958 diary or her 1991 journal, of another aspect of her introduction to sexual intercourse, one that she frequently spoke of later: namely, that it had relieved her physical pain. Most likely, though, her discovery of sex as a pain killer occurred later, especially as she herself often stated that it was a result of the sustained high that accompanies (at least for women) buildup, crescendo and coasting down, not the "wham-bam thank you ma'am" of this first venture with Don. It is also not clear how much, if at all, Judy's college years were plagued with the chronic health problems of her earlier youth; she made no reference to these illnesses in her 1958 diary.

Just a few days after this momentous event, school started again, and Judy was signed up for classes in Speech, Political Science and Art. She also started working two jobs, one in the cafeteria and another as an assistant in the drama department. After having slipped seriously in her studies during the spring semester, receiving mostly C grades and only two Bs, she began to buckle down more in the fall.

Along with her partying and sexual experimentation, Judy kept close ties with her family, even if she did not inform them of all the details of her escapades. What they did know—the partying and social whirl—worried them enough, and she had some fights with her mother over her lifestyle. Still, she visited with her sister Chris from time to time, and socialized with her family quite a bit during the summer, when she lived at home.

It was just after Thanksgiving that her parents moved to San Diego, having bought the doughnut shop there in September, and Judy and Chris went down to stay with them for a few days and help them get settled in.

Religion was also still important in Judy's life, even if only as a habit. She continued to attend church at least periodically, and made frequent references to God in her diary musings, although generally only *after* she made decisions rather than *before*. More than one Sunday morning found her blearily sitting in a pew after attending a party that had lingered into the wee hours. On Christmas Eve she was disappointed at not being able to find a late-night church service after she had spent the evening making out with her latest boyfriend.

Although most of her social life revolved around sex, Judy did manage to tend to a few other activities. She and several girlfriends, in typical 1950s fashion, formed a tongue-in-cheek "sorority" they called GDI—Gold Diggers, Inc. Judy designed a clever sweatshirt: deep rose with gold logo and motto "Always looking for the best," which they silk-screened on. They held a contentious meeting to elect officers, and became a well-known entity on campus, hosting an open house on May 21st. Although there was officially no liquor at this event, there were trips out to various cars for swigs of wine, along with dips in the pool, dancing and plenty of food. And no doubt plenty of making out as well.

For many months, Judy continued to vacillate between Don, who had a compelling hold on her, and Walt, of whom she was growing fonder and to whom she was becoming more attracted. She found out to her surprise that Walt was not a virgin; he had almost married a woman who claimed (falsely, it turned out) that he had gotten her pregnant.

By Christmas Eve, Judy was feeling closer to Walt: "Wow has he changed—is now quite a lover."[7] Walt spent Christmas with her and her family, and gave her presents: red shoes and a matching purse. Judy met his mother over the phone. Walt had just gotten the news that he had won a full scholarship to the University of Maryland (a school that then, as now, actively recruited students from the military) when his term in the Navy ended.

Judy and Walt spent New Years Eve together as well, attending a party at a nearby inn where they doubled up with another couple. Judy managed to pass for age twenty-one, and they all had a great celebration at the bar.

Judy's 1958 diary ends here, with the observation:

> I had more of a taste of life this year than ever before...
> more wonderful and exciting than I ever expected. Also
> shed many tears... The most important thing gained was

---

[7] The meanings of words like "sex", "lover", etc. did not, in the 1950s, necessarily refer to sexual intercourse.

> to know that I am capable of falling in love again... My
> only hope is that I will never regret the sometimes
> surprising and questionable actions I took... May God
> forgive my sins and lead me to better things in 1959.

While Judy kept no written record of 1959, her later references
indicate that it followed a pattern similar to that of 1958, especially in
regard to her romantic adventures. The most notable event of 1959,
of course, was turning twenty-one in July, when Judy was able to get
the diaphragm that she later claimed to have obtained prior to her
deflowering with Don. She and her friend Sheila, who had also
recently passed the age-of-majority milestone, celebrated their new
legal status and sexual liberation with an evening at their favorite
bar, the Forty-Niner, where they picked up two randy sailors "for a
night of laughter and lust."

It was in the following year, 1960, that Judy met her future husband—tall, blond, curly-haired, Bob Watt, with his intriguing New
York accent. They met at the beach, probably in Alamitos Bay. Judy
spent quite a bit of her free time at the beach when the weather was
decent, including late-night beach parties, which were quite the thing
in Southern California at the time. But it was a beautiful sunny day
when she met Bob.

Bob was taken immediately, as most straight men were, with
Judy's beauty and vivaciousness. He was also struck by the warmth
and friendliness of her family, who were with her on this particular
occasion.

Bob was a Navy man, like Walt (it is not clear what became of
Walt, but presumably he and Judy drifted apart after his move to
Maryland), and was assigned to the ship *Windham County*, then
docked in San Diego. As Judy, still a student at Long Beach State, was
living at the time in Venice, it was quite a trip—about a hundred
miles—to visit her, but Bob made the journey almost every weekend.

As with all the other romances Judy had been bouncing through
for the previous several years, she was swept off her feet, and the
young couple fell madly in love. They spent long luxurious days and
nights getting to know each other, both in the privacy of her apartment when her roommate was away and in various entertainment
venues. They both loved good food and good music—primarily
classical and jazz. Bob bought and assembled a small hi-fidelity set

kit, with a Garrard turntable, and they listened to dramatic music in the small apartment while they explored each other's bodies. They had long talks about philosophy, politics, civil rights, and the coming sexual revolution.

With this more stable relationship and reliable contraception, Judy was now free to explore her own sexuality, and the male body, more safely and at a more leisurely pace than she had been able to do with Don. This may also have been when she discovered the pain-relieving power of sex—a benefit she often touted in her later public pronouncements.

Judy with Bob Watt, whom she later described as having the body of an Adonis. Photo: Carr/Pettit family collection.

When not spending intimate time together in the apartment, Judy and Bob took advantage of the many charms of late-1950s California —both geographical and cultural. They drove up and down Pacific Coast Highway, walked on beaches, marveled at sunsets, and cuddled and made out in sheltered hollows among the dunes as the moonlight cut a ragged path across the waves. They discovered quaint little restaurants where they ordered exotic-sounding dishes. It was a great time for jazz lovers, and the young couple heard Nina Simone, Ron Carter, and Dave Brubeck in person. On a trip to San Francisco, they ate at the Top of the Mark restaurant at the Mark Hopkins Hotel and wandered the city visiting various jazz clubs, including the Blackhawk, where they heard Miles Davis and George

Shearing perform live. In short, they reveled in being young and sensual, in having the great adventure of life before them.

But in November of 1960, Bob's ship set sail for Japan and the young couple were separated. Although Judy quickly moved on to other lovers, writing Bob off as just another romantic interlude, Bob had a very different reaction, realizing, after a couple of months, what a treasure he had left behind. He wrote and invited Judy to follow him to Japan, offering to pay for her passage, and suggesting that they could get married if it would reassure her family.

Judy was stunned and delighted. This invitation elevated Bob back to the level of fascinating and romantic, and she danced exultantly around her apartment, waving the letter in her hand and yelling, "Yes! yes!" Although she was in her last semester at Long Beach State, very close to finishing her degree, she could not resist the lure of such an exotic proposition. Surely living in a foreign culture would be more of an education than plodding along at a state college. Not to mention getting away from her family, whose influence twenty-two-year-old Judy found more oppressive than supportive.

So it was that on Wednesday, 15 February 1961, Judy boarded a plane for Tokyo. Her international adventures were beginning.

4
"When in Rome ..."
Going Native in Japan

Judy's sendoff to Japan was "utter confusion and hurried good-byes." A traffic crash on the freeway delayed the Carr party on the trip to the Los Angeles airport; they arrived two minutes before departure time (Japan Air Lines actually held the plane for her), and everyone was in a panic of disarray. Her mother drove the car off to park it, with some of Judy's luggage still in the trunk. Luckily, Judy had loaded herself down with her wedding dress, her coat, a bulging purse, books, a bottle of champagne, a gardenia and a telegram from Bob's parents. She was in a daze, bemoaning her forgetfulness at leaving a critical item—her vanity case—in the car. It contained not only the makeup that any self-respecting middle-class woman of the time needed to make herself publicly presentable, but, more importantly, the critical diaphragm. (Her mother shipped the case to her by express; it was waiting for her in Tokyo when she arrived.)

When Judy calmed down enough to notice where she was, the plane was high above the Pacific, although the water was not visible below the puffy cumulus clouds. Glancing about, she noticed that most of her fellow passengers were Asian. The tourist section was only about half full. The cabin motifs and crew dress were Japanese, rich in color and design. The seat pockets were full of useful Japanese items: slippers, fan, postcards and travel literature. Sumptuous Japanese meals were served with a hot towel for pre- and post-meal hygiene. Already, Judy was finding sensuous delight in her surroundings. Exhaustion overcame her excitement for a time, though, and she drifted off into a much-needed nap.

After two refueling stopovers—one in Honolulu and one at Wake Island—the plane landed in a frigid Tokyo at 11:35 p.m. on Thursday, 16 February. With her clumsy load of riff-raff, Judy was held up at customs longer than any other passenger. Although she spied Bob waiting for her, with a shy smile and a wilted bouquet, she could do no more than wave to him as she negotiated with the customs officials. When at last she was free, they fell into each other's arms and enjoyed a proper hello.

After gathering up all her luggage and re-distributing the unpacked last-minute items she had carried on, Judy and Bob sped away down the darkened highway in a taxi, arriving at two a.m. at the house Bob had rented for them in Hayama, a small fishing village. Stepping out of the cab, Judy was overwhelmed by the mixture of heady, pervasive aromas—saltwater, drying seaweed, fish entrails, open sewage trenches, and smoke from both wood and coal fires. Exhausted from her trials, with little energy left for processing yet more novelties, she almost threw up. No time for that, though: they only stopped long enough to drop off Judy's luggage before continuing on, again by taxi, to the nearby home of Walt and Marion "Mickey" Riley, civilian friends of Bob's. Too keyed up to sleep well, Judy dozed and watched the sun rise over the house tops.

Up at six-thirty in the morning, the couple had no time to go back to their house for clean clothes, and had to re-don their previous day's garb. After a quick coffee, they set off by bus to the Tokyo train station, traveled by train to Yokohama, then took a taxi to the naval base. On board the ship, they waited for half an hour to pick up papers, then to the lab for blood tests for Judy, then off to buy flowers for the ceremony and a ring for Judy. Next, back to the American consulate at Yokohama, for a civil marriage ceremony. The American consulate was about to close, but their intrepid Japanese taxi driver was undaunted. With one hand on the steering wheel and the other on the horn, he careened along the narrow, picturesque streets, running up on the sidewalk or veering onto the wrong side of the street when necessary, delivering them to their destination five minutes before closing time. After that it was on to the Japanese ward office to record the marriage, get the certificate for the religious ceremony and send telegrams to their families. Next stop: the Yokohama Navy Exchange to buy a ring for Bob. Finally, the couple headed back to Tokyo by train. They stopped briefly at their house to pick up a change of clothes and went to spend the night at the (heated) Kanko Hotel, where they had a third-floor room "practically hanging over the ocean." The hotel was pure luxury for those days—large window, private bath, futons, room service, kimonos and slippers—all for $6 [$48] a night.

They arose at eight a.m. for green tea. Bob was required to be back on base at ten a.m. for a ship's party; they barely made it. Back at the Rileys' home afterward, they ironed their wedding clothes, then were off to the hotel again for a rehearsal, followed by the ceremony and reception, with wedding presents of some useful household items.

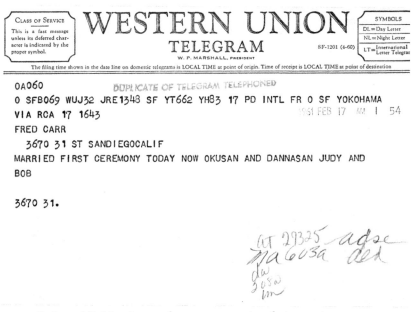

Judy and Bob's telegram home, announcing their marriage

As they dashed off to catch a train, still in their wedding clothes, it suddenly dawned on both of them that they were now married! They looked at each other, stopped in the middle of the busy side-walk, wrapped themselves in each other's arms and kissed, much to the horror of passersby; such sensuous displays of affection were taboo in Japan. Nevertheless, they escaped reprobation—probably being dismissed as crazy Americans—and went on to board the train, which they rode to Yokosuka and another hotel, so exhausted they barely made it through a bath and dinner—their first real meal in thirteen hours. Bob collapsed on a tatami mat on the floor. Judy, with help from the room boy, tried to get him into bed, but to no avail. The next morning Judy awoke to find Bob in a corner, submerged under a pile of futons. Apparently she had risen in her sleep and opened all the windows, letting the freezing winter air, driven by 30-knot winds, pour into the room.

Hurriedly dressing and checking out, Bob and Judy made the trip back to their still unheated house to find two friends of Bob's huddled around a hibachi pot, the only thing that could possibly pass for a heater. Aside from the cold, though, the house seemed luxurious to Judy: a hand-carved teak chest from Singapore, a four-track Sony tape recorder, hand-carved wooden figurines, hand-painted porcelainware, a ninety-five-piece set of bamboo-patterned crystal, assorted kitchen utensils, a two-burner hot plate and a top burner oven, a cupboard and refrigerator stocked with food, and on a low, carved redwood chest—the only piece of furniture in the dining room—yards and yards of five different types of brocade and a vase of flowers. Judy was so happy she cried.

Judy and Bob's wedding, and at home with their presents. Photos: Carr/Pettit family collection.

The first dinner at home required some resourcefulness, as, despite the many utensils, there were no saucepans or sharp knives. Judy boiled water for coffee in a bottle warmer and fixed a three-item dinner—hamburgers, French fries and peas—in one large skillet by sectioning it off with aluminum foil.

By Tuesday, Judy was sick—a result of the cold, the lack of food and sleep, and the typhoid shot she had gotten earlier in the day. Nevertheless, they traveled to the small fishing village of Zushi, a quaint and thoroughly Japanese town near their residence, to shop and eat lunch.

On Thursday, their kotatsu (kerosene stove) arrived, but given that it had only about an hour's worth of fuel, it did little to dispel the cold. Friday brought no relief, and Judy had no clothes appropriate for the weather. She and Bob walked half a mile to the bus stop, waited twenty minutes in the bitter cold ("It must have been 10°") for the bus, then went on by train and taxi to the base. Judy had to pick up an ID, which she had finally acquired after much hassle. Bob's ship was to depart that day for a three-week cruise.

After a grueling morning running errands and trekking home ("I'll match the trip from Yokosuka to Hayama with any Marine training obstacle course"), Judy collapsed in bed, still sick. Mama-san, the landlady, made her some miso and brought the hibachi over to the bed, but it had little effect.

The next day, Saturday, sufficient fuel finally arrived but Judy could not get the stove going. Mickey Riley and a friend, Elizabeth, came by and eventually got it working. "Ah, blessed heat..." Judy drifted off to an afternoon nap in a warm house. That evening, Bob's ship having departed, she sat on a zabaton (large cushion) beside the kotatsu, sipping green tea, listening to Mantovani on the small tape player, and watching a light snow cover the camellia bush in the garden.

"I miss Bob but love him and my new home—Japan."

It was the beginning of a great adventure, one befitting a drama queen like Judy. Yet, as night fell, she could not help feeling abandoned, left alone in a strange country of whose language and customs she knew virtually nothing. It suddenly hit her, what she had gotten herself into, leaving behind everything familiar to come live in a foreign culture, with a man she now felt she hardly knew. And then, suddenly, even he was gone. Excitement and resentment battled within her, and she spent the night alternately sobbing and trying to reassure herself, finally falling into an exhausted sleep.

Alone in her new home for the first time, Judy awoke to morning sounds as the pale dawn light filtered through the closed shutters, casting fluid shadows on the tatami-covered floor and up the walls. Outside, children laughed and chattered on their way to school, housewives clattered along the hard-packed dirt street in their geta (wooden shoes), bamboo branches creaked against each other in the light morning breeze, and finches sang in the bare plum tree outside the window. Three loud gongs from the large brass bell at the nearby Shinto temple, announcing morning prayers, indicated that it was seven a.m. Forcing herself to brave the cold, Judy dressed hurriedly in several layers of clothing, started the stove, and went about exploring her new abode.

The house was primitive by U.S. standards, but had a simple and tranquil beauty that appealed to Judy's artistic tastes. A grid of smooth, slim wooden ceiling rafters supported sheets of coarsely woven rice paper, and one wall consisted of a series of sliding screens painted with delicate cherry-tree branches, behind which were stored clothes, linens and even the futon when it was not in use. In the main room was an alcove which featured a hanging scroll, a vase of fresh flowers and a small Buddha sculpture. In the middle of the room itself was a low, square polished wooden table surrounded by four cushions, with a rice-paper lamp suspended just above it. Judy climbed the ladder up to a small loft that would have been the maid's room if they had been able to afford one. From the tiny window she could gaze out over her new neighborhood. Fishing boats were heading out to sea, their decks covered with ice visible even at this distance. Nearer by, a grocer was opening up his shop, setting out baskets of fruits and vegetables. And to the west, over the roof tops and across Sagami Bay, rose majestic Mt. Fuji, its snow-capped peak rosy in the light of the rising sun.

It being not much colder outside than inside the house, Judy decided to venture out to explore the yard. Bundled in her bulky clothing, she descended back to the ground floor and pushed aside one of the heavy floor-to-ceiling wooden shutters that covered the entire front of the house. Frost shimmered on the straw roof and along the top of the high fence surrounding the property. The heavy shutters gave the house a fortress-like appearance. Their elderly landlady's cottage was on the same property, close enough to provide Judy some feeling of security against her loneliness but hidden by sheltering trees. The entire lot was, in fact, typical of those in any small Japanese town, the houses deliberately secluded, hidden within small groves, and almost impossible to see from the paths.

Hayama, the village Bob had selected for their home, was a small fishing village on the eastern shore of Sagami Bay, almost due south of Tokyo, and a short trip from the Great Buddha of Kamakure. It was nestled between the shoreline to the south and mountains to the north, and was largely wooded, mostly with pine trees. There was only one real street in the town, a road that led to Yokosuka, on Tokyo Bay, to the east (where Bob's ship was docked when it was in port), and to the town of Zushi to the west. The other "streets" in Hayama were really just footpaths, and most of them were steep, leading up toward the mountains. Judy, amused by the ruggedness and simplicity of the village, referred to Hayama, tongue-in-cheek, as the "Miami Beach of the Orient" in her letters to her family. Indeed, it was a popular tourist stop for Japanese families, and the imperial family of Japan maintained a villa there.

It was only a short walk from Bob and Judy's house to the beach where fishing boats were hauled up at night. Although there were a few buildings that might be characterized as stores, these were primarily porches or lean-tos attached to houses, where residents sold fresh produce, seafood, and a few sundries. Elderly people of both genders visited with each other during days of good weather, squatting Japanese-fashion on the porches or along the roadside and conversing for hours, while toddlers ran about virtually unsupervised. Males urinated publicly in "benjo" ditches that ran along the sides of the streets.

The beach in Hayama. Photo: Carr/Pettit family collection.

The nearby village of Zushi, while still quaint and thoroughly Japanese, was a larger town with multiple streets, traffic both vehicular and pedestrian, and many stores and restaurants. It was there that Judy and Bob did most of their shopping, including purchases of traditional Japanese household goods and clothing.

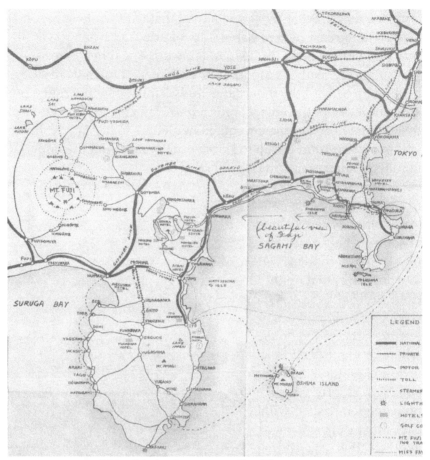

Map of the region surrounding Hayama

Judy and Bob enjoyed "going native" as much as possible, eating the local foods, learning enough of the language to negotiate in the small restaurants and markets, and wearing traditional apparel, at least some of the time. Judy enjoyed browsing in the small markets, marveling at the strange fruits and vegetables and fresh-caught fish loaded into the boats pulled up on the sand. There were carrots as small as a little finger, cabbages as large as a wrestler's head, strawberries the size of a fist and fish of bizarre and iridescent colors. She became fairly adept at communicating with shopkeepers, although she never went out without her little red English-Japanese pocket dictionary. Her efforts to learn their language and culture impressed

the locals, and people were invariably kind and helpful once they
ascertained her sincerity.

Sometimes colorful celebrations intruded directly into their lives,
as when a large festival at Morito Shrine, a few hundred yards uphill
from their house, spilled over into their immediate neighborhood.
Judy accidentally got caught in the middle of the frantic procession,
and was surrounded by inebriated young men snake-dancing
through the village carrying a small shrine on their shoulders. "It is
impossible to describe the color, exuberance, and noise," Judy wrote.
Later in the evening, there were sumo wrestling matches and
traditional Japanese plays.

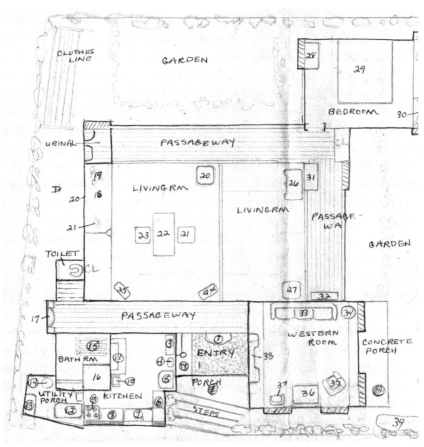

Floor plan Judy drew of one of their houses in Japan

While Judy and Bob were not the only Westerners resident in Hayama or Zushi, they stood out more than others because of their height and their blond hair. Judy was five feet six inches tall, and even taller in either Western-style high heels or Japanese geta. She was a show stopper wherever she went, which no doubt appealed to her need for drama and attention, although there were also times when it was annoying, such as when she would be asked to pose for photographs, usually with large Japanese families or tour groups.

By early March, Judy was settling into her Japanese house and beginning to adjust to married life. "Never in my life have I been so peacefully content," she wrote to her family on March 7, "...each day filled with the immeasurable joy of just being alive, in good health, near to Bob, and in this remarkable land of warm hearts and friendly faces." Sometimes, hardly able to believe she was really living this romantic life, she immersed herself in the sensuousness of just being in this new environment. She watched the ever-changing play of light and shadow against the walls and floor of the house, felt the smoothness of the tatami mats under her feet or the texture of the silk kimono against her skin, and listened to the swish of her slippers as she walked along the polished wood corridors, the hissing of the wind through the narrow gaps between the shojii screens, or the calls of the fire watchman as he walked throughout the village, banging two sticks together and calling out "Hi-no-yo-jin!" [Mind your fire!]

Being a good Japanese housewife, however, was no easy task, especially for someone not brought up to deal with the many inconveniences. This first house she and Bob lived in had a sixteen-mat living room, two entry rooms, a dining room, one bedroom, one bathroom with a separate shower room (neither one heated), a kotatsu room, a laundry room, a small hallway, and a kitchen with one cupboard, a sink and refrigerator, but no counter space, table or drawers. The walls in Japanese houses in those days were made of either plasterboard, mud, or cardboard, and offered little insulation.

The house had a typical Japanese floor toilet, with a big wooden bucket called a benjo, which was changed about once a month by honey-bucket carriers who brought a new bucket, put a lid on the old one, loaded it onto a hand-drawn cart and proceeded on to the next house. In the more rural areas families still emptied their own, on their gardens. In most public buildings toilet paper and hand towels were not provided; you had to bring your own; this was known as "bosom paper." Judy described all this in letters to her family: "And to really shock you—may I reveal that I prefer these toilets... They are really a blessing when struggling with a girdle...[although] you rarely have to wear a girdle or hose or heels or a bra."

Dishes and laundry were washed in ice-cold water, as hot water could only be obtained from a boiler, located outside the house and heated with a hand-tended wood fire beneath it. This task in itself was a major production: "Remove your slippers, step into outdoor shoes, rummage for burnable trash paper, stuff it under the boiler, then pile on kindling wood followed by logs, light it, fan the flame, cough, wipe your smoke-filled eyes and then return to civilization." Judy's friend Mickey let her use her washing machine for sheets and towels, but everything else had to be done by hand, including chopping the wood for the boiler. Judy was building up strong arm muscles.

A Shinto temple Judy visited with one of her American friends. Photo: Carr/Pettit family collection.

Hot water and washing were not the only challenges, though. The kerosene stove, the only source of heat, had to be lit every morning and turned off every night. Beyond the glass doors in the passage were the heavy shutter doors that had to be closed each night and re-opened in the morning. Each one had to be slid back into its housing unit at the end of its section of windows—just so—or they would not all fit. Cleaning included dusting the shoji screens, which took more than an hour, and the wood-floor passage that separated the shojis from the sliding glass doors had to be swept every day, and frequently washed and waxed. As for the tatami mats—well, there was a project: wet and wring out newspaper, tear it into shreds, scatter it on the floor and then sweep it up. This picks up the dust. Then get down on your hands and knees and wipe them with a damp cloth. (Keep in mind that the whole house was carpeted with tatami mats.)

Cooking was like an adventure over a campfire. The kitchen had a 2½-burner hot plate and an oven that operated by placing it over a burner. Their only cooking supplies consisted of two saucepans, one bottle warmer, an electric skillet, two pie pans, a set of mixing bowls, and a few cooking utensils. "But you'd be surprised at the good meals I can prepare." Since the Japanese typically used human waste for garden fertilizer, the Navy recommended soaking all Japanese vegetables in bleach solution, but Judy was not convinced: "...people are too squeamish. I'm not dead yet and I have done most of my shopping in the Japanese market. Let the Americans practice their ridiculous sanitation methods—I'll go native, thank you!"

Trash had to be separated into four different categories—cans and bottles, garbage, paper to burn in the boiler ("nothing goopy or real dirty as you must dig into it with your hands and put it under the boiler"), and dirty trash which must be burned outside: "Put it into a heap, light a match and then hope it doesn't burn down the house...This is an unpleasant task—foul-smelling, smoke in your hair and face and blowing into the house plus keeping constant guard on the fire which takes considerable time."

As for shopping, it was not the straightforward errand that it was in the States. If you saw something you might possibly need, it was best to buy it, because it might be your last chance for several months. And transportation was certainly different from the way it was in the U.S. "I walked over two miles today... Boy was I ever lazy with my car in the States," Judy noted, adding that "a collapsable hand cart would be helpful, if you can find one and send it over." Her family did manage to fulfill this wish.

With all the challenges, though, Judy wrote, "I'm not complaining; I am having the greatest time of my life. I don't have time to be sick or worried or too lonely... The only thing that bothers me is the constant quiet, day in and day out" except for the banging of the glass doors in the wind and the tromping of rats in the attic, which "gets eerie." Judy got through some of the more difficult times in these early months by pretending that she was an actress playing an Asian housewife.

Still, there were times when she suffered nostalgia for American culture. She and Bob had no close English-speaking neighbors and no radio, and only three tapes of classical music. They eventually acquired a Sony transistor radio, so that Judy could listen to classical music, and, when she found the Jack Benny Show, she finally felt a connection with home.

During Bob's first ship-out, Judy was left on her own to finish much of the marriage-related paperwork—getting the rest of her shots, having her passport changed to her married name, acquiring an ID card and a Navy ration card.

Financial struggles plagued the young couple while the paperwork for Bob's extra marriage allotment dragged on. They spent almost all their money on food and bare essentials. When, on March 24, after being in port for only a few days, Bob's ship left again, suddenly and unannounced, on a top-secret mission, Judy was left stranded with very little money until Bob's April 1st paycheck.

To keep her mind and hands busy, Judy sewed velvet and gold brocade curtains and kimonos for both Bob and herself. She was looking for an art tutor, and for a language teacher so that she and Bob could learn at least some basic conversational Japanese. Judy was picking up a little informally, of course: "I know about 20-30 words now and can make myself understood in most situations." Those situations were probably only the most basic ones: shopping, asking directions, discussing the weather, etc.

In April, they finally acquired enough money, or at least enough Military Payment Certificates, to purchase a few more items for the kitchen: some corning ware and a set of four graduated mixing bowls, for a cost of $3.50 U.S. [$28]. A couple of months later they bought a Trio Deluxe Stereo AM/FM radio and adaptor, a coffee percolator, a toaster, a set of zabutons, some clothes for Bob, linens, and for Judy a Lady Hamilton diamond watch. "I have never had such nice jewelry."

Toward the end of April, the couple moved to a slightly smaller but nicer house—two stories (the second story being a new addition), with a sun porch off one upstairs bedroom, and a deep tiled Japanese bathtub, heated by building a fire underneath it, like the boiler. Three sides of the upstairs were glass doors, offering a magnificent view of Mount Fuji on clear days.

Downstairs was a combination living/dining room (18 X 27 mats), a hardwood corridor with no separation between it and the dining area, and glass doors that opened directly outside. In the living room were a low table, zabutons, and two stereo speakers; in the dining room, a tiny utility table and china cupboard. The kitchen was small but cheery and freshly painted, and had two cupboards, two drawers and a counter top, a linoleum floor, a tiled sink, and a stove with a real oven.

In spite of her remarkable adjustment to her new home and culture, though, Judy's body began to complain of the change in environment: "I've had trouble sleeping for the past two weeks, and often wake up four or five times a night." She also cycled through some strange food cravings—for sweets, then fish, then grapenuts, then mashed potatoes with gravy. (A note in the margin of one of her letters: "No, I'm not pregnant.") Later, in December, she needed a hernia operation, the result of the strenuous work and the heavy loads she had to carry. She was not in pain, but her movements were restricted, and with Bob away so much, she needed to be able to continue to function at a fairly high level. All the medical procedures were gratis from the Navy. Needless to say, Judy experienced a great deal of trepidation about going to a hospital, after her childhood experiences. And while this visit was not as traumatic as those earlier ones, it was not pleasant, either. Judy was glad to get out as soon as she could.

Aside from this incident, though, Judy was healthy, maintaining her weight at 123 pounds—slender for her 5'6"—and her shapely figure of 37-25-36. The Navy had also provided her with about $200 [$1600] worth of dental work for free, to correct an overbite. "I should have had braces ten years ago."

It was not long after their arrival that Judy began to get a taste of Japan's weather extremes. By the end of March the winter cold had dissipated and the rainy season had begun. It rained regularly about half the time, with sunny days in between. The heart of the rainy season, though, was June; it brought unremitting humidity and severe storms. While the humidity aggravated Judy's arthritis, she hardly had time to focus on this discomfort, as many other challenges faced her. "The mud is ankle deep... geta (wooden clogs) are a must, as this mud is no match for even sturdy galoshes... One never leaves the house without an umbrella in June... [and] the wood is too wet for a fire in the boiler."

With Bob away, Judy faced her first real Japanese typhoon alone. She wrote to her family:

> It has been close to a nightmare. This is the sixth morning of the storm and there has been no break from the torrential rains. Last night's news listed 264 dead, 293 injured, 195 missing, thousands homeless, and over 55 million dollars [$437 million] in property damage... Our home is undamaged, only our yard is torn up. Others in this area were not so fortunate, as rivers, drain-offs, and benjos overflowed, mountainsides gave way and driving rains crumbled homes. Trains were stopped, tunnels filled with water, and many roads were impassable because of mud and landslides. It was literally impossible to travel from here to Yokosuka. Bob was in port that night but was unable to make it home.

The next night the rain started becoming more intense, and the benjo that ran only two feet from the house overflowed. The landlady hired three men to pack mud and stones against the openings in the wall, in a frantic attempt to channel the water away from the yard, but flooding was inevitable. Judy went to her neighbor Rose's house for the night, a hundred yards away. She barely made it there before the town fire horns started blaring away, warning of high tide. The wailing continued for five minutes, until the electricity went out, silencing them.

Even after the storm, hardships continued. The humidity stagnated at close to 100% for days on end. Everything soured and mildewed—curtains, linens, clothes in closets and drawers, the mattress, their shoes, the refrigerator, the shower. Judy washed their clothes, but they never dried. All the firewood was too wet to burn; the boiler could not be used, and there was no hot water except what could be boiled on the stove. "The house is hot, sticky and sour but the windows must be boarded with wooden shutters or the glass will break and the wood warp."

Later in the summer, warm and pleasant weather was more the norm, with temperatures in the high 80s. Judy bought a new coral-colored bathing suit. "I am in my bathing suit sitting on the sun porch soaking up the rays. In spite of the onslaught of bugs, spiders, mosquitos, centipedes, etc. it is good to feel the sun after such a bitter winter."

Judy's lifelong love of cats finally manifested itself with the acquisition of a new kitten, red and white, with a crook in the tip of its tail, evidently typical for Japanese cats. A few months later, unfortunately, it followed her to the bus stop and was lost.

Although Judy was learning to adjust to the Japanese lifestyle, challenges still assailed her from time to time.

> This 5'6" blob of protoplasm has been cut, scratched, burned, gouged, slashed, crushed, pounded and bitten more times in the last 4 months than the sum of all such injuries in the past 22 years. Three weeks ago I was carrying Chris, age 3, on my back (Japanese style) and stumbled in my geta as I approached our back door and went head first through 2 panes of plate glass. I emerged with only a few small surface cuts, but thoroughly shaken. I was lucky I wasn't killed. [Presumably the toddler was not harmed.] Then recently I got a large burn on my forearm from the iron. The next day as I was burning the trash, I accidentally opened it and it got infected from the smoke and ash particles. To complicate its healing, Bob would always inadvertently grab at this part of my arm. Wednesday I about cut my finger off by dropping a full [glass] bottle of rubbing alcohol on the bathroom sink, breaking the sink and ramming my hand into the broken tile to break my fall...there are many situations and hazards one encounters over here and especially in this

house that we are not used to. I just hope I am in one
piece when we return to the States.

With September, the weather changed; although the storms
continued, they were milder and more intermittent, thunderstorms
interspersed with sun. "These thunderstorms strike without warning
—and just as you finish running madly around the house closing
windows and wooden shutters, the rain ceases and the sun appears."
The days were muggy but the nights were already noticeably cooler.
"An all too brief summer—reluctantly slipping away!!!" Judy had to
put a blanket on the bed. Fall housekeeping included sweeping out
the sand and setting the tatami mats, and even the futons, out to air.
Judy was amused to wander down the streets and to see all the colorful futons hanging out of windows, over porch railings, or from bamboo frames. Glimpsing these intimate furnishings gave her the feeling that she was sharing her neighbors' beds.

It was in September, too, that Judy had her first encounter with
one of Japan's notorious saucer-plate-sized spiders, a "kumo." She
had heard about these monsters; her friend Mickey had killed seventeen during a three-week period the previous year. While not poisonous, they were certainly frightening, especially to an arachnophobe
like Judy.

The incident began while she was eating breakfast one morning;
she glanced down and saw one of these impressive creatures on the
floor. She ignored it until she finished eating, then retrieved the
insect spray and prepared to attack it. Kumo, however, apparently
wise to this trick (or perhaps just sensing danger), went on the attack
and came leaping toward her. Judy did a fast sprint across the room
and jumped up on a stool. There ensued a twenty-minute battle,
which Judy evidently finally won, although perhaps the spider
simply retreated into a safe hiding place.

Unfortunately, Kumo was not the only disagreeable creature to
share the house. One morning Judy woke up to find a cockroach
crawling along her arm, even though Bob had assured her that these
ubiquitous insects shunned human beings and that she need not fear
their intrusion onto her person. So much for that theory. Another
morning she found a three-inch-diameter crab lurking in the bathroom sink. This did not faze her, though; she simply shooed it down
the drain and pushed in the plug.

Elderly Japanese shopping in the produce market in Zushi. Photo: Carr/
Pettit family collection.

Another plus in September was finally finding a Japanese language teacher, elderly Mr. Kato. Before World War II, Mr. Kato had
been a professor of English at Tokyo University. During the war he
had been captured by the Americans, and had taught Japanese to the
GIs while imprisoned. Judy found him while out shopping one day;
he rescued her when she was having a particularly difficult time
explaining her requests to a shopkeeper. Along with another couple,
Judy and Bob began taking lessons from Mr. Kato, paying only 26¢
[$2] for each one-hour session for the four of them. Since Judy had
more time to devote to her studies than did Bob, she became more
proficient at the language. She enjoyed the lessons immensely and
felt that she was progressing quite nicely, "but it will take at least two
years of diligent studying to be able to talk fluently and to understand other people. The latter is most difficult," especially dealing
with slang. "But I like the challenge, and am determined to master
the language." Both she and Bob mastered conversation much better
than reading or writing.

In early October, another typhoon was headed for Tokyo, and the locals were preparing for the 136-mph winds expected at the center of the storm. Sounds of hammering filled the air as people boarded themselves up. Judy had to draw reserves of water in case their supply got disrupted, re-stack food in the refrigerator so that water dripping from the freezer wouldn't spoil anything, and remove breakable items from high shelves. She went to the Rileys' house to wait out the storm, while Bob and Walt stayed on the ship. "It was really exciting, but truthfully I wouldn't want to repeat it. It is a dreadful feeling knowing that when you return home your house may be gone." Luckily, the center of the storm bypassed them, swerved and headed out to the Sea of Japan, and the winds reached only 85 mph. Even so, 170 people were killed, scores were injured or left homeless, and damage was in the millions. "The following day was clear, warm and beautiful with only scattered evidence of the typhoon; debris-littered shoreline, collapsed fences and mangled flora. Our house was dirty but undamaged... Summer is definitely over."

With the approach of winter, Judy wanted some indoor activities to fill up her time and to continue to expand her horizons. She had originally hoped to take college classes at Sophia University in Tokyo, but abandoned that idea because of the cost, not only of tuition, but of travel. Instead, she hired private tutors, and studied Japanese art, flower arranging ("ikebana"), pen and ink brush drawing ("sumeai") and folk dancing. She also took on her first job as an English conversation teacher.

One autumn afternoon not long after the storm, while she was sitting on the back porch enjoying the late fall sunshine, the front door bell chimed. When she opened the door, there stood five young men dressed in dark blue school uniforms. At her appearance, they removed their caps and bowed in unison. One of them stepped forward, held up a piece of paper and read a short prepared speech, explaining that they were university students attending a wrestling camp next door. "Please excuse our rudeness, madam, but from which foreign country do you come?" When Judy replied that she was from the U.S., big smiles broke out on every face. Their spokesman went on to ask very formally if she would be ever so kind as to practice English conversation with them while they were at the camp. "We have all studied English at school many years, but because our teachers are Japanese our speaking ability is poor. We will be most grateful for your assistance." So began Judy's English as a Second Language (ESL) teaching career.

Flower Arrangement

I placed the two peonies and twisted lotus branch on the low table next to the green porcelain vase, knelt on the tatami, picked up and deftly clipped off the end of the branch and placed it in the vase.

It was early morning, my favorite time of day. The sun cast shadows through the shoji screen onto the straw mats. The fishmonger's cry could be heard in the lane behind the house as I held up one peony and guessed its length, snipped it off exactly 1½ inches and carefully threaded it into a space in the branch.

The second flower, exactly one third shorter than its sister, was placed to the left and front.

My masterpiece was finished; I set it in the takanoma to the right of the hanging scroll, stepped back and smiled, pleased that I, a foreigner, had mastered the art of ikebana—even the name sounds like beauty and simplicity.

Thirty years later I still arrange my flowers according to the ancient tradition of balance between earth, sky and water.

-- Juliet Carr

Every evening for the next two weeks, Judy's students would arrive at her door promptly at seven p.m. Removing their shoes, they followed her into the only warm room in the house: the kotatsu (stove) room. In the center was a large square hole equipped with an urn holding hot coals. Over this hole was a table covered with a thick quilt that draped over the sides. Judy and her guests sat at the edge of the hole, their legs under the table, the quilt keeping in the heat. They wore heavy padded jackets and sipped hot tea to keep their upper bodies and hands warm. The young men were the soul of courtesy, for although Judy was sure that her beauty and exotic outsider status excited them, they extended her the respect due a married woman, an "oksan." They practiced their colloquial English with her and she practiced her elementary Japanese with them. She was delighted with both their company and the opportunity to learn more about Japanese culture and customs. Not to mention basking in male attention, something she missed from her madcap single days.

Shortly after this interlude, just when the students' camp ended, Judy and Bob moved again, into a house they had coveted for some time, previously inhabited by their friends the Scribners, who had decided to move onto the Navy base because Mrs. Scribner was pregnant and they felt it would be safer there. The new house, about a hundred yards away from their first one, was only two years old, and was luxurious by Japanese standards: it boasted a semi-automatic gas boiler in an enclosed service porch, where the kerosene was also stored, "so you don't have to traipse out in the rain to get it." The kitchen walls were wood-paneled, with tile and carved woodwork. Other rooms had wood floors and beams, and the garden held flowers and a fish pond filled with bright orange carp. As in the first house, there was a maid's room on the second floor, which Judy planned to use as an art studio.

They hired a housekeeper, Misa San, who came in twice a week. She was a hard worker, and although she spoke only a few words of English, Judy was able to converse with her well. Misa San did all the washing (by hand), the ironing and cleaning, working from nine to five, with only a half-hour lunch break, for 400 yen/day ($1.10 U.S. [$8.75]).

Even with all the physical, financial and language struggles, Judy and Bob found time for social life. Their friends the Rileys were stalwarts, and Judy went to church with Mickey and the children, caring for their youngest, Jef ("he is as cute as a button") and carrying him to church so that Mickey, who taught Sunday School, could go earlier with the older children. They also met another American couple, Ed and Jennine Peoples, about same age as Bob and Judy but with three children. Most of their activities were quiet ones, staying at home, having dinner together, listening to music. Even so, Judy found them to be "as unconventional as Bob and I, and we are doing the weirdest things at the weirdest hours, like swim-ming in the bay at 2 a.m."

Once, Judy and Bob were invited to the home of a well-to-do Japanese family, owners of a large lumber and pulp factory. The son had gone to Kieo University in Tokyo (then the most expensive university in the country), then on to Yale for his graduate degree. The imposing house was an architectural masterpiece, a blend of contemporary and traditional styles, plush yet characteristically simple in the Japanese style. It was wired with an intercom system— unheard of in those days. There were rare objects of art and a beautiful garden, with the house on the garden side completely open in summer, presiding imposingly over a sweeping lawn and several ponds, dotted with decorative stone lanterns.

From the minute the young couple arrived, the two housemaids kept up a constant food service, all the items delicate, delicious, and artistically arranged. These were only the hors d'oeuvres, though; a twelve-course dinner was served starting at about six p.m. The matriarch of the house kept an antique bell at her side for calling the maids (evidently the intercom system was not to be used for such lowly folk). In the evening, the garden was lit with soft blue lights, and classical music played in the background. The entire family were refreshingly intelligent and charming, and everyone but the matriarch spoke English well.

Judy traveled to Tokyo from time to time, both with and without Bob. This bustling city was, by the early sixties, one of the most Westernized in Japan, with international food and entertainment offerings. At the end of April, Judy and Mickey saw the English Royal Ballet perform, and in late September, Judy went with Bob to see the American Holiday on Ice show, Swan Lake, preceded by a meal at a German restaurant in Tokyo. After the show they stopped for coffee at a lovely hideaway cabaret in Shinjuku. About a week later they went to see "Carmen" at the Tokyo Takarazaka Theatre, presented by a French company. This was Judy's first opera attendance, and she loved it.

Unfortunately, their after-show homeward trek was another disastrous Japanese adventure. It was pouring rain and they had not taken their umbrellas. It took them over an hour to get a cab, by which time they were thoroughly soaked, and Judy lost her hat in the cab. Attempting to catch the train home, they got trapped in the rush-hour stampede. "Dripping wet, tired, Bob with a splitting headache, me with throbbing feet and sit-down-spike-heeled shoes, we were herded into the train along with thousands of others—and couldn't even see the seats, much less sit in them." The train kept making unusually long stops at each station and there were unintelligible announcements coming over the intercom system. Two hours later—instead of the usual 45 minutes—they arrived at Kamakura, and passengers started disembarking. "At last, a seat!" they thought as they slumped wearily onto the green cushions. "Ha, ha, no such luck!! A wizened old man tugged on our arms saying 'Dozo ... sayonara ... train ... domme!!' At first we thought we were just to change trains. Then we saw the multitudes swarming to the exits. The scene was a confusion of rain, buses, loud-speakers blaring, umbrellas, cars, and weary people. I thought my feet were going to give out and Bob was sure his head would fall off—but we hobbled to the nearest umbrella shop, departed with umbrellas but 1300 yen ($3.50 U.S. [$28]) less in our pockets, hiked up a few mud alleys to try and flag down a taxi before it reached the other thousands of needy, stranded passengers. Some time later, Bob saw a car coming and signaled to it. It came to a screeching stop and the driver yelled, 'Doko desu ka?' (Where are you going?) 'Zushi!' we replied. 'Daijobu' he answered ... so we hopped in. About ten minutes later I noticed it wasn't a cab. Mmmmm, this could prove interesting, I thought, if not fatal. On our way to Zushi we saw the trouble ... a train had derailed. From the looks of the situation, I'm sure there must have been a number of injuries. We arrived safely at our destination and the driver charged us the regular cab rate. The following day we learned that many private cars had been called to help the stranded passengers." Japan was still Japan, Western influence or no; the old informal business networks yet under-girded the modern industrial economy.

Although by October Bob had finally started getting his marriage allotment, with back pay, the couple was not out of the woods financially. "The honeymoon is over! We put ourselves on a strict budget last month." They needed to save for Christmas, after several months of spree spending. "Since I've come to Japan it has been a 'monetary-fairy-tale-existence.' ... Actually, [though,] I am an ichi-ban (#1) budgeter, as I've had many years of practice before this marriage."

This resolution did not seem to last long, however, as a few days later she wrote, "I splurged and fulfilled a lifelong dream... a fawn-colored suede jacket." She also bought some olive green and black mohair material, at $8 [$64] a meter, for a tailored coat. This cost a total of $40 [$320] including labor, but she had a $125 [$995] coat when it was done.

Judy had not abandoned her obsessive need to buy new clothes, although she was becoming somewhat more practical about them. Her Christmas requests to her family included "a terry-cloth robe for Bob, and for me knee-length fur-lined slippers (I freeze even in mukluks), and a very warm fleecy coat-sweater, with a hood. Also some full-length spun nylon/ flannel gowns, "minus all that rosebud and babyish garbage print (if there is such a thing as a sexy winter gown...it's for me). In Japan one cannot escape the winter cold; houses are not heated here as there."

Judy and Bob in their traditional Japanese garb. Photo: Carr/Pettit family collection.

Yet she was also learning the practicality of re-using clothes: "I am having almost my entire ward-robe altered. This includes numerous outfits that Chris has given to me over the years. Things that she either didn't like, got tired of, didn't fit her or wore only twice. 90% of my winter clothes are her generous cast-offs made to fit me. I'll still have them when I return to the States. You'll be surprised how many things you will remember as once belonging to Chris." She had a hard time finding shoes to fit her, though, as she wore a size 8, and 6 was the largest available in the Japanese stores.

The Navy did not stock anything acceptable, although they could special order items. Judy preferred to ask her family to send her shoes from the States.

By early 1962, the young couple's finances had finally improved enough to allow Judy to enroll in some courses at the university, and she started attending two days a week, taking a class in Japanese art history. She made some friends among the students, and accompanied them on a few skiing trips on Mount Fuji. And once again, she traded help with English for assistance with Japanese, as she had with the young wrestling students.

While Judy never was much of a political animal, she did take some interest in the subject, and made occasional references in her letters home. She read *The Ugly American*, and noted, "I can see it happening over here—all the blunders made by the service men and their families in their dealings with the Japanese. It just sickens me. But I and a few others are fighting our campaign, as small as it may be, against the injustice of inequality and the pompous, false superiority displayed by so many Americans."

And in a later letter: "*How much do you really* know about Cuba? Americans are screaming that Castro is a murderer and the Cubans are Communists. But do you know what prompted the revolution and what forces created the Cuba of today? How much do you know about Bautista's Cuba? I was screaming along with the rest of the uninformed Americans until I read C. Wright Mills, *Listen, Yankee*. He is one of the few respected yet outspoken authors left in this mess we call civilization. READ IT!"

When it came to family and relationships, though, Judy was truly passionate. She worried that her 18-year-old sister Chris was rushing into a relationship with Bob Pettit (to whom Chris has now been married for over fifty years).

And her mother's alcoholism was an ongoing family issue. Evidently her mother had queried Judy about her feelings about it, for one of her letters addressed the issue forthrightly, although with the judgmental approach that she continued to use toward her family for many years:

> Mother you are always putting me on the spot
> about the cause and effect of your illness. ..after this
> letter I will answer neither in the *affirmative* or the

negative. It will be impossible for me to lie to you if I
refrain from making *any* comment. Do not mistake
this attitude for apathy or a lack of love for you. It is
just the opposite. I love you too much to hurt you any
more. So please don't put me on the spot any more
because I'm afraid I will not respond.

Four years ago I got out on my own because of
several things: a fierce desire for independence (I'm
the restless, unconventional type); a clash of personalities between you, Mother, and me. (This has nothing to do with love. Often those whom you love the
most you cannot live with; your nerves upset me and
my ileum.) Moving closer to school was just the convenient factor that made my break possible.

And for the hundredth time, Mother, I will tell you
that the whole family knows that your drinking is only
the *obvious result.* There is always a *cause* for excessive drinking. Drinking is only one of the many escape
mechanisms people use to erase their problems. What
is most upsetting to the family that loves you is that
you let your problems and griefs torment you so and
that you are so unhappy."

This was only the beginning of Judy's many letters and phone
calls abjuring her family to get their act together; it would be a sore
point, especially with Chris, for many years.

In May, 1962, Bob got orders to return to the States, and he and
Judy began to sort through their acquired belongings, to minimize
what they had to carry and ship back, although in fact they kept
quite a bit. They had, after all, just set up housekeeping. They took a
few of their kitchen items, most of their clothes, and a number of
futons and zabatons, shipping the bulk of their possessions and
flying back with only a few suitcases.

Judy had been in Japan for little more than a year, but the short
adventure had changed her life. She was now a young married
woman, had developed many new skills and learned a great deal
about herself and her capabilities, and had come to appreciate the
Japanese values of harmony, balance and subtle beauty. Although she
never set foot in Japan again, she carried with her fond memories of
the quiet gardens in Yokohama, the exhilarating crisp winter days on
Mount Fuji, the haunting music and the fluid sounds of the Japanese

language. She also left Japan with mixed feelings about returning to the easier life of middle-class 1960s America. Relieved to be freed from the hardships, Judy was nevertheless regretful at leaving the excitement and the frequent challenges that had functioned to divert her from any emotional pain she might otherwise have had to confront.

Florida would be quite another story.

5
Moving On

Judy and Bob traveled separately back to the states, as he had to make a stop in Alaska first. Judy went straight to Hialeah, Florida and found them a small house to rent. After about six months, they moved to a two-bedroom apartment on Southwest 74th Street in Miami, just a few blocks from the University of Miami campus, where they quickly fell in with a motley crowd of about a dozen young people much like themselves, college students and young married couples.

Housing was still relatively cheap in those days, even taking inflation into account, as the Baby Boomers, with their high expectations, had not yet invaded the housing market. Young people could still survive comfortably on irregular employment. Indeed, Bob seemed to be the only one in their circle of friends with a steady job. While this was not exactly the Beat crowd, they were on the fringes, trying their best to imitate the lifestyle, and they fancied nearby Coconut Grove to be a sort of tropical Greenwich Village.

Bob and Judy in their small home in Miami. The roundish white object in the background of the right-hand photo, just to Judy's right, is a Japanese lamp. Photo: Carr/Pettit family collection.

One of the young men in this group, Ty, the scion of a wealthy family, provided whatever funds they needed for luxuries. He had set up a sort of mock coffee house in his den, and it was here that the group gathered to hang out and smoke weed while Ty played folk music on his guitar. Ty's wife Carole was sensuous and earthy, and Judy admired how comfortable she was in her body. Judy, however, could not bring herself to go without makeup or to wear loose-fitting, unglamorous clothing as Carole did.

Another couple, Mel and Susan, both redheads, looked so much alike that they were often mistaken for brother and sister rather than husband and wife. They kept three pet monkeys in a cage in their living room. Then there was Liv, tall with rich brown tresses, a student from Norway, and her boyfriend Attilla, who usually went by the nickname Pete (to avoid the "Hi, Hun" jokes).

Ty also had a friend, Jim, who knew how to capture poisonous snakes, which could be sold for $25 [$190] each to a company in Miami, where their venom would be extracted and sold to pharmaceutical companies for producing antivenin. (The snakes were then released back to the wild.) Judy, always ready for adventure, accompanied them on at least one of these expeditions into the Everglades. They traveled in Ty's Jeep until the trail became too narrow, then proceeded on foot, in protective hip-high wading boots, khaki slacks and helmets. The slough sheltered all kinds of exotic creatures, from panthers to wild boars to the water moccasins they sought, and the trio made their way cautiously, ducking under the orchid vines trailing down the trunks of stately cypresses, sloshing through the muck, alert to dangers both real and imagined. Mosquitoes were ubiquitous, naturally, and the heavy layer of repellent they slathered on provided only a slight deterrent. The snakes could be found sleeping in mud holes just out of the midday sun. It took two people to capture a snake: one to hook the head with a forked stick, the other to grab the tail, and both of them to stuff the creature into a burlap bag. They could collect four or five snakes per trip, netting as much as $150 [$1,150].

Once, Ty decided to hunt alligator, and Judy went along on that expedition, too, this one by boat through the Everglades. Jim tried unsuccessfully to lasso a large gator, who fortunately escaped rather than turning on his would-be captor. Then they spotted a smaller one swimming across a quiet pond. Judy, determined not to let this one get away and heedless of the danger, threw herself out of the boat on top of the animal. This one, too, proved shy, and slipped away, while Judy's consternated hunting companions hauled her back into the boat and tended to her hands, which were cut and bleeding. It was all in a day's adventure, though, and the unsuccessful hunting party headed back to town in Ty's Jeep, passing around bottles of beer and a joint, which Judy managed to manipulate with her bandaged hands using a wire clip as a holder. They stopped and bought alligator steak at the supermarket.

(Although Juliet related this hunting adventure in her later journals, she hedged about its veracity: "Did it really happen or is it just another tall tale I love to tell?" The snake tale, however, is corroborated by Bob Watt.)

Judy and Bob host Judy's sister Chris and her husband Bob for a Japanese dinner in their Miami home. Left to right: Bob Watt, Bob Pettit, Chris, Judy. Photo: Carr/Pettit family collection.

In another attempt to make money, Bob and Ty cultivated several marijuana plants, starting them in large tin cans in the bedroom. Judy carefully set them out on the side of the building each morning, so they would get some sun. Although this area was in full view of all the neighbors, few people in those days could tell a marijuana plant from a tomato, and as soon as the plants grew to about four inches in height, the men transplanted them to a place near the edge of the Everglades, going out to water them them twice a week. Alas, later that summer they were burned in a weed-control fire. After that, Judy and Bob decided to stick to petunias.

Not that there was a shortage of smoking material; Ty saw to that. And in an effort to make their small apartment into a hippie pad, Judy painted the living room ceiling in iridescent colors and studded it with stars. The pot-heads would lie on tatami mats, zoned out, floating in the music emanating from the large speakers Bob had installed in the corners of the room. Occasional trips to the nearby convenience store kept them in Chunky's chocolate bars and Cheetos.

Judy also had a family connection in the area, as her sister Chris had moved to Nassau, the Bahamas with her husband Bob Pettit. Now that the sisters were each established in their own lives, Judy's childhood jealously of Chris was fading, and the two of them were able to enjoy each other's company. Judy took a number of trips to the islands, and Chris and her husband spent a few weekends with Judy and Bob as well. The young couples made some friends among the well-to-do American tourists, and enjoyed swimming, boating and snorkeling in the warm Atlantic waters.

Informal nude photographs Judy had Bob take for her. Later, she paid a professional photographer to help her create a portfolio for modeling work. Photo: Carr/Pettit family collection.

In addition to all her partying and adventures, Judy managed to find time for real life. She attended classes at the University of Miami, hoping to finish up her degree, and drifted through several mundane jobs to supplement Bob's Navy income—cocktail waitress, clerk at the airport Avis Rent-a-Car office, receptionist at the Burger King headquarters. She also sought modeling work, even paying a professional photographer to shoot her for a portfolio, including some nude (artistic, not erotic) shots. Judy was a natural model; her beauty, tall slender frame, innate sense of drama and knowledge of art composition were exactly the qualifications studios were looking for. Yet, surprisingly, she never broke into the modeling field with enough steady work to support herself.

Eventually, she decided to go to a trade school to supplement her office skills, and found a secretarial job with Sepy Dobronyi, a highly successful Hungarian jeweler who also seemed to engage in a number of questionable activities on the side. He appeared to be involved in organized crime, or at least to have some connections with it, and lived a lavish lifestyle, residing in the Coconut Grove mansion previously owned by the valiant World War I aviator Eddie Rickenbacker. Sepy frequently traveled, most often to Europe, and during his absences allowed Judy and Bob the run of this impressive 24,000-square-foot brick Mediterranean-style residence. The place boasted a three-car garage (palatial in those days), a formal dining room that could seat at least twenty, and a kitchen with every gadget available at the time. Judy and Bob lived like royalty, cooking sumptuous meals, helping themselves to the well-stocked liquor cabinet, and cavorting in the Olympic-sized pool and on the ornate bed in the master bedroom. Chris and her husband Bob enjoyed the mansion's delights on a few occasions as well, when they visited from Nassau.

Sepy also maintained a photography studio in Coral Gables, which he rented to free-lancers, including model-turned-photographer Bunny Yeager, who shot the first *Playboy* centerfolds. This studio rivaled the Eddie Rickenbacker mansion in unique decor, inside and out. It was a small building hidden at the end of a lane edged with colorful tropical plants. It included an upper-story bedroom extending out to a balcony dramatically carved to resemble the prow of a Viking ship. This balcony overlooked the back yard, which was secluded behind lush vegetation and contained a small swimming pool. The studio itself was downstairs, along with a small office, changing room and kitchen. Like the Rickenbacker mansion, it was well stocked with food and liquor. Judy and Bob spent many of their spare hours here as well, including a few overnights in the eclectic bedroom. A number of parties were hosted here, attended by creative and off-beat personalities—friends and acquaintances of Sepy's, including *Playboy* founder Hugh Hefner. Judy loved the romance and adventure of both the place and the company.

It was through Sepy's connections with these early pornographic photographers that he eventually became a director of some of the early "sexploitation" films—rather lame affairs showing nudists at play without revealing any significant body parts. Judy had a small role as a clothed police officer in one of these films. At that time, though, it would never have crossed her mind to seek any major role, or to extend her search for modeling work to the budding porn photography business. She still saw herself as a respectable middle-class woman and looked askance at such trends. Nor would she have considered exposing her body in public, even within the limitations imposed in the early 1960s.

One of the most positive effects of working for Sepy, though, was Judy's dawning realization that she had an appeal to upper-class men. Not only was she beautiful, she was also poised, intelligent and well educated enough to handle herself in upper-class social situations, at least in the short term. Whether Judy responded positively to any moves Sepy made on her, at least in these early days, is not clear. But it was probably through him that she met a man she referred to as Chas, a wealthy Sicilian, with whom she later had a romantic connection.

It was in their small apartment in Miami where Judy heard the news, on Friday afternoon, 22 November 1963, of JFK's assassination. Bob was out running errands, and Judy was off work for the day, at home listening to the radio. When Bob returned, she was in tears. Like most Americans, Judy and Bob spent the next several weeks in shock, sorrow and disbelief. Having no TV themselves, they visited friends to watch some of the incessant newscasts, including the funeral procession, live cast from Washington, D.C.

In early 1964, partly to help make ends meet and partly to help out a friend who needed housing, Judy and Bob took in a roommate, a 19-year-old college student named Cheryl. With Judy gone much of the day, and given Cheryl's irregular class schedule, Cheryl was often alone in the apartment, although Bob sometimes came home earlier than Judy, or stopped by for lunch. Their encounters evidently turned physically intimate, for in May, Cheryl announced that she was pregnant, and named Bob as the father. Since he evidently did not deny that this was possible, there was no doubt that he had at least had sex with her.

Naturally, Judy felt deeply betrayed. She had no idea that Bob had not taken his wedding vows seriously enough to refrain from acting on any other attractions he might have. And, to add insult to injury, he asked Judy not only to help find an abortionist, but also to hock her wedding ring to pay for the procedure. She complied—the ring was meaningless to her now, after all; in fact, it reminded her of her pain. And Sepy was able to find a back-alley Cuban abortionist in Miami, even driving Cheryl to the appointment—after, of course, taking his own fee in the flesh from her.

Decades later, Juliet realized how much of a victim Cheryl had been as well, but the pain never went away. Bob was the first man she had really loved and trusted, and her sense of betrayal was deep. She never entirely forgave him, just as she never forgave her parents for preventing her from pursuing a career as a child actress. Well into her fifties, Judy was still obsessing about both of these betrayals.[8]

Despite her recriminations, though, Judy's interpretation of this incident may have been somewhat over-dramatized. Bob's importance in her life had been primarily as a ticket to get away from what she considered her mundane life, to sweep her off her feet and out of the U.S., to the romantic land of Japan. Her "love" for him was more about the experiences he could give her than about truly caring for him. Furthermore, Judy may not have been leading an entirely sterling life herself. A list of men she had sex with, drawn up decades later, includes Sepy, although whether that particular coupling occurred before or after the Cheryl incident is not clear. Truth be told, Judy and Bob were drifting apart, no longer needing each other's support through the challenges of living in a foreign country, nor sharing enough long-term goals and values to commit to a lifelong

---

[8] Bob Watt denies any memory of this entire incident.

relationship. And Judy had no real interest in being a military wife; she sought bigger adventures.

Whatever the exact circumstances surrounding the Cheryl incident, though, it precipitated Judy's and Bob's separation. Judy moved to a one-room mother-in-law unit in Hialeah, while Bob returned to base housing. In October, he was reassigned to Bainbridge, Maryland, and in July 1965, back to Japan, having by then impregnated another woman, Susan, whom he later married. Judy numbly initiated and carried through the divorce proceedings, with neither resistance nor participation from Bob; the divorce was final in August 1965. Bob evidently did feel some remorse, as his 1965 Christmas card to Judy, sent from Japan, includes the short notation "I'm sorry I failed."

With the breakup, Judy's finances took a dive. Bob left her the car, but also the payments, which her small budget barely covered. She was still struggling along on her part-time clerical work, supplemented by occasional modeling jobs she was able to find. Depressed and wanting a change in scenery, Judy jumped at an invitation to vacation in Mexico with the Sicilian she called Chas, whom she had started dating. He called her from Acapulco and asked her to fly out and join him and another couple "for a week of romance in the southern sun." Since it was difficult for him to wire her money from Mexico, Judy borrowed the plane fare—$200 [$1,530]—from her parents, not telling them why she wanted it (they assumed she needed an abortion) because to them it would have seemed irresponsible to be running off to Mexico.

Acapulco was beginning to burgeon into a tourist town for well-to-do Americans, and the two couples stayed in a hotel bungalow perched on a cliff overlooking the sea, bougainvillea spilling down its white-washed stucco walls and climbing the lattices enclosing the patio. Judy, like Chas, knew enough Spanish to make her way around, and the small party meandered down quaint lanes lined with expensive boutiques, fish stalls, souvenir shops and outdoor restaurants, the smell of the heat-baked streets mixing with the salty air. In the mornings, uniformed waiters traipsed over the lawn from the main hotel building next door, bearing huge plates of fruit, steaming coffee and warm pastries for their breakfast on the patio.

Chas took her shopping for some clothes appropriate to the climate, including a sexy bikini—a real treat for her, as she had been getting by on thrift-shop clothes and feeling deprived, as she had as a teenager. The local American Penney's store was so plush that it featured an outdoor restaurant partially encircled by a swimming pool, with terraces leading down to a well-kept private beach. The young tourists sipped Mai Tais as they lounged under blue-striped umbrellas, watching the deep green-blue breakers roll in.

> I enjoy being a temporary kept woman. Chas is easy to please, a sharing of some simple sex ... Last night we went to a fabulous party at the home of the CEO of Coca-Cola in Mexico—a palatial hacienda on the lip of a cliff jutting out to sea. 'Beautiful people' mingled around a lit pool upon which floated a platform supporting a live Mariachi band. I felt like Dorothy in Oz but successfully faked enough sophistication to fit in. Uncomfortable being viewed as a whore, I pretended I was an English teacher who collected dashing decadent gentlemen.

This aristocratic lifestyle did nothing to protect Judy from the local water supply, however, and she suffered a bout of dysentery during her short stay, putting a real crimp in her activities for about a day and a half.

At the end of this glamorous week, Judy boarded the plane back to the States. Yet she was not really prepared to jump back into her struggling lifestyle. Since she had a layover in Mexico City, she decided to contact a Mexican she had met on the plane on her trip down, an auditor in IBM's Mexico City office; she had kept his business card. He was in the office when she called to suggest that he come over to the airport and take her out for a drink. As they sat in the airport bar, José twirling his swizzle stick in his rum and Coke as he offered to guide her around the city, Judy could tell that behind his friendliness lurked unadulterated lust. No matter; "far from being offended, I regarded a little sex as a fair trade." Although she did not find the middle-aged paunchy José attractive, "I had nothing to rush back to Miami for, and here was another adventure."

Without admitting it, she had entered the sex business.

So it was that Judy retrieved her luggage from the plane and prepared for an extended vacation in Mexico City. José, who turned out to be Spanish rather than Mexican, found a room for her to rent from another IBM employee, Romano, a young married man with two small children, in a suburb of the city. Judy would join the family for a coffee-and-pastry breakfast each morning, then accompany Romano to work, and spend her mornings wandering the streets, before José took them both out for lunch. She spent the rest of her day sightseeing: to the museum, the Pyramid to the Moon Inca ruins, the floating gardens. Then to José's apartment for an evening fuck, followed by a shower, dinner and either a show, dancing, or just strolling in the park. José would then drive her back to the two-story tract house for the night.

Judy hated José's apartment, a dark, cramped basement flat near the IBM headquarters building, where Judy could smell a gas leak although José could not. "But no point in protesting; it was part of our agreement. He showed me the sights and bought me meals, I fucked him. I was naturally passionate and loved sex, so I almost always had a good time sexually with men, even if they weren't skilled lovers. I was mute orgasmic" [then], "affectionate and exuberant and didn't depend on my partner

Judy expressing her exuberance, at the beach
Photo: Carr/Pettit family collection.

to make me happy. José, like most of my sexual partners, thought I was great."

Yet Judy encountered pain and degradation in Mexico—other people's, not her own. Her most vivid memory was of poor women with their children in tow, crawling on bloody knees up the stone steps of the cathedral, rosaries in hand, crossing themselves and praying to a male god for forgiveness for the sin of being a woman with too many hungry mouths to feed. (At least, that was Judy's interpretation of the ritual.) The scene filled Judy with such horror that, after her first exposure to it, she closed her eyes every time she and Romano drove past on their way into the city.

After a while, the romance and intensity of this exotic vacation began to wear thin, and Judy wanted to get back home to Miami. While it was fun to be a kept woman, the dependency went against her grain. And José was beginning to be a problem. He was mistaking her lust and her willingness to be romanced for love, and was soon begging her to return to Madrid with him. He even hired a Mariachi band to serenade her at three a.m., much to the amusement of her hosts and the neighbors. She packed up and left after three weeks.

This short vacation in Mexico City was the only basis for Juliet's later entry, on her resume, "1965-1966: ESL teacher in Mexico City, for employees & execs of IBM" and her claim, on her website, that "I lived in Mexico City where I taught English at IBM and explored the country." While

Sam's yacht, which he planned to sail around the world. He invited Judy to accompany him. Photo: Carr/Pettit family collection.

she may have helped her host family with a little English practice, to call this interlude an ESL job was nothing more than another one of Juliet's "enhancements of reality."

Back in Miami, Judy was able to land a less glamorous but more stable job as executive secretary for Breakstone Designs, a small husband-and-wife-owned architectural and interior design firm in Miami. Judy did the bookkeeping and payroll, and performed various secretarial duties. She enjoyed working with this intelligent, professional couple, and, with her natural artistic talent, she began to develop an eye for interior design herself.

But Judy was restless. Was she going to spend the rest of her life working office jobs? Surely there were more adventures ahead. At some point, perhaps on one of her Bahama weekends, Judy met Sam, another well-to-do man who owned a forty-foot yacht, in which he was planning to sail around the world. He invited Judy along, and in September 1966, she flew to Lisbon to meet him. Instead of accompanying him on this adventure, however, she abandoned him there in Portugal. Another man was about to grab her attention.

6

Passion and High Drama in the Mediterranean

No information survives on the details of when and how Judy met the greatest love of her life, Nikolas. He has said that they met through their mutual involvement in underwater archeological expeditions off the coast of Greece, probably in the fall of 1966. Her passport indicates that she first arrived in Athens on 14 October 1966.

Her sojourn in Greece is the period of Judy's life that she talked about least in later years, either publicly or privately. None of her closest friends in the U.S. knew any of the details, and many did not even know she had lived in Greece. Her public statements about this time in her life were brief. She said that she worked as a photo-journalist, studied Greek art and history at the University of Athens, and taught ESL, in addition to the underwater expeditions; and that she "had the most powerful and transformative love affair of my life during this time." Given Judy's propensity for fabrication, we cannot be sure how much of this was true, especially the university studies, ESL teaching or photojournalism work; she often used these ruses to give an air of legitimacy and independence to her activities, when actually she was primarily busy being a consort.

Even her private writings contain little information—only an admonition to herself in 1991: "Write about meeting Nikolas—the concrete details!" She never followed through on this intention, however. "I can't write about Nikolas," she lamented elsewhere in her journals. Although she wrote frequently to her family during the one-and-a-half years she was in Greece, those letters have been lost. Her family remembers only that they were filled with stories of drama and adventure, not all of which they took seriously. Only two postcards from this time in Judy's life were among the epistles she kept—one written in 1966, shortly after her arrival in Europe, and one in early 1968, a few months before she returned to the U.S.

It is indeed surprising that Judy spoke so little about this time, because it was obviously the most dramatic and exciting period of her life—due, for a change, more to external circumstances than to her emotional turmoil or usual embellishments. Even for a country that had experienced little economic or political stability since the early nineteenth century, 1967 and 1968 still stand out as years of upheaval in Greece.

In the 1960s Greece, like Japan, was still recovering from the aftereffects of World War II, when it had been occupied by the Germans. King George returned from exile in September 1946 but died within a few months, succeeded by his brother Paul, since his son Constantine was only six years old at the time. Yet the country was still in the grip of a civil war that had begun even before Germany's defeat, in September 1944, when the British helped drive out the invading Germans. Guerilla Communist forces battled several other factions, both leftist and more conservative, including those who supported the monarchy; the monarchy faction finally prevailed in October 1949.

Like all civil wars, this one was bitter and divisive. Nikolas's own father was killed by one of the leftist factions. Nikolas was a teenager at the time, and nursed a lifelong bitterness against the left.

It was not until October 1952 that Greece reached any real political or economic stability. There was controversy, for example, about trade with defeated Germany; whatever their failings, the Germans provided a steady market for Greek tobacco, one of the major exports. Still, Greece joined NATO and the Organization for European Cooperation and Development (OECD), and later the European Economic Community, during the early 1950s. King Paul died in 1964, succeeded by then-twenty-three-year-old Constantine, whose mother Frederika (of German ancestry) remained as queen.

The mid-1960s, however, ushered in new hostilities. The young king soon embroiled himself in a conflict with Prime Minister Papandreou, ultimately dismissing him and forming a new government. This rash move destabilized the country almost to the point of revolution. Parliamentary elections were set for May 1967, but the population, still suffering from economic woes, were restless, as was the military.

Nikolas, a remarkably young admiral in the Greek navy, was caught up in the chaos. The scion of an upper-class Greek family, he was very well educated, spoke fluent English, and was a skilled seaman; his family had been navy people for generations. He was only in his mid-thirties in 1966; Judy was twenty-eight. While not strikingly handsome, he had rugged good looks, with a solid build and thick, curly dark hair. He loved the sea, and spent much of his free time sailing, swimming and diving. The underwater archeological expeditions were a passionate hobby, bringing together his love of country and the sea.

Although Judy left behind few details about her relationship with Nikolas during these years, we can imagine a plausible scenario for her trip to Greece and their meeting.

Judy had flown to Lisbon, where she met up with her latest sugar daddy, Sam, who had sailed his forty-foot yacht across the Atlantic without her; we can certainly assume this much because she would never have neglected to recount the dramatic story—probably much embellished—of crossing the Atlantic in a yacht. With no specific plans to return to the U.S., Judy had gotten rid of most of her possessions, sending a few to her parents in California for safe-keeping.

While Judy did not elaborate on her reasons for dumping Sam in Portugal, these most likely involved some dispute around his expectations of her role on the voyage. Perhaps he made it clear that her job on the around-the-world sail was to be chief cook and bottle washer. Nothing could set Judy off like expectations of performing house-wifely duties; she had had her last fling at that in Japan. She was an artist, a free spirit, a liberated woman, although not above using sex to manipulate men, as long as her duties were limited to mad, passionate love-making, which she loved anyway.

Unburdened from Sam, Judy decided to do some traveling around Europe. After all, she was there; that was more than half the battle. She had some money saved up, and may have prevailed upon her parents to supplement these funds. Traveling in Europe was easier and cheaper in those days; youth hostels were a modest and readily available type of lodging, and she availed herself of these as she made her way across southern Europe.

She began with a train trip from Lisbon to Madrid, seeing a few sights there, and thence to Barcelona, on the coast. The weather was wonderful in September, and she spent long days on the beaches and ate in quaint restaurants or brought groceries back to the hostel. It was in one of the hostels that Judy met another young American woman, Kitty, who was also traveling alone. Kitty was headed for Athens, where she had a job working for an American company, and she invited Judy to travel with her. Why not? Judy thought. She had always wanted to wander among the ancient Greek ruins about which she had learned so much in the classical education she had received in American public school.

Pula, the coastal Yugoslavian town where Judy and Kitty vacationed on their way to Athens. Photo: Carr/Pettit family collection.

Judy and Kitty got on the train in Barcelona and traveled along the southern coast of France and through Italy, stopping briefly in Milan for a respite and a little sight-seeing, then continuing on to Zagreb, Yugoslavia, staying there for several days, and finally moving on to Pula, at the tip of the Istrian Peninsula, making it their home base for another week. Ah, to be young and free and on an adventure! Judy was in love—with the countryside. The welcoming Mediterranean climate matched that of her southern California home, but this was a foreign country—exotic, beckoning. Although Zagreb's architecture made it look like a medieval town, it had modern conveniences like art galleries, wonderful restaurants that served rare dishes like fried octopus, night clubs with fabulous rock bands, and plenty of shops. The countryside was scenic, too; Judy and Kitty rented bicycles and pedaled along the Sava River, passing through farmland and small villages.

But Pula—now *there* was a paradise. Situated directly on the "incredibly clear Adriatic Sea," it was the gateway to a "perfect escapist holiday": swimming, lazing on the beach, exploring. They went scuba diving and explored coral reefs, took a hydrofoil boat over to romantic Venice, joined an excursion up a fjord, and visited a nudist beach. This was Judy's first exposure to the more laissez-faire European attitude toward nudity and sexuality, and she loved the feeling of freedom and acceptance of the human body.

Then on, finally, to Greece, traveling by ship down the Yugoslav and Albanian coasts, through the Gulf of Pátra, reaching Athens on a sunny October afternoon. Dirty, noisy and crowded, the iconic Greek city was a stressful contrast to the lovely Adriatic coastal towns, and Judy at first wondered if she had made the right decision. But surely not all of Athens could be like the miserable downtown area that surrounded the port.

Disembarking, the young women made their way to the furnished flat that Kitty had already arranged to rent. Over the next few days, Kitty started settling in, buying household goods and getting to know the neighborhood, as her job was to begin in less than a week. She urged Judy to think about staying on for at least a few more weeks; she was welcome to live at the flat if she could contribute to the rent. Why not? thought Judy, once again. She had nothing to go back to in the States. Maybe some kind of work would turn up here and she could avoid going back to a boring life in the U.S.

Exactly how Judy became involved in the underwater archeological expeditions is unknown, but it is certainly the kind of activity that would have appealed to her passion for adventure. And she had been snorkeling and scuba diving since her Miami days, during her recreational trips to the Bahamas.

It was in late October that Judy went on her first dive with the group. Although the days were getting shorter, there was still plenty of warmth and sunshine, and Judy looked stunning as usual, in her skimpy body-hugging swimsuit, her long blonde hair tousled by the wind. As often when she was nervous, she covered up her trepidation with joking and flirtation, at least with those in the group who could speak English.

Nikolas, for his part, was noticeable in an entirely different way. Long used to being in command, he was taking charge—giving directions, taking care of technical glitches on the boat, and being treated deferentially as befit his status. He could not help noticing Judy, though; she stood out because of her appearance as well as her ignorance of the language and a certain degree of uneasiness. Ever the perfect host, Nikolas came over to welcome her as soon as his duties permitted.

Judy was smitten almost immediately, although she was somewhat intimidated by his self-confident manner. She could not know his true status, of course, dressed unpretentiously as he was in baggy chinos and a worn T-shirt. He told only her that he was a Navy man (like Bob Watt, she thought at first: "Do I need another sailor?"). He offered to accompany her on her first dive, an invitation she gratefully accepted.

At day's end, Nikolas asked her out to dinner for the following evening. He would not come to pick her up in person, though; he would send his personal driver. It was then that Judy realized he was a man of some means, and that she might be headed into another consort vacation, like the one in Mexico. Little did she know how much more intense this would be.

Judy was swept off her feet by Nikolas, but in a different way than she had been with her early college heartthrobs. Although she was of course impressed when she found out, during that first dinner date, that Nikolas was not just rich but politically powerful, it was not these qualities that thrilled her most. Nor was it his obvious intelligence and worldliness, nor his attentiveness to her, although those traits certainly did help to endear him to her. It was, rather, what she perceived as his personal magnetism.

Nikolas was intense, and Judy was drawn to intensity, while at the same time intimidated by it. Great manipulator though she was, she still felt somewhat awkward in Nikolas's presence. He was older than she, firmly established in his career and in his life as a person of social worth. Judy had never been personally acquainted with anyone of such standing—someone who knew who he was and where he was going in life. Indeed, one of his charms, for Judy, was deep and abiding financial stability; despite her oft-voiced desire to be a free spirit, she craved the protection of a man who would relieve her of the burden of working for a living.

As for Nikolas, he was drawn first of all to Judy's beauty, but also to her ebullience, her warmth, and her innocence. Although by this time Judy had been around the block a few times, and had traveled enough to observe first-hand some grinding poverty and misery, she had still been living largely in the bubble of middle-class white America, with no direct knowledge of privation or physical violence. Nikolas, on the other hand, had lived his entire life in a politically unstable country; even his high social status had not protected him from some of the suffering of his fellow countrymen. Judy made him happy, and he had not had much happiness in his life.

By the end of their first evening together, they felt deeply connected. It was a bond that would last for the rest of Judy's life, despite—as it turned out—the brevity of their time together.

The only surviving photographs of Judy with Nikolas. A note on the back of the picture on the right describes the water as deep aqua, the rock formation as pink. Photos: Carr/Pettit family collection.

It was not long before Judy became essentially a kept woman, although she may not have thought of herself that way. She probably harbored thoughts of marrying Nikolas, since that was the frame of reference she was familiar with. Although she had had her flings, she still thought of long-term commitment in terms of marriage—nothing less. For Nikolas, though, marriage with Judy would never have entered his mind. She was not marriage material for him: neither Greek nor upper-class, and clearly too emotionally unstable to handle herself consistently in high society. On the other hand, it was perfectly acceptable, even expected, for him to keep a mistress. Not publicly, of course, but among his circle of male friends and relatives, it was an arrangement that would not be frowned on.

The Room in the Greek Villa

White walls, warm, smooth, reflecting light, holding
me in their soft womb of an early pink dawn.

Beyond the window the brilliant Mediterranean
shimmering, potted red geranium on the sill. Twisted
pieces of driftwood, shells I found, trinkets hung on the
walls, a multi-colored hand-woven shawl draped
across a stiff-backed chair. Bread crumbs and strong
stale coffee in a tiny cup sit silently on the table
waiting for mice or a brave bird to make a feast.

I liked to lie on the low narrow bed and watch the
shadows paint the naked ceiling—an ever-changing
scene—fluid, illusory. When the moon was full I would
set objects in the window—ribbons, wheat grass, bits
of glass, bottles and paper sculptures—thru which the
light would cast shadows on the walls and ceiling.

My theatre, my four-walled shrine, my altar, a canopy
of ever-changing fantastic shapes, ever new.

-- Juliet Carr

These differences in perception, alas, would lead to heartbreak. Nikolas was the number one priority in Judy's life (aside from her passion for adventure). She, however, was fourth in his—after family, country, and the sea. It was in the long run a recipe for emotional disaster. Portentously, although inexplicably to Judy, her arthritis flared up the day after that first dinner date. This physical pain was a warning she ignored.

Nikolas first set Judy up in her own apartment in Athens. That city was where he spent most of his time and where he could easily drop in to see her whenever he had an afternoon or evening to spare —which was not often enough to satisfy Judy. Satisfaction, in fact, was never part of Judy's experience of Nikolas. He turned out to be a poor performer in bed. Not that he had any potency problem, but he lacked staying power. Evidently no one had ever informed him that a woman might want that, and Judy was far too intimidated to speak up for herself. Nikolas was intense and powerful, and she was emotionally and financially dependent on him. "I willed myself to be satisfied," she would later write of her frustrating experiences with him.

Yet Nikolas kept her entertained in other ways, buying her gifts, paying her way to the sights of Athens and on trips all around the northeastern Mediterranean, although it was rare that he could find the time to accompany her, and he hesitated to be seen with her in public, at least in Greece. Judy was often lonely and frustrated, but she so lived for their moments together that she was willing to put up with the scraps of attention he threw her.

Later, in 1978, Juliet wrote in her journal at great length and with the dramatic superlatives so characteristic of her, about her intense feelings toward Nikolas:

> It is a passion beyond passion, a love beyond love, a wonder beyond description...We cannot escape our oneness...the force of this love blinds me with tears...I cannot get enough of him; the more I have the more I want, yet the more I get the more dissatisfied I become. I am constantly frustrated. Nikolas answers a very basic need in me and still he leaves so many other sides unfulfilled that it is an impossible relationship.

Not long into their relationship she was also made aware of how many restrictions were going to be placed on her behavior. After one of the diving expeditions, she wanted to change into street clothes. Since they had had to disembark hurriedly and there was no private changing area at the beach, she draped a large towel over herself and changed underneath it—a technique that she and other female relatives had often used on beach expeditions back home. Nikolas was horrified, however, and admonished her, "You must always act like a lady, Judy. Never bring shame to me or my family." Judy was chagrined and ever after felt that she was under strict scrutiny.

Soon, however, there would be far more serious matters to worry about. On 21 April 1967, just a few weeks before the scheduled elections, tanks rolled into the streets of Athens. A group of colonels in the Greek army, fearing that the left wing would win the elections, was staging a military coup.

Despite Judy's love of drama, this real-life scenario was more than she had bargained for. She was frightened, huddling in her apartment for security. And she could not get hold of Nikolas. It was several days before he resurfaced. When he did, he sent for her to meet him at a villa he owned on one of the small islands in the Aegean. His love-making that night, while no more enduring than usual, was certainly more intense. And afterward, he wanted to talk. Clasping her so tightly to him that she could feel his warm breath on her hair, he told her of the ordeal he had gone through the night of the coup.

Pacing the deck of his destroyer, he had wrestled with his options. Should he speak for or against the navy's joining the coup?

He hated the colonels. There was not a man among them that he had any respect for or trust in. And yet, if the navy opposed them, would the country not degenerate into civil war again? He knew what that was like; his entire adolescence had been overshadowed by it; it had taken his father from him. And the leftist scum who had murdered his father were the only alternative, he felt, to what came to be known as the Regime of the Colonels.

The admirals would be meeting in the morning. Which course would he speak for; how would he cast his vote? Dawn came without an answer.

In the end, although neither the navy nor the air force supported the coup, the country did not, fortunately, erupt into civil war. Yet the threat hung in the air for months. Nikolas moved Judy several times, for safety, finally settling her in another villa—this one on the Isle of Khios, just offshore from Turkey. Her letters home told of sudden displacements, often at night, when she would be told to pack and move with only an hour's notice. Her family, while entertained, suspected her of exaggerating, but for once, she may not have been. Her family were not particularly politically savvy, and whatever news reached them about Greece at this time would have been overshadowed by the more dramatic Six-Day War in Israel in early June. It was a volatile time in the Mediterranean.

Judy with the octopus she and Nikolas caught while diving off Skopolos Island. Photo: Carr/ Pettit family collection.

Nikolas himself became even less available, disappearing for days or even weeks, with little communication. Still, he looked after Judy as best he could. From her safe haven in the east, she was able to continue recreational travels. She herself had but little interest in the political situation. Her friend Kitty, or one of the other two or three women she had been able to connect with in the short time before she met Nikolas, often accompanied her; Nikolas paid expenses for them all. And in November, he delighted and surprised her with a special formal dinner. Although few Greeks were even aware of the American holiday of Thanksgiving, Nikolas had learned enough about it to understand how much it meant to Judy.

In the midst of all the political upheaval of late 1967, he took the trouble to procure a wild turkey (hunted especially for the occasion) and have a feast prepared for his lady. He had temporarily moved Judy to a small cottage on the island of Skiathos, near where his destroyer was anchored, and he sent a boat to pick her up. Judy met the dinghy on the small weather-beaten dock, on a clear cold Thanksgiving Day. A young sailor stood in the bow, tall in his dress navy blues as the boat drifted to the dock. The pilot, a rank seaman, sat at the tiller and silenced the motor, and both men greeted her with a polite "Kalematias Neiti Carr." Vasilis, Nikolas's first mate, helped her on board. The dinghy threaded its way through the floating debris and the bobbing fishing boats at anchor, and headed out to sea to their destination, the Greek destroyer anchored just beyond the bay. The small white-washed buildings on shore, nestled along the curve of the bay, smiled in the sun. Judy's two-story pension abode stood proudly, with its red-tiled roof and a flower pot on the railing, like a decked-out mother hen hovering over her brood of smaller cottages. Donkeys and black-clad women were moving specks along the curve of the quay. Judy, dressed up for the occasion, shivered in the wind on the small boat.

Nikolas greeted her formally on the deck of the destroyer—trim, handsome, in blue dress uniform with brass buttons, high collar and visored cap. Judy knew how much he hated formal attire, much preferring the casual garb he had worn at their first meeting; his uniform itself bespoke his respect for her, his lover and guest of honor at this specially prepared American Thanksgiving feast. Judy wobbled across the deck in infrequently worn high heels—she reciprocating Nikolas's respectful formal dress—the wind whipping under her skirt, biting her thighs.

In Nikolas's stateroom a long table had been set with crystal, candles, and fine china embossed with the royal seal. Six naval men, also formally dressed, stood stiffly at attention behind their chairs along either side of the table. As she was introduced each man bowed with a serious "Welcome, Miss Carr." Judy was seated at one end of the table, Nikolas at the other.

The occasion began in formal silence as the steward poured the wine. Toasts were then made: to Greece, to King Constantine, to American President Johnson, to Commander Nikolas, and to Judy, and to the feast they were all about to enjoy. The tension broke then; the mood changed and formality gave way to laughter and big gulps of wine. Everyone was amazed at the food. Here in the Aegean between Greece and Turkey in a floating dining room, was a turkey, imported cranberry sauce and yams, along with rice, Greek salad, cheese, bread and lots of wine. For most of the diners, except Nikolas and Judy, it was the first taste of these exotic American foods.

Judy understood Greek well enough to share in the stories and understand some of the jokes. Everyone ate and drank too much, and they would all have hangovers the next day. But, ah—that was another day. Today they were celebrating an American Thanksgiving, giving thanks for the food and friendship made possible by a gallant commander, a generous and ardent lover who went out of his way to make it a memorable day for Judy. It was to be one of her few gratifying memories of Nikolas.

Despite this celebratory respite, the political situation in Greece continued volatile. While the navy and air force supported King Constantine, the young monarch's ill-advised attempt at a counter-coup in the early weeks of December failed, and he fled to Rome, not to return for another seven years, shortly after which the monarchy itself was dissolved.

Judy, though, was blissfully unconcerned about these political details. She never was much into politics, anywhere she lived, being only vaguely aware of events and issues, and holding no strong opinions. While she would probably have described herself as moderately left-wing, she never discussed political issues unless they directly affected her, and she kept company with some fairly politically conservative people over the years. In Greece in 1967 and 1968, she led the life of a high-class courtesan, expressing no interest in politics, and that was fine with Nikolas, who expected women to confine their energies to more intimate spheres. Judy continued to be a woman of leisure; her time in Greece, aside from the occasional midnight adventure, was like one long vacation.

Early in 1968 Judy took another trip at Nikolas's expense. Again in the company of her friend Kitty, she meandered around the Mediterranean, exploring the ruins of Knossos on the isle of Crete, and visiting Ephesus, riding a donkey up to a small cliff-perched village on the coast of Turkey. She was planning a ten-day trip back to the

U.S. in a few weeks, via Brussels and London. She expected to return to Greece. Alas, these plans changed radically.

Nikolas accompanied Judy during the European portion of this overseas trip. Most likely this excursion was part business trip for Nikolas, as he was still far too busy to indulge in lengthy vacations.

As with many relationships based on emotional dependency, Judy and Nikolas both had impossible expectations, and it was inevitable that these would eventually clash. What exactly happened in London is unknown, but it was traumatic enough to end Judy's liaison with Nikolas. She described it later as a domestic violence incident. Apparently, another man, probably a servant or lower-ranking naval officer, assisted Nikolas: "They almost killed me," Judy claimed, years later, but did not elaborate in any of her writings. Nor is there any indication of whether her injuries required medical care, or, if so, where she might have obtained it in London. But on 11 March 1968 she landed in New York. Presumably it was either Nikolas or her friend Kitty who packed up her belongings in Greece; Nikolas paid to have them shipped them back to the U.S.

That Juliet never wrote in more detail about this trauma, despite her many flashback journal entries in later years, is no doubt an indication of the level of genuine pain the incident and breakup caused her. It was beyond words, and for Juliet, that was saying quite a bit. Unlike many battered women, though, she did have enough self-esteem, and financial means, to leave.

7
Starting Over

Judy returned to the United States with a heavy heart. She had found amazing adventure with the greatest love of her life and yet it had all come crashing down. She was adrift again, and heartbroken. For although Nikolas's violence in London had struck fear into her heart, it had not driven out the passion. She had always been slightly afraid of him, and always would be. She had lived with that fear, and had accepted the crumbs of sex and affection Nikolas doled out, bound by her emotional dependency on him. The pain was more than she could bear to deal with right now, and she would have to put it off. Like Scarlett O'Hara, she would think about it... tomorrow.

Meantime, what to do with her life? She had had three major international adventures—in Japan, in Mexico, and in the Mediter-ranean—and two unsuccessful major relationships—a marriage and a passionate though ill-fated love affair. She had done virtually nothing toward building a career, despite her dreams of using her creativity. Well, here she was in southern California again, just four months away from her thirtieth birthday. She could pick up the pieces of her life and try to find fulfillment through her talents rather than through a man. Best to start by finishing her degree.

But she decided to wait until the fall semester for that. Now it was spring, and she would have six months to get settled and save up some money before starting school again in September. Since she planned to go back to Long Beach State College, she settled in Long Beach, renting a small apartment not far from the campus and work-ing at temporary clerical jobs while she looked for something more permanent.

Long Beach, twenty-two miles south of downtown Los Angeles, is a relatively quiet outpost of the metropolitan area. While the city boasts one of the world's largest seaports and a Naval shipyard, and is a major oil producer as well, life in Long Beach is slower-paced than in Los Angeles. The downtown is much smaller and less bust-ling, and the outlying residential neighborhoods evoke a quieter ambience; those directly on the coast, like Naples Island and Belmont

Shore, resemble any beach town, with pastel stucco residences lining the sunny but secluded streets.

The beach in Belmont Shore, looking toward downtown Long Beach, on the right-hand side of the picture; oil-rig island on the left. Photo ©2011 by Marian Rhys.

In earlier days, though, Long Beach was a busy recreational area, and home to The Pike, one of America's largest amusement parks, with its famous Dual Ferris Wheel and dual-track wooden roller coaster, the Cyclone Racer. Although the park was shut down in 1969, when Judy arrived in Long Beach The Pike was still up and running, and the luxury ocean liner the Queen Mary had steamed into Long Beach Harbor in December 1967, just a few months earlier. The ship soon became a major tourist attraction and luxury hotel, reflecting the shift to higher-income patrons that followed the prosperity of the 1960s.

In 1968, relatively cheap housing was still available in Long Beach, and the city served as a refuge for artists and other creatives. Not all of the locally owned businesses had been replaced with franchises; there were still mom-and-pop stores and restaurants, some of them down at the heel but nevertheless surviving, providing goods and services to the hippie fringe who had drifted down from Venice. The long, wide beaches that gave the city its name were never hectic or crowded; office workers from Los Angeles who could afford the commute jogged or strolled along the water's edge, before or after work. The air was deceptively clear, for although the offshore breezes kept it free of visible smog, Long Beach, then as now, was one of the most polluted cities in the country. Its port was one of the busiest on the West Coast, if not of the entire U.S., and oil rigs (disguised by clever landscaping) stood like sentinels off the coast. For Judy, it was a good place to sojourn for a while and plan for the future. It was certainly a refuge from the tumultuous political events of 1968, and Judy had experienced enough tumult in her own life in the previous year or so, thank you very much.

In the fall, she managed to land a teaching assistant job with the Long Beach public schools, which was actually the largest employer in town, despite the other thriving industries. This was the best Judy could do without a teaching credential, but the work was light enough to allow her to attend college part-time. Her first assignment was assisting in a kindergarten class.

Children always loved Judy. She was irreverent and full of fun, and her short attention span and high energy matched theirs. Her duties were

Judy in 1970, in Long Beach. Photo: Carr/Pettit family collection.

fairly simple: teaching the alphabet and counting skills, helping with arts and crafts projects, and supervising play activities. And for every holiday, she designed decorative displays for the windows and classroom walls, incorporating the kids' creations into the layouts.

Judy recommenced her own studies just a few weeks after the start of public school, around the end of September. Since kindergarten classes ended shortly after noon, she was able to take both afternoon and evening classes at the college. Having developed a little more practicality by now, she decided to major in English with a double minor in art and education. She loved to write almost as much as she loved to create art, and a degree in English would make her a little more marketable than a degree in art. With the education training, she could teach either subject.

Judy on vacation in Mexico, Thanksgiving 1968.
Photo: Carr/Pettit family collection.

Going back to school was a shock for Judy. The partying and cutting up that had so thrilled her from 1958 to 1960 now seemed vapid, and she looked with pity at the younger students who were still caught up in it. One thing, however, had not changed—her incessant pursuit of men. Despite her heartbreak over Nikolas, she was soon involved with a new man, Denny. Over the Thanksgiving holiday, they took a quick camping trip together to Mexico, riding burros into the wilderness. Denny had joined the Peace Corps and was soon sent to Cambodia; Judy kept in touch with him for a while.

After Christmas vacation, Judy was assigned to supervise the English and Reading Laboratory at a high school for "problem" youth who could not function in a regular classroom. Then, during the summer of 1969, she worked with fourth-graders with learning disabilities, who were trying to catch up so that they could attend regular school in the fall. When the summer session ended, Judy realized she needed more income to get by on, and reluctantly sought full-time employment. She found a job as assistant office manager at a company called Financial Communications, in Culver City; they printed and distributed various types of financial data. Taking only evening classes was more challenging, but she managed to stick with it, attending the summer session at Long Beach State that year, and finally got her degree in September 1970.

One of the benefits of Judy's living in southern California was being able to visit her parents, who were still living in San Diego, and sometimes her cousin Pam, who was now married and living in Redondo Beach. Sadly, an incident related to one of these visits led to a family rift that was never healed.

Pam's father Bob, Judy's uncle by marriage, was an engineer at General Dynamics, and he sometimes he gave Judy a ride from San Diego back to Long Beach, letting her join the carpool with several of his co-workers. In fact, since two of Bob's co-workers held pilot's licenses, there were even a few occasions when the group rented a small private plane for the trip—an added benefit that obviously appealed to Judy's sense of drama. On one of these occasions—whether traveling by ground or by air is not clear—Judy claimed that Bob made sexual advances toward her. Bob's version of the story, however, was that Judy made moves of her own, on some of the other male General Dynamics employees in the group, and he was so mortified by her behavior that he never spoke to her again, banning her from future family gatherings. Bob's wife Barbara, Pam's mother, took her husband's side in the squabble, while her sister Dottie, Judy's mother, took Judy's side. Where the truth lay no one knew, except presumably Judy and Bob, but the quarrel was never re-solved, and it added fuel to an already smoldering contentiousness between the sisters Barbara and Dottie. The feud eventually resulted in a permanent estrangement. Although the younger generation—Pam, Andy, Dan and Chris—tried on numerous occasions to bring their respective parents together again, they never succeeded, and the issue festered, making for some awkward situations over the years. And Judy, feeling eternally wronged, certainly never attempted to repair any bridges.

At some point during her sojourn in Long Beach, Judy met her next heartthrob, Ed Brown. It is not clear exactly where she met him, although it was most likely at the college; he may have been an instructor there. Following her usual pattern, Judy was swept off her feet, as they led a life of "carefree abandonment" for several months, topped off by a romantic camping trip over the Fourth of July weekend. With her usual hyperbole, Judy described her feelings about Ed: "[I]t is more than passion, more than dependence; he is simply my other half, without whom life would be very bleak. I want our love to survive and to live together, more than anything else. I hope to God I don't blow it." At thirty-two she was no more capable of distinguishing between lust and love than she had been at nineteen. She overlooked any undesirable character traits she saw in Ed, such as his too-quick temper. She abhorred his smoking habit, but figured she could cure him of that.

Ed was African American, and had decided to leave the States and go live in Europe, where he hoped there would be better opportunities, without racism to hold him back. (He may also have been dodging the draft, although he was probably over twenty-five, which was the upper age limit.) He had chosen Finland; exactly why is not entirely clear. Judy, of course, was always up for living abroad. Besides, she had decided that she actually wanted to lead a more traditional life, to settle down with one man, and have children. Ed would do as well as anyone else, and his ethnicity allowed her to feel that she was still rebelling against society.

Leaving most of their belongings in California and packing only a few boxes and one large chest in addition to their regular luggage, Judy and Ed loaded up his battered white Volvo station wagon, and set out in high spirits on 21 December 1970. They had been delayed two days by a fender bender and the consequent repairs to Ed's car that were required, and were now anxious to make good time, as they wanted to arrive in Philadelphia, where Ed's family lived, in time for Christmas.

They didn't get on the road until three p.m., and they drove through most of the night. The first challenge was crossing the San Bernadino Mountains, which had received sixteen inches of snow that day; some of the roads were solid ice. They stopped to put on chains as they entered the high country. Judy dozed while Ed drove, but she was rudely awakened at two a.m. to find the car in a terrifying spin. Despite the chains, the heavy load in back had made the car difficult to manage. Fortunately they ended up in a ditch rather than falling off a cliff, and two passing motorists stopped to help pull them out. They finally arrived in Flagstaff, Arizona, and checked into a motel, exhausted.

After rushed showers and a mid-morning breakfast, they headed off, driving through the night once again. And once again, they were forced to stop when Ed realized he was falling asleep at the wheel. At four a.m. they pulled over onto a wide shoulder, bundled themselves up warmly and managed to fall asleep in the car. They were awakened at six a.m. by a roaring snow plow. Ed got into a shouting match with the snow-plow driver; it would have come to blows had he not been in his stocking feet and unwilling to step out of the car. He and Judy did rouse themselves, however, and they drove on for another twenty miles, stopping again to sleep in a supermarket parking lot.

They awoke to a bright and clear desert morning and headed out. The road was clear, too, and straight as well, and they made

Judy and Ed, Christmas 1970
Photo: Carr/Pettit family collection.

good time until the car chains broke. Replacements cost $14 [$86]. Then, as night fell, both headlights went out and Ed had to labor for over an hour in 20° weather to fix them. He was not a happy camper at this point. Neither was Judy, as her recently-pierced ears were becoming painfully infected. To top it all off, the next morning she discovered she had lost her sunglasses for "about the 4,000th time," drawing more ire from Ed.

These trials behind them, however, they made good time across New Mexico, averaging 75 miles per hour even at night. After a two-hour nap at a rest stop, they crossed into the Texas panhandle in the wee hours of the morning. Ed had a CB radio in the car, which he kept tuned to the police frequency. They heard with trepidation an order to track down and hang a man, most likely an African American. Ed was glad he was packing a gun in the glove compartment. They were relieved to cross into Oklahoma at sunrise. They finally stopped at a motel again in Tulsa, shelling out about the same amount as they had spent on the new tire chains. Still they felt like new people after enjoying a good sleep, love-making, showers and a picnic breakfast.

Missouri was frigid—14°F—but the roads were clear and the rolling farmland that continued on through Indiana and Ohio had a peaceful and time-worn beauty. Large weather-beaten farmhouses dotted the fields, and pigs and sheep grazed in the thin winter sunlight. They finally stopped for dinner at a truck stop in West Virginia, then traveled on into Pennsylvania, where they checked into a motel again. Judy immediately headed for the shower, precipitating a fight with Ed the next morning over her "inconsiderateness," whether for not giving him the opportunity to do the same or because she had not helped him unload the car, is not clear. It was Christmas morning now, and they made good time on the almost-deserted roads, arriving at Ed's parents' apartment in Philadelphia at three p.m., starving. They had been unable to find an open eatery (evidently having overlooked the Chinese restaurants).

Judy was charmed with Ed's family: "What gracious and wonderful people!"[9] The whole family enjoyed a turkey dinner with all the trimmings, and the Browns had even gotten Judy a present: a red and black woolen muffler, a practical gift she could use in both Philadelphia and Finland. The sexual liberation movement not yet having taken full effect in mainstream society, Ed and Judy had to sleep separately while staying with the Browns. Judy got a room to herself at his parents' place while Ed slept at his brother William's apartment in the same complex.

---

[9] Ed's family may have been white rather than African American, as Ed is the only black person in some surviving photographs from this trip.

Ed and Judy lingered in Philadelphia for several weeks before setting off for Finland, and the Browns' behavior soon began to grate on Judy. Now his brother was "stingy and self-centered." Family members were suspicious that Judy and Ed might be surreptitiously shacking up, as they probably were, and Judy felt she was being spied on. There was a family phobia about using any mechanical objects, from the blender to the juicer to the car, for fear they would wear out. Judy sought to escape this toxic atmosphere by going to the gym and sauna daily. "I never felt so unwelcome in my life," she wrote in her journal. So much for gracious and wonderful.

Ed Brown with unidentified persons, presumably his family members. Photo: Carr/Pettit family collection.

Ed and Judy took a short tour to Baltimore and later to New York City, partly because it was quick and cheap to travel to both places by train. They had originally planned to fly to Finland on January 11th, then moved it up to the 7th and then back to the 21st. Ed's father was scheduled for cancer surgery on the 18th, and his brother wanted him to stick around for that. In fact, though, they departed on the very day of the surgery. Petulant William refused to drive them either to the airport or to the port where they could put their heavier luggage on a ship; they had to take taxis for both trips.

Despite all the stresses, however, Judy was sure that her new life in Finland would be wonderful. Another overseas adventure, another great love affair. Now thirty-two, she had a happy picture of her future as a wife and mother.

8
Girl of the North Country

Why Ed had chosen Finland as a place to resettle (and it was, indeed, Ed's decision, not Judy's) is not clear. It was certainly a contrast to the U.S. More agrarian than urban, and sparsely populated (4.6 million people spread out over three million square kilometers), Finland had seen many ups and downs over centuries of European wars and migration waves. At the time Ed and Judy arrived, the country was not caught up in any major political upheavals. Like Japan and Greece, Finland had been deeply affected by World War II, and particularly by the Winter War of 1939-1940, in which she lost some of her prime forest and agricultural land to the Soviet Union, which extended along her entire eastern border. But in the early 1970s, Finland was beginning to grow and prosper.

Finland sits at the lowest elevation of all the Nordic countries, and water encroaches on the land ubiquitously; there are over 60,000 lakes—not to mention the many inlets and fjords. While its northern reaches are above the Arctic Circle, Finland is protected to some extent by the higher-elevation northern lands of Norway and Sweden, and the Atlantic Gulf Stream brings more warmth to its southwestern coast than either of the other two countries enjoys. The countryside itself is stunningly beautiful—about two-thirds of the total land area is forested (Finland's "green gold"), interspersed with many lakes and small farms. Judy described the view from the plane on one of her autumn vacation flights to the interior: "A patchwork quilt of reds, yellows and greens, the river cutting its way through dense and colorful forests... an endless succession of rising and falling fells, cut here and there by the river gorge or small lakes." Such hills as exist are low and rolling, except in the far north—Lapland—the only area that can support a downhill skiing industry; elsewhere, cross-country is a major sport.

Most of the population lives in the south, where the climate is milder and economic opportunities abound. When Judy lived there, manufacturing was actually the largest employment sector, with 57% of the population so engaged; wood, paper, textiles, glass and stoneware, and metal and engineering products, were the main outputs. Nevertheless, forestry was Finland's primary industry, and agriculture its second, with a fair amount of food exports: dairy products and reindeer meat, as well as some grains and vegetables, with potatoes topping the list.

Ed and Judy arrived in Helsinki in late January 1971, in the dead of winter. The sun rose at 8:45 a.m. and set at 4:30 p.m., although the light was returning fast, adding almost three minutes to every morning and evening by the early weeks of February. Yet mists still crept over the tranquil white-blanketed countryside and dense green forests in the evening, lingering into the morning hours. Judy had plenty of time to notice details of the scenery as she rode the aging, slow-moving trains between Helsinki and the countryside. The local populace were friendly but reserved, and when out of doors they were usually bundled up in dark clothing against the cold. It was not uncommon for daytime temperatures to hover well below zero Fahrenheit. Still, frigid weather was a predictable challenge, unlike the earthquake that hit southern California on February 10th. And the Finns knew how to deal with snow; the plows and ice breakers, as well as individual householders, always went straight to work at the first sign of a snowflake.

Ed and Judy managed to find a small fifth-floor flat to rent—a significant accomplishment given the pervasive housing shortage in Helsinki—and both of them started looking for work right away. As she had done in Miami, Judy hit up all the modeling agencies, and, as they recognized that she had a wonderful voice as well as visual beauty, she soon landed her first television gig: narrating a documentary about Norwegian ships. Near the end of February she also procured two teaching jobs, both part-time: the first as an ESL instructor at the food import company Kesko—the largest company in Finland—and the second, drawing on her experience in Long Beach, at a private kindergarten run by the firm Inlingua, under the auspices of the Finnish-American Society. The school was attended mainly by Finnish children whose parents wanted them to acquire English-language skills—a real benefit in the increasingly U.S.-dominated world economy. Judy's first few weeks on the job were lessons in frustration, as the lack of a common language between her and her charges made for some pantomime challenges. Judy lost eight pounds during her first month on the job. One of the benefits, though, was free Finnish-as-a-second-language classes. Although of course the children learned English much faster than Judy learned Finnish, the passing months did bring better communication, both ways.

Ed also got a job in mid-February, as a histological technician in the pathology department of a hospital. He would have preferred a job in woodworking, a fine craft in Finland, but his refusal to learn even rudimentary Finnish was a major handicap.

Judy was studying the language assiduously, although she

Judy with her Finnish kindergarten charges
Photo: Carr/Pettit family collection

was making slow progress compared to her efforts at Japanese or Greek. Both she and Ed found the language frustrating. Finnish, a Uralic language rather than an Indo-European one, is complex and particularly difficult for adult learners; even Japanese is easier for native English speakers. Judy was further handicapped by using English almost exclusively in her work and social interactions. Still, she was persistent. In May 1972, more than a year after arriving in Finland, Judy wrote to her sister Chris: "In spite of being a lousy student that rarely studies I amazingly am making some headway with this SOB language."

Ironically, her lack of language skills was belied by her Nordic appearance. One major advantage of Finland, over both Japan and Greece, was that Judy fit right in, visually: she looked like a native. No more stares or requests for photographs. Yet it was not long before Judy discovered the down side of this situation: many locals assumed she was fluent in either Finnish or Swedish, and were not infrequently taken aback by her blank stares in response to their attempts at conversation.

It was not long after arriving that Judy started critiquing Finnish culture. As in Japan and Greece, she soaked up the local color. "The pace of life here is beautifully relaxed, violent crime is rare, air is clean, Helsinki a small but modern city, the countryside minutes away, the land lovely and the people genuine." Litter was a rare sight; people actually used the public trash receptacles, and the vigilant street maintenance crews compensated for those who did not. Finns smoked a lot, though; they had the second highest lung cancer rate in world. And as in all northern European countries, there was a lot of alcoholism. In fact, the major duty of the police force seemed to be rounding up drunks. The solitary (male) beer drinker, for some reason always dressed in black, was a common sight in bars.

Commercial streets were lined with small shops—dairies, bakeries, groceries, florists, and stores selling cosmetics, paper, clothing, or general-purpose gadgets; yet surprisingly downtown Helsinki had only one hardware store. Shop hours were eight to four-thirty Monday through Friday, and nine to three-thirty on Saturday; everything was closed on Sunday in this heavily Lutheran country. Vehicle drivers were "insane"; traffic seemed to careen randomly through the streets. Pedestrians turned to jaywalking for survival; it was an accomplished art. But public transportation was rapid and efficient; a ride anywhere around town cost only about 12¢ [70¢]. Judy and Ed soon acquired a car, an old Volvo, but used it only in good weather, storing it during the heavy winters, as did many Finns.

Helsinki had only recently embarked upon an ambitious new public transit project: a light-rail system called Metro, part subway, part above-ground. It would connect Helsinki with its outlying suburbs, and was to be primarily a commuter service, although it was flexible enough to serve recreational needs as well, cutting in half the 30-minute average private-vehicle travel time into the city. Construction began in 1973; scheduled completion was 1979. Tunnel construction was particularly slow because of the solid rock foundation under the city, and much of Judy's time in Finland was colored by this major construction project in downtown Helsinki.

Traditional Finnish bedroom (museum display). Photo: Carr/Pettit family collection.

Clothing and fashions were, of course, among the first things Judy critiqued, and fortunately they met with her approval. Fashions were modern and tasteful, although the winter colors were drab, mostly black and brown. Women wore practical midi-length coats and fur hats. Judy dreamed of having a suede coat trimmed or lined with fox fur, with a fox-fur hat to match. Her winter footwear was limited to boots for outdoors and slippers around the house. Chris later sent her a leather outfit from El Salvador: a midi-length skirt and suede belt, and a leather vest for Ed. Judy had to make adjustments to the latter; not an easy job, sewing leather, but she was skillful enough for the task.

Their dark winter clothing notwithstanding, the Finns arrayed themselves and decorated the interiors of their houses with bright colors and intricate designs. Judy loved shopping for fine fabrics, especially Marimekko—a brightly colored but sturdy and practical fabric just recently patented. She sent many bolts home to her mother in California and to her sister Chris in El Salvador and later Brazil. She also decorated her own small flat with orange, purple and white

Marimekko curtains, vividly colored candles, house plants, wall prints, and orange bedspreads.

The Finns were also very practical in their household design. Bathrooms—always shared, in an apartment building—invariably had a drain in the floor, to catch stray splashes from the tub or shower (although their original purpose may have been for toilet overflows). Kitchens sported built-in dish-drying racks instead of cupboards: stack your dishware into the slots and then close the cupboard door; your dishes air-dry and are already put away. Houses and apartments were well insulated against drafts—a must in a frigid climate. Windows were double-paned and swung outward to open, a design that made them easy to close and latch securely against drafts. In fact, part of the reason for the high cost of housing was the quality of the insulation and building materials, which increased prices that were already high because of the housing shortage brought on by a growing urban population.

Beds were somewhat of a challenge. They were invariably extra-firm—an initial adjustment for Judy although she soon came to prefer them. "Double" beds were actually singles that could be pushed together. The possibility of falling through the crack between the beds was enough to give one pause before cuddling up. Bedding, at least in the winter, consisted of large brightly colored sheets sewn together to make a bag, into which one stuffed a bulky quilt—sort of a featherbed with a removable cover. "Pussi-lakkanas" they were called, or just "pussis" for short (the 'u' was long rather than short; hence not to be confused with "pussy"). While this bedding kept one warm, it did not always fit tightly around the body, and cold air could creep in if one was not assiduous in tucking the bedding closely around one's neck and shoulders. Yet Finns were in the habit of always keeping a window cracked open even in the dead of winter, and Judy followed this practice as well.

Public spaces were equally well appointed. There were huge indoor swimming pools, in buildings that included restaurants and of course that essential Finnish commodity, a sauna—including hot rocks, water buckets and ladles, although saunas in the urban areas were electric-powered rather than heated with the traditional wood stove. For the Finns, the sauna served as the major bathing facility, not just as a sweat lodge. Most city apartment buildings had a sauna in addition to the shared bathroom.

And of course, there was the food. Although the boiled potatoes that were served with almost every meal could be tedious, the meats were tasty—ham, beef, sausages, and lots of fish. The meat industry was highly regulated; beef, for example, had to be sold the same day it was ground, or else it was discarded. No hormones or food coloring were permitted in meat, and meat from an animal that had been treated with antibiotics or chemotherapeutic substances could be used for human consumption only if the slaughtering took place at least six days after the cessation of treatment. Dark breads were commonly available, and delicious; cardamom and caraway were in wide use as seasonings. There were seventeen varieties of milk and countless cheeses. The yogurt was scrumptious. Sweets were lightly sugared and pastries delicately flavored. The Finns were great coffee drinkers—it being one of the new imports they took to with great enthusiasm—as well as beer drinkers and smokers. Despite the delectable food, though, Judy managed to maintain her slender frame at one hundred twenty-five pounds and her critical feminine measurements at 36-26-37, according to a letter she sent to Chris asking her to send clothing.

The Finnish version of a laundromat was semi-self-service. An attendant supplied the soap and operated the machine. Two loads of washing took fifty-five minutes and cost about $1.60 [$9.40]; the resulting cleanliness of the clothes was impressive. Judy, like most of her Finnish neighbors, did the lighter laundry by hand, hanging it up on a line strung across the kitchen. Hot water, fortunately, was readily available; she did not need to struggle with firing up the boiler as she had in Japan, or limit her use to those hours when the water heater was running, as in Athens.

As for entertainment and recreation, the Finns were great party-goers, especially at the beginning of every month, right after pay day. Holidays, too, were an excuse for partying, and hardly had Judy and Ed set foot in the country before they experienced their first Finnish holiday—Runeberg Day, February 5th, honoring the nineteenth-century Finnish national poet Johan Ludvig Runeberg. Flags flew everywhere; Runeberg's statue in Helsinki was lit with torches at night and decorated with garlands of spruce and flowers (despite the still-frigid weather). Runeberg's poems had an effortless simplicity and clarity, and idealized the Finnish national character: simple, blunt, inarticulate, withdrawn, yet stubbornly loyal, honest and courageous.

❖   ❖   ❖   ❖   ❖   ❖   ❖   ❖   ❖   ❖   ❖

Harvesting Potatoes

The whole gang—family and friends—rumbled out to the fields in the old truck at 5 a.m., the sky already light in the endless rays of the Arctic summer. Three American women volunteers, along with the Finnish farmers—mom, dad, the kids and the neighbors—harvesting three acres of potatoes and cukes. Breakfast served from the back of the flatbed truck: a flask of hot tea served with milk and sugar, chunks of rye bread with butter and jam. Sitting on the ground in the shade of the truck I took off my shoes and squished the heavy dirt between my toes. Nothing smells so elemental as fresh earth, and I would rather sit or lie on it than on a feather bed in a luxury hotel.

Then out to the field to start the harvesting. Kneeling on the moist freshly turned earth, digging with my hands down through the rich red soil to unearth the potatoes, tossing them into a sack. Midday sun hot on my back and bonneted head, no breeze off the Baltic. Two workers to a row, digging and tossing golden jewels into burlap bags. Sweat trickled down my face and chest, my pants damp around the waist. Dirt clung to the hairs on the back of my arms. Insects buzzed in my ears, my back hurt, my mouth was dry, but with the delicious ache and dryness of work-ing the land.

At noon the truck's beep-beep gathered us in for lunch. Nothing fancy: potatoes of course, cold and plain, eaten like an apple, along with a hunk of swiss cheese, dense dark bread, cucumbers, sausage. No trees for shade, so we crawled under the truck and lay down to eat and nap.

Out in the fields again for a few hours, the sun high, never giving us a clue of the time. I got slower and slower, arms and back and legs aching, dirt in my ears and nos-trils. Bending, kneeling, sitting... it all hurt. When would it be time to quit? I was volunteer labor, could leave whenever I chose, but was determined not to be a sissy, and to stick it out with the others. Finally the horn sounded, the truck came to life and traversed the field to pick up the bags of potatoes and the workers. We flopped down on top of the lumpy load; never mind the uncomfortable seating —just hold on. We bumped and swayed back to the farmhouse.

A hot sauna was waiting. The three American women went first because we were guests. We tore off our clothes and entered the hot cavern in silence. Deep sighs of contentment as we settled onto the benches. The heat penetrated our flesh, brown rivulets of dirty sweat trickled down our bodies. Water on the rocks, a rush of steam down the back, engulfing our poor tired dirty bodies. Then a dash to the sea, wading thru oozing mud at the shore, plunging into the icy water ... a shock, a thrill, breath taken away — hot, cold, a scream, giggles, steaming bodies trudging toward shore.

Then the unpleasant part—scrubbing off the dirt with large-bristle brushes while standing on large flat boulders at the water's edge, shivering and scrubbing, then one more plunge to rinse, then a hurried scramble back into the sauna; all the day's aches melted away. A final rinse in the sea, then washing our clothes while standing naked in waist-deep water; spreading the clothes on rocks to dry, dressing and going to the farmhouse for the evening meal of—you guessed it—potatoes! Small yellow smooth-skinned Finnish potatoes, so sweet and flavorful as to be eaten plain from pot to mouth, or slathered in butter and sprinkled with dill, rending me speechless in a hedonistic stupor, roused only with equally delightful strong black coffee served in chipped china cups. For dessert, strawberry short cake ... yumm!

❖   ❖   ❖   ❖   ❖   ❖   ❖   ❖   ❖   ❖   ❖

One of the main things Ed and Judy missed when they first arrived was the really good music they were used to, aside from opera; most of what people danced to regularly was polka and tango music. As in Japan, the acquisition of a radio provided a link to what they considered civilization, including a greater variety of musical selections. Theaters, fortunately, were a better source of recreation. Finnish theaters, after suffering a long decline since 1958, were starting to make a comeback as an entertainment venue. The largest chain was buying up and renovating old theaters, upgrading them while retaining much of their ethnic charm and decor. They were also beginning to show a good selection of foreign movies, including American ones. Judy noted that there were also X-rated movie theaters, which were open twenty-four hours a day. She never dreamed, though, that she herself would ever have any connection with such venues.

Outdoors, winter sports were of course immensely popular. Cross-country skiers thronged the parks and children sledded down the mild hills. Intrepid toddlers hardly big enough to walk set off confidently on ice skates, fell, got back up with a laugh and repeated the process until they began to master it. Judy, a cross-country skier since her college days, had plenty of opportunity to indulge herself.

With spring came the next major holiday, Vappu—May first, exuberantly celebrated in this land of long winter darkness. As with most Finnish holidays, Vappu was an excuse to eat and drink. On the night of April thirtieth, every bar and restaurant in Helsinki was bursting with customers. Just before midnight, thousands would gather at the market square for the big event: the capping of the Havis Amanda statue—a naked maiden standing in the middle of a fountain. At the stroke of midnight, a bold male college student would climb the statue to place a white student cap (similar to a graduation mortarboard) on the statue. The next day, May Day, saw the resumption of revelry, at least by those not too hung over, with plenty of eating, drinking and dancing around the May pole, dark winter clothing now replaced with bright spring colors.

Midsummer, too, was a major celebration in the land of the midnight sun. Houses, cars and railroad engines were decorated with birch branches and colorful flags. Helsinki was practically abandoned as citizens flocked to the countryside for feasting, dancing and athletic contests. During the height of midsummer, music rang out until late at night in the Finnish countryside, often near huge bonfires reflected in the lakes. Lapland came into its own in midsummer—the only time the otherwise dark and frozen land was welcoming; here inside the Arctic Circle the sun shone continually from the ninth of June to the fourth of September, never dipping below the horizon. At midsummer, there were lumberjack logrolling contests and races on the swiftly flowing Ounasjoki River, spectators lining the banks. The bolder of the young men shot the rapids on logs.

Throughout the summer, there were festivals in the larger cities. Some focused on music and dancing, others on handicrafts, lectures, drama or films. At the Kaustinen Folk Music Festival, dancing went on long into the night; Judy danced until three in the morning one year, in the dew-wet grass.

It's Saturday

our weekly magazine which started in September has already received very nice comments from listeners. Thank you! We try to bring you interesting items on various subjects to entertain you on Saturday evenings. In each magazine there will be greetings included to listeners in a certain country, and we will tell some facts about the country and its relations with Finland. So far we have greeted New Zealand, Romania, Scotland and Greece.

It's Saturday has got a new producer to place Susan Sinisalo, who will still continue in Letterbox. She is Judy Carr, an American girl, who has settled in Finland this year. The other producers are: Martha Gaber, Colin Narbrough and Donald Fields.

Judy Carr

By April of 1971, Judy was well established as a radio personality, co-hosting the English-language show "It's Saturday!" once a month, and by the following year she was co-hosting three additional monthly shows: "Letterbox"—whose format included answering letters from listeners—"Finnish Forum," and "Made in Finland." These shows followed a basic magazine format, with one or several topics presented during each show, enlivened with bantering between the co-hosts. The shows had an international audience, and were geared toward potential English-speaking tourists, touting the virtues of Finland as a travel destination, while also discussing interesting tidbits of everyday life in the country. Judy's responsibilities included rounding up her own material and writing scripts; often, she also chose her own topics. One of the benefits of this steady work was that she could give up teaching kindergarten, a job she had come to detest: "Having charge of eighteen 4-year-old screaming banshees doesn't really help my nerves." Teaching was the only one of her jobs that required her to keep a strict schedule, something she also hated. In her other work "I'm mainly my own boss, the routine varies, I can use my artistic talents, organizations are small and personal... and I can arrange my work so as to take off for a few days or weeks if I want to." This need to be unfettered she would continue to emphasize for the rest of her working life.

Judy supplemented her more regular income with free-lance work as an editor for a translation bureau, cleaning up the English in translated papers, and later as a journalist, contributing articles to *Look at Finland*, an English-language magazine. She interviewed Ray Charles on his 1974 Scandinavian tour, following up with an article about vocational opportunities for the blind, including massage. During her first summer in Finland, Judy also got an ESL job at the Finnish-American Society's summer sports retreat for teenagers, and Ed accompanied her there for a short vacation.

Throughout her time in Finland, Judy kept up with her far-flung family—her parents back in California, and her sister Chris, who lived first in El Salvador and then in Brazil. During her first two years in Scandinavia, Judy's main focus seemed to be exchanging products: Chris could get leather goods fairly cheaply in El Salvador, while Judy could get fine dinnerware in Finland, and they shipped items back and forth, or were sometimes able to get travelers to take them along for free in their luggage. As time went on, though, Judy's focus shifted more to her aging parents, now turning sixty. They had given up the labor-intensive doughnut shop and were managing a motel in Palo Alto, but, finding the stress too much, abandoned that also after less than a year. Too young to collect Social Security, their financial situation deteriorated, although they did have some savings. Chris helped them out with rent money. Judy worried about them, too, but not enough to consider going back to the States to be nearer to them. In fact, she felt deprived by her family's unwillingness to come and visit her, despite her letters extolling the virtues of vacationing in beautiful Finland. She bewailed her inability to meet

her new niece, Monica, to no avail. Her parents' health was beginning to deteriorate as well; in August 1974 her father underwent
surgery for prostate cancer. Judy wrote to tell him he should have
come to Finland for the treatment; it was so cheap that it would have
been worth the cost of travel. This was par for the course for Judy;
for the most part, her interactions with her family consisted of either
giving them advice or asking them for help, including, on more than
one occasion, money. And, while on the one hand she praised their
parenting ("I agree with you, we really have super parents who have
been through a hell of a lot and still managed to keep their wits
about them," she wrote to Chris in October, 1971), she had also come
to believe that her childhood illnesses were entirely emotional rather
than physical, even claiming in a postcard to her mother, "Arthritis is
a symptom, not a disease; it no longer bothers me." Perhaps not at
age thirty-five, but later, as she aged, it manifested again as a major
problem in her life.

As for Judy's emotional life, it continued to be a roller coaster.
While the financial and cultural stress she and Ed were under
precipitated not-infrequent fights, she was still full of romantic
dreams. "What's important to me [is] first of all, a great love, which
gives meaning to my whole existence." Then the rest of life: a "free
environment, chance to expand my mind, utilize my artistic talents
and live in a stimulating environment with bountiful and appreciated nature, the healer of the psyche. I can't fathom living in an
apartment or a city for much longer. The tranquility and the active
participation which rural living demands are key to my sanity." Then
she immediately contradicted herself by adding, "But if Ed and I can
be happy together, place is irrelevant."

Life with Ed, in fact, was becoming less and less happy. His
moods were often black, and their fights were more frequent. Ed's
stress level was high for a number of reasons. His father had terminal
cancer and Ed worried about him. His family considered his geographical distance an act of abandonment during the crisis. And life
in Finland was a much harder struggle than he had ever imagined it
would be. He hated his boss; the Finnish language was impossible;
the cost of living here was insane, with prices too high and wages too
low. He threatened to move them to Nigeria. No way, said Judy; she
had spent a miserable year and a half in a country in the midst of

political upheaval, and she had no intention of jumping back into that kind of fire. She would live in a civilized country.

Logging a Tree

One of my greatest accomplishments was logging an entire tree. That experience gave me an intimate connection with the land and affirmed my ability to do an ordinary but important task that had been repeated millions of times throughout the world by many types of people. Just me, an ax, saw and wheelbarrow—no fancy machines or gadgets—steady, hard, rewarding work on the land.

It was a medium-sized pine tree, perhaps two feet in diameter at the base. Mimi helped me fell it, with her grandfather's saw—she on one side, I on the other— back and forth, stopping many times to rest. After the tree went down with a mighty roar, I sawed off the branches, cut them and the trunk into logs, hauled them down the hill to the chopping area, split the logs and chopped up the smaller branches for kindling. It took me three days. Even though I was sore, blistered and tired, I was full of light and joy, free—and yet bound to all humankind with this ancient ritual of labor.

-- Juliet Carr

The Recreational Riches of Finland

Porvoo

Only 30 miles from Helsinki, across the Porvoo River, this town is at least 700 years old. Its still-maintained old section has steep narrow lanes lined with low houses, surrounding a cathedral first built in the 1300s. Originally a trading center, it was a military post as well; earthwork fortifications built in 1200 are still visible.

The cathedral's stone vestry wall is attached to exterior ones of whitewashed stone and red brick, supporting a high peaked roof. Here Alexander the First of Russia gave Finland autonomy, leading to its eventual independence in 1917.

Porvoo was the home of Finnish national poet Runeberg; he lived here for 25 years until his death in 1877.

Turku and the Åland Islands

Nowhere in the world is there a concentration of islands quite like that in the central Baltic Sea, and none has a clearer identity than the Åland Islands—"the land belonging to the sea." Midway between Stockholm, Sweden and the arch of Turku in Finland, they lie low on the water and first appear as no more than a mirage. Their broken rim of granite glows coppery red on a bright day, capped by the dark green line of the forest.

The approximately 9,000 islands in the chain are scattered between the capital city of Mairehamm on the west and mainland Finland on the east—treacherous channels of rocky islets and reefs through which ships twist and turn. The barren reefs of the outer islands are unoccupied save by sea birds and the occasional bleakly perched home of a pilot.

Turku is Finland's richest province for flora, and insect and bird life are correspondingly abundant. It has been settled for over 5,000 years, and holds many secrets: buried ship-wrecks, Dark Age hill forts, formidable medieval churches.

Turku Castle, on an island at the mouth of the river, was founded in 1280. In the 17th century it was gutted by fire and abandoned. Since being restored, it is used as a chapel and a banquet hall, and there is a music festival in the main courtyard in summer.

The Recreational Riches of Finland

Tornio

This city, located at the tip of the Gulf of Bothnia where Finland and Sweden meet, has always been an important trading center. Its oldest and most valuable building is a 17th-century wooden church, among the best examples of Finnish wooden church art, with a rectangular basilica design, a high shingled roof, and a richly decorated interior. Its tall steeple long served as a landmark for sailors. Dedicated to Hedvig Elenora, queen of Sweden in 1686, it was still in use in the 1970s.

Kuopio

Located in eastern Finland, in the lake district, Kuopio rises 730 feet above the surrounding Kallavesi lake system. A restaurant perched on the hill revolves once an hour, looking out over thousands of square miles of water and islands. With a population of 74,000, it is the business center of eastern Finland, sustained by its woodworking and textile industries. It hosts a dance and music festival in June and a strawberry carnival in midsummer.

Kuopio hosts attractions both old and new, with an Orthodox Church Museum and one of the largest indoor swimming pools in Finland. Tourists can tour the lakes on a steamer, rent a cottage or stay at a farmhouse, go sein fishing, mushroom hunting or blueberry picking. Its signature cuisine is a fish and pork pie with a rye crust.

Kuusamo and Pyhätunturi

These two towns—the first just south of the Arctic Circle and the second just north of it—constitute a sort of gateway to Lapland. Kuusamo got its start as a fur trading center but is now best known for its ceramics and other handicrafts.

Pyhätunturi has become a popular downhill skiing destination. Its polar slope is 6,500 feet high. On a bright winter day, the snow glows with a gold and white shimmer, interspersed with twisted trees in grotesque shapes. There are magnificent views from a hotel halfway up the slopes, looking out over sheer drops into the valley below.

Nearby is the old Lapp village of Suvanto, the only one that escaped German occupation in World War II.

Restaurants serve a Lapp specialty: sliced reindeer meat with mashed potatoes and ligonberry preserves.

The Recreational Riches of Finland

Lapland

Northern Finland is at its best for a few weeks in September, with blazing autumn colors, still warm days, beautiful scenery, vast stretches of unbroken wilderness, clean water and good fishing. Networks of fell huts offer shelter to hikers and hunters. From the hills or a plane one can look down over a patchwork quilt of reds, yellows and greens, the river cutting its way through dense and colorful forests, an endless succession of rising and falling fells, cut here and there by the river gorge or small lakes. Outdoor enthusiasts come here for river rafting and backpacking.

The farther north one goes, the narrower the roads, and the shorter and more intensely colored the trees—birch, aspen and rowan inter-mixed with pines. Roads are expensive to build because they have to withstand the severe winter weather.

Local food delicacies include salmon, trout, whitefish, reindeer meat, cloudberries, new potatoes, and a scrumptious dessert of Lapp cheese bread served with hot lingonberry sauce.

Tunnari, central Finland

In the northernmost province in the lake district of eastern Finland, the countryside around Tunnari is characterized by hills, deep forests, rapids, and unspoiled fishing spots. Its well-maintained national parks and preserves protect rare species like the wood grouse.

Well-preserved wooden churches built in the wilds in the 18th century still stand, and there is an old mill restaurant where patrons can smoke their own fish catch. At the Luhuja Cottagers Museum are huts built for specific tasks—milking, spinning, fishing, baking, etc. Also nearby is a farm that functions as a bed and breakfast, with separate cottages for guests, and twelve saunas, one of them a special smoke sauna with a cozy hearth room, fireplace and rustic furniture. For less adventurous travelers, there is also a modern hotel and rental cottages.

The Rehabilitation Institute, for those with long-term but not debilitating illnesses, offers exercise and nutrition classes, a restaurant, and a sports and swimming hall—a huge dome-covered structure. The pool is actually three in one: an outside ring with a continuous one-directional current, for exercise swimming; a conventional pool; and a children's pool. One entire wall of the building is glass, looking out on fields and forests.

Judy's emotional dependence on Ed, however, was too strong for her to consider getting away from him. His anger, or even just his silence, triggered a primal panic in her. She must find a way to keep him happy, or she would die of loneliness. She begged and pleaded with him, wrote out her troubles in her journal, or simply left the apartment for greener pastures—the library, the gym, shopping, or just walking the streets. As with all dysfunctional relationships, the increasingly infrequent "good" times sustained her. After all, if the sex was good, the relationship must be worth saving, right?

And so they plodded on, month after month. Judy was sure that the relationship would work if she could just figure out how to manage Ed's moods. And in early August one of her dreams came true: she was pregnant. Thrilled, she went out and bought a crib and a high chair. Her preparations were premature, however, as in late October she miscarried, spending several days in the hospital, always a traumatic place for her, let alone under those circumstances. In later years, she sometimes referred to this event as an abortion, subtly implying that it was elective rather than spontaneous, while never explicitly stating so. This seems unlikely, though, since at the time she was hopeful that she could try again; the histological report was encouraging. She had feared that her failure to maintain the pregnancy might be due to chromosome damage caused by the X-rays she had been subjected to as a child; this was not so. Her later references to "abortion" were most likely due to her usual need to be dramatic, to sound more politically correct, or to take on some responsibility for the "failure."

Actually, her desire for a child may have been driven partly by some lingering jealousy of Chris, who on February first had given birth to Monica, who would remain an only child, as Chris could not bear the thought of subjecting anyone to the kind of sibling rivalry she herself had experienced from Judy. Yet Judy did not in fact conceive again with Ed, and as time went on she gave up the dream of motherhood entirely, for reasons having nothing to do with her difficulty in starting or maintaining a pregnancy.

Meanwhile, though, Judy had found an outlet for her maternal affections with a cat. Although her first feline acquisition fell out the window of their fifth-floor flat and disappeared—a real heartbreak for Judy—someone responded to her lost-cat ad in the paper with an offer of a replacement, a stray they had picked up but could not keep. With some trepidation, Judy took a long tram ride to an out-lying suburb to take a look at the creature. Homely though he was, with multi-colored splotched fur and crossed eyes, he won Judy over instantly by snuggling into the crook of her arm and purring. She named him Laikku, Finnish for "irregularly spotted." Laikku was a gregarious cat with a loud insistent meow and a habit of inviting himself onto any available human lap without so much as a by-your-leave. He especially loved parties, with the multiple opportunities they offered. He was an adventurous soul as well; Judy often took him on skiing trips, wrapping him up in the front of her ski parka, keeping both of them warmer that way. And in summer they took long walks in the woods together, a pattern she would follow with future feline companions years later in the foothills of the Sierra Nevadas.

Laikku was a great comfort to Judy when Ed finally abandoned her, not long after her miscarriage. About this same time she got a scare with a lump in her breast. Dark indeed seemed Finland now, with her health problems, the shortening days (sunrise at eight, sunset at four), Ed's departure, and the still-strange culture. Yet Judy was never a quitter, and once the worst had happened, she picked herself up and plodded onward, eternally hopeful. The breast lump, fortunately, turned out to be benign; a harbinger perhaps of better times ahead. And for about six months Judy actually went regularly to a psycho-therapist, although she implored her sister not to tell anyone. In those days, seeking any kind of mental health treatment was still considered shameful.

As it turned out, while Ed left her he did not leave Finland, and after a few months they began to socialize as friends from time to time. In February 1972, they were hired together as counselors at a ski resort for teenagers, the winter equivalent of the Finnish-American Society's ESL seminar where Judy had taught the preceding July.

The summer seminar became an annual job for Judy, in fact, and in 1973 she met another heart-throb there. Knut was a Swedish jour-nalist, handsome and virile, but rabidly communist and anti-Ameri-can. He and Judy spent their first meal together glaring at each other across the dining table, heatedly debating the merits of capitalism versus communism. Yet as the long summer evening wore on, Judy's beauty and charm worked their magic, and these political differences evaporated; in the gathering mists of the midnight sun antagonism gave way to lust. Over the next two weeks, they coupled wherever they could sneak off to—the deserted sauna, a secluded spot in the birch forest, a rowboat drifting among the reeds. Once Knut even climbed through the window of the women's dorm, risking his very job at the camp.

Knut invited Judy to visit him in Stockholm the following winter. He was living communally with a group of young communist college students, in a rambling dilapidated house. Knut had the attic to himself, and his living space revealed his real-life values; neither beauty nor order were among them. The attic had no windows, and the dismal room was in total disarray: books and papers scattered everywhere, a lumpy unmade bed standing in one of the darkest corners. Judy found her passion evaporating as rapidly as lust had dissipated their initial antagonism that first evening in camp.

Nor was the rest of the communal atmosphere pleasant. The heated political conversations over dinner were carried on in Swedish, of which Judy knew but few words. Just as well, as she was totally outnumbered and her views were disdained. Knut was embarrassed by her presence and apologized to his housemates for having let a corrupt capitalist into the house.

Judy took the hint, leaving on her own on the third day, after penning a note to Knut reviling him for his cruelty to her. Bereft and low on cash, with her flight back home still a week away, she managed to find a cheap boarding place—a university dorm in a village just outside Stockholm. She spent her remaining vacation time alone, wandering the streets and trying to find entertainment enough to salvage the trip. She did stumble onto one gem—erotic art in an obscure chapel. Enough to provide fodder for her later dramatic claim that she had researched erotic art in Europe.

Judy had more success with women friends she met in Finland. The first was Leila, another American expatriate, who became her roommate after Ed left. Leila had access to a lovely country cottage in mid-Finland, and they often vacationed there, either together or separately.

Spring in Finland

Never did I so crave the sun on my naked body as in Finland. It was a desperate longing thru the long dark cold winters. That first June in Finland, when the sun first appeared, only briefly, thousands of otherwise staid citizens stopped whatever they were doing, came outside and paid mute homage to the return of the Sun god. Leaned against windows, packed park benches; silent, reverent, grateful, their faces toward the glow, with eyes closed and radiant smiles of intoxication, in something akin to a pagan rite to the Sun God.

White button daisies strewn across the sleeping lawns, heavy damp and brilliant green from the recent rain. Baby's toys scattered across the verdant carpet. Overhead recently bare cherry-tree branches now bursting with bright pink blossoms.

I weave a path between these visions of spring, my toes sinking in the spongy grass, water and mud seeping between my toes, clouds tumbling across the sky, creating a light show of shadows among the trees.

I remember that day in early summer, my first year in Finland, when I was so ecstatic with the warmth that I asked Ed to stop the old red Volvo, as we explored a country road, so I could lie in a field of dandelions and daisies, took off my clothes to feel my body pressing into the sweet earth, stroked by the long sharp grass. A brilliant blue sky blessed me and sun baptized my innocent body, white from months burdened with layers of warm clothes. I inhaled the fragrance of unpolluted air, a deep sense of connectedness, of joy and reverence. As I lay still, insects resumed their scurrying and birds their songs.

It was one of the happiest times of my life. I didn't notice the cold or the nibbles, or Ed calling me. Pure contentment! I could have died happy at that moment.

One of my greatest sensuous pleasures is being naked outdoors.

-- Juliet Carr

The woman Judy became closest to, though, was Mirja Kajalo; they were to remain friends for many years, as Mirja relocated to the U.S. in 1976, even before Judy returned. It is not clear exactly how or when Judy met Mirja, but the most salient incident in their relationship in Finland was a disastrous roller-skating excursion. Mirja wanted to learn to skate, and since Judy had been an avid roller skater in her childhood, she figured she should give Mirja a few pointers to start her out. Never mind that she had not actually been on skates since her college days, nor that she was terrified of skating; she had visions of a severe fall that could make her a paraplegic or worse. She had to prove to both Mirja and herself that she was competent and courageous.

So they headed for the small plaza in the park near Judy's apartment. They both strapped on their skates and Judy struck out bravely, Mirja following cautiously. Just as they were headed down the sloping path to the Shakespeare Garden, picking up speed, a small boy darted out in front of them. Judy swerved to avoid hitting him, lost her balance and fell sprawling on the pavement. The pain was incredible, even to Judy, who was no stranger to real pain.

But her fear was even greater. She was torn between wanting to move in order to determine whether she still could, and not daring to budge, lest she cause herself permanent paralysis. Mirja was solicitous, removing Judy's skates for her and taking off her own light jacket to wad up under Judy's head, then staying with her, holding her hand and reassuring her with her calm quiet voice. Judy dared not even turn her head as she heard the wailing sirens, then saw a mounted policeman looming over her. "Am I crippled for life?" she wanted to ask but was too embarrassed.

She was not, of course; it was "just" a fractured pelvis, but the sirens, flashing lights, and ambulance ride did not bring up pleasant memories, nor did the hospital gurney, X-rays or emergency-room environment. After her surgery, two weeks of bed rest and plentiful pain killers pulled her through. Judy's inner voice was less kind: "Fool! Show-off!" She attempted no more roller skating, for the rest of her time in Finland.

In 1974 Judy made another friend, Anita, a woman who hired her for English language instruction. As part of her studies, Anita invited Judy to a week at her country house on the shore of the Baltic Sea; it was to be an English immersion experience for her. A week to laze around in luxury, Judy thought, but agreed to go only if Laikku could come along. Anita, not a cat lover, reluctantly gave in, and was not pleased when Laikku took his revenge for being left in the car at a shopping center by peeing on the salami. Anita came around, though, after a day or two in the country and a few glasses of wine, appreciating the humor of the situation and warming up to Laikku's outgoing personality. As for Judy's visions of a stately country mansion, however, these were shattered as they drove up to a decrepit two-story affair overgrown with runaway foliage. Inside was no better; mildew and dirt covered the walls and floors, electricity and running water were technologies the house had not yet been graced with, and the bedroom she was to sleep in had to be shared with both rats and bats. Not Judy's style at all. She decided she preferred the porch, and hauled her mattress out there.

The house, Anita explained, belonged to her grandfather, but was not maintained now (who could guess?). It was only occupied for a week or two each summer. Undaunted by the mess, she set about unpacking their food, sweeping a thick layer of dirt out the door and building a fire in the wood-burning stove. At least the sauna worked; what Finnish house would be without one, after all? Finnish saunas were impressive: capacious, and noticeably hotter than any Judy had experienced in the U.S.

The two women spent a week roughing it at the house, and Judy came to appreciate at least the solitude and some of the simplicity. She strolled in the woods with Laikku and had long talks with Anita. They went fishing with primitive rods—bamboo poles with a line and hook attached. They dug up worms, attached them to the hooks, and sat naked on a large boulder waiting for bites (from the fish, although they probably experienced some bites of their own from mosquitoes). When they snagged a catch, they pulled the whole line up and flipped it backward over their heads. Judy caught three fish and Anita several as well; they cleaned and cooked them over the wood stove back at the house.

Not only did they go fishing in the buff, they spent most of the week that way. It was wonderfully freeing after being confined all winter, either huddled indoors or bundled in heavy clothing, and Judy was beginning to appreciate the European acceptance of nudity in appropriate circumstances. She was beginning to awaken, in fact, to a more easy-going attitude toward the body.

Finnish attitudes toward sexuality and relations between the sexes were actually still mixed in the 1970s, however. While married couples—both men and women—always wore wedding rings, the men at least were nevertheless available, although chauvinistic: the typical Finnish husband would sit at the kitchen table and summon his wife from an adjoining room to fetch him a beer from the refriger-ator. One symptom of the shifting attitudes toward sexuality was that many men, while welcoming the increasing availability of wo-men for sex, literally could not perform without being the aggressor. Judy discovered this phenomenon after she had gotten up the nerve to initiate an encounter or two. The irony and hypocrisy did not escape her attention, or her disgust. "Invariably they have never before met such an erotic and experienced chick as I and it may please but shock, upset and limp-dick the guy."

Early in 1973, Judy met two men who attracted more than just her passing attention. It had been more than a year since Ed had left, and, despite her awakening sexual independence, she was still alone and beginning to panic. Emotionally independent she could not be, nor did she ever really try. Despairing of finding an appropriate man in Finland, she started to make plans to leave, going so far as to start sorting through her belongings and packing. Then Velic Pekku, "a handsome engineer," walked into one of her classes at the Finnish American Seminar, and she was hooked. "He courted me from his cubicle at the language lab," she wrote in her journal. He went by the nickname VeePay, and it was as "VP" that she always referred to him in her letters to family and friends.

VP was recently divorced from a nine-year marriage, and had just become the father of a son, Sasu. Not an unusual pattern—a long childless marriage not surviving the stress of a new addition (al-though Judy's sister Chris's marriage had in fact done fine in just such a situation). VP moved in with Judy in June, although their relationship was open and they were almost more roommates than partners at that point. For someone else had caught Judy's eye: John Zaradin, a British professional solo guitarist whose career was just about to take off—"a lovely, wonderful man...very talented, sensitive and capable." Exactly how or where Judy met John is not clear, although it may have been through her journalistic connections.

At any rate, John invited her to accompany him on a trip to London and the continent. Judy was thrilled at the possibility of visiting Greece and seeing Nikolas again, and since she had a free ticket from FinnAir that she needed to use before it expired, she accepted with delight. The trip, unfortunately, was an almost unmitigated disaster.

"The past three weeks can only be described as an 'ordeal'," Judy wrote, a jumble of "accidents, mountains, fog, bodies, hunger, being lost and deserted." They started out with five days in London— August 16 to 21, a portion of the trip eagerly anticipated by Judy; she would visit art galleries, see a ballet and go to a play at the Royal Shakespeare Theatre. But the crowds, noise, filth and high prices put a crimp in those plans. Some respite arrived in the form of a one-night stay with some friends of John's in the seaside town of Bexhill, and with another stop in a plush restored Victorian hotel in the resort town of Eastbourne. They were also able to spend a quiet day with Chris, who had come over from Brazil via the U.S.; they walked in the park, dined and went to a play. "What a darling sister I have," mused Judy.

Nevertheless, Judy could hardly wait to get away, on to Yugoslavia and the "sunny Adriatic Sea," where they would swim, lie in the sun and partake of the delicious food she remembered from the summer of 1966. They crossed the English Channel at night, in a ferry that had no berths, so that Judy arrived in France exhausted from trying unsuccessfully to catch a few winks sitting in the uncomfortable seats. The worst part of the trip, though, was the drive through France, Switzerland, and Italy in their rented Mercedes, a car that impressed everyone they encountered but was not necessarily the most reliable form of transportation. They crossed northeastern France along the border with Belgium and Germany, collapsing in a motel in Nancy the first night—their first good sleep in two days—then headed into Switzerland, careening along tortuous mountain roads with no safety barriers, shrouded in mist and fog (which made it impossible to see any of the scenery) and thronged with irresponsible drivers of all kinds of vehicles, including trucks and buses that John passed on curves at ninety mph. Upon reaching

Italy, the car overheated and they had to stop at the first place they could find, which turned out to be a third-class pension in a small hamlet, with over-priced food and no bathroom.

More harrowing poorly-maintained roads took them into Yugoslavia, where they drove along the coast through the continuing rain. Rather than spend more money on lodging they spent the next night in the car; late at night they were accosted by a pack of wild dogs ominously circling the vehicle and howling (at least, that was Judy's story). Back on their way in the morning, they managed to take advantage of a few hours of sunshine and take a dip in the "sunny Adriatic"; their only swim of the entire trip. After a picnic of spoiled yogurt, tasteless white bread and tomatoes, they proceeded, driving through many seaside villages but finding nothing worth stopping for.

Bassano del Grappa, Italy, where Judy and John enjoyed a short respite. Photo: Carr/Pettit family collection

John had some business to take care of in Belgrade; Judy spent their two days there feeling sick. On to Zagreb and "the filthiest motel imaginable," a far cry from her delightful sojourn there with

Kitty in 1966. Finally they stumbled on the small town of Bassano del Grappa, Italy, picturesque and undiscovered by the tourist crowd; they had a lovely three-night stay at a hotel there, with excellent food, friendly people, and ... sunshine! By this time, though, their funds were running so low that they had to cancel their plans to visit Greece, Judy's anticipated high point of the trip.

The trip back, through Austria, Germany and France, while not quite as miserable as the trip down, had its challenges. A fuel leak in the car subjected them to gasoline fumes, even with the windows open, and the weather was but little improved. Still, Paris was nice, John spoke fluent French and had friends there, and they managed to find "a darling attic room in a quaint but luxurious hotel," where they stayed for three days.

Judy returned to Finland in a state of exhaustion, agitation and disappointment, sad to leave John because "who knows when I will ever see him again?" (she never did), but relieved to be back in "my beloved Finland, peaceful, uncrowded, civilized, clean... My globe-trotting days are over; I simply don't enjoy being a stranger in a foreign land and will gladly turn in my folding toothbrush and currency conversion card for a little house in the country with flower garden and sauna... Finland is a part of me, she is in my bones, the first place I've ever been homesick for."

As for the man situation, she and John had a lifestyle conflict; he was a night person, she a morning one, and he was "married to his guitar." No matter. "VP is so dear to me that I cannot enjoy being with another man no matter how charming he may be." In fact, on the 20th of October she married VP, although she claimed to her family, who were appalled, that it was the only way they could get decent housing together, which may well have been true. Her warm sentiments started to wane in less than three months; by January 1974 she was full of recriminations against her new husband. Although they did move to a small house in Haukilahti, six miles from downtown Helsinki, their home life was anything but quiet. There were communication problems because of the language barrier. While VP's English was better than Judy's Finnish, they shared no adult emotional vocabulary in which they could discuss issues (although, given the problems she had had with Ed, it is not likely that

this made much of a difference). Judy was insanely
jealous of the attention VP
gave his son Sasu. And, despite VP's claim during their
courting days, that he was
drawn to her intelligence and
independence, he was in fact a
typical macho Finnish male.
Judy did not take kindly to this
discovery. She was not a beer
fetcher. Nor did she warm to
his family or Finnish friends,
who had similar attitudes; a
college class reunion and his
brother's "old-fashioned,
country-style farm family"
wedding were both dismal
affairs, with the men drinking
too much and the women singing sad songs of advice to the

Judy with her Finnish husband, VP
Photo: Carr/Pettit family collection

bride at the latter event. She felt that VP was showing off his beautiful American wife, and she did not like being a trophy. "Being mute
for two days was an ordeal let me tell you." One can imagine.

On the bright side, Judy took up a new job in early 1974; she was
hired by the Finnish tourist board to travel to various venues and
write up glowing reports for the board's journal; the series was called
"Out and About," and catered to English-speaking visitors. These
ventures took her from the Soviet border on the east, to Norway in
the west, to Lapland in the far north, visiting small towns, farms,
landmarks, museums and various historical or ethnic attractions,
including a castle in Turku (an ancient and colorful city a short distance west of Helsinki) whose courtyard was used for opera performances, and a restaurant in the form of an over-sized Lapp tipi,
complete with a smoke hole in the roof ("through which moonbeams
shone"). Judy also got to interview local celebrities and eccentrics: a
female reindeer herder, and a famous raanu rug weaver who worked

in her hundred-year-old log house. Drama, adventure and creativity: right up Judy's alley.

Finnish restaurant in form of tipi. Photo: Carr/Pettit family collection.

A vacation with another woman friend, Mimi, provided some calm and relaxation amidst Judy's busy travel schedule. Mimi, like Anita, had access to a family-owned summer house, this one much better kept up, on a small island just offshore from Turku. Although it was late October and the Arctic light was fading fast, taking the summer warmth with it, the two women enjoyed a sensuous respite there. The house itself—a two-storied white frame affair—had already been prepared for its winter hibernation: furniture covered with sheets, beds stripped, cupboards bare, lower halves of the small-paned windows protected with shutters. The very walls seemed to be gathering in the cold night air, filling the rooms with chilly sighs, yet holding memories of the laughter, warmth and joy of summer visitors, and of the aroma of new dilled potatoes, sausage, and blueberry pie. Judy and Mimi camped out in the still usable sauna, down the steep hill that sloped toward the sea. They huddled in makeshift beds in the dressing room at night, and cooked soup and porridge, and brewed strong hearty tea, over the wood-burning stove in the sauna room itself.

The days were short and bone-chilling, the winter afternoon sun hugging the western horizon over the sea, the Arctic wind whirling through the dry dead leaves. The women spent their days chopping firewood and foraging for mushrooms, stopping for tea breaks in the always-warm sauna. As the sunlight faded each afternoon, they'd strip off their sweaty work clothes and luxuriate there, dumping ladle after ladle of water onto the hot stones, filling the room with steam. Then they'd swat each others' backs and legs with birch twigs, gathering their courage to run naked down to the dock for an exhilarating plunge into the frigid sea—skin tingling, but heads clear and alert—after which they'd run back again to the over-heated sauna, repeating this ritual three or four times before a final wash-up and donning of flannel nightgowns. Then steaming hot tea and dark crusty bread smeared with rich jam, partaken of by soft candlelight. And finally, utter darkness, silence except for the crashing sea, and blissful sleep.

Judy's love life, however, was less satisfying. By April 1975, her relationship with VP was a train wreck. Hoping that some time away might help, she managed to scrape together enough money to take a vacation home to the States in June, even visiting with ex-husband Bob Watt in New York. "We were both amazed that we enjoyed each other's company so much after 11 years [since their breakup]... I realize how lucky [it was] I met him so early in the game and how much of an influence he had on me." Upon her return to Finland, however, she and VP separated, and soon after, divorced. Tired of her struggles and fearing a life of loneliness (i.e., one without a man), Judy once again began to consider returning home to the U.S. Contradicting her earlier pronouncement that Finland was part of her, body and soul, she now proclaimed in a letter to Chris that "Finland has become an albatross ... I must make a new life else-where and the only logical choice is the States." Yet, despite having made this decision, she delayed putting it into action. She needed more time. And money. On May thirtieth the Freelancers' Union, a Communist organization, declared a strike against her major em-ployer, Yleisradio, cutting off her main source of income. Judy was furious, as she was not allowed to join any union, being a non-citizen, and therefore could get no financial help from them to ride out the strike. Despite her pronouncements against debting ("I have an aversion to borrowing but if I must...well I must."), she in fact survived the first month largely by doing just that.

Desperate for work, she took on a job with a survey company to evaluate Lapland's qualifications as a tourist destination. She was to pose as an American traveling alone in northern Finland with no knowledge of the language or culture. Following a carefully defined timetable and armed with a stack of questionnaires, Judy set off for the far north country. Unlike her "Out and About" job, however, this one did not afford her the freedom to roam, interview interesting people or explore destinations that intrigued her, and although she did find some high-quality facilities and helpful locals who spoke English, the negatives overwhelmed these positives, in the reports she was required to write up. Restrooms were often dirty, public drunkenness was prevalent in the bus stations, and Finns who spoke no English were more rude than helpful. This kind of reporting cast a black mark on her journalistic name, and the negativity later came back to haunt her, blocking her further advancement in the Finnish journalism market.

Within a few weeks, however, things had returned to more-or-less normal. Judy still had her editing and ESL work, which was enough to sustain her for a while, and after the strike was settled she returned to her regular radio work. She acquired a new roommate, Klara. She was able to take advantage of the wonderful Finnish summer weather and enjoy a cheap vacation, taking a bicycle tour of the Åland Islands between Finland and Sweden, near the city of Turku where she had visited Anita's summer house. And she again served as director at the Finnish-American Society's summer sports retreat (where she had cavorted two years earlier with Knut).

In the fall of 1975, Judy had another romantic fling, this time with an Englishman, Brian, whom she picked up in a bar and took home to pleasure her for the night. Their next rendezvous was at an opulent hotel in Stockholm, where they sipped champagne while lolling in an antique clawfoot bathtub. For Christmas, Judy invited him to spend a week in a cottage in the isolated forests of Lapland, one of the darkest, most snow-bound and frigid places on the planet. No running water or plumbing, although the cottage did have electric heat, thankfully, and in typical Finnish fashion, was well insulated. They skied over the six-foot snow pack, cut their own Christmas tree and trudged out to the woodshed for fuel for the wood-burning sauna. Wash water had to be obtained from the nearby lake, a task that required negotiating the icy shoreline to dip the water buckets, hoping that one did not slip and fall in. Potable water for drinking was even more of a challenge, requiring a one-kilometer trek to a well and hauling the heavy buckets back to the cottage. (Water weighs eight pounds per gallon.) Nights they spent on a mattress on the floor in front of the fireplace, tossing down schnapps and nibbling on lox and French bread slathered with generous amounts of creamy butter. And of course, they would finish

Judy making her way through the snow during her glamorous 1975 Christmas vacation at the isolated Finnish cottage. Photo: Carr/Pettit family collection.

off the evening with wild and abandoned sex.[10]

Come spring, Brian invited her to vacation at his English countryside home; he paid her air fare there. The first morning Judy awoke early to the idyllic sound of birdsong and the fragrance of roses. Mist rose from the gentle green hills. A school bus filled with laughing children rumbled down the lane. And then: "Mother's been ill and hasn't been able to iron my shirts, so do them for me, would you, love?" Brian asked, giving her a peck on the cheek on his way out the door to work. Judy was too stunned to respond with anything other than an incredulous stare. She fumed the entire day. When Brian returned and found the task undone, he whined, and Judy, while inwardly rebelling, complied by ironing one shirt, insisting, though, that he immortalize the moment with a snapshot

---

[10] Judy recounted this adventurous vacation on her radio show the following week, neglecting to mention, however, that she had a companion; instead, she painted a dramatic story of her lone struggle against the elements, extolling the rewards of solitude and self-sufficiency.

from her own camera, a picture she kept for the rest of her life. Later that day she took the remaining pile of shirts to a laundry in the

village, returned to the house to leave the claim check on the dining room table along with a recriminating note, packed up, took a rose from the garden to garland her hair, and left. She took the train into London and joined an Armenian family on a barge trip down the Thames. Or so she claimed in her journal.[11] So much for Englishmen. It did not occur to Judy to reflect that this was the second time she had dumped a man after traveling to visit him in his home.

A couple of months later, in May 1976, Judy took a last vacation at the summer cottage she had first gone to with Leila, alone this time

Judy resentfully ironing one of Brian's shirts. This incident put an end to their relationship. Photo: Carr/Pettit family collection.

except for a feline companion, Mildred—"a black spirit of contentment asleep in the rocking chair." Her roommate Klara dropped her off with a plentiful supply of food for both woman and cat. Time for Judy to take up her pen and journal, reflecting on her life, Finnish culture, humanity and its foibles.

---

[11] Barges plied the Thames River for centuries, carrying small cargo loads, but by the mid-twentieth century, these had been supplanted by larger corporate cargo ships. Some of the small-time barge operators were able to survive by offering excursion trips to tourists.

Judy and her English lover Brian enjoying fleshly pleasures. These are probably the earliest photographs of Juliet that might be called erotic. Photos: Carr/Pettit family collection.

Much of her time on this vacation was spent in rigorous physical labor. There was no particular need for her to do so, as the cottage was only rented for two weeks, but Judy always needed to mold her physical environment, and the activity helped clear her head. The warm weather allowed her to indulge her love of nudity or near-nudity; she labored on the grounds in bikini panties, yellow rubber boots and work gloves, her hair unkempt. She wanted to clear an overgrown path from the cottage down to the lake, and pruned away tree branches, dug up roots, raked the ground even and set flat stones in the muddier areas. She prepared a garden plot, getting dirt under her nails as she mixed peat moss into the soil. Then she dug up and hauled away impressively large boulders, fencing the entire area with some of the extricated stones. She washed the cottage windows so that she could better appreciate the view. She shook dust out of the rugs and washed her laundry, and herself, in the cold waters of the lake. She prepared sumptuous meals on the wood stove, falling into bed each night deliciously tired.

During breaks in the work, and before falling asleep at night, she mused on her life, her relationships, and her work. Nikolas had written to her a few weeks prior; he was now married and held a prominent position in the newly stable Greek government. Judy had mixed feelings: relieved that she was not the one he had married, and thus not subject to all the pressures attendant upon an upper-class Greek wife, but at the same time, jealous. She still yearned for him. Should she call him? "How much I loved him and always will."

A handwritten weekly schedule:

Monday   Tuesday   Wed.   Thurs.   Fri.

Monday:
1. Call Silvinomen re: interview on WHO
2. Call re interviews on Meat program
3. Studio record 9-12 nm "Out & About"
4. Lesson: 3pm Dr. Wiikeri
5. Lesson: Bush. Disc. Groups 5-6 30 pm
6. Evening: Write prelim meat script.

Tuesday:
1. 10 30 meat interview #1
2. 12 00 meat interview #2
3. Lesson: Statistics Bureau 2 pm
4. Lesson: (same) 3 pm
5. Lesson: Ins. Co 4 30
6. Lesson: Dr and wife 6 30
7. Concert 8-10

Wed.:
1. 9 30 Lesson Doctor
2. Trans- lation Bur. 11-2
3. Finnish lesson 3-4 (for me)
4. Lesson: 3 ladies 4 30
5. 6 30 8 Disc. Group at FAS

Thurs.:
1. 10 30 Lesson Doctor
2. Massage 12 30-1 30
3. Lesson: Lawyer 3-4
4. Lesson: Ins. Co 4 30
5. Evening: write "Topic" script

Fri.:
1. 9 30 Finnish Lesson 10 30
2. Studio 12-1 record "Topic"
3. Translati Bureau 2-5

8 hr + concert   7½ hr   5 hr.   5 hr.
7-8 hr day

plus cooking cleaning washing, shopping and TLC to Jaikku & V-P U

This is as typical a weekly schedule as I can give you. But times and jobs change constantly. I have to be an expert juggler. Some we[eks] I have more or less radio work and more or less work correcting translations. I try always to take 2 hr/wk Finnish lessons.

Judy wrote up this typical weekly schedule for her family.

Relationships: they were the bane and yet the necessity of her existence. Her time in the more enlightened Scandinavian countries, and perhaps moving into her thirties, had enabled her to think outside the strictures of the Puritanical culture that had prevailed in

1950s America, when she was coming of age. She was beginning to realize that sex could be decoupled from love, and that women should be able to take more initiative, rather than passively waiting for male attention or drawing it to them through manipulation and intrigue. She decried the hypocrisy of women who pretended they were looking for respectable love when they were actually just horny: "[It's] OK to act like a whore behind closed doors with a man you kidded yourself you loved (no matter how fleetingly), with excuses of looking for a husband." She realized that she herself was "an erotic, sex-loving woman who would suffocate in a conventional relationship, in marriage and the prison of child-rearing."

Yet she wanted financial security, and did not seem to be able to attain that on her own. "[I] wish I could shake off the yoke of needing to work to support myself. Freed of this necessity I think I would like to try to write. But I have no one to fall back on for support, to pay my debts. I like the good luxurious life too much, [have always been] a hedonist."

After about a week and a half alone at the cottage, Judy took a chance on following through with her newfound determination to be a sexually liberated woman. She invited Matti, a real hunk she had met a few weeks prior, to come and spend a night with her. He jumped at the chance and showed up with a roast chicken and three bottles of wine. After dinner and a dousing bath on the porch, they lay on the reindeer-skin rug before the fire. This encounter was a major disappointment, however. Matti, a typical insecure Finnish man, was a grabber who could not deal with Judy's assertiveness. He didn't even like her sucking his cock; although he admitted it felt great, it put him in too passive a position to respond. Nothing in Judy's impressive arsenal was able to bring his rod to more than half mast. Furthermore, despite his stunning build and good looks, his cock was small as well as limp, much to her dismay. "I need a large stiff dick to touch my happy button deep down," she wrote later although of course she did not tell him so.

Matti spent the night, and was almost silent through breakfast, embarrassed by his poor performance of the evening before and obviously eager to be on his way. The next night, Judy tried masturbating with only her hands, for the first time in her life. She vowed to get a good rubber dildo as soon as she got to San Francisco; the plastic one she had brought with her was too cold and hard, but it was all she had been able to find in Finland.

Judy spent the last couple of days at the cottage finishing up the garden work, planting tomatoes, celery and dill. Although her work-worn hands were now like sandpaper, she was proud of her first garden. She washed her work clothes at last; the water got so dirty it "looked like the Ganges."

By March of 1977, Judy was planning her return to the U.S. in earnest. She would fly to Toronto and then on to Las Vegas, where her parents would be vacationing. Her finances were still weak; she had to borrow from several people, including her cousin Andrew, to get enough money to come home.

She landed in Toronto on April 8th. Her sojourn in Finland had ended, and two more major relationships had failed. She still had hopes for her future, but the picture was fuzzy.

9
Coming Home

When Judy returned to the U.S. in April of 1977, she was almost a stranger to American culture. She had lived half her adult life abroad —nine out of eighteen years. She had missed an intense period of U.S. history: the Vietnam War protests, the oil crisis, George McGovern's heart-breaking presidential campaign, the entire Watergate scandal. And the preceding six years, she had spent in a lightly populated country, more rural than urban, and removed from some of the more tumultuous worldwide political activity. "It now seems like a long hibernation," she commented in her journal. Indeed, she had in some ways been hiding out—not just from the world, but from her own life.

Now she was adrift. And alone. Wondering where she was, who she was, and what the hell she was doing, anyway.

Judy was undergoing a classic midlife crisis, searching for an identity and a path in life. For something that would make her feel grounded, that she belonged somewhere, that she was loved and appreciated. And perhaps more than anything else, for a livelihood, a life calling that would sustain her financially and define who she really was.

Since childhood, Judy had defined herself more by who she was *not* than by who she *was*. Her painful childhood hospitalization experiences had made her determined not to be an invalid or a victim. She was not a "good girl": she had rebelled against that stereotype in college, becoming a wild woman at a time when there was no such popular archetype. She was not a housewife, although she enjoyed keeping a home and savored the sensual part of marriage. After her kindergarten teaching disaster, her unsuccessful pregnancy, and the painful experience of step-parenting, she no longer had any desire to be a mother. And while she certainly loved attention and drama, she was not happy being a mere trophy for a wealthy and prestigious Greek politician. And she was not, above all, a materialistic, parochial middle-class American.

What Judy knew about herself at this point in her life was that she was creative, resourceful, highly intelligent, adventurous, hardworking, sensitive and sensual. That she needed warmth, nurturing, and a lot of physical contact. That she was lonely. And that no one, not even she herself, really understood her.

In this state of ambiguity, Judy returned to the U.S.—for good, as it turned out. Never again would she live abroad.

She began her repatriation, as planned, by joining her parents for a short vacation in Las Vegas. She had been eagerly anticipating this trip; it would be a wonderful warm, sunny vacation—a perfect break from Finland, which was still cool in the early spring. But, although she had fond memories of hanging out with Chris in Las Vegas while their parents gambled, Judy discovered that she now hated the place. It represented the worst of American culture: "throngs of loud, obese, garishly clad tourists and camera-toting Orientals [Asians]... walking stomachs, both male and female... spoiled, pampered, friendly but uncouth, naive, materialistic." She felt herself "superior, aloof from the masses," opining that "at 38+ I'm in fantastically better shape mentally, emotionally and physically than most 25-year-olds." Always a connoisseur of male attractiveness, though, she could not help but notice that some of the casino workers were worth a second look: she admired the "sensuous hands (and asses) of the dealers" [at the gambling tables], and noted that the young men in service positions had an "apparent innate gift of wit, chatter and friendly flirting." And she did enjoy being with her father, whom she described as being "witty, happy and out of pain."

For all her complaints about the U.S. and its backward culture, though, Judy expressed relief at being back. "Don't miss Finland; should have left years ago," she wrote, although she missed her privacy: "Here it is a sin to be alone and *enjoy* it!" Yet she was beginning to settle into life in the American southwest. Her first purchases were "white sandals, white sweater, swim goggles, skin care products, health food and vitamins, swim clogs and towels, hair dryer, iron, ironing board" (despite the shirt incident with Brian).

After the brief sojourn in Las Vegas, Judy moved on to the Bay Area, and by the 26th of April, she had settled in Palo Alto with her friend Mirja, who had moved to the states the preceding September.

Here she relaxed, tried to readjust to U.S. culture, and pondered what to do next with her life.

A major issue was sex: "[I] realize how important regular, *good* sex is to my well-being." Finding a partner who could meet this need was a major challenge, however. She bemoaned the lingering double standard, which dictated that even "if a woman is sexually liberated [men] still want to take the initiative." The "waiting princess" role was definitely not her style. "When I'm sexually frustrated I am very aggressive.. and scare men off."

Judy was envious, but at the same time judgmental, of her friend Mirja's promiscuity: "Why not to bed with every male one meets? Wrong only because it brings her no satisfaction. [She has a] Don Juanita complex—conquer and leave."

In fact, at this point in her life, Judy's standards for engaging in sex were surprisingly mainstream feminine, at least on paper: "Good sex is only communication in intimate form and to be really satisfying to both partners, feelings are involved. How many people can you really feel close enough to, respect enough to expose your body, your guts, your primal feelings and emotions? My sexual partner is a mirror image—an extension of myself. Discrimination is essential."

Yet her actions belied these words, as her main hunting grounds seemed to be the bars. And despite Judy's later claims, she does not seem to have had the problem of not being able to get laid "no matter how hard I tried." Her actual difficulty was in finding lasting, satisfactory sexual relationships. Most of her relationships were very short-term, many only one-night stands: Bob and Clark, musicians she met through her one of her temporary sales jobs; Al, John, Roger, Franco, Gary and Charles, worth only passing mention in her journals. Her old Swedish flame Knut did pay a brief visit, accompanied by his friend Pauli. But this visit ended in heartbreak, too, as Knut declined to renew their sexual relationship, and Pauli, after a sizzling three-night stand, dumped her cold.

The truth is, Judy was confused about her own needs and desires. She wanted unattached relationships with good sex, but she also wanted the security and validation, both social and personal, that comes with long-term commitment. While on some level, she knew that "[I] have a desperate need to touch and be touched," she struggled just as she had during her first year of college, to envision the style of relationship that would meet these needs. She still had not discovered that her true nature was sensuous, rather than merely sexual, that she had a need for a consummate physical intimacy that few men, especially younger men, could fulfill.

This confusion led her into a lot of pain. While she had no trouble finding passion without attachment—bar-hopping took care of that —her need for a steady companion who would hold and caress her regularly, went unmet.

Typical of Judy's sexual behavior during these months was her relationship with a thirty-year-old named Francisco: "so warm, cuddly, touchable, sensuous, sexual, intelligent. What doesn't he have? ... I've a real passion for him... we melt into each other... am working to make it a long-lived friendship." She reveled in "a night of love and a day in San Francisco—lunch, aquarium, tea garden— perfect in every way." At the same time, she reaffirmed to herself her commitment to unattached sensuality with Francisco: "[I] don't want to pressure him as he has work and other women."

Yet for all her proclamations, she realized on some level that she was, in fact, needy and insecure: "[I] must see him more often than once a week or I suffer... I need him more often than he needs me." And less than a week after the wonderful San Francisco day with him, she was bummed out over his "squirming out of" a dinner date with her and Mirja, having a "disquieting feeling he is not being honest, and it hurts." She claimed it was this lack of honesty that hurt, not that he had "other lovers and interests." He was "*too* nice to everyone, and sadly it smacks of insincerity."

And about ten days later, the ax fell. She thought they had a date to spend Sunday afternoon at the beach together, but when he failed to show up or call and she finally called him, he claimed there had been a misunderstanding about the day, and then added, "I met the most wonderful girl last night," a beautiful 22-year-old. "A knife to the heart," Juliet described this blow, especially harsh on the heels of her jubilant anticipation of a delightful day with him.

She reacted just as she had during her college days when her heartthrob Bob—the young man who had taken her mind off her lost love Jerry—had snubbed her. She collapsed into tears, followed by recriminations, as she berated him over the phone, hoping to guilt-trip him. "Let him suffer awhile."

The weather cooperated with her, unleashing a deluge of rain. Dramatically, Judy took the opportunity to drive her unreliable car up Mt. Diablo, where she slid off a road shoulder and spent $25 [$98] getting towed out. She returned to Alice's Restaurant, where she drowned her troubles in beer and shared a chili dinner with a "spaced-out hitchhiker." At least it was a little male attention.

She returned home to find flowers from Francisco, with a report from Mirja that he had called multiple times. Ignoring both, as well as the frequently ringing phone (answering machines were rare in those days, and they did not have one), Judy finished off half a bottle of red wine and retreated to bed. "Even though suffering, [I am] enjoying the extended drama," just as she had at age five when she discovered that illness could garner the attention she was always craving. "I want to suffer for a few days; it equalizes me."

A few hours later, in a sleepy daze, she forgot her resolution and answered Francisco's call. She agreed to meet with him. That turned into a sexual encounter, "an expected and welcome release" which she sensed Francisco viewed as a solution to the problem even though she knew it was not. Especially after finding out later about his overtures to her friend Mirja.

Judy woke up early the next morning and left him sleeping to return home, feeling "great sadness at another person who has betrayed my trust and love. How do I always find these types of men?" Probably by being drawn to those who seemed too good to be true and not having developed the judgment to discern this, as most people would have by age thirty-eight.

Following the disaster with Francisco, Judy traveled to Lake Tahoe to renew her tryst with Jim, a guy she had met some weeks earlier. But his attentions were erratic, waxing only when he was horny, with no concern for her needs. He was, moreover, "too cocky, a braggart; he needs constant praise of his cock.. his large cock." Although he had learned to ask a woman what she wanted, he didn't follow through on it. His response to any compliment was "Of course!" After a few days of frustration, Judy returned home to her vibrator ("a man can't do as well on a clit").

Despairing of ever finding an emotionally satisfying relationship, Judy and her friend Mirja decided to "pursue rich men in a dedicated well-thought-out way and stop wasting our time on poor students and stingy hustlers," a strategy they apparently either did not follow through on or were unsuccessful at.

One relationship that lasted a little longer was with a man named Harry, who at the time Judy got involved with him was either still married or had only recently separated from his wife. Harry was quite well off, and seemed to be something of a professional entre-preneur, starting and ending new businesses with rapidity. He ap-parently helped her out financially, although not enough to support her. She also described him as alcoholic and emotionally cold. He continued to pass in and out of her life for the next year or so.

Throughout all the emotional ups and downs of her romantic life, Judy tried to settle into her new life in the States. At some point during the summer, she left the Palo Alto apartment she shared with Mirja and moved into her own place, a third-floor studio apartment in North Beach. The city, the East Bay and Marin were more cul-turally aligned to her tastes than Palo Alto ("elite... beauty and brains, youth and snobbishness"), and she started taking hikes on Mt. Tamalpais, going to the opera, browsing the bookstores in Berkeley. And job hunting.

It is not clear from her journal what this search consisted of, as she took a break from journal writing between May and September. Despite her later claims that she had come to the Bay Area to get into documentary film-making, she made no mention of any such pursuit in her writings. And if she applied for regular jobs as a journalist, she was not successful, whether because of fierce competition or from her lack of skill in selling herself to an employer. After all, she had been self-employed for most of her life, as had her parents—her primary role models. She may, in fact, have had the perception that only mundane jobs, like her mother's secretarial work or her own jobs at the phone company and teaching, could be regular, 9-to-5 stints, working for wages; professional work was, according to her definition, self-employment.

This she did pursue. Building on her extensive journalistic experience in Finland, she sought out interesting topics she could write up and sell. She toyed with the idea of visiting a "male brothel" and selling the story to *Playgirl* magazine, and of writing a book on the topic of saliva, or more grossly put, spit—"all uses of, historical side, medical properties, chemical breakdown, advertising possi-

bilities ('how does your spit taste?')" and of course the sexual benefits. She did land a temporary job with the radio and TV station
KCBS in San Francisco, presenting a sales training program to their
employees.

To cobble together some income, however sporadic, she worked
at several commission-only sales jobs, one of which entailed selling
advertisements on matchbook covers. Companies she mentioned
working for include BKE, Banner, and Cal Pacific Signs, probably a
billboard company.

None of these projects, though, generated long-term secure
employment, and as the months dragged on, both her economic
situation and her social life went from bad to worse. She was on food
stamps and MediCal, and by September she was $4,500 [$17,640] in
debt. She had vague feelings of guilt about her lack of motivation
and perseverance, but "not enough to spur me to action."

The stress was beginning to take a physical toll, too—diarrhea,
acne, and backaches that even massage did not alleviate. She tried to
keep up some regular physical exercise, jogging, swimming, and
hiking on Mt. Tamalpais, but she was sinking into depression. She
had "a miserable sex life, no close friends, and no money... But surprisingly I go cheerily on, getting further in debt, eating on food
stamps, climaxing with a vibrator, trying to keep the five jobs
separate, desperately needing affection, rapport, material support
and a satisfying job."

In November, Judy had a "light-bulb" experience, and decided
that her romantic rejections were caused by her "putting everything
into a relationship because nothing else is going right in my life
now." That kind of pressure was a turn-off to potential partners, she
concluded. "Henceforth I must let love develop *slowly* and naturally,
and not equate it with sex. When I need a fuck, get a good one but
don't confuse sex and love, don't make sex more than a good time
with no strings or future commitments." Yet, "I cannot forgive a man
who refuses to come to my bed... if only to hold and comfort. It is the
ultimate cruelty."

Adopting Snuggles

Harsh overhead fluorescent lights, pale green cement walls and row upon row of caged cats. Pitiful meows trembled in a silence heavy with the despair of the abandoned. I'd been up and down the aisle several times, peering into the small dark cages. How could I possibly decide which cat to take, knowing the ones I left behind most likely would be killed? For one I'd be a savior, for the rest, a murderer.

They were all so cute—a playful striped gray, a shy calico, two long-haired black angoras huddled at the rear of their cage in fright, an elegant Siamese. How could I possibly choose?

I was about to leave this chamber of horrors at the SPCA catless, to find a furry companion at a pet shop or even at a Saturday morning give-away at a Safeway, rather than make a choice here. But at the doorway I paused; something had made me turn, like a tap on my shoulder.

A small white leg protruded through the bars into the aisle between the cages, waving, pleading with me to return. I didn't have to choose, after all; it chose me, the white front leg. I asked the attendant to open the cage for a better look. A small bundle of pink and white cotton leapt into my arms and purred, "Take me, please take me."

-- *Juliet Carr*

A few days after this revelation, suffering from long-term feline deprivation, she acquired from the SPCA the two-month-old solid white female kitten who would be her companion for the next nineteen years—first named Lumi but later Snuggles. "Something breathing to come home to, something to sleep by my side."

After six months back in the U.S., Judy was still adjusting to the middle-class American lifestyle of the 1970s, not sure where she fit in or where she wanted to go. She vacillated between philosophizing and survival. A list of priorities in her journal shows "freedom," "self respect" and "touching" near the top, "quiet," "friends" and "money that gives freedom" near the bottom. She fantasized about her ideal life. Entries included a "Happiness is" list (a cat; sunshine; privacy; quiet; massage; good food; hot shower; clean silky sheets; giving head to a gorgeous cock belonging to a gorgeous, sensitive, responsive man; love), and two versions of "The Perfect 24 Hours"—the first, with a lover (lazy, tender wake-up lovemaking; breakfast on veranda; long hike; outdoor lovemaking; picnic; dinner in an elegant restaurant; snuggle up and sleep); the second, alone (breakfast in bed with a good book, a day outdoors, sauna and massage, good music, good meal, evening entertainment, playing with cat, satisfying myself with vibrator, early to bed). These were balanced by a list of "turn-offs" regarding men (long boxer shorts, body hair and flab, farting, snoring, unruly eyebrows, jumping up to wash off after fucking, refusal to use public transportation).

Despite these attempts to visualize her ideal life, reality had a way of intruding. By March of 1978, her situation was desperate. None of the five jobs she had was satisfying and even in total they were not sustaining. "The roof was falling in."

The breakthrough came one Sunday when her friend Erkki was visiting. After bemoaning her situation to him at some length, Judy pled, in desperation, "What can I do?"

"What are your options, Judy?" he asked. He picked up the Sunday paper and ran through the classifieds. The first section was Performing Arts. Perusing the page, Erkki read aloud an ad that caught his eye: "Alex de Renzy needs attractive girl for live soft-core porno show. Fun, short hours and good pay."

Judy's first reaction, of course, was: "No, not me!" But Erkki urged her to think about it, and she ended up making an appointment for an interview. Why not, she decided, use the only assets she hadn't exploited: her body and her uninhibited sexuality?

Even so, she was full of indecision about whether to keep the appointment. While she had always been curious about the "seamy side of life," she feared it as well. During her six years in Finland she had been completely out of touch with U.S. culture in general, and thus knew nothing about the Golden Age of Porn that had been blossoming in the United States during the 1970s. "I thought [porno films] were amateur productions catering to the perverted tastes of no more than a couple of hundred degenerate men, clandestinely made and mailed in brown paper wrapping. I was an experienced traveler and uninhibited sexual adventurer, but very naive about professional sex." Thus she approached the scheduled interview with a mixture of apprehension, anticipation, and no doubt some relief at the prospect of solid employment.

As she jogged in Golden Gate Park she went through a mental tug-of-war: "Yes I will, no I won't, yes I will, etc... Plainly, I was scared of rejection. I thought I was too old, my body too flabby." But she did keep the appointment, mitigating her nervousness by pretending she was a journalist researching sex work for a news article. She wore red pants, a black T-shirt and a black cape to the interview. Milka, the "extremely ugly nineteen-year-old Spanish/ Japanese dyke theatre manager" took one look at her and said, "Can I see your breasts, please?" Judy pulled up her shirt (she had gone bra-less since her Japan days), and Milka responded, "Aahhh! You're hired. But," she warned, "don't tell my boss, Alex, your real age because you don't look thirty-nine; you actually look younger than me. And thirty-nine is considered too old for this kind of work. But don't worry; everything will be OK."

Although Milka had warned Judy that it might be several days before Alex got back to her, he actually called her that very night to ask if she could come in the next day, as he said Milka had been very impressed with her.

The interview with Alex took place in the dingy basement of the porno theater, the Screening Room (now the Century). Since the advertised job was for a stripper in the "Playpen," Alex took Judy to view the show. The Playpen was on the main floor of the theatre, and consisted of a small room with eighteen plush pink upholstered seats and a raised platform, open on three sides with a mirror along the entire back wall, where the strippers performed. Although customers were not allowed to touch the performers, the shows were very explicit.

As they sat there eating oranges and watching the other women perform, Judy was intimidated. She wondered how she would "have the stomach to push my pussy in men's faces." Nevertheless, as she began to take tentative steps in the direction of sex work, she became more and more intrigued. "At first I was motivated by money, then by money and curiosity and finally by enjoyment and money."

Instead of hiring Judy for work in the Playpen, though, Alex decided to offer her the part of the maid in the movie *Pretty Peaches*. The original script had called for an Asian housemaid, but Alex changed the ethnicity to Scandinavian to suit Judy's Nordic looks. "When I accepted the part I had no idea what I was getting into... but I needed the $200 [$730], so I gulped and plunged."

The very next day, one of Alex's assistants escorted Judy on a shopping expedition to buy lingerie for the Swedish maid character. She was then driven to the filming site, at Alex's home in Marin, where she met the other two actors, John Nuzzo (better known by his later stage name, John Leslie) and a very young woman named Flower. The script called for Judy to hop up on the bed where Flower lay waiting with her legs spread, and start eating her pussy. Although this was the first time Judy had ever had any sexual contact with a woman, she kept her nervousness to herself and plunged in as if she had been giving women head for years. Her efforts were highly effective, for both she and Flower got so into it that Alex had to cut the scene to bring John in. His role was to immediately start fucking Judy, doggie style, and Judy threw herself wholeheartedly into that encounter as well. "There I was with this gorgeous, sexy man's stiff cock buried deep inside me, rubbing my G-spot and cervix," she wrote on the biographical page of her website years later, then went on to recount how, just as she was getting close to coming, Alex called out, "Cut!"

"Cut?!" she exclaimed. "Why cut?"

"This is a film, Judy," Alex explained. "It's not real life. We need to cut here, then you fake your orgasm, and then we get on to the next scene."

"Fake?" she responded. "I don't need to fake it."

"Now, Judy, I realize that this is your first film and you don't know how we do things, but that's how it is. Just do the orgasm and then we'll move on."

"No, just give me three minutes, Mr. de Renzy, and I'll give you a real orgasm."

Alex was dubious but finally gave in. "Yeah, yeah, OK. I'll give you four more minutes, max. Just remember to moan and breathe heavily." He demonstrated the proper vocalization techniques.

So Judy got her way. John picked up where he had left off, thrusting heartily, and Judy hungrily accommodated his still-stiff cock, riding the wave of rising energy, ecstatic with the opportunity not only for uninhibited sex but also for exhibitionism, reveling in being the star, the center of attention. Within two minutes she climaxed, not just once but three or four times, letting out all the stops—moaning, squirming and yelling to her heart's content.

After Alex yelled "Cut!"—for real this time—a stunned silence filled the room, punctuated only by Judy's and John's heavy breathing and laughter.

So began Judy's porn career, and the birth of Juliet Anderson. The long and circuitous journey to her real identity was over. "After years of physical frustration, feeling trapped by my own sexuality, unappreciated, neglected... I had come home."

10

The Not-So-Golden Age

The American porn film industry was at its peak when Juliet arrived on the scene in the spring of 1978. It had its roots in the late 1950s, when Juliet was coming of age, with Alfred Kinsey's research, the invention of more effective contraceptives ("the pill"), the coming of age of the Boomer generation, and the consequent loosening of sexual mores. In the mid-1950s, Bunny Yeager, a high-fashion model in Florida, turned photographer and started shooting "bathing beauties"—voluptuous young women in extremely skimpy bikinis. Among her models was the "notorious" Bettie Page, who, like Juliet, brought a joyous ebullience and a wry sense of humor to the business.

Some semi-professional filmmakers took the idea of photographing skimpily clad or nude models on to moving pictures, inventing the "nudie cutie" and "sexploitation" films. Some of these early films were pretty tepid, featuring people playing nude volleyball or lounging around swimming pools. No genitals could be shown, and scenes often had to be re-shot so that male actors exposed only their backsides. The first real film was *The Immoral Mr. Teas*, released in 1959, shot in four days on a $24,000 [$196,000] budget.

It was Dave Friedman who, in 1960, came up with the idea of shooting 10-minute shorts and selling them to burlesque theaters. Although he met some resistance from the theater owners at first, they took to the idea when they realized it would solve their perennial problem of unreliable strippers; you never knew whether they would show up, or be in condition to work if they did (many had substance abuse problems). It was cheaper, too, for both the producers and the theater owners; producers made their money on volume and theaters could run each film multiple times.

Films conferred some benefit to sex workers as well; you only had to show up once for the filming, you got paid right away in cash, and you could move on to another job or another city—an advantage that suited the vagabond lifestyle of the majority of sex workers. Pay started at $100 [$800] per day for women and $75 [$600] for men.

(Women generally know the value of their sexuality better than men do.) Anal sex garnered bonus pay for the bottom actor.

These early films were fairly crude, with actors often doing double duty as cameramen for scenes they did not appear in. There was usually only one sound person and one lighting person, and editing was minimal. The idea was to shoot the whole movie in one day, at one location—often a warehouse that could be rented cheaply, or someone's apartment. These short films eventually morphed into the "loop": a twelve-minute film that could be run over and over at a peep show, with the customer charged twenty-five cents for each two-minute segment. Loops were actually a more lucrative business (for the producer) than full-length films, bringing in an estimated four times the revenue.

Meanwhile, still photography became more explicit as well, and captured a growing market. Paul Johnson, later one of Juliet's close friends and a wonderful fuck buddy for her, shot the pictures for the 1970 book, *Sex in Marriage*, ostensibly a marriage manual but really intended as a porno book. It was, in fact, the first truly hard-core publication to be sold in adult bookstores in the U.S., effectively launching the Golden Age of Porn in the United States. Paul is a fascinating figure in his own right, as his life is a veritable history of the porn business, to which he made significant contributions. He invented "point-of-view" porn photography—pictures shot from the point of view of a participant (the participant always being, of course, a straight male, the assumed bulk of the market). Juliet would have liked to produce some point-of-view photographs from the woman's point of view, but although she and Paul discussed this idea, they never got around to implementing it. Truth be told, there may not have been much of a market for it.

A few more explicit porn magazines began appearing during this time as well—*Jaybird, Bachelor, Titter, Wink, Cavalier, Nugget, Fling, Sunbathing* and *Escapade*, among many others. Some of these publications were actually designed to challenge obscenity laws, in order to push the envelope. Despite the emergence of films, still photography continued to make up the bulk of the pornography market, even throughout most of the golden age of porn. It was only the invention of cheap videotape, whose sales started to take off in the early 1980s, that shifted the balance to action performances.

Nevertheless, there was a vibrant market for porn films. In 1970 Alex de Renzy produced his first porno movie, *Pornography in Denmark*, a sort of documentary about the legalization of adult pornography in that country in 1969. When (to many people's surprise) this film was not censored in the United States, it opened the door for the explosion of the hard-core porn film industry here. De Renzy was also the first director to incorporate real story lines, albeit minimal, into porn films. With more professional productions and improved technology came the opportunity for porn to become a real art form, and it began to draw some truly creative talent along with the vagabond element that is always drawn to short-term easy work with immediate pay.

Yet despite this introduction of better-quality production, there was always a tension between quality and commercialization, even during the height of the Golden Age. While many actors and directors, including Juliet, were sincerely dedicated to doing a professional job, the owners and distributors were often catering to a market of heterosexual men who were angry at women and craved porn that showed the women being degraded or exploited. Sometimes good dramatic scenes were edited out of the productions, frustrating both the professionals and those audience members who did want a higher-class act. As with so many consumer goods, the most lucrative segment of the porn industry was that which catered to the lowest class of consumer. The investors were evidently convinced— rightly or wrongly—that that was where the most money was to be made, and enough of it rolled in to validate their beliefs. There were also enough sex workers to provide the required services.

Juliet often ranted over the custom of paying porn actors only by the hour or the day, rather than giving them residual fees from the films' profits, as actors in regular films receive.[12] Yet there were good reasons for this practice. For one thing, porn actors were rarely more than glorified extras, usually doing only one shoot per scene with almost no rehearsing, and engaging in minimal dialog—in other words, not really acting very much. Furthermore, because porn films were shown at small independent theaters, who did not have elabor-

---

[12] Juliet, once she established herself, was able to set going rates: $50 [$145] for a short loop, $75 [$217] to $100 [$290] for a long one, $150 [$434] for an elaborate one, $200 [$580] for a supporting role, $300 [$867] for a lead.

ate systems in place for monitoring sales receipts, there was no way to keep truly accurate track of profits or royalties. The porn business, although legitimate, has always been more loosely run has than has the mainstream film industry. It has also tended to draw its participants primarily from the population of drifters looking for quick and easy money, not inclined to plan for their futures. Ironically, when Juliet produced her own film *Educating Nina*, she also paid her actors strictly by the clock.

As soon as it became clear that there was big money to be made in porn films, organized crime got involved, and they were behind most high-profile films like *Deep Throat* and *Debbie Does Dallas*. The Peraino family, Reuben Sturman ("the king of smut") and Robert DiBernardo (Di-Be) were some of the larger producers and distributors—not one of them someone you would want to get on the wrong side of. Mickey Zaffarano, owner of the Pussycat Theaters, was another shady figure who at least had connections with the mob, whether or not he was one of them. Mickey died of a heart attack on Valentines Day, 1980, while trying to escape arrest during a major porno sting operation; DiBernardo was killed by renegade mobsters in 1986. Reuben Sturman[13], one of the more forward-thinking entrepreneurs, is credited with inventing the peep booth—where customers could view loops via a coin-operated machine—and was also the first to recognize, in 1974, that the future of porn lay in videotape. After managing to evade numerous pornography charges, Sturman was finally convicted of income tax evasion in 1989, and later of extortion and jury tampering, and sent to federal prison in Kentucky; he died there in 1997, of natural causes.

One of the major directors for the organized crime moguls was Gerard Damiano, the director of *Deep Throat*, who actually aspired to be an independent filmmaker. He directed porn films because at that time it was the only area where you could actually make a living as an independent producer. Since he got paid a flat fee for each movie, he was exploited as much as any of the actors, although of course his fee was considerably higher than theirs. Juliet worked with Gerry

---

[13] Homer Young, an FBI agent who participated in obscenity investigations for decades, believed that Sturman had consistently fought to keep organized crime out of the porn business. Sturman himself vigorously denied having any mob connections.

Damiano in 1980, in *Beyond Your Wildest Dreams,* and hated him, claiming he was the sleaziest of all the directors she ever worked with. However, she rated the movie itself as one of her favor-ites, probably because of the shower masturbation scene. Damiano lived to age eighty, dying a natural death in 2008.

Most of the porn movies with ties to organized crime were produced on the East Coast, primarily in Florida. While they had some people in Los Angeles, these tended to be the renegade family members, and the production and distribution of West Coast films was not as tightly controlled, nor were they as lucrative. Organized crime never really got a foothold in the West Coast pornography scene.

The biggest names in pornography on the West Coast were the Mitchell Brothers, Jim and Artie, in San Francisco. Their beginnings were modest. Jim was studying political science at San Francisco State University when he decided to take some classes in filmmak-ing. He took a job at the Roxie Theater just to see what was going on in the film world, and from there got the idea of making skin flicks, to bring in some extra money. When Artie got out of the army, he had some money saved up, and they decided to go into the porn film business together. They bought a used movie camera, learned how to use it, and made a few short films, recruiting their actresses from strip clubs. Encouraged by the ease of this new venture, they got the idea of making a full-length movie, *Behind the Green Door.* Selecting a very young Marilyn Chambers as the female star, and powerhouse Johnny Keyes as the male lead, they started filming. The young stars brought their vibrant energy to the film, and to the filming: in one scene, the crew got so aroused watching that many of them got into the act and a veritable orgy ensued; some of the footage shot there was used in the movie.

Behind the Green Door did well, garnering $30,000 [$170,000] in one week at the box office in New York City, but it was not until Marilyn Chambers was revealed to be the woman on the Ivory Snow box—the quintessential wholesome mother image—that the film took off. It was shown at Cannes, and Marilyn Chambers was nom-inated for an award for the best sex scene ever shot. After the film became a hit, Marilyn and Johnny were able to re-negotiate their contracts, and actually received residuals for their work—an extremely rare occurrence in the business. Juliet worked with Marilyn Chambers on *Insatiable II*, and did not like her, pegging her as one of the most egotistical actors in the business.

Meantime, only three weeks before starting to film *Green Door*, the brothers had opened the O'Farrell Theater, and had to interrupt filming to deal with an obscenity bust there—their first of many. The theater became an icon of the San Francisco sex scene. It was there that Juliet premiered her live stage shows, in 1981, and she counted the brothers among her friends and colleagues, even testifying on their behalf in a sexual harassment suit against them in 1986. Although the brothers were involved in many sex-related cases, both civil and criminal, they never lost one; their high-priced New York lawyers saw to that.

Jim murdered Artie in 1991, during an argument over Artie's substance abuse. After spending three years in San Quentin Prison—1994 to 1997—Jim moved to Petaluma, in Sonoma County, where he died of a heart attack in 2007.

Another director Juliet worked with was Sam Weston, a.k.a. Anthony Spinelli.[14] Born Sam Weinstein, he took the same stage surname as his successful actor brother, Jack Weston, hoping for a big break himself. Failing at acting, he turned to directing porn instead— an easy gig, requiring only a modest amount of up-front money and some good connections. As directors go, he was neither among the worst nor among the best, in terms of either skill or character. Juliet was mildly disgusted by him but felt that he only moderately mistreated her. He did not, for example, press her for casting couch privileges, although he did ask her for them. She declined.

Juliet's favorite directors were Alex de Renzy, whom she worked with first, and, even more, Ron Sullivan (who used the name Henri Pachard for both of the productions Juliet acted in), a gay man about Juliet's own age. Sullivan had been in the business a long time, having directed a few of the early sexploitation films, and continued for some years after the Golden Age, doing mostly S & M films. Ron was a real professional, and treated his crew and cast as such. He won Juliet's trust and admiration.

---

[14] A pseudonym Weston may have adopted from an O. Henry story, "The Coming Out of Maggie."

While Juliet worked with most of the big-name male stars—Jamie Gillis, Richard Pacheco, Billy Dee, Mike Horner, Mike Ranger, Johnny Keyes, Ron Jeremy, and of course John Holmes—her favorite movie partner was always her first, John Leslie. Despite the sleazy characters he often portrayed, John understood sensuality, not just sexuality. The two had a rapport together, and both were among the more professional of the porn actors. John died in late 2010, about ten months after Juliet.

Excessively-endowed John Holmes was probably the best known and most notorious of Juliet's male colleagues. Although he was, according to some accounts, a warm and loving person before he embarked on his porn career, his cocaine habit destroyed him, changing his personality and sucking up most of the money he made from films. (He was one of the few actors who did make a lot of money from porn.) It was also his cocaine habit that led to his disastrous and traumatic involvement in the Wonderland murders, on 1 July 1981. Although he was acquitted of conspiracy in those murders, the trauma destroyed what was left of his emotional health. There was certainly no love lost between Juliet and Holmes. His passing merited only a terse one-sentence paragraph in her journal, on 17 March 1988: "John Holmes died of AIDS."

Besides Juliet, the only women who began their porn careers somewhat late in life were Georgina Spelvin and Kay Parker. Spelvin played the lead in Gerard Damiano's 1973 film *The Devil in Miss Jones*; she was thirty-two at the time. Georgina, unlike Juliet, had a background in straight acting, including *The Pajama Game* on Broadway. *Devil* was also one of the few films that actually had a real story line; it almost didn't qualify as porn. Juliet would have loved to star in a classy film like *Devil*, but never got such an opportunity.

Kay Parker, a British actress who had relocated to the U.S., entered the porn film business at age thirty-three (still six years younger than Juliet), appearing in Sam Weston's *Sex World*. She worked with Juliet in Weston's film *Vista Valley PTA*, as well as in the first two *Taboo* films. Despite their common late entrance into the business, Kay and Juliet could hardly have been more of a contrast; Kay was reserved and serious, and had entered the business only reluctantly. Yet their personalities blended well, and they later became close friends; this was one of the few gratifying relationships Juliet maintained, and it lasted for the rest of her life.

In addition to the films themselves, there was plenty of advertising for, and commentary on, the pornography business. The magazine *Cinema-X* was launched in London in 1969; Juliet later wrote reviews for their American spin-off, *Cinema Blue*, not too long before *Cinema-X* itself folded. A similar but longer-running and more successful U.S. publication was *High Society*, published by Gloria Leonard, who indirectly started the phone-sex business, although she never received any income from it. In the late 1970s, about the time that instant credit-card verification was developed, Gloria started recording the outgoing greetings on the *High Society* office line, promoting the upcoming issue. So many people called up to listen to the recording that the phone line was overloaded. It was but a short step, then, to setting up phone-sex lines: first pre-recorded ones and later live ones. By the mid-1980s phone sex was a booming business. Juliet began her phone-sex work in 1983 when she was hired by a small start-up; she was their star attraction: "Chat live with Aunt Peg!" She got $50 [$120] per call, far above the average operator's $3 to $5 [$7-$12].

Juliet's phone-sex skills were minimal, however, for even though she had a lovely voice, verbal sex, unaccompanied by action, was not really her thing. A recorded video of her supposedly doing a phone-sex call—obviously staged, with no real caller on the line—is mediocre, her delivery embarrassingly stilted. Indeed, Juliet never did well with solo performances; only the stimulation of interaction with other people brought out the best in her. The staged call was unrealistic in other ways as well, as Juliet is dressed in sexy lingerie and masturbates during the call, whereas most phone-sex operators—including Juliet, according to her later private writings—usually dress sloppily while on the job and only pretend to be participants in the sexual activities they describe. After all, it can be hours between calls; one cannot sit by the phone dressed up for sex during these sometimes interminable intervals. Nor can anyone be sexually "up" for every call.

In addition to films, peep shows, and phone sex, more explicit live performances also took off during the late 1970s. East Coast versions of the Mitchell brothers O'Farrell Theater included the

Palace Theater, near Boston, and New York's Plato's Retreat, Melody
Burlesk, and Show World Center, where a number of big names
performed: Annie Sprinkle, Vanessa del Rio, Veronica Hart, and
Annette Havens. While strip clubs had been part of the American sex
scene for many decades, their number—and the explicitness of the
acts performed in them—increased dramatically during the Golden
Age. Juliet performed at some of these venues when she developed
her live stage shows.

     The Golden Age of Porn began to fade for a number of reasons.
The primary one was the invention and wide availability of videotape, which was so easy and cheap to produce and distribute that
one could make considerably more profit than with conventional
film. Another problem, ironically, was the resulting market satura-
tion. It was difficult for a single producer to compete in this vast field
and make enough money to survive for very long. A similar problem
arose in the phone-sex business. The costs of both advertising and
credit-card processing became exorbitant (much higher rates are
charged for "adult" businesses), and only large companies could
make it. While for a brief time the Internet reversed this trend, making it possible for small enterprises or even individuals to maintain
adult websites or phone-sex services, that did not last, as the end of
commercial net neutrality meant that search engines began to ignore
independent websites, and the costs of credit-card security began to
skyrocket. Most independent adult performers now rely on social-
networking types of sites for their business, cutting their overhead
but also forcing them to compete in a saturated market. Although
prostitution, always the mainstay of the sex business, can still be
profitable for an independent provider, pornography—the poor
man's "Rosie Palmer" prostitute—is not, as the effective monthly rate
of pay is too low. The financial winners in the porn industry are the
people at the top: the production companies, distributors, and corporate executives. Most of the lowly workers, whose bodies and
minds are put on the line, make effectively well below the minimum
wage. Even the authors of pornographic books make little money;
Sam Steward, a gay man who wrote porn novels in the 1970s, under
the pseudonym Phil Andros, received a flat fee of $400 [$2,000] per
book, with no royalties.

By 1990, the so-called Golden Age of Porn was dead and gone, remaining a memory for those who had partaken of it, either as performers or as customers. Like many of the late-twentieth-century cultural ventures in industrialized nations, it was primarily a product of the Baby Boom generation, and a victim of its own success. In a capitalist economy, the most lucrative enterprises are those that appeal consistently to the lowest common denominator, placing profit over quality, and the sex business has been no exception. While pornography certainly remains a booming business, there is no longer any pretense to quality or to dealing with the complexity of intimate interactions, at least in the U.S. scene, although a few directors have made some strides in this direction.

Moreover, for all its vaunted freedom, from both legal restrictions and inhibition, the Golden Age did little to improve the American cultural view of sex. That swung from one extreme—repression—to the other—exhibitionism: both unrealistic and in their own ways negating. Acceptance of sexuality as a healthy part of everyday life—sometimes celebratory, sometimes humorous, sometimes manipulative, sometimes truly intimate, sometimes simply mundane—is as distant a goal now as it was in 1960. Juliet dreamed of such a shift, tried to implement it, and failed, except to a small and appreciative audience. "I thought I could change the industry," she lamented in 1985, after her retirement from films. Alas, she could not, and her disappointment was bitter.

11

Beyond Her Wildest Dreams

The day of the *Pretty Peaches* filming was certainly a defining moment in Juliet's life—one that she often recounted later, and no doubt relived in her own mind many times. Although she had intended to try only this one brief foray into the adult entertainment business, to make some much-needed money and then get back to her "real" life, her emotional response to that experience led her in another direction.

Alone in her North Beach apartment the night after the filming, she lay awake, her mind racing. In one way, the path ahead seemed clear and straight, as though her whole life had led her to this point. Judy, the confused, frustrated young woman who had struggled with her childhood self-image as an ugly duckling, who had rebelled against middle-class propriety by immersing herself in the 1950s Southern California college sex scene, who had followed three different men to two different continents and had suffered through four failed relationships, had finally become Juliet, the sensuous, joyous, self-confident beauty who reveled in life and sexuality, her magnetism drawing admiration and longing from men young and old.

Yet despite feeling that she had come home to her true self, the unfamiliarity and intensity of this new world overwhelmed her. "Nothing in my 39 years had prepared me for taking this road," she wrote in her journal. She felt ungrounded, as if she were floating away on a river of intensity, carrying her she knew not where. What exactly had she gotten herself into? How was she going to remain true to herself while being open to this new experience and all it entailed—finding her way around, connecting with new people, learning new skills?

And what, specifically, were those skills? She got out of bed, sat down at her desk, and wrote down a list of things she believed she would need to do and learn in order to play this new role of sex star. She would need to experience stripping, prostitution, and S & M, including B & D (bondage and discipline). She would need to study erotic literature and art, and the history of prostitution and the sex goddess archetype; she would need to view porn films and write some of her own scripts. The very fact that Juliet took her new job this seriously put her head and shoulders above most, if not all, other sex workers of the time. Rare indeed was one who even had enough work ethic to show up, in condition to work, on any regular basis; even rarer, one who saw herself as a professional, who realized she needed specialized training and skills, who felt herself connected to a sacred legacy.

Yet despite her trepidation, Juliet jumped into her new role with both feet. She got her first taste of stripping the very next day after the *Pretty Peaches* filming, working in the Playpen section of the theater where she had originally interviewed with Alex de Renzy. "My first experience [of sex work] was so positive, so empowering, that performing live was [my] next eagerly anticipated step into this forbidden, glamorous, exciting and unknown world of porno." On staff at the Playpen were about a dozen women, all of them much younger than Juliet—so young, in fact, that they immediately nick-named her "Mom" even as they took her in hand to show her the ropes. They escorted her to Frenchy's Adult Bookstore on Polk Street to buy porno magazines, for some pointers on poses and vocabulary. And, as anyone who has ever seen Juliet perform knows, she took to this new work with unbridled enthusiasm. She loved "looking beautiful, getting naked, dancing around, [getting] plenty of exercise, caressing soft bodies, turning men on and being sexy and uninhibited. *And always being in command.*" Yes, this work fed into Juliet's desperate need, developed during those terrifying ordeals in the hospital as a child, to be in control—of her body, her surround-ings, and the other players in her life. In a sense, it was like being self-employed, as she could select her hours and choreograph her own stage routines. "Turns out that I like being a nice tease, like being the aggressor and even like intimidating assholes. I love to make men laugh and squirm with my dildo." The pay was good, too —$100 [$365] a day for five hours' work.

Juliet's age also gave her status among, and some control over, the younger workers, and she was soon handing out advice on everything from hairstyles and makeup to sexual relationships. She tidied up the closet-sized dressing room, and enforced the "no smok-ing, drugs or perfumes during work hours" rules.

Underneath this facade, though, Juliet felt no more grown up than her co-workers, having been a late bloomer because of her long illnesses as a child. "I was emotionally [in my] early thirties and fortunately had a body to match." Meeting the younger workers at their own emotional level made it easy for her to make friends, and she had soon developed a deeply affectionate relationship with one of them, a nineteen-year-old lesbian named Lisa. A refugee from the midwest, Lisa had found her way to the Bay Area via Los Angeles. "Street tough on the outside, sweet and vulnerable on the inside," Juliet described her. With her tanned body, small breasts, firm ass and flat stomach, and sporting a rose-and-heart tattoo on her inner thigh, Lisa made a good partner for Juliet on stage, despite their four-inch difference in height. The duo developed a sensuous mirror dance, moving opposite sides of their bodies in unison as they alternately entwined and drifted teasingly apart.

Lisa soon became Juliet's frequent companion offstage as well. During work breaks, the pair often dressed down from their stripper costumes and makeup and headed off to Al's Bar and Grill in the Tenderloin, one of Lisa's favorite hangouts. An avid pool player, Lisa was determined to bring Juliet into that fold, too. Juliet was non-plussed by pool, but she was fond of Lisa and willing to be led along into yet another adventure. While she had been a nighttime bar-hopper since her college days, she was a novice to the daytime, hard-core drinking scene. The first time she followed Lisa into the dimly lit tavern, she was temporarily blinded, and put off by the smell of beer, piss and tobacco smoke. Vaguely aware of a few dark forms hunched over their drinks at the bar, Juliet and Lisa made their way to the pool table at the back of the room. Lisa lit a cigarette; the smoke swirled into the cone-shaped lampshade over the green felt table. "I'll make a pool player out of you in no time," she pronounced, leaning her 5'2" frame over the table, jeans stretched tight over her ass, to rack the balls and scatter them with a breaking shot. She showed Juliet several ways to hold the cue stick and how to hit the balls.

Juliet was awkward and self-conscious at first, but with the bar almost empty in the mid-afternoon she felt free to try and fail without fear of criticism, and Lisa was a supportive teacher, joking, teasing, and praising her every time she pocketed a ball. While Juliet never became a hotshot, she mastered enough of the game to enjoy these lazy afternoon forays with her young friend.

From time to time they would stop by in the evening, in between shows. On one of these occasions, just as they were starting to play, a brash jock came up to Juliet, laid a hand on her shoulder, and offered to show her "some tricks." This display of male solicitation lit a fire under Lisa, who crossed the room at record speed and slammed into the offender's chest, knocking him backwards into the nearest bar stool. "Keep your fucking hands off my girlfriend!" she shrieked at his astonished crumpled form. The entire room lapsed into a stunned silence. "Having any trouble, Lisa?" Big Al asked from the far end of the bar. "Not that I can't handle," Lisa replied loftily, as she shriveled the cowering male with an imperious glance. Returning to Juliet, she put her arms around her and gave her a sweet kiss, and they went matter-of-factly back to their game. After this incident, the men in the bar gave the duo a wide and respectful berth.

Juliet kept in touch with Lisa, even after they had both moved on from the Playpen. Sadly, Lisa died of a drug overdose in 1982, at the age of twenty-three.

Although Juliet reveled in the Playpen work, and made quick and easy money at it, she was drawn more and more to film performance. However, it was only Alex de Renzy's professionalism that convinced her that porn acting was her true field: "With Alex at the helm I was steered to success."

Juliet had mixed feelings toward Alex, which is not surprising because Alex had two sides to his character. A skilled director who appreciated good work in others and who could remain calm even after a grueling twelve hours of shooting, Alex could be also "macho and tense"; there was a harshness about him. While he sometimes gave performers a great deal of latitude, soliciting their feedback and encouraging them to find their own unique brand of self expression, at other times he could be autocratic: "Women are bodies, not minds." His face spoke of cruelty and suffering, and he wore a single jade earring, giving him somewhat of a pirate appearance. He had apparently suffered a personality change after an accident that left him mentally and physically scarred. Juliet was also put off by Alex's obsession with Desiree Cousteau, who, like many sex workers, had a substance abuse problem as well as an overblown ego, and whom

Juliet considered only a mediocre actress, a body without much of a brain.

Still, Juliet noted later, looking back on her film debut, "If my introduction to porno had been with anyone besides Alex, I probably would have bolted in disgust. Yet this grand master of diplomacy... made the experience fun." Generally, he treated both actors and technical crew with respect—a rarity in the business, as Juliet found out later, working with other directors.

And move on she quickly did. Word soon got out about Juliet's beauty, energy and enthusiasm, and she started getting calls from other directors. Over the next several months, she performed in five more porn movies: *The Curio Shop, Hot Lunch* (later re-named *Lisa's Diner*), *Caught in the Act, Bad Company,* and *Tender Trap.* The next year, she worked with de Renzy again in *Summer Heat,* filmed at Lake Shasta, and performed as well in *Tangerine, Shoppe of Temptations, Inside Desiree Cousteau,* and *Perfect Gift.* It was around the end of 1978 when she created the "Aunt Peg" character, from a line in the Swedish Erotica series. She was cast as "Peggy Norton," a movie producer showing her "niece" around the set. The niece (played by Sharon Kane) exclaimed, in response to her first sight of John Holmes's cock, "Oh, Aunt Peg, it's soooo big!" The moniker had subtle incestuous overtones, too—always a popular theme in pornography geared toward straight men.

However, it wasn't until later that Juliet adopted her official stage name. It took her a while to realize that she needed one; she was too excited just to be living out her dream of being an actress. At first she either worked uncredited or was billed with her real name, Judy Carr. Then, realizing that she was not ready to come out to all her friends, family and acquaintances, she experimented with a number of stage names—Judy Fallbrook, Alice Rigby, Judy Callin, Julie Morrow, and Ruby Sapphire (a combination of her and her friend Harry's birthstones). In February of 1979 she finally settled on "Juliet Anderson." She chose "Juliet" because she wanted to keep her first initial, J, and because she related to the title of the Fellini film *Juliet of the Spirits,* as she felt that there was a spiritual dimension to her sex work. "Anderson" was just a good Nordic surname, and she knew she had a very Scandinavian appearance (although according to her sister Chris, the family ancestry is in fact a mixture of Scottish, English and Irish).

It was, of course, Juliet's age—along with her obvious enjoyment of her work and her refreshing sense of humor—that set her apart. "The public was tired of young airheads, and when I came along—a mature, bright, articulate uninhibited woman—they could identify with me, their fantasy mom, sister, aunt, co-worker, wife; it was instant lust for them ([both] men and women)." Indeed, Juliet's later protegé Nina Hartley remarked that Juliet was "the original MILF" (mother I love to fuck).

Sex work transformed Juliet.

> With that movie [*Pretty Peaches*] and later after great popularity with other porno directors, actors, actresses and my great success at the Playpen, my ego was given the boost it needed. After seven years in Finland my sexual self esteem was at an all-time low. Now I was not only having a great time, living out my dreams of acting, having an assortment of beautiful, sexy men and women to participate with sexually, being impulsive and uninhibited, my sexual desires fulfilled, turning on to women, being without clothes, and exciting even the most jaded of porno stars (e.g., John Holmes) but getting paid for it too... It's a real turn-on to excite young studs, who I know are woman-wise, with my unself-conscious sexuality. Wow! A porno star is born at 39.

Meanwhile, her social sexual encounters proliferated as well. She fucked a number of the porn actors off-screen, to the point where the directors actually became concerned that she would wear out the men and ruin their ability to perform for the camera. When filming the movie *Tangerine*, her co-star Mike Stapp (Ranger) was provided with a chaperone to keep Juliet away from him. No problem; Juliet substituted Billy Dee, who was on a break from filming.

Juliet also acquired lovers among the film crew. Keith, a truck driver, was always good for a fast fuck ("[we] fucked our brains out in corners, closets, and under the brass bed"; at home, her neighbors complained about Keith's enthusiastic vocalizations). And there was her star lover, Ali, a twice-divorced dress designer. Ali had a sense of romance as well as sex, and he and Juliet wandered the Bay Area seeking both respite from their high-paced work, and adventure. In a typical escapade, Ali once called her at two in the morning and asked her to meet him on Union Street. Hailing a taxi from there, they drove to the top of Nob Hill and down the long semi-circular flag-lined driveway of the Fairmont Hotel, San Francisco's most ostentatious lodging edifice. Alighting from the cab, they strolled through the red-carpeted lobby, past the imposing oak-banistered staircase, and made their way to the always-open dining room with its panoramic view of the sleeping city, where they indulged in an early breakfast. Then home for a quick fuck and a nap, and out again to meander along the coast of West Marin. Strolling on the beach at the south end of Tomales Bay, they met a fascinating young boy, an eight-year-old genius (musician, photographer, inventor), out with his artist mother and fisherman father. Both he and his parents regaled Juliet and Ali with yarns of his impressive accomplishments. On to Marshall for lunch at the seafood house there, then back down to San Francisco for a walk down the beach to Fort Point. They finished off their glamorous day with a languid and delicious fuck and a much-needed restful sleep.

Ali was not available the next day, but Billy Dee, whose partner was out of town, graciously stepped in again. Juliet met up with him at a nudist camp, where they spent a leisurely few hours before returning to the city to get stoned and go disco dancing. A great lead-up to a night of fantastic sex: "Rarely if ever do I get off by getting head," she wrote, but "Billy made me climax clitorally several times and then fucked my brains out. After a few hours of sleep of the dead I awoke him by putting his soft cock in my mouth, getting him hard and riding him home! Our fucking that night was the most fantastic I can ever remember with anyone." (Which probably didn't mean too much, as Juliet made similar comments about many encounters over the years.)

In effect, Juliet was repeating the partying pattern she had developed in her college years, only with more sophistication. While she no longer confused a passing sexual attraction with romantic love, she was still cycling through men as fast as she could. And making up for deprivation again as well, only this time it was the deprivation of not expressing her full sexual self during her earlier adult years, rather than of being hospitalized and isolated during her childhood.

While these intense couplings never lasted long as relationships, Juliet did form at least one long-lasting friendship during this time. It was only a few months after her *Pretty Peaches* debut that erotic still photographer Paul Johnson heard about Juliet. A new woman in the business, older, and *hot*! Paul was no young sprite himself, being two years older than Juliet, and he was intrigued by the prospect of a mature porn star. He contacted her and arranged for a meeting. Interviewing her in her North Beach apartment, with Snuggles scampering around the cat runway a few feet below the ceiling, Paul was instantly charmed and knew he had to shoot her as soon as possible. They booked a session at a friend's well-appointed home in the Oakland Hills. Paul shot Juliet in a hot-tub scene there with Peter Bent. Paul was so impressed with Juliet's performance that he promptly booked her for another shoot in Sausalito—a double with Holly McCall. Paul, in fact, got into the action himself with his point-of-view photography; his assistant Christine shot those scenes.[15] This auspicious beginning led to a long fuck-buddy friendship and working relationship between the two middle-aged sex connoisseurs.

Within a year, Paul's assistant Christine had moved to Hawaii, and Juliet took over her position. She had coveted that job ever since the first shoot, when she watched Paul and Christine jump into the hot tub together for an off-the-record friendly fuck. Paul and Juliet made a great team. Juliet brought her disciplined work ethic, excellent eye for staging and warm sense of humor; Paul brought his years of experience, professional photographic skills, and ability to engage his subjects. Between them, they were able to produce erotic photographs with a level of authenticity and spontaneity that was rare in the world of pornographic photography. And of course, their professional relationship never deterred them from engaging in a warm, friendly fuck whenever they needed some R & R. "Paul is the *only* person I can relax with, love with and joke about sex with, and he *understands*, especially sexual overtones," she wrote in 1983.

In addition to acting, stripping, and assisting Paul, Juliet lost no time in diversifying her skills in the sex industry. Although she at

---

[15] See Paul's DVD, *Juliet and the Bears*, for these photographs.

first claimed "I can't turn tricks," before long she was accepting a few select call-girl assignments. "A hundred dollars [$365] for four hours is not bad pay" (although it actually was; the going rate in 2004 was $300 per hour). The clients were well-to-do and vetted by people she trusted. And in 1983, she added phone sex to her skill set, although it was never her best venue; Juliet was a doer, not a talker; a physical actor more than a verbal one.

Of course, sex work had its down side as well. Juliet was not getting the regular, non-sexual exercise she needed, and she worried about putting on weight. She was also doing more drugs than she ever had before, and keeping later hours. Her health suffered as a result, and her Crohn's disease began acting up. She missed spending time outdoors, too; the forays to West Marin were rare interludes rather than regular recreation. She decided to back off on the unhealthful food, drink, and inebriating substances, and she went to a homeopath and started taking natural remedies. "I'm getting disenchanted with drugs because of the aftereffects. *Reality* is pleasant for me." She had obviously not inherited her mother's substance abuse tendencies.

Working conditions were not always as sterling as they had been in *Pretty Peaches*, either. The sex scenes in *Hot Lunch* took place on the wooden floor of a "disgusting, filthy cafe," and the underwater sex scene in *Summer Heat* was anything but hot, Lake Shasta having an average summer temperature of below 70°—cold enough to trigger hypothermia if they had not cut the sessions short and warmed themselves up quickly afterward. And then there were the unscrupulous directors—she missed getting a part in a Mexican-directed film by refusing the casting couch—and the egotistical male co-stars: Johnny Keyes, Jerry Heath and John Holmes came in for some pointed barbs in her private journals. Not to mention the occasional occupational hazard: John Leslie called her in July to tell her he had gonorrhea. She also contracted a vaginal infection from oral sex with one of her female co-stars.

Then there were the people in her old life. She panicked at the thought of how her family and old friends might react to finding out about her sex work. This issue came up less than two months after she started her new career, with the arrival of her fortieth birthday. She wanted to celebrate—not just the milestone age, but, more importantly, her newfound identity. Yet how could she tell her old circle about her new life? Most of them would be horrified, she was sure. On the other hand, how could she celebrate entering a new decade of life and not mention her joy in this wonderful new path? To complicate matters, Chris's husband Bob Pettit was planning to join Chris and Monica on their upcoming summer vacation to California, and although Juliet felt she might be ready to inform Chris of her new work, she did not want Bob to know of it. This situation precluded inviting Chris to the birthday party, and Juliet reluctantly restricted her guest list to her new circle of friends, swallowing her guilt and disappointment, and visiting quietly with Chris, Monica and Bob later.

Perhaps the most incongruent facet of Juliet's life at this time was that underneath her public persona, she retained a surprisingly mainstream feminine attitude about pornography—at least its more passive form, still photography. Her response to seeing photographs of herself on some film box covers in an adult store was that she "looked very strange. [I] haven't yet seen the magazines, but I expected to be disgusted. I like making porno but not looking at it."

She felt better watching her movies, where she was active—a living being, not just a static photograph. She was struck, in fact, by what an intense presence she projected on set. "I realize I'm a very strong character and I should subdue my actions because just my presence is a strong statement." No one who has ever watched a Juliet performance could disagree with that statement.

For all her adventurous new life, though, Juliet had not left her past entirely behind. Nikolas was calling her, more frequently than she cared for. He wanted to see her again, and was offering her an all-expense-paid trip to Athens.

12

Leaving Old Loves, Embracing a New Life

There is probably no sadder chapter in Juliet's life than her frustrating relationship with Nikolas. Her feelings for him were always more all-encompassing than his for her, although he clearly did care for her in his own way, keeping in touch for decades, and inviting her and footing the bill for her visit to Greece in October 1978.

Her anticipation of this trip had been fraught with both fear and longing. Being in Nikolas's arms again would be a thrill beyond description, but what if he found out about her porn career? He was now in political office (and, ironically, was an anti-vice crusader). Juliet recalled again his warning early in their relationship: "Always act like a lady... never bring shame to me or my family." With her usual drama, Juliet envisioned the blaring headline: "Cabinet minister sends for and shacks up with porno star." She would be a stain on his honor, and in the heat of passion he would have to have her killed. As she well knew, he was perfectly capable of violence, even against her. "Once intimate with a woman she is yours and you must cut out any offending spot. HEAVY!"

When Nikolas called her at 12:30 in the morning on the night of September 16th to 17th, they talked for half an hour discussing the trip, and the conversation kept her wakeful the rest of the night, as the full moon shone in through her window. He wanted her to buy her own plane ticket; he would reimburse her, he said, but wanted no direct record of his having paid her way over.

Despite Nikolas's precautions and her own misgivings, though, she felt she must accept the invitation. "The significance of the trip is that I feel this is the obstacle I must overcome to progress to a higher plane of existence than in my former life... [I feel] compelled to take one last journey into the past—then [I] can close the door and start anew."

It was going to be a two-and-a-half-week trip, lasting from the 7th to the 23rd of October. Juliet bought a small journal to take with her—one that she could easily slip into her purse. And now that she was actually on her way, her detached attitude of a few weeks earlier had evaporated. On the way over, she wrote about her still-intense feelings toward Nikolas: "The heart/psychic link between Nikolas and me is as strong as ever—a bond that neither man nor God can break," as well as her continuing frustrations: "It is an impossible relationship."

Nikolas was now in his late forties and married to a woman about twenty years younger than himself. It was more critical than ever that he keep his liaison with Juliet secret, not only because of his political prominence but also because of his marital status. And fortunately, he did not find out about Juliet's porn work. He actually had little time to focus on her while she was there, being preoccupied with family and public responsibilities.

Yet Juliet, lost in her pink cloud, turned the situation into a fairy tale: "I shall be known as an actress visiting her lover, a busy and famous (mystery) man. We must meet clandestinely and because of his position I am alone most of the time."

Despite this initial dramatic spin on the trip, the truth is that it was an almost unmitigated disaster for her—frustrating in that she had very little opportunity to spend intimate time with Nikolas, disappointing because of the negative changes that had come to Greece since her stay there in the sixties, and stressful on her body (she came down with two colds and had several digestive episodes, partly because she had a hard time finding food she could tolerate). And, after having been pain-free for twelve years, Juliet was once again suffering from an arthritis flare-up like the one she had experienced in 1966, when she had first arrived in Greece. "Why now?" she wondered.

The trip started off with a bang, as Nikolas did not show up at the airport to meet her. In anticipation of their meeting, Juliet had donned a flimsy dress and high heels, rather than something more comfortable and practical. The weather was stifling, no service people were available to help with her luggage, and she could not reach Nikolas, having evidently been given the wrong phone number for him. She caught a bus to the hotel, but it was not air-conditioned and the one-hour ride was miserable. Tired, sticky, her feet hurting, Juliet was finally met at the hotel by Mr. Zefiriou, Nikolas's secretary, who escorted her to the flat Nikolas had rented for her.

It was a comfortable studio flat, furnished with the essentials but without a view, and with neither radio nor TV. It was private and quiet, set up so that she could cook meals, and stocked with a generous supply of liquor, some pistachio nuts, and, of course, condoms. It reminded her of the apartment she and Kitty had stayed in on her first night in Athens in 1966.

Kitty, who had settled permanently in Greece, came by and took her out for a drive and dinner, but she was in the midst of a family medical crisis and was not going to be able to spend much social time with Juliet. Nikolas finally came by the flat around nine p.m., but he was only able to stay for about an hour, just enough time for "a brief but passionate coupling—and he was gone."

The next morning, a Sunday, Juliet arose at six, had a light breakfast, read until about eight and then went out for a walk in the quiet morning. Most of the locals were sleeping in, and the morning sounds of wooden shutters being opened and occasional coughing added to the atmosphere of domestic tranquility.

That afternoon Nikolas took her for a sail in his yacht, but, probably to deflect any aggressive paparazzi, he took along a friend as decoy; Juliet was to appear to be with that man rather than with Nikolas. Juliet was painfully frustrated at not being able to be demonstrative. Later that evening, back on shore, Nikolas slipped in for a surreptitious liaison (at Juliet's insistence), but "he simply lay back and let me minister to his needs. I willed myself to be satisfied."

Juliet slept for eleven hours that night, and on the following day (without Nikolas but at his expense) began a four-day cruise around the Aegean islands and to Turkey. Because of the need for discretion, Juliet was introduced on board as a guest of the cruise line owner, Mr. Potamianos. She was ostensibly a journalist friend of Mr. Zefiriou (Nikolas's secretary, who had picked her up at the hotel). Although she had a double stateroom to herself, she felt awkward, as it seemed to her that almost all of the four hundred passengers on board were in couples.

At the same time, the secrecy appealed to Juliet in a perverse way. "Nobody really knows who I am. If they knew of my relationship with Nikolas, I would have rose petals scattered in my path," she mused with her usual sense of grandiosity. "The role of Mr. Z, the go-between, appeals to my sense of drama."

Juliet played tourist at the ports they visited, tromping around ruins, shopping, wandering along streets in old villages—places she had visited before and which still held some of the old-world charm she had remembered. Once, she got lost and had to take a taxi back to the ship, but her limited Greek landed her a mile from the port and she had to walk the rest of the way back.

Her apparent unattached status of course drew the attention of men. A clueless steward persisted in trying to pick her up. At the ship's bar, an unattached doctor tried his luck. He was looking, he said, for a Scandinavian wife (he believed they were independent but hard-working, and he needed a mother for his son); Juliet certainly looked the part. Had any of these men known of her attachment to Nikolas, it would have given them pause, but she could make no public claim on the connection.

Overall, the cruise depressed her. She felt confined on the ship and hated the crowds. "I need natural space, trees, clean air, sunshine, water, small creatures, QUIET, a hard bed, clean linens, proper lighting, warmth, a comfortable chair and writing space, hot water, simple but good food, books, typewriter, paper, music, loose clothing, a CAT."

Back in Athens, she waited hours that evening for Nikolas to show up; he finally arrived at 9 p.m. for another hurried fuck. Juliet asked if he could arrange for her to go to London for a few days; he was annoyed but said he would try. After he left, loneliness stalked her. She busied herself writing postcards ... "not cheerful ones, I am afraid. I really need a friend to share my troubles with. What I really want is to go home." She contacted four friends, including Mirja, to see if any of them would be able to join her in London; the last solicitation, to a male friend, finally yielded a positive response, but the trip did not materialize.

Juliet finally began to relax, though, and feel a little more at home in the neighborhood. She shopped and went to the park, but was hit by an attack of diarrhea and barely made the mile walk back to the flat. Later that afternoon, another of her friends, Henrietta, took her to a camping spa she and her Greek husband owned just outside Athens. Although this outing provided a respite from the city crowds, Juliet found the place boring, and the other guests' limited English made conversation difficult. She chafed to get back to Athens.

Another encounter with Nikolas the next day was a little more satisfying. They actually spent about ten minutes in caressing and foreplay, then "I again gave him good head and assumed the superior position (no genital foreplay for me) but this time he lasted thirty seconds [instead of his standard ten] and I was able to climax."

The day after that, they went sailing again, apparently alone at least part of the time, and Juliet recorded the following conversation between them.

Juliet: I'm curious; tell me about your wife. How old is she?
Nikolas: Twenty-nine.
Juliet: And beautiful!
Nikolas: What makes you think so?
Juliet: You always liked beautiful women—you chose me, after all.
Nikolas (with a smile): Yes, she's nice looking.
Juliet: Did you know her long before your marriage?
Nikolas: Yes, four years.
Juliet: Won't you have more children?
Nikolas: Of course, I think two is a good number.
Juliet: You had better hurry up—don't let them be far apart.
Nikolas: I'm working on it all the time. In fact I think one is now under construction. I hope so. I started so late in life I can't lose any time.
Juliet: I will never have any children.
Nikolas: Why not?
Juliet: I never wanted children without a stable marriage and I never found a good husband. I conceived a child once.
Nikolas: Why didn't you have it?
Juliet: I lost it at four months and was very sick. Now it is too late for me.
Nikolas (sadly): Very sorry, Judaki-mon.
Juliet: Why did you wait so late to marry?
Nikolas: Marriage can be a trap and if you marry young you lose your freedom. If I cannot have my freedom within the

marriage I would divorce. A couple always together is worse than hell.

Juliet (inwardly: A man's world; pity his poor wife not 'cause he demands his freedom but denies the same to her. Keeps her trapped at home with children, catering to his beck and call. I doubt if she ever gets her way except by coercion): I prefer love to marriage.

Nikolas: Ah, Judaki, it is hard to keep love alive.

Juliet: Yes Nikolas-mon, only when the lovers are not together often, like you and me.

Even with this rare interlude, though, Juliet was beginning to find the whole journey tedious. Nikolas resumed his busy schedule and she was left on her own again, and being a tourist was boring. "There is nothing I would have preferred more than spending this rainy day in bed fucking my brains out... This trip seems so out of whack with my life." As it was. It must have been a rude shock to jump from her dramatic and sex-filled California playground into this pool of loneliness, boredom and sexual frustration. Despite her continued obsession with Nikolas, her mind kept returning to her San Francisco truck driver lover, Keith. "To visit Greece with him would have been delightful. Surprisingly he is the only one [of my California lovers] I have thought about."

Athens itself depressed her; it was neither physically nor socially the city she remembered.

I hate the changes—the noise, traffic, pollution, smart shops, crowds... Athens was designed for a population of 350,000; it is now 3 million (in 1966, it was 1.5 million). Combined with the fiery Greek temperament, it is chaos! Athens is one vast parking lot and blaring horns. With my aversion to noise and crowds I am almost neurotic... Roller skates should be introduced as a means of transportation, except that the sidewalks are too crowded and uneven in most places. The average speed of cars is 7 mph, and in rush hours, less. The center of Athens is a scene from Dante's Inferno. So dirty, tacky, loud, aggressive, pushy... Greeks swagger in the streets blocking traffic. Communism will never succeed here as the cooperative spirit fails... Athens is one of the last places on earth I'd choose to live.

She had a low opinion of the population as well. "I find the Greek women unfeminine and offensive. Behind stylish clothes and shoes lies a harpie—shrill, over-bearing and ungraceful. The men are even less appealing; crude and arrogant." Nor were they sexually appealing: "My guess is that a Greek man considers himself a great lover because he has a cock and knows how to put it in an orifice. The thought of a woman enjoying herself never enters his mind."

Her encounters with Nikolas did not rate any higher on her scale. "He is still fixated with assholes—mine and his." (Is there some factual basis for the sex business's use of the term "Greek style" for anal sex?) "[Nikolas] probably doesn't even know the clit exists... I wonder how his wife gets along? Maybe she is inexperienced and doesn't know any better and as a Greek woman doesn't expect more." But, she went on, "I can't picture *ever* telling Nikolas how to be a better lover."

Her sexual dissatisfaction with Nikolas is poignant in light of her obvious addiction to him, and her compromises seem pathetic: "He finds momentary peace in orgasm, but I never climax because it is so hasty"; however, "by centering my thoughts on my love for him I can achieve some satisfaction and also by caressing him I am touched vicariously."

Finally her time in Greece began to wind down. October 22nd was another rainy Sunday and Juliet had a sore throat. "I paint my nails, dissect my life, count the hours to my escape from this trap, this suffocating experience of entombing the Judy of subservience and helpless submission to a love horrifying in its enduring intensity and debilitating in its unfulfillment. I couldn't bear another day of this madness... My only solace is whiskey, the canary's song and pouring out my guts into this journal."

At eleven a.m. she went out "and my hostility abated as soon as I walked thru the Natural Gardens and then into Plaka. Being Sunday it was quiet. The sun broke through the clouds and the air was clean and the panorama breath-taking. I rambled above the Ancient Agora at the base of the Acropolis and my nerves were soothed. I even treated myself to lunch at a vine-covered patio taverna. The service was insufferably slow and the meal took my last drachmas but it kept the beast of loneliness away. No male accosted me, fortunately, because I was ready to kick him in the balls if he did."

She had one final encounter with Nikolas, and

"surprisingly enough our last evening together turned out well... aren't I getting cynical? He came over at 6 as planned and stayed a whole three and a half hours. And even though fucking was inadequate (he came in 10 sec) the closeness, tenderness and TLC was lovely and left me satisfied... We talked, touched, drank herb tea and he even laughed and told me funny stories about his childhood. I never got around to voicing my sentiments because he studiously avoids sentiment. For me to tell him that I have loved him for twelve years and will go on another twelve and yet another twelve and that he has been the only man in my life who is both stronger than I am and yet is tender and loving with me—to say this to Nikolas would be like entering a room of fully clothed people stark naked... Our commitment to each other is a wordless understanding.

After he left, she read until midnight, long enough to finish *Small Changes* by Marge Piercy ("sometimes becomes tedious, preachy and radically feminist, [but] she writes exceptionally well and has some important points to make").

Her departure the following day was a vast improvement over her arrival. "I was so eager to get out of Greece that I got to the airport two hours early... but got to wait in the VIP lounge—spoiled by the pompous ass of an airline official fawning over a supposed important passenger. Get this—lounge to airplane via limo. Ta, ta!"

On the plane she sat across the aisle from an American couple whose daughter had been won over by the same doctor who had tried to pick up Juliet on the ship; he had given the daughter an engagement ring. Juliet informed the three of them of the doctor's intention to find a stepmother for his son, a wrinkle they had not been aware of.

Juliet was immensely relieved to be leaving. "I plan never again to visit Greece," she vowed. [She never did.] Even New York City was preferable: "Ah, the USA... even the subway and filth were tolerable." Leila, her friend from Finland who had also returned to the U. S. and was now living in New York, picked her up and took her to her apartment; they stayed up talking until after midnight.

The next day, Juliet looked up two "sexy bachelors" a friend had told her about. One was out of town, but the other, Gordon, was eager to meet her, and he invited Juliet and Leila to dinner at his house. He was a great chef. They smoked some good weed and had a threesome, but unfortunately Leila was a reluctant participant. She could only handle the situation by getting drunk, and Juliet realized she had to protect Leila by holding back and being more inhibited than she really wanted to. After a frustrating two hours, Leila insisted on leaving, and Juliet, disappointed, felt obligated to accompany her home in the taxi at three a.m.

The next day, Juliet had some leisure time to explore the city. A nip in the air signaled the approach of fall as she strolled on the Promenade, taking in the stunning view of Manhattan. In the evening, she took the train to Briarcliff Manor with her cousin Andy Saunders, where she spent three days with him, his wife Sharon and their three kids. Juliet designed and sewed Halloween costumes for the children, as her mother had done for her and Chris decades earlier. The costumes won first prize in the local Halloween parade. On Saturday, after a sumptuous Finnish-style lunch with Leila and her parents, Juliet got a tour of the Astor estate "from the grand dame herself." That evening she returned to New York and met Gordon, alone this time. They had "several hours of some of the best sex I've ever had, but he wouldn't eat pussy. That pisses me off. Oh they like their cocks sucked but 'retch' not pussy!"

Juliet next visited her ex-husband Bob Watt in Westbury. She was bored, though, and felt uncomfortable in his home with his twelve-year-old daughter Laura. Put up in a bedroom whose door didn't close properly, her senses were assaulted by the ubiquitous orchids, constant cigarette smoke and classical music. Juliet and Bob took a ride together and talked, "but ran out of things to say... Bob's a 40-year-old kid with his head still in the clouds, still not knowing what to do with his life."

They slept together in the same bed but did not fuck ("I couldn't muster up the desire"). The next morning, after getting Laura off to school, "I intended to take him back to bed after breakfast. I wasn't the least interested in having sex with him, but felt obligated—stupid but true—but Laura spoiled our plans by coming home sick." Later they went to Leila's and fucked there, relieving Juliet of her feelings of obligation. "Another chapter is closed."

Upon her return to New York City, Juliet called the previously out-of-town bachelor (another Bob), intending just to say hello over the phone, but he insisted on meeting her. She had been described as a "HOT, DYNAMITE LADY" and he couldn't let the opportunity pass. So she rescheduled her flight back to California and went over to his place.

This Bob turned out to be a great fuck. He had invited a beautiful young model over for a possible threesome, but when she turned out to be a prude they dismissed her and had a most enjoyable twosome instead. Then Juliet put together a sexy costume, cutting up a $40 [$145] silk shirt of Bob's to make a G-string for herself. With the addition of beige high heels, diamond-shaped jewelry and a red carnation in her hair, she was a hit with "the beautiful jet-set deca-dent coke-snorting rich" Halloween party crowd at Studio 54, the most elite club in New York City. The company, though, were sur-prisingly "classy and smooth," and the venue was impressive. There was a laser light show, great music and acoustics, a fog machine, lights, balloons "and me in my sexy costume that drew admiration from both men and women. I literally danced my ass off. The coke made me very sensual and I felt beautiful, exciting, and desirable." Her host's "code of chivalry was impressive: he always paid atten-tion to me... even if he had another girl on his knee... I never felt deserted." Other guests were in costumes, too, although nothing to rival Juliet's stunner.

A group including Juliet and her host finally departed to some-one's apartment, but there was no sex because "the drugs had made the men limp." So back they went to Bob's for the night, to a king-sized bed with a mirror on the ceiling, plenty of women's toiletries in the bathroom, but no food in the fridge! A friend of Bob's came over and she sucked them both and fucked Bob, but by this point was get-ting tired and wanted to leave. Fortunately, the start of her period gave her an excuse. She cleaned up, dressed, caught a cab back to Leila's, packed and left. She slept for most of flight back to San Fran-cisco. "I'm full of travel and excitement for a while."

Or so she thought. A call came in the next day to do a two-girl session for a movie producer in Southern California, and soon she and Sharon Kane were on a plane to L.A. After a "sensual bath in his [the movie producer's] huge tub," they fucked, slept, and awoke to the sun streaming through uncurtained leaded windows in "this lovely Spanish-style mansion with a superb view of Beverly Hills below." She and Sharon went shopping on Wilshire Boulevard to pass the time until their flight back.

Despite her tiredness from the trip, this interlude gave Juliet a lift, for she reveled in being a call girl; it fulfilled her dream of being independent, creative, and sensuous, and getting paid for it. "Sex for money is to me a business deal. The man may get his rocks off thinking he is possessing an inferior and enjoying degrading a woman by paying for it, but for me, I know I am my own boss, can accept or refuse... No one will ever own me... Perhaps possess me momentarily but only with my permission." She offered a good service, with clear boundaries: "I have something beautiful to sell, like a hand-crocheted shawl, feminine and luxurious. I am classy, I am good and the customer gets his money's worth... I offer the certainty of moments of grace, warmth, sensuality and uncomplicated sex. No sexual blackmail, no teasing, nothing to prove, just pleasure." There was a poetry in these encounters, at least for Juliet. "I am the wind, the climbing of the high hill, the swimming naked in clear seas, the sun bringing warmth. I am the cat, affectionate at her own bidding, the bird flying freely to the topmost branches." Sex work had given her, at last, a venue where she could take advantage of the assets she most valued. "I have been lucky enough to have been born in a free country, with good looks, intelligence and a creative and inquisitive mind; it would be a crime, a sin, not to exploit my talents."

When she finally got home for good, Juliet had a chance to rest and reflect on the whole trip: the frustrating weeks in Greece, the fun times in New York, the tying up of loose ends with Bob Watt, and, finally, the glamorous whirl in Southern California. She compiled a list of what she had learned. "A return to the past is not wise; I am several different selves and must compartmentalize my life; I do live an exciting, writable life." Although she had always prided herself on complete honesty, she realized that she now had to hide parts of herself. "But honesty is relative. Each identity has its own morality."

Another insight was that the strain of the urban life in Athens had drained her. She longed for rural peace and quiet, and reflected back on the serenity she had felt in the gardens of Hayama and in the cottages and farmhouses of Finland. "I must move to the country, have a garden, a few animals, a fireplace, a lover or two. I must now pursue whatever means necessary to reach that goal—soon."

It would take her seven years.

13
All in the Family

For all her delight at finding her true calling, Juliet lived in fear that her friends, or, even worse, her family, might find out about her new life. In response to any queries from her family about how she was earning her living, she fudged, lying by omission: "reporting, interviewing, editing, film production." Knowing that she would be visiting her cousin Andrew and his family on her way back from Greece, however, she summoned up the courage to write to his wife Sharon, announcing her new career with pride. Being a sex star, Juliet explained, was a channel for self-expression and a celebration of sexuality, a way of bringing pleasure to others and helping them to accept this part of their lives as not only healthy but fun. While Sharon did not castigate Juliet, she remained unconvinced. She asked Juliet not to say anything about her career to the children while visiting; Juliet complied with this request. Sharon's husband Andrew was more accepting, and had apparently already found out about Juliet's porn work.

It was not until May 1979 that Juliet summoned up the courage to tell her sister and her parents about her sex work. She decided it would be best to approach Chris alone first, and pulled her aside on one of her visits home. Although Chris had been a *Playboy* fan for years, she was not at all enamored of truly hard-core pornography, which she saw as merely gratuitous, without *Playboy's* redeeming intellectual value. Taken aback by Juliet's abrupt announcement, Chris at first recommended that she simply not tell their parents, or possibly she could make some vague back-handed confession, like, "If you don't want to know about everything I've been doing lately, don't read the magazine *Cinema-X*" (a British publication founded in 1969, devoted to news about the porn business); a strange suggestion, for why would their parents be likely to read it anyway?

At some point, however—exactly when is not clear—Juliet did inform her parents. A story she sometimes told about that encounter was that Fred already knew, as he had seen Juliet's photo in adult stores that he patronized, and that Dorothy, after a long pause,

responded with a philosophical, "Well, as long as you're safe, dear."
Fred's supposed reaction is likely another one of Juliet's fabrications,
however, as it really does not jibe with his sensitive, artistic personality, nor with Juliet's later remarks in her journal that her father was
mortified by her involvement in porn work. Furthermore, Chris
denies that Fred ever demonstrated any interest in pornography;
when as a teenager she went snooping around the house, hoping to
find some, she had been completely unsuccessful, turning up nothing more questionable than a few crime novels and magazines. Fred
was never angry or recriminating about Juliet's involvement in porn,
though; it was simply painful for him, and Juliet was pained in turn,
not having wanted to hurt him. After her confession, therefore, Juliet
and her father never again referred directly to the issue, returning to
their prior relationship as much as possible.

Of all Juliet's immediate family members, Chris was probably the
least comfortable with Juliet's confession, because she saw sex work
as exploitative and degrading, and she simply preferred to avoid
negativity in general. Even as late as 1990, when Juliet was out of the
film business but had begun doing erotic massage, Juliet noted that
Chris "listens politely to my talk about sex but she is [clearly] uncomfortable." And Juliet believed that Chris's husband Bob was even
more unaccepting of her porn work. She was sure, when her eight-
year-old niece Monica visited her briefly in San Francisco in 1979,
that Bob would never have allowed the visit had he known about
Juliet's career. Whether this was actually true, though, is doubtful, as
Chris and Bob let Monica visit her aunt frequently even after they
found out about her profession, having faith that, whatever her
living circumstances might be and whomever her social crowd might
include, Juliet would shield her niece from any unsavory people or
circumstances. And she did. Monica was always safe in her aunt's
care.

Juliet's cousin Pam may have been the last family member to find
out. Ironically, it was Pam who ultimately became the most accepting
and supportive of Juliet's porn career, viewing all of her movies and
even attending a rehearsal of Juliet's scene in *Ageless Desire*.

Pam, ten years Juliet's junior, had always been in awe of her
older cousins Judy and Chris. As teenagers, tossing about their long
blonde ponytails, they had seemed so sophisticated to eight-year-old

Pam. They knew how to dress and how to apply elaborate makeup, even curling their eyelashes—a skill that simply amazed young Pam.

After Judy and Chris grew up and left home, it was Pam who stepped in and became like a third daughter to her aunt Dot, working in the doughnut shop after school and on weekends, and frequently spending the night at the Carr house. Pam often felt closer to her aunt than to her own mother, Barbara, who was one of the rare introverts in the family.

Unfortunately, Pam married young, and badly. By the time she was twenty-five, she had two daughters of her own. Although in the late 1970s Pam started hearing whisperings among the family that Judy was "into something questionable," no specifics were discussed, nor did Pam particularly care to hear them. Neither did she question Juliet, preferring not to know anything that would lower her opinion of the cousin she thought so much of.

It was not until 1980 that Pam's husband Llew (short for Llewellyn), a biologist with Southern California Edison, discovered Juliet's secret and broke the news to Pam. One afternoon, he called her at home and insisted that she immediately get a sitter for the kids and come meet him in downtown Redondo Beach. Though she protested the inconvenience and questioned his imperiousness, she finally agreed.

Llew took her to the local porn theater. "Oh no, I'm not going in there!" Pam demurred. "It's OK; you'll be fine," he insisted, taking her by the arm and leading her in.

Pam entered the theater with great trepidation, sat down and, when the movie started, covered her face with both hands. Yet, slowly, curiosity got the better of her, and she peeked through an opening in her fingers. She was taken aback by a view of a woman's hand, wearing a ring she recognized as one that her aunt Dot had given her cousin Judy. Then she heard Judy's voice, and, hardly believing her eyes or ears, stared openly at the screen. Llew grinned at her, delighted at his victory.

Pam did her best to try to accept this part of her beloved cousin. When she took the time to think about it, she got over her initial shock, reasoning that Juliet's life was her own business and the work she was doing was not hurting anyone. And frankly, by this time,

Juliet's family was used to her eccentricities; this was just another one.

Llew had a different approach. He bragged about his connection with Juliet whenever he could, and his boundaries around sexuality, never very good to begin with, became even more slippery. He barely escaped being fired from Edison for sexually harassing a co-worker (resigning instead), and, after promising Pam that he had learned his lesson, repented and changed his ways, he moved the family to Seattle, where he quickly found another job. It was not long, however, before he was running around again. Pam eventually left him, taking the kids with her and buying a house on the north shore of Lake Washington. Their divorce was final in 1983.

Pam had always been an active outdoors person, and she found a job with a small outfit just outside Seattle that offered horseback riding and rafting trips to tourists, run out of an old restored hotel. There she met Skip, the stepfather of the owner, who became intrigued with her when he found out about her connection to Juliet. With this auspicious beginning, as well as their mutual interest in the outdoors life, Pam and Skip soon developed a warm and loving relationship that lasted for the rest of his life, although they never married; she had had enough of that. Pam's family had almost as much trouble accepting this relationship as they did Juliet's sex work, strengthening the bond between the two cousins.

Skip eventually moved to Vallejo, in the Bay Area, which gave Pam an excuse to see Juliet whenever she came down to visit Skip. Pam remained Juliet's primary connection to her family of origin; it was Pam that Juliet most often called when she wanted to catch up on family news.

Pam's brother Andrew—the first family member to find out about Juliet's sex work—continued to be very accepting of it. Andrew acquired copies of all of Juliet's movies; his teenaged children managed to find and watch some of them on rainy days when they were bored. "*Of course* we've watched Aunt Judy's movies," they confessed years later. Their mother Sharon was not happy about this, feeling that Andrew should have taken more care to store the videos securely enough to prevent their being found.

Pam and Andrew did make some attempts, from time to time, at bringing along the more disapproving family members, but they did not push the point. Family members, after all, are not responsible for each other's behaviors or lifestyle choices (at least, not in this culture), and there was no need for the family to weigh in with their opinions, one way or the other. To them, Juliet was still Judy, as she had always been. Actually, the fame (or notoriety) of an individual in any family is rarely an issue or a topic of interest to that family, unless it affects interpersonal dynamics. And it was only in that regard that her relatives were affected by Juliet's sex work.

For it was not really her career that was difficult for Juliet's family, but her personality. She had always been self-absorbed and given to over-dramatization—of both her feelings and her life experiences. Her film career only provided more fuel for that fire. As a child, she had used illness to gain attention and to manipulate people. Now she could use her fame and eccentricity. In fact, as she aged, Juliet seemed to feel that her role in the family was to play the eccentric elderly aunt ("What are eccentric relatives for, anyway [if not to be irreverent]?" she once wrote in her journal). While most of the family accepted Juliet's choice of lifestyle, they experienced her compulsion to talk about it at every possible occasion as an intrusion. And as her friend Carolyn Elderberry astutely observed, Juliet suffered from a total inability to not make an entrance, wherever she went. Sitting quietly at a party was not within her capabilities. Not being the center of attention seemed to trigger a sort of panic in Juliet, and, despite her best intentions to "behave herself" she almost invariably drifted into sharing the dramatic aspects of her life with whomever she fell into conversation with. And of course, what could be more dramatic than being a porn star?

Family gatherings could be particularly dicey. It was usually Pam who monitored Juliet at such events, keeping close to her and deftly changing the subject whenever Juliet started off, before she could get into the really juicy stuff. This technique generally worked fairly well, especially as Pam became more skillful over the years. But it did serve to make Juliet a high-maintenance guest.

Typical was Juliet's behavior at her niece Monica's wedding reception in 2001. She and her friend Mirja both looked lovely in their white dresses and straw hats, and Juliet started out calmly enough, sitting and chatting with cousin Pam and some of the other guests. It was not long, however, before Juliet was queried about her livelihood. And, as usual, she could not resist the temptation to enliven the conversation by explaining her unconventional career choice. Neither Chris nor Monica was pleased with the revelation; this was a wedding—Monica's wedding—not a promotional event for Aunt Judy, nor an adults-only gathering; there were children present. Pam moved in to perform damage control, corralling Juliet and spiriting her off the premises with as much speed and grace as possible.

While her family members were relieved to have Juliet safely escorted from this scene, Juliet herself was so angry and hurt over what she perceived as rejection that, on arriving home, she rounded up one of her photographer friends and had him take some porno-graphic pictures of her in her wedding-guest finery, although she was careful to first remove the locket she wore around her neck, with its photo of her parents inside, replacing it with a string of pearls. She looks sad in these photos, though; the rebellious act apparently did not comfort her.[16]

It was not only Juliet's tendency to grab attention, however, that troubled family members. She also had an uncanny way of finding out about family events she had not been invited to, and showing up anyway. This was most painful to Bob, her aunt Barbara's husband, who never forgave Juliet for the incident in 1969 and refused ever afterwards to speak to her. Juliet, equally intransigent, if not more so, seemed to delight in taunting him with her presence.

Juliet enjoyed pushing the envelope in other ways as well. On one occasion when the family was vacationing at a beach house, she managed to sneak into the hot tub nude, when everyone else was wearing swim suits. Approaching the tub covered with a capacious towel, she doffed it at the last second and slipped into the tub before anyone realized what was happening.

Another "Juliet problem" was money. She was continually asking for financial help, and would turn to almost anyone to borrow money, family being one of the primary sources. Although she eventually wore out her welcome with everyone on this issue, she was likely to approach any new family member—usually unsus-pecting in-laws or children who had recently reached adulthood. It

---

[16] See http://xhamster.com/user/oldsurfer_99/posts/390708.html

was not until Juliet started collecting Social Security that she attained the means to at least decrease, if not entirely eliminate, her requests for financial assistance.

While many family members had struggles with Juliet, the most volatile combination was Juliet and her mother Dottie. Both were sure they were always right about everything, and they rarely agreed on anything. Fireworks of various kinds often ensued. On one occasion when the two of them were traveling with Pam to visit Pam's daughter in Montana, Dottie—the front-seat passenger—had tuned the car radio to a country-western station, music that Juliet abhorred, as in fact did Dottie; apparently her desire to annoy Juliet was stronger than that abhorrence. Juliet asked Dottie to turn the volume down. Instead, Dottie turned it up. Juliet, in the back seat, responded by plugging her ears with her fingers and singing and humming alternative tunes.

Whether because of her frustration over this incident or simply out of contrariness, Juliet continued her difficult behavior after they arrived at their destination. Pam had arranged for her to stay at a bed and breakfast, as there was limited space at her daughter's house. Juliet did not approve of the way the manager was running the place, and toured the house pointing out errors to her hostess. After all, Juliet knew how a bed and breakfast should be run. Pam, with mortified apologies to the poor woman, moved Juliet to the family quarters and placed another house guest at the bed and breakfast instead.

Most of Juliet's family, obviously, experienced her as difficult, as did many other people. But she was family, and she was accepted into that fold, included in family gatherings whenever possible. To them she was always Judy: impulsive, ebullient, and entertaining (they often wished she were less so), but also recriminating, self-absorbed and immature. She made them uncomfortable—less for her unconventional career than for her frequent and inappropriate references to it, and her need to take charge everywhere she went—but they took her as she was.

As Juliet aged she began to take this acceptance more and more for granted, while at the same time her behavior became more and more difficult to put up with—for everyone. Yet she was who she was; her behavioral habits had been set long ago, and despite all her therapeutic insights and New Age self-talk, Juliet was stuck in a narcissistic rut. That these patterns persisted unresolved was one of the great sorrows of Juliet's life, and of the lives of her family as well. She was, as her niece Monica so aptly noted, easy to love but almost impossible to like.

14
On the Inside, Looking Out

By the end of 1978, the glitter was beginning to wear off Juliet's glamorous new life. As it turned out, becoming a porn star had not solved any of her problems or even changed her basic lifestyle. She was still impulsive and self-absorbed, still mired in financial worries, still unfulfilled both professionally and romantically. The only difference was that she was more hopeful. She was sure that her ship would come in any day, and ignored any evidence to the contrary. She nurtured a vision of a sex performance industry that would celebrate the real joy and creativity of human sexuality, showing both women and men in a respectful light; this was the mission that guided her through the often sordid waters she had jumped into.

Professionally, she had many irons in the fire. She took every opportunity to network, meeting many of the "biggies," as she referred to them, in the adult industry: directors Bob Vosse, Sidney Neikerk, Ralph White, Ron Sullivan (Henri Pachard), and Jerry Abrams, as well as other influential people: *Eros* magazine publisher Harry Matesky; *High Society's* Gloria Leonard; *Screw* magazine editor Al Goldstein; Bob Wolfe, owner of Centaur Distributors; Phil Smith, vice president of operations for Shubert Corporation; Joe Steinman of Essex; and Jimmy Johnson of the American Film Awards Association. She took on almost every film role she could land—demurring, however, at any that were too degrading or low-paying.

She ventured as well into various sidelines in the sex industry. For a while, she continued to do a little stripping, but finding it too physically demanding and time-consuming, she finally gave it up for good. She landed a one-shot job doing voice-over moanings and groanings for a porno film shot in France, netting $25 [$82]. In May, she accepted a $300-per-month [$985] job as a reviewer for the British magazine *Cinema-X*; they were starting a U.S. West Coast edition called *Cinema Blue*. Her first review was of one of her own films, *Summer Heat*. Juliet also continued to work as Paul Johnson's assistant; he paid her $100 to $150 [$325 to $490] per shoot. At this time in Juliet's life, Paul was a steadying influence financially as well as emotionally.

Probably her most lucrative work, though—at least in terms of money earned versus time spent—was as a hooker. She went out on a fair number of calls, doing occasional doubles and threesomes, along with domination work—always a mainstay of the sex business. She took on some Japanese businessmen visiting the city, through connections with a tour guide who wanted to pick up a little extra commission on the side; she was a hot item with the Asians, who were as thrilled with a tall blonde as they had been when she lived in Japan in 1961. She received two job offers from houses of prostitution: one from a madam who was setting up a house on Nob Hill and offered to hire her as a regular; the second a more tentative offer from a prospective backer who proposed helping her set up her own house in Marin. Apparently, though, neither of these prospects materialized.

In June, she did a bachelor party double that threatened to turn violent. The original deal was $100 for each woman, $450 if it turned into an overnight. The young Thai architect groom-to-be, however, had not been informed of this treat, a friend having arranged it for him as a surprise, and he was too shy to perform with them until after the guests left. To pass the time the two women offered to dance on the table top, stripped down to garters and hose. But the young Asian men at the party were ill-mannered. They didn't like the lingerie and wanted total nudity; Juliet and her companion complied, although they felt degraded by the demand. The atmosphere was beginning to get tense. Juliet picked up on their feelings of pent-up sexual frustration combined with a contempt for "loose" women; for a while she feared it might turn into a gang rape. Fortunately, however, things calmed down, the guests did leave, and both women spent the night. The overexcited groom-to-be, now released from the need to impress his friends with his prowess, spent the night jumping back and forth between the two of them. "We earned our $400 [$1,300]," Juliet asserted ($50 from each of their fees went to the agent).

Lucrative tricks like this were rare, though. "I wish I had a steady john," Juliet mused, because that would be "an assured $100 [$325] a week." But it was not to be. Sugar daddies are hard to come by. Ironically, the government was still paying her $93 [$305] a week in unemployment benefits—about the same amount she sought from a regular john.

Still, all of this income, put together, was insufficient to meet what she perceived as her needs, especially given that her employment was erratic. Although her rent was fairly reasonable—$195 [$640] for her San Francisco apartment plus another $63 [$205] for the garage—she continued to spend money on luxuries, especially clothes, partly to support her inflated self image, and sometimes because she needed costumes for film roles, for which she did not always get the reimbursement she expected. Her debts from the previous year's struggle remained unpaid and she was constantly playing a cat-and-mouse game with a collection agency, managing to elude them and get her $1,030 [$3,375] U.S. tax refund, which she was afraid they might be able to take. The tax refund from Finland finally came through as well, but was only $233 [$765] rather than the $1,000 [$3,280] she had been expecting.

Her future prospects, however, still looked bright; success seemed to shine on the horizon. The "Aunt Peg" series was particularly promising. Director Bob Vosse hinted that Swedish Erotica was interested in an exclusive contract with her, and in March backer Sidney Neikerk bought the rights, agreeing to make the series into a feature, with a three- or four-day set of additional shots at $350 [$1,150] per day for her. This work was released as *Aunt Peg, Aunt Peg's Fulfillment* and *Aunt Peg Goes Hollywood*. It was a good one-time deal, bringing her total income in April to close to $2,400 [$7,875], but it was not the guaranteed ongoing $600 [$1,970] a month she had wanted.

There were other indications of imminent fame and fortune as well, at least to Juliet's way of thinking. In March 1980 she attended the Third Annual Erotic Film Award ceremonies at the Hollywood Palladium. Juliet outdid herself here; riding a rented horse and wearing a long blonde wig, she appeared at the venue as Lady Godiva—whether scantily dressed or entirely nude is not clear, but she apparently did not encounter any opposition from the Los Angeles vice squad. At the ceremony itself, she donned some real, although minimal, clothing: a red gown with only one shoulder strap, split high to the hip on the left side. She left the ceremony in a white limousine, accompanied by Vanessa del Rio, some journalists from *Cinema-X*, and their own photographer. A reporter from the Japanese version of *Playboy* interviewed her; to her surprise and delight, Aunt Peg was as big a hit in Japan as in San Francisco, perhaps even more so.

Juliet also had her first try at directing a film: *All the King's Ladies*, shot in Las Vegas. Her acting role in this film was "the wealthiest, hottest most glamorous madam in Las Vegas," and she received $800 [$2,625] for two days' work. She was impressed with the scene where a string of pearls was pulled out of her ass, and she hoped the audience would be, too.

Yet for all the up sides to her sex work, there were disappointments and even degradations. She was sure she was perfect for the lead, Barbara, in a new film to be directed by Dave Arthur, believing that it would be "the plum of my career," but Annette Haven got the part instead, leaving Juliet with a $100 [$325] bit part. She also lost much-needed income whenever any of the main actors—never a reliable bunch—failed to show up for a filming and the shoot was canceled. Then there were the sometimes disgusting filming conditions. Director Bob Wolfe hired her for two back-to-back loops, but they were shot at a converted schoolhouse in Santa Rosa that was not only filthy but also freezing cold, and the film crew were so incompetent that it took about five hours to film each twelve-minute loop; the second filming ended at 1:30 a.m. Her exhaustion and disgust tempted her to swear off films for good, but of course she couldn't afford to.

In June, director Sam Weston (a.k.a. Sam Weinstein, Anthony Spinelli) finally came through with a major part for her in *Vista Valley PTA*. However, Juliet was not crazy about the script, as it included a mother-daughter incest scene (which she reluctantly performed), and she flat-out refused to do another scene in which she was to beg for a load in her ear ("the only orifice that had not received one"), offering in trade a full Lotus-pose fucking position. She was also disappointed at getting only $300 [$985] per day rather than the $350 [$1,150] she had asked for. Grossly overweight Sam was also pressuring her for casting couch privileges, but she put him off by promising sex if he would lose a hundred pounds. (To her dismay, he actually managed to lose thirty pounds by the end of June, but fortunately he never made it all the way to a hundred.) Sam's health was not the best, either: he collapsed during the third day of filming and John Dirlam, the lead cameraman, had to take over directing.

Other areas of Juliet's life were less than ideal as well. Her health continued to be a source of stress. She tried to keep up regular exercise, but this had its drawbacks. In early September, she fell while roller skating in Golden Gate Park and broke her tailbone, leaving her with $3,000 [$9,850] in hospital bills as well as three weeks of pain. She continued to swim regularly, but often took long breaks because she was too busy or exhausted. She signed up for both aerobic dancing and Yoga classes, but discovered that "I have two left feet" and couldn't follow the dance steps, and she got distracted by attractive men in the Yoga class, once getting caught by the cook at the Yoga center, making out with one of these hunks in the kitchen. "This is a spiritual organization!" he admonished them.

Juliet's ambivalent approach to food and diet also became more dysfunctional during this period of her life. While she tried to stay on a diet of healthful, organic, mainly vegetarian food, she frequently fell into junk-food binges, purging later with water-and-juice-only fasts (better than vomiting, of course, but still clearly a bulimic pattern). In truth, although she was a stunning success as the oldest porn star in the American market, she felt tremendous pressure to keep in superior shape. While she was no longer disgusted at pictures of herself in magazines and on film box covers, she looked at these depictions of her body with critical eyes: "Saw myself in first magazine layout (*Swedish Erotica*) and I look great. Only a few wrinkles at neck, no flab showing. Damn I have beautiful breasts." But "[I] am getting freaked out trying to keep in the competition with slender young beauties (in films). Hope I can hurry up and get famous and rich so I can get out of having to be beautifully naked."

Despite all the stresses of her new life, Juliet maintained her ebullient sense of humor, sharing it with those around her whenever she could. Telephone answering machines were just beginning to become popular at this time, and Juliet delighted in leaving whimsical greetings on her machine, changing them almost every day.

Creative Answering Machine Greetings

This is Judy's almanac service. On this day, March 28, in 1797 the washing machine was invented. In commemoration Judy has taken her dirty duds to the laundry.

I'll make an attempt to put in a full day's labor to commemorate this day in 1910 when the U. S. government adopted the 8-hour work day.

On this birthday of Jean Paul Sartre I'm pondering the nature of existentialism. When I determine the implications of "I think therefore I am," I'll call you back.

I'm strolling thru the Tenderloin playing my flute to commemorate this day in 1284 when the Pied Piper lured 130 children into oblivion.

I've gone to visit the little prince and his rose because today is Saint Exupery's birthday.

I'm making bathtub gin to commemorate this day in 1919, the beginning of Prohibition. If I don't fall in and get pickled I'll return your call.

To commemorate this day in 1970 when the Supreme Court found *The Tropic of Cancer* not obscene, I've gone to the bookstore to read dirty books.

Warning to the foolhardy: don't do anything rash on the anniversary of this day in 1815 when Napoleon met his Waterloo.

To commemorate this day in 526 when an earthquake in Antioch killed 250,000, I've gone to picket the San Andreas Fault.

With garlands in my hair and bells on my toes I've gone to the village green to dance around the Maypole; call you when I return.

This is Red Riding Hood Judy. Grandmother has the sniffles and I'm taking her some sesame tahini and alfalfa sprout soup. The woods aren't very deep so I'll be back soon.

To commemorate this day in 1904 when the U.S. purchased the unfinished Panama Canal from France, Judy has gone to get a malaria shot.

Creative Answering Machine Greetings

[After starting Daylight Savings Time] I've gone to look for the hour I lost yesterday.

I've gone to play that newest California game: "Gasoline, gasoline, where's the gasoline?" The search and the waiting in line may take a while, so leave me a message.

In observation of this day in 1648 when Manhattan Island was purchased for $24 by Peter Stuyvesant, Miss Carr has gone to buy Alcatraz Island, to which the Tenderloin will be transferred as part of the Beautify San Francisco project.

I'm blowing up balloons for the True Mind Temple Evolutionary Transitional Church of Hedonis' annual picnic. When I've run out of hot air ...

This is Judy's psychiatrist. To help Miss Carr recover from the trauma of trying to find gasoline on Sunday, I've prescribed a long soak in a hot tub. If she doesn't drown she'll call you back. But for heaven's sake don't hang up as it will create further anxieties in my patient.

On the anniversary of the founding of Las Vegas in 1902, Judy has gone to the back room at Ernie's pool hall to shoot some craps. After the beep leave any ol' message but preferably a hot tip on the horses.

This is Judy's campaign manager. On recognition of this day in 1950 when the first woman was nominated for President, Judy has gone to declare her candidacy. Both messages and campaign contributions are welcome.

Captain Kidd was hanged on this day in 1701, which should be a reminder to any of you callers contemplating dastardly deeds.

On this day in 1502 Columbus was returned to Spain in chains for mistreating the natives of Haiti. What more *apropos* occasion to talk with my boss about better working conditions?

Juliet was also developing an active, if superficial, social life. By now an expert at getting rich men to wine and dine her, she took advantage of many such opportunities, whether the reward was food, entertainment, or just being the center of attention. While her escorts of course expected sex as a reward, Juliet, now more sophisticated than when she was romping around Mexico in 1965, often managed to weasel out of such payment, with no pangs of conscience. After all, she was a famous porn star now; her stunning presence should be payment enough. She had actually become, in a way, the gold digger she had joked about being in college.

Most of these encounters were brief—dinner and theater dates—but one included a trip to New York City, to celebrate the ending of 1978 and the beginning of 1979 with Gordon, the "sexy bachelor" she had romped with on her way back from Greece in October. How romantic, spending New Years Eve in New York City! Except that the trip was an unmitigated disaster. While this assignment paid enough for her to feel that sex should be part of the bargain, Gordon was actually apathetic about it, preferring unsatisfying (for Juliet) hand jobs, and, furthermore, he left for three days in Philadelphia on December thirtieth, the day after she arrived, thereby abandoning her for New Years Eve. Although he arranged for her to attend a party hosted by a friend of his, her substitute escort was no improvement over Gordon. When Juliet volunteered to help with party prep, he delegated to her the whole task of cleaning his filthy house and expected her to jerk him off as well. The party guests were a "bunch of bar-hopping phoneys [sic]." She left the party in disgust, in the company of another guest, with whom she attended two equally bad parties. The glamorous New York vacation was really nothing more than a bad week-long trick. Not very different from her "lamentable journey to Greece" two months earlier.

Back in the Bay Area in April, she attended a somewhat more successful although much briefer event—an officer initiation party for the Elks—as the guest of Raúl, a sixty-year-old politically conservative Venezuelan. Attiring herself in a "smashing, sexy" green-and-white sun dress and white shawl, she "agreed to attend because I knew I'd be a sensation. As expected I caused a stir. 'Where did you find that gorgeous woman, Raúl?' "

She was also willing to make exceptions to her no-casting-couch rule, if she found the director in question non-repulsive enough. She carried on a weeks-long affair with Leonard Kurtman, a New York porn actor turned director who temporarily relocated to the Bay Area in late March; Juliet spent many days and nights at his impressive rented villa in Sausalito, which overlooked the bay. Not a bad deal, even though Leonard was not quite up to Juliet's standards: "It's no great passion but I feel comfortable with him. He fucks well and is a great cuddler but I'm having to teach him how to caress me tenderly instead of pouncing." The bloom was soon off this rose, however, as the only work she got out of the arrangement was a bit part, paying her only $100 [$325], and Leonard had to give up the house to return to New York when his father died in May. And, truth be told, this interlude was not all opulence and romance: the Sausalito house was ill-kept, and Leonard lived on junk food; Juliet had to supply her own meals. As some consolation, she did manage to pilfer a few valuables from the house before she left.

During a break in her filming schedule, in early June 1979, Juliet accompanied Paul Johnson on an outdoor shoot for his "Let's Pretend" series at Point Reyes National Seashore. This trip, far from being a relaxing diversion, was in fact a telling commentary on the not only unglamorous but often downright miserable conditions under which slick- and exotic-looking pornography is actually produced. The party gathered at Five Brooks Stables, where they loaded up their equipment on rented horses and headed off up the Olema Valley Trail to the shooting location. A series of mishaps followed: Ken, another assistant, dropped a camera on a rock, breaking the expensive lens, and later one of the camera magazines got broken as well, destroying vital footage that had been laboriously shot. Not to mention the stinging nettles that proliferated in the shady areas, or that it was the height of the tick season. Since Juliet did not mention the ubiquitous poison oak in this area, presumably either they managed to avoid it, or no one was allergic to it. On the way back, Juliet had to ride the horse that Ken had ridden out, because he was too saddle sore to tolerate another minute on horseback. (Whether this left an extra horse that had to be led, or whether some of the party had hiked in rather than riding, is not clear.) It was only the second time in ten years that she had been on horseback, and she neglected a critical detail: adjusting the stirrups to fit her. Between this oversight, her fatigue and her being out of riding shape herself, she had a miserable trip back, traveling twice the distance necessary because her riding companion, Jen, tried some "shortcuts." They were racing against both the approaching dark and a menacing fog bank rapidly moving in from the ocean—a common weather pattern at Point Reyes in June.[17]

Back in the car at last, their troubles were not over. Ken took a wrong turn along the winding country roads and they did not get back to San Francisco until eleven p.m. And it was only after Ken dropped Juliet off at her apartment that she realized she had left her bag, with her keys in it, in his car. She spent the night with John Dirlam—lead cameraman for *Vista Valley PTA*—instead, but he was tired and grumpy, and they both had to be back on the set the next morning, exhausted and irritated after far too little sleep.

It was in fact John who became Juliet's major romantic project of 1979. She had taken notice of him when he had to step in and finish directing *Vista Valley* after Sam Weston collapsed on the set, and she was soon swept up into another of her heart-breaking relationship addictions.

For, despite her newfound fame as a sex star, Juliet's love life remained in the same state of wreckage it had been for most of her life. Although she enjoyed casual sex and had all she wanted, she still sought a serious relationship that encompassed intimacy and com-mitment in addition to sex. For this prize, she was sometimes, al-though not always, willing to spend some time getting to know the man in question before jumping into bed with him—say, three days to a week. Her first 1979 venture in this direction was Franco, the one bright spot in her New York City vacation. It was lust at first sight for them both; they could hardly wait to be alone together. And Franco somehow tapped into her desire to be submissive: "He is the only man ever able to dominate me outside Nikolas and I am captivated. I want to be his love slave." They engaged in some light B & D in addition to hot and heavy conventional sex. But Franco lost interest after a few days, standing her up on her last night in New York.

---

[17] This narrative is entirely from Juliet's 1979 journal. Paul Johnson has no recollection of being involved in any such expedition. Juliet may have been mistaken about who in fact participated.

So it was that by the time John Dirlam came along, in mid-April, Juliet was again looking for a soul mate. This relationship followed her usual pattern: long hours of mad, passionate sex, with Juliet completely losing herself in a pink cloud; John's withdrawal as her emotional demands escalated; Juliet's tears and recriminations; her partial acceptance of the situation for a few weeks; her attempt to revive the relationship; its brief re-birth; and its death, followed by her grieving and final nonchalant acceptance: "Oh, well, I guess he wasn't the One." But never any self-examination on her part, or lessons learned. It would simply be a matter of time before the next drama.

Self pity there was aplenty, though. "My love life is still the pits. The irony of it is that thousands of men are jerking off nightly to my picture and yet the sex star 'Aunt Peg' is lonely and sleeps alone." (Not an uncommon pattern among sex workers: a painful, if ironic, place to be.) "I need an intense relationship with a man. Where is he?... I've used my vibrator so much that I can't get relief from it any more." Her rationalizations, on the other hand, were creative—"I scare men off because I am too damned self-sufficient," or "Why [can I not find a mate]? Not because I am not up to it but because my partner is not,"—and only occasionally interspersed with insights into her own ambivalence:

> I am terrified of love, yet wither without it; I have too much to do in life to waste time on debilitating experiences. Yet I believe so strongly in love that I can't avoid encounters for fear of pain. It must be [an] intense relationship or none at all; I keep falling into deep waters... I come up choking and shivering and vomiting dirty water; the emotional side of my nature is stumbling along thru an unfamiliar forest, proceeding ahead and even coming into an occasional sunny patch, but still most of the time in alien and unfriendly territory full of wild beasts and snares.

Even aside from the emotional turmoil in her life, Juliet was actually beginning to tire of the intensity of living in San Francisco. In April 1980 she moved out of the city to Piedmont, near Berkeley— away from the intensity and rush of the city, although she was still in a largely urban area. Her rent was no cheaper, but she got more for

her money in the East Bay: a pleasant two-story house on a quiet
street, in a more secure area, although with less privacy as it was a
shared house; she had two roommates. Soon after, she moved to
another, even more impressive shared house, the Jack London House
on Blair Avenue, where the famous author had spent his early married life. Built originally in 1883 as a Worcester-style bungalow, it had
been upgraded and added on to by London, and was one of the
better-appointed places Juliet lived, although not quite up to the
level of Sepy's mansion in Florida or the Greek villa on the Isle of
Khios.

Life was a little slower-paced here in the East Bay, and she needed a place to withdraw to from time to time. And it appealed to her
that Berkeley had been a hotbed of the social and sexual revolution
that had swept the world in the 1970s. Much of that energy lingered;
there were fascinating people and cultural events, though these had a
somewhat more subdued and intellectual flavor than in the City.
Aside from her five years in Placerville, Juliet would spend the rest
of her life in Berkeley and Oakland.

It was shortly after this move to the East Bay that Juliet met Frank
McGrath, a photographic technician who had begun assisting Paul
Johnson, and they soon began a sexual relationship. Unlike most of
the partnerships Juliet had been churning through during these
years, this one endured for close to two years. While they never lived
together, nor were they monogamous, Juliet and Frank were acknow-
ledged as a couple until early 1982, when Frank moved on to another
partner. Frank's easy-going personality calmed Juliet, and his being
outside the sex-work sub-culture helped her maintain some distance
from it as well; he provided a respite from the intensity and volatility
of Juliet's career. Theirs was more a sexual friendship than a romantic
partnership, allowing Juliet to appreciate their intimacy without the
extreme emotional dependency she tended to develop with the
charismatic but unstable men she was most easily drawn to.

Frank accompanied Juliet to the Annual Erotic Film Award
ceremonies, and also joined her in the Bahamas in the spring of 1981,
after a filming job there went awry. A porn photographer had hired
Juliet for a shoot in the islands, paying for her travel and lodging, but
the project went south when Juliet objected to conditions she considered demeaning. The photographer left, but since the rented yacht

and its captain had already been paid for, he allowed her the use of them for several more days. Frank flew down, and he and Juliet spent two days on the boat, drifting lazily among the islands, then moved on to a small hotel bungalow for several more days. They spent almost a week basking in the sun, strolling through markets, enjoying the local cuisine, and making lazy love in their cozy abode. It was a welcome break from the intensity and craziness of the porn film scene, and Frank was the perfect companion for such an interlude.

Juliet and Frank McGrath, on their vacation in the Bahamas in 1980. Photo on left by Frank McGrath. Photo on right probably by Juliet.

Through all of the ups and downs in her emotional, physical and financial life during these first few years of porn film work, the one consistently bright spot for Juliet was the work itself—at least when she was actually on the set, acting in a scene where she felt free to express her true sensuality and love of sex, and from time to time even use her sense of humor, which often enlivened otherwise dull scenes. In *A Girl's Best Friend*, for example—a film that included a fair amount of slapstick humor—she quipped, as Robert Kerman fondled her breasts, "They're originals"; this was in response to his preceding line, "This is the original"—referring to a supposedly rare and expensive sculpture he was trying to impress her with. Later, as she moved into sixty-nine position on top of him, she taunted, "And you thought I was a natural blonde," referring to the fact that her pubic hair was light brown rather than blonde. (Juliet was, in fact, a natural blonde, as all her fans knew.)

This movie was actually her favorite, as director Ron Sullivan (Henri Pachard), being gay, had no interest in taking sexual advantage of her. Moreover, he had a truly professional attitude toward directing. "There's nothing I would not have done for [that crew]," she asserted years later, because they treated her well, giving her the feeling of safety and comfort she needed to deliver a stellar performance. She also reveled in the elegant costumes she wore for that production— silks, satins and furs, and several stunning hats, including a pert pillbox with a veil (which she sometimes wore even in the sex scenes, enhancing her already authoritarian air).

Juliet all dressed up for her role in *Girl's Best Friend.* Photo: Carr/Pettit family collection.

Juliet loved "being in command," as she had noted at the very beginning of her sex-work career. This tendency often manifested in her films; she had an almost regal stage presence. Early in *Taboo 2*, for example, she sets up and directs the encounter between Kay Parker and Kevin James, not only initiating their coupling but urging them on into specific activities and reminding them how much they are enjoying themselves. And later in the film, in the party scene, she plays her hostess role to the hilt. She places many of the other actors in specific locations, building a ring of naked bodies, and then, as they writhe on the floor, she stands above them, still clothed in her royal blue gown. When she does condescend to become a participant, she slips off her gown, selects the man she wants from among the crowd and sits erect on his hard cock, far above the madding crowd, still partly clothed in garter belt and stockings, drawing attention to herself as she rides him and exhibits her obvious enjoyment through facial expressions and vocalizations.

Yes, Juliet loved performing, loved being in her body, high on endorphins, driven by her vision of the gifts she could bring to her audience. "I feel that my true calling is teaching and opening others to love, adventure and the desire to explore one's own uniqueness... to show people their untapped potential for love and pleasure. How the spirit and mind and body can be raised to new levels of energy and joy." However, she was also aware, at least intellectually, of the pitfalls of pride: "I am not selfless; quite the contrary. I give because it pleases me, and it incidentally gives pleasure to others."

As indeed it did. Juliet truly loved sex—and, even more, she loved showing off, drawing attention to herself, and being in control. Porn film work offered her these opportunities, and she brought a level of not just professionalism, but true enthusiasm, to it. Her own performances so contrasted with those of the other actors that rare is the person who, watching her films, has not remarked on the difference. While most of the performers seem lukewarm at best, Juliet was hot. She knew what to do, when to do it, and how to do it, to bring a genuineness to any scene she was in. She was being herself, having fun, trying to engage her fellow actors, and catering to her audience. In short, she was *present*. Her beauty, her sparkle, her love of life and sense of humor—all are manifest in her work. And it was in these early years of 1979 through 1982 that she was most engaged, feeling most fulfilled in this amazing career she had chosen.

And so, despite heartbreaks and disappointments, the sky seemed to be the limit on where her sex career could go. "Aunt Peg is San Francisco's most popular series. [Next] I want to be a spread in *Penthouse*," she wrote in early March. Setbacks were only temporary bumps in the road. "I have great self confidence. If one door closes, another opens." If anyone seemed envious or resentful of her, it was merely "a sign of accomplishment... They're afraid of my abilities."

On location (actors unidentified); Juliet taking a break at the beach. Photo: Carr / Pettit family collection.

As it happened, the years 1980 and 1981 would mark the high point of Juliet's film career. A fourteen-foot cut-out of Aunt Peg stood on the marquee of New York's Pussycat Theater for several weeks in the spring of 1980, when Juliet was in town both filming and doing personal appearances "and meeting a lot of big shots." Photographs and interviews of her filled many porn magazines, and she was on several covers: *Starlet*; the British journal *Knave* ("Porno Princess Juliet Anderson - America's Favourite Auntie"); *Stag* ("First Lady of Lust"); and *Stag's Best*, pictured as the (obviously not distressed) victim of King Kong. She got some decent roles, too, performing one of her hottest sex scenes ever with John Leslie in *Talk Dirty to Me*, and playing opposite *Green Door's* Johnny Keyes in *Aunt Peg's Fulfillment*. "My career is taking off like a rocket," she wrote to her sister Chris in May, 1980, "and I couldn't be more pleased. It's finally happening. I've got[ten] rave reviews...starred in a couple of big ones and there are a couple more lined up."

However, Juliet dreamed even bigger dreams. "The X film biz is a means to something else, writing probably. Or maybe photography, or being an agent. So [what if] I came thru the back door? So did many a great lady." Ultimately, she wanted to bring forth a new form of erotic entertainment—more refined, more life-affirming, with a more respectful image of women and their sexuality. "I would like to do point-of-view [pornographic photography] from the woman's point of view... I want to produce erotic and sensual realism. All I need is the backing. I'm becoming known by the biggies in the film industry, but have to convince them there's a market. Investors are only interested in returns not reforms." Quality, though, was the touchstone. "Whatever I do, I want to do with professional skill and pride and be the best!"

Juliet performing her stage shows. Left: The White Widow; Right: Cassie the Cook. Photos by Annie Sprinkle.

Her first real step in this direction was the development of her live stage shows. Juliet had been stripping since her first week on the job with Alex de Renzy, but she wanted to take it to a new level. Why not make it a story, a show, rather than just a quick strip and dance? Although the glory days of strip-tease were gone, and along with them artists like Gypsy Rose Lee, who wore elaborate costumes and stripped them off languorously and enticingly, Juliet felt that she could revive some of that classiness. And so, as she moved into her second and third years in the porn business, becoming increasingly dissatisfied with its seamy side, she worked to develop a set of characters, with names like Helen the Housewife, Cassie the Cook, Nurse Naughty, and the Executrix,[18] and then pitched the idea to her friends the Mitchell brothers, at whose O'Farrell Theater she had already stripped a number of times. Jim and Artie, always open to new ideas and presentations—if they felt there was a market for them—readily agreed, and Juliet debuted her stage shows there in the fall of 1981.

And these were real shows, not just strip routines. Juliet started out in character, fully clothed, surrounded by a few props, then acted out some simple tasks appropriate to the character—sometimes with dialog and sometimes without. She moved on to stripping (accompanied by plenty of seductive looks and moves), until she was nude except for some sexy lingerie (which did *not* cover the critical body parts—nipples or genitals). She would then do a more-or-less standard dance routine, building to a spell-binding climax. She usually did three or four characters at any given performance.

After her routine, she would throw on a scanty robe, sit on a stool on the stage and answer questions from the audience. These questions could be about her, the live performance, the porn film industry, or even technical questions about sex. Finally, she would move to the theater lobby, where she made herself available for photo sessions with interested customers, for an additional fee; the fans could leave with an autographed Polaroid of themselves with Aunt Peg.

After her debut at the O'Farrell Theatre, she took this show on the road in the winter of 1981-1982. She was now well enough known to get the publicity necessary for performing at some high-profile venues: the Palace Theatre near Boston; the Pussycat; Plato's Retreat, Melody Burlesk and Show World Center in New York; the Oak and Festival theaters in Chicago; and another Palace Theatre in Seattle, among others.

It was through Juliet's show tour in New York City that she first met Annie Sprinkle, with whom she shared a birthday as well as some personality traits. Annie put Juliet up during her stay in the city, and also functioned as photographer for Juliet's performances.

Annie arranged one of the most enjoyable escapades of Juliet's life, as well: an erotic photo session with a male artist and his life-

---

[18] See Appendix C for a complete list of shows and characters.

sized sculpture of a stallion. The sculptor painted Juliet's face and body, depicting her as an Amazon warrior, and Juliet posed in erotic positions both on top of and underneath the horse; Annie shot the photos. It was a magical afternoon—a chance for Juliet to combine her love of art, sex, and performing, immersed in creative energy with two kindred spirits. It was certainly the high point of that tour, and a precious memory she always treasured.

Juliet posing seductively in her red macrame dress, and made up as an Amazon warrior, posing with the artist whose horse sculpture she was about to cavort with. Photos by Annie Sprinkle.

Unfortunately, not all of the tour was as uplifting. Not long after her romp with the horse sculpture, Juliet had her first encounter with obscenity law, while performing her afternoon show at the Oak Theater in Chicago on Friday, 2 July 1982—the fourth day of her six-day run there. Part of her Suzy the Secretary routine included play-ing seductively with a bright yellow toy telephone. She had toned this scene down somewhat for Chicago, having been informed by the management that city law forbade public touching of genitals, even in a porn theater. She was simply bending over with her back to the audience and running the receiver up and down the inside of her legs. Although she assiduously avoided going all the way up to her crotch, a plainclothes policeman planted in the audience believed she had broken this law. After the show, when she was out in the lobby during her picture-taking session, he arrested both her and the lighting technician (although what his crime was, was not at all clear). Juliet was allowed to send someone to fetch her purse from her dressing room, and she was able to throw on the negligee she had been wearing for her Q & A session, but she had to go off without her shoes or jacket. She was taken to the Maxwell Street Station (of "Hill Street Blues" fame) for booking; the charge was "lewd display of genitals."

Both the arresting officer and the station lieutenant apologized for the arrest, saying that they admired the classy and clean act she had put on, but that they had orders from "higher up"—evidently it was an election year in Chicago, always bad news for sex workers. The cops then hauled out several adult magazines they had confiscated from book-store raids and asked her to autograph some of the photos of herself in them. Although she was disgusted at their hypocrisy, she obliged. She was not in a position to assert herself.

After her booking, she was taken to the city jail in a paddy wagon, along with a load of prostitutes (all of them black, she noted in her writings, revealing her covert racism), where she spent a miserable nine hours in a cold cell (despite the summer weather; it was in the basement), her neighboring detainees "raving, banging on the steel doors with either hands or head, or throwing up." All of them were released hours before she was. When at last she was allowed to pay the $100 [$246] bail, which theater manager Joel Ross had given her in cash before she was taken in, she was exhausted and felt filthy. But she had a midnight show to do, and only barely enough time to get back to her lodging and take a quick shower. After finishing the remaining two days of her run at the theater, she tried to put Chicago behind her. Yet she still had to deal with the charges; the fallout from her arrest would drag on into early 1983.

Since the theater itself was also cited, Ross suggested that Juliet contact their attorney about representing her. But, after all, she was only a whore, as far as the legal establishment was concerned. The attorney refused; he was working on "more important cases," and referred her to a private attorney, a woman. That attorney advised her to take a plea bargain of six month's supervision (if she had no other arrests during that time, her records would be expunged), but

Juliet was outraged by the whole incident and wanted to fight the charges. To do so, she had to return to Chicago in November, at her own expense, and she still lost the case. Whores, after all, have no credibility, while cops, as we all know, never lie under oath. Never did the Oak Theatre offer her any help, other than paying her original bail. Neither Joel Ross nor his attorney would even return phone calls made by Juliet or her attorney.

She attempted an appeal but did not have the resources to follow through. She even wrote to Sam Weston, then president of the West Coast Producers' Association, pleading for his intervention, but despite her cordial relationship with him, he declined to get involved. All she could do was to put out the word on the sex-worker grapevine, informing her fellow workers of the incident and urging them to boycott the theater. A lost cause, as most of them were clueless and zoned out, if not actually in a drug-induced stupor most of the time, and thus rarely even aware of being mistreated. Juliet, however, with her narcissism and high expectations, viewed her failure to mobilize these scattered troops as yet another betrayal. Even her fellow workers would not stand behind her.

While the Chicago bust was the most traumatic of her traveling show experiences, none of her stops was a bed of roses. The theaters, being basically strip clubs, were not equipped to put on professional live shows. Her requests for experienced stage hands were often met with laughter. Some of the stages, designed only for bumping and grinding, were too small to accommodate all of her props. The lighting was often poor. She was frequently propositioned after the shows, either for a quick BJ or for full service.

Nor were her accommodations anything to rave about. She often had to stay with other sex workers with whom she had only a passing acquaintance, and many were not sterling people. Their apartments were often chaotic, not only physically but emotionally.

Typical were her sojourns with Annie Sprinkle, who, despite her understanding and support in creative ventures, proved less than satisfactory as a hostess. Annie welcomed a motley collection of sexual renegades into her New York apartment, which she thought of as a temple and meditation center. To Juliet, however, it was "a magnet for pimps, freaks, transvestites, transsexuals, tattoo artists, [and] junkies."

Juliet was performing five stage shows per day at "sleazeville" Show World Center. Enduring that venue was an ordeal—"the struggle to keep beauty, truth [and] gentleness alive in me, to keep the beasts of lust and greed gone wild at bay"—and staying at Annie's was like jumping "from one pen into another." Juliet seemed to be

> the token porn star, wedged in between two sofas and a mattress on the floor, cats and queers and sexual revolutionaries clustering in the dining room; the windowless bedroom with its aquarium, stuffed with clutter—goddess costumes, a bicycle, books and photos; bathroom in day-glow pink, smelling of douche, shaving cream and cat shit. Hostess Ellen [19] eagerly feeding her guests miso soup and brown rice from a closet-sized charrette—the sweet Jewish mom feeding her children... [Juliet tried to sleep with] my head beneath a pillow, wax in my ears to try to deaden the roar of Lexington Avenue, hissing pipes, and the endless parade of artists. [My] legs flung out from the covers... [it was] always too hot, too noisy, too frantic, too crowded. But here I fit, was loved, accepted and cared for [by] mom and fellow radicals. It took two weeks, though, to unjangle my nerves when I returned to Oakland.

Still feeling contaminated from the dirt and disorganization, Juliet went on a cleaning binge once she was back in her own space.

But even when she had her own private accommodations, they were often designed more for sex parties than for living. In Westchester, Massachusetts, for example, where she performed during a frigid December, in 1981, the decor bordered on the bizarre. The heavily lined orange and white flowered drapes blocked out any outside light; the ceiling, woodwork and radiators were all painted black; the overhead light bulbs were bare; the TV adjustments were missing their knobs and had to be operated with pliers; and the antenna was a coat hanger. The bathroom wallpaper was metallic silver and aqua interspersed with yellow and orange geometric patterns; the bathtub was lavender and completely enclosed with a dark blue

---

[19] Referring to Annie's original name, Ellen Steinberg

shower curtain; the only towel rack was broken; the towels a well-worn locker-room white; the tile floor an ugly black-and-white geometric pattern, and dirty. The lack of light gave the whole place the aura of a prison; there was no sense of the passage of time. Not surprisingly, the double-bed mattress thrown on the floor was quite comfortable, albeit made up with ugly brown, black and white sheets and moth-eaten flannel blankets.

The general area she was staying in presented some challenges as well. It was hard to find a restaurant open late at night, when she was returning from her last performance of the day. And John, the theater owner as well as proprietor of the local adult bookstore, had been reluctant at first to let her perform, as his regular clientele were not used to such a classy show and he feared they would be put off. His fears were unfounded, however, as Juliet received no complaints and in fact got a lot of compliments. Some men drove twenty-five miles to see her, although attendance was somewhat depressed because of a snowstorm; the memory of the blizzard of 1978 gave them pause. Some potential customers, too, were put off not by Juliet's lack of sleaze but by John's excess of it: he was arrested for selling child pornography at the bookstore, and attendance at the theater the next day was noticeably down.

Back home after the Chicago bust, Juliet received some good news that helped offset the trauma of her travels. It was in the spring of 1983 that a local phone-sex start-up contacted her about working for them. They explained the format: she could call in to their office whenever she wanted to work and simply sign off when she didn't; the calls would come in to their office, where they would collect the payments via credit card, then the dispatcher would patch the call through to her. She would be a great addition to their line-up as they could use her name in their advertisements. Even if she was not available for a customer who specifically requested her, he could usually be talked into chatting with another performer.

Juliet loved the idea, and took to it with enthusiasm. Although voice work was not her best mode, she was sure she could do it. And, given the low expectations of most phone-sex customers, she did fine. This work helped sustain her, in fact, for a good five years, even after she had dropped out of the rest of the sex-work scene.

Hence by early 1983—five years into her new career—Juliet's life revolved around sex and sex work. She continued to act in films, although she was much more choosy now. She had had two tries at directing. She had single-handedly put together her stage shows— writing and choreographing, designing the sets and costumes, producing and performing. She still worked with Paul Johnson, and still enjoyed a warm fuck-buddy relationship with him. She was a phone-sex operator. And she continued to supplement her income by turning a few tricks here and there.

Yet she was also growing older. Where, ultimately, was this road going to lead?

15
Fame and Its Discontents

By the spring of 1983, ambiguity had taken up residence in Juliet's life again. True, she was settled in her porn career, knew what she loved and what she hated about it, and was able to pick and choose the work she would do. With her live shows, she had actually created some of those performances herself, blending truly sexy entertainment with her image as an intelligent, in-charge mature woman. She had finally found a venue for her creativity, and was getting her ideas out into the world, fulfilling a life-long dream.

Yet fame had its price. Loss of privacy was the one that stressed her out the most. It was worse than being a tall American blonde in Japan; she was often recognized in public, photographed against her will, or asked for autographs. And she was tired of living up to other people's expectations. She had thought that being famous would give her the freedom to do as she liked, but her continued success depended on doing what her audience liked. Her audience loved her for her exuberance, self-confidence, and sense of humor—certainly important aspects of who she was. But she could not show her dark side—her fears and insecurities, her need for love and intimacy.

And, despite her many irons in the fire, she still did not have the long-term financial security she wanted. She had built a solid foundation for herself in the sex business, but the business itself was not solid. Like all businesses dependent on addiction for their long-term survival, the adult film industry depended on intensity and constant change: new faces (and body parts), more extreme activities. It was beginning to dawn on Juliet that being a porn star was not actually a career path.

Yet this was her identity—the only one she had found in her forty-five years. The sex-work subculture, despite its shortcomings, was a home for her, as was the Bay Area with all of its multi-cultural opportunities. She had begun to find many like-minded people, and even some good friends, in her new life. One afternoon in the summer of 1981, on a stroll down Berkeley's San Pablo Avenue, she wandered into "the first [and last] annual erotic art show," put on by Kat Sunlove and Layne Winklebeck, both of whom had recently started working at *Spectator Magazine*, the Bay Area weekly with news, views and advertisements on the sex scene. Juliet was entranced: a marriage of art and eroticism—just what she was looking for! Chatting with Kat and Layne, Juliet recognized two kindred spirits, and she returned to the makeshift gallery many times to visit with them, meantime meeting up with other interesting people who wandered in.

One of these was Michael Rosen, an artistic photographer who wanted to bring eroticism into his work without going into explicit pornographic photography; the erotic art show was displaying exactly the kind of work he wanted to do, and he was delighted to find a venue for it. Michael later did some fine photographs of Juliet; she was a great subject, being not only a professional model, but also an artist herself, with a good eye for composition and posing.

Kat and Layne were wonderful social connections for Juliet, and she quickly became entranced by this free-wheeling, intelligent, well-educated couple, so comfortable with sexuality, in an exuberant and wholesome way. They were among Juliet's longest-term friends, keeping in touch with her almost to the day she died. (They moved to Costa Rica in 2009 and lost contact with her during her final few months.)

When Juliet decided it was time for her to experience S & M, it was Layne whom she approached for a partner. Although light domination had of course been part of her escort and phone-sex work, she had not played the submissive role, and felt that she would not be a truly experienced sexual professional until she had added this skill to her repertoire. Layne was more than accommodating; he had always admired Juliet for her adventurousness, seeing her as a wonderful role model for women who wanted to claim their sexual freedom, to be as licentious as men if they so chose. Kat did harbor some apprehension about the encounter—not jealousy, but apprehension. "Now you be good to Juliet," she admonished Layne. "Don't you dare hurt her!" Of course the encounter went fine: both Layne and Juliet were well acquainted with the S & M ground rules of "safe, sane and consensual." Juliet did conclude, however, that this realm of sexuality did not particularly interest her. She was essentially a plain vanilla sexual performer, with a few garnishments thrown in for color. Artificially heightened intensity was never really her thing; with her energy and enthusiasm, she could make regular sex as intense as she or her audience needed.

Actually, it was not just Juliet's friendship with Kat and Layne, but also her connection to *Spectator Magazine* itself that became a major social as well as professional connection for Juliet. The newspaper was the mouthpiece of the sexual liberation movement in the Bay Area. It got its start in 1979, as a spin-off from the *Berkeley Barb*, when that newspaper, under public pressure, stopped taking ads for sexual services. (The *Barb* folded not long after.) Later, in 1987, Kat and Layne bought the major share of *Spectator* when it was offered for sale to the employees. They eventually bought out the remaining shares, and owned the paper until 2001; it folded in 2005.

It was a year or so after the *Spectator* connection, late in 1982, that Juliet met Carolyn Hardies (later Elderberry), soon to become her closest friend. Carolyn had attended Ray Stubbs's massage workshop in Arizona, on integrating sensuality and sexuality—another theme dear to Juliet's heart. Back in the Bay Area, Carolyn was conducting half-day mini-workshops promoting Ray's work, and it was at one of these events that Juliet and Carolyn first met. When she came across an ad for Carolyn's workshop in *Spectator*, Juliet was immediately hooked on the idea. Combining sexual and non-sexual touch—exactly what she had been trying to do all her adult life! She signed up immediately.

And Carolyn and Juliet connected at first sight; they both knew that here was a kindred spirit. That impression was sealed when they participated in a dyad together on the theme of death. It was the beginning of a lifelong friendship and sometime business partnership. They shared many interests and values, and seemed to be on similar life trajectories as well. They even started going to the same therapist, Maureen Namen,[20] with whom they would maintain a long-term connection.

---

[20] This is a pseudonym, for reasons that will become clear in a later chapter.

After knowing each other for about a year, Carolyn and Juliet decided to rent a house together, on Richmond Boulevard in Oakland, along with two other women sex workers. Paul Johnson claims that the quartet were known as "Paul's girls," although he himself may have been the only one who referred to them as such; Carolyn demurs at the term. The house was a two-story, four-bedroom 1940s-era structure, not far from the 580 freeway, in an area known as the Lower Piedmont. Not the kind of quiet neighborhood Juliet preferred, but the yard and street trees muffled some of the freeway noise and provided a little privacy. And it was cheap, especially split four ways. Not long after they moved in, the owner resurfaced the driveway; Juliet could not resist the temptation to write in the wet cement "Aunt Peg lived here - 1983."

It was also in 1982 that Juliet, through one of her more disastrous experiments, met Greg Franke, a gay man who became a dear friend and staunch companion. Tired of being recognized in public, she decided to perm her hair and dye it bright red. Alas! it turned out purple instead. In the early twenty-first century, she would have fit right in, but in 1982 this was a fiasco. Desperate for a rescue, she found Greg, a hair stylist that her Jack London housemate Sandra Klein had discovered on a random walk down Piedmont Avenue. He was able to adjust the color closer to what she had actually had in mind, although her redhead phase was a short-lived experiment.

Greg had just started out in the hair-styling business, but he was a natural, and Juliet had always been able to recognize and appreciate artistic talent. Except for the period when Juliet lived in Placerville, Greg cut and styled her hair for the rest of her life. He was unique among Juliet's circle of friends: she did not meet him through the sex industry—either directly or indirectly; and there was of course no sexual charge between them, nor any emotional or financial dependency, nor did they need to compete in any way. It was a good mix of professional distance combined with mutual respect and warmth. They each had their own lives, their own social circles, but they truly cared for each other, and shared a love of beauty and harmony. Greg and his partner Lee's house in Rockridge was a place of refuge for Juliet, a haven from her sometimes tumultuous life. She often house-sat for them when they were away on trips; she could bask in the quiet solitude and simple elegance of the place, away

from the heavy energy that sometimes pervaded her own living/
working space.

These new friendships provided Juliet some solace when her
relationship with Frank McGrath ended in the spring of 1982. Frank
was suddenly making himself scarce, failing to return her phone calls
and making excuses for breaking dates they did have. Juliet finally
pinned him down for a lunch date and confronted him. Frank then
somewhat sheepishly admitted that he had begun keeping company
with a younger woman and wanted to end his relationship with
Juliet. She took it well, at least on the surface, only admonishing him
that she would have appreciated his coming forward on his own.
Whether she actually felt more hurt and abandoned is not known,
since she was not keeping a journal during this time and did not
refer to her relationship with Frank in her later writings.

Juliet also began to broaden her recreational horizons during
these years in the Bay Area. Paul Johnson introduced her to Wilbur
Hot Springs; they spent many long weekends there, escaping from
the frenetic city life. Juliet kept up with her cross-country skiing, too,
with trips to Lake Tahoe, and discovered some of the bed and
breakfasts in the foothills of the Sierra Nevadas—knowledge that
would later prove useful in an unexpected way.

Another refuge Juliet discovered was Raamwood, a communal
farm in Mendocino County. Originally begun as a sort of spin-off
from the hippie commune movement of the 1970s, Raamwood was
now kept up solely by Shirley Lewis, whom Juliet had met through
Paul Johnson and with whom she had become warm friends. The
land comprised a hundred acres, presided over by a restored Finnish
farmhouse originally built around 1850. The property had purposely
been kept rustic, off the electric grid and furnished instead with a
gasoline-powered generator that could be cranked up to run power
tools, the washing machine or the vacuum cleaner when needed.
There were also a few guest cottages, so that the place functioned as
a bed and breakfast part of the time.

Juliet also continued to visit with her family when she could. In
the summer of 1983, Juliet's cousin Pam was planning a get-together
at her place in Seattle, and Juliet felt this would be a good opportunity for a long vacation. She wanted to spend some time bicycling
around Vancouver Island, relax, write in her journal, and think about

her long-term plans. By happy coincidence, Paul Johnson was about
to head north for a trip to visit his family in Walla Walla, Washington,
and Juliet asked if she could ride along with him. Paul enthusiastically agreed, and, piling their equipment into his van—including a
ten-year-old slightly dinged-up yellow bicycle Juliet had recently
acquired and spiffed up a bit—they set off on July 21st, just two days
before Juliet's forty-fifth birthday.

They got an early start, traveling up Highway 101, through the
"golden, rolling hills" of Sonoma and Mendocino counties, then
through Garberville and the stately redwoods. Just south of Eureka
they turned west on a back-country road to Ferndale, setting up
camp just beyond the naval station there, a "lovely well-preserved
Victorian Gothic structure." Leaving the main highway for the back
roads, they worried about running into illicit pot farmers, but had no
trouble. Not that they were without a few small problems. Juliet's
bike was strapped to the back of the van, and a tailgater caused some
minor damage bumping into them. Nothing that couldn't be fixed
before Juliet had to take it on the road the following week, though.
And of course they had time to stop for a quick fuck, with the "good,
warm sun beating down on our naked bodies lounging in the doorway of the van."[21] The trip was a time for the friends to cement their
emotional intimacy as well. "Paul blew me away by revealing that he
had learned a lot from me these years. I really love Paul, as crazy as
he is."

The beauty of the coast made up for the minor glitches they
encountered along the way. "The ecstasy is unrivaled... the last rays
of sunshine, surf crashing, fog wisping across the dunes, I'm high,
relaxed, sexually satisfied, hungry." Juliet prepared a gourmet meal
over the camp fire and Paul did his part by washing the dishes. In
the morning, the upper back pain that had plagued Juliet was gone,
although her lower back still hurt. She had also had an ileitis attack
the night before, but decided that "shitting in the woods is a religious
experience" (she was probably stoned at the time).

After enjoying Juliet's gourmet breakfast ("scrambled eggs with
cream cheese and green onions, topped with crumbled corn chips,

---

[21] See http://paulsfantasy.com/Pauls_fantasy_site/Juliet_memorial.html for
photographs of this trip.

kosher sausage, strong coffee") they set off, crossing into Oregon just before noon. The stretch between Newport and Portland offered a quiet time for reflection. Juliet wrote in her journal while Paul drove. She enjoyed this interlude, reflecting on the trip: "Been high a lot, good sex, food and reminiscing between two old mature pornographers." One of the best parts was getting to be "Judy" again: "I'm going incognito this trip. Great to be scruffy in baggy sweats, T-shirt, sandals, dark glasses and no makeup or groomed hair, chipped dirty nails... Am longing for my communal farm family[22] to take me home where I can write: papers, books, poems, scripts, everything! I want fame to be internal, not decided by a fickle, cliche-ridden, guilt-tripping society."

At Portland's Union Station, Juliet and Paul parted ways. She boxed up her bicycle and checked it along with her other luggage, then climbed onto the train to Seattle while Paul headed on out to eastern Washington. Juliet spent most of the ride looking out the window, drifting along along the Columbia River, then through verdant farmland to Puget Sound, with mountains looming to the east: first, recently truncated Mount St. Helens, and farther down the tracks, Mount Ranier. She mused on other train trips she had taken: to ski in Japan, through Spain and Italy, on her way to Greece and Nikolas. Trips in which she had tried to escape her mundane middle-class American identity, wanting to be the "respectable rebel, to get away, be free, flee home, family, country, make up for all those years of pain and suffering," always seeking intensity, "always the *ultimate* experience, the *unique* adventure, suck up life, fast," panicking that she had lost too many years already and had to make up the time. Yet her past illnesses had also given her a gift: "Having had that cross to bear has given me courage and curiosity, perseverance but not tenacity, inspiration and vision. But I still have some closets to unlock, drawers to clear out, junk to throw away." She would not have time to do that until after getting out of the porn business two years later.

Her mother and Pam met her at Seattle's King Street Station, their brightly colored clothes—Dorothy in purple and turquoise, Pam in red—giving them a warm and welcoming appearance. Pam and

---

[22] Probably a reference to Raamwood.

Llew, along with their two daughters, then ages twelve and ten, had only recently moved to the area and were still trying to make a go of their marriage, although Llew was already running around again and Pam had recently met Skip, who was to become her long-time companion. Pam's house was delightful, on a large lot with lots of trees; she kept a small menagerie, including a sheep, two dogs, five cats, and two ducks. Later she would add some horses.

The Pettits arrived shortly. Twelve-year-old Monica was "tall, tan and gorgeous" and Chris "as lovely and relaxed as usual," and, like Juliet, brightly clad in pink and purple. Pam's husband Llew was in Alaska; his presence was not missed. Settling in on this first evening, Juliet noticed to her surprise that she was more centered than usual around her family. Perhaps because she was free from the pressure of being Juliet Anderson with them. "I felt very loved and lucky to have such a fine family," she wrote in her journal.

The next day, Saturday, was Juliet's forty-fifth birthday, which she celebrated by cooking dinner for the whole crowd: chicken simmered in wine and homemade pesto and pasta. Her mother, in a show of support for Juliet's new identity (although her work was never openly mentioned) gave her a black teddy, cut high to the hip bone. But the sexy outfit would not be for work; Juliet would keep it for private, personal use.

By Sunday, the family dysfunctions had started kicking in, with Dorothy getting drunk and sinking into a crying jag, lamenting about her estrangement from her sister Barbara (which had happened some years earlier and was never repaired). Juliet stayed up with her until one a.m., even though she had to get up at five to catch the steamship to Vancouver Island.

Now began the part of the vacation Juliet had really been looking forward to. After quick good-byes to the family group, Juliet boarded the ship and almost immediately fell into conversation with an attractive Englishman. Despite her claims that she wanted to be incognito on this trip, she responded truthfully to his query about what kind of work she did, with the expected results. The next night, at dinner, a video store owner recognized her in the restaurant. Juliet reveled in the attention ("[he] acted as if Mary had descended"), feeling validated that people recognized her no matter where she was or how she was dressed.

Juliet settled into a boarding house, sleeping with the house cat at her side and awakening to the raucous cries of ravens, the major bird species on the island, since the quail and song birds had been decimated by the large population of peregrine falcons. Aside from the birds and an occasional ferry whistle, though, the boarding-house refuge was so quiet that she could hear water dripping in the bathroom and kittens romping down the hall. The midsummer days were long and slow-moving, with the sky lightening at three a.m. and darkening at ten p.m.

Juliet spent a week on Vancouver Island, staying at various inns and bed and breakfasts, wandering through tourist areas, enjoying good food, beer and wine, and engaging in conversations with various people she met, mostly other tourists. Her intention to use her bicycle as her major means of transportation was frustrated by the many steep hills (she had neglected to investigate the island's topography) and she ended up using public transit more than she had expected. And spending more money, too: many things were more expensive in Canada, from food to lodging to spare bicycle parts—for, despite her infrequent use of it, her bicycle broke down twice during her brief stay.

While downtown Victoria was overly touristy, Juliet did revel in two of the popular destinations: the Museum of Natural History ("best I've ever seen besides [the] one in Mexico City"), where she spent three and a half hours, collapsing that evening from sensory overload and an aching back; and the Butchart Gardens ("one of the most beautiful places I've ever visited... [where] all one's senses are wrapped in beauty: colors, textures, fragrances, waterfalls and fountains"). The latter reminded her of the gardens of Hayama. "I realize how flowers, a garden, a pond with running water, soothes my soul. I must include them in my future plans." The sensual experience that day lasted through her evening back at the B & B, where she was surrounded by antique furniture and the smells of lavender, talcum and and Avrame cologne, with an evening snack of English muffins and homemade strawberry jam to finish off the day.

Before leaving the island, Juliet took some time to reflect. Overall, Canada had been disappointing. "No reason to come this far for a holiday; [there is] better scenery in northern California." And even the limited bicycling had triggered pain in her hips. Still, Victoria might be worth returning to, but only during the off season, without a bicycle, and in the company of someone interesting.

She made another of her lists:

expand my consciousness thru workshops, meditation, retreats, reading and associating with people of similar interests; move to the countryside; simplify my life with few material possessions; make work an integral part of my life; let more love into my life; open my heart for a primary relationship (I yearn to be in love again).

She included some practical actions to help implement some of these goals, including hiring some clerical help, limiting her stage show work and depending more on phone sex and still photo shoots for her primary income. And her dream: producing her own Aunt Peg film.

Her last day on the island, Monday, August 1st, she awoke to sunshine streaming in the window, and (finally) freedom from back pain. She went down to the barn and greeted the horses before indulging in a hearty English breakfast. Off then to Seattle, to meet Barry, a baseball trainer who was as eager to romp as she. He had mentioned his connection with her to many of the players, and "of course several are pornophiles; in a way I'll be having sex with the whole team. Wow!"

In Seattle she checked into Barry's room at the Hilton, took a long luxurious bath and unpacked. She was excited about Barry's returning, wondering what would happen. She had specified no sex at first, just holding and nurturing touch; they would move on from that if and when it felt comfortable. When he came in she was asleep, but mumbled a few nothings as he greeted her with a tender kiss. They cuddled and snuggled for a long time. "My god it felt good, just a delicious warmth, not horniness, sleep and content, warm... mmm. Hadn't realized how much I miss the feel of another body next to mine."

The morning was marred by a call from Barry's partner. Juliet answered the phone the first time it rang; she dispelled the awkwardness by pretending the woman had reached a wrong number. Barry swore he had kept their liaison under wraps, while also admitting that it was one of hardest secrets he had ever kept. It was exciting for him to think about coming back and finding her in his bed. At the same time, it was wondrously comfortable to sleep next to her without having the pressure to perform. "Ditto for me!" Juliet confessed. Leaving his room later, as he slept, she was careful not to let anyone see her. She left him a note telling him she looked forward to getting to know him better.

Cousin Pam picked her up and took her to meet Roger, owner of the Palace Theatre, with whom she had a lunch date. But it turned out that he was deeply disappointed she had not come to spend the night with him. Apparently he had thought such a visit was likely, for he'd roasted a turkey and arranged with a female fan of hers to give her a manicure, pedicure and massage. He was even going to serve her breakfast in bed. Juliet apparently felt no guilt, however, and they discussed business over their lunch. Juliet squelched his ideas of turning his theater into a full-time live show place; there was not enough available talent, and his costs would be too high, she told him.

The next day was spent wandering around downtown Seattle with Pam and her two girls. During this walk Pam told Juliet that she had learned a lot from her, and that she felt Juliet was a good role model for her daughters; Juliet was showing them that a woman can be independent and powerful, and did not need to live her life through a man. Juliet was gratified, especially given how little acceptance she got from most of her family. Despite the ten-year difference in their ages, the cousins were becoming closer.

Her vacation over, Juliet got on a plane back to San Francisco. Mirja met her at the airport at 11:30 p.m. and helped her get her bike home; she fell into bed exhausted at 1:30 in the morning. The next day Paul took her to the mechanic's to pick up her car. The mechanic "about shit in his pants when he found out whose car he'd been working on." Juliet gave him an 8X10 glossy autographed photo. "Being a star is so weird!"

16
The End of the Yellow Brick Road

Films, stage shows, directing, phone sex, photographer's assistant: Juliet had built for herself a decent living. But her dream was
still to produce her own work, to get her own ideas out there in the
world. And now that dream seemed attainable: a movie of her own, a
story line that would both entertain and inform, that would portray
sex and sensuality as joyful, and would show that a woman could be
straight, sexy and powerful.

In the fall of 1983, after returning from her trip to the northwest,
Juliet started writing her script. *Educating Nina* would not, after all,
be an Aunt Peg movie; it would star a younger woman. Juliet had
had the story line in mind for some time: A young graduate student
decides to write her masters thesis on real people's sexual fantasies,
offering to act out the fantasies and videotape them for the contri-
butors.

The movie would need investors, and Juliet set about rounding
these up. She consulted one of the porn film producers she felt she
could trust; he gave her a referral to a professional investor, and
coached her on the art of sucking up to such people. Unfortunately,
he did not realize that such men were not, at that time, accustomed
to dealing with women in business, and that his approach would not
work for Juliet. Juliet tried to follow his instructions: take the potential investor out to dinner at a nice restaurant, explain your project
and why you think it will be a success, and be sure to bring along a
copy of your limited partnership agreement, all in order and ready to
sign. Also, arrange for a young whore to join you for an after-dinner
drink; he can then take her back to his room when the deal has been
signed (a sort of signing bonus).

The evening, alas, turned out to be a complete fiasco, largely
because of several unforeseen glitches, but even without these it
would probably not have been a success. "Mr. A" was not used to
having women—even older ones—wine and dine him; he knew
nothing about the film business, erotic or otherwise; he thought porn
films were stupid and boring; he hated French cuisine and preferred

McDonalds; he had been in business meetings all day and was looking forward to an early bedtime; he had no interest in the young
whore; etc., etc.

Almost nothing went as planned, either. Juliet decided to take
BART over to the city because of inclement weather. She stopped by
the photocopy shop to copy the partnership agreement on the way,
but found it closed, so that she had to make do with her original.
Then the train was late, causing her to miss her connection to the
next train, and she could not call Mr. A to inform him because the
only pay phone at the BART station was out of order (this was long
before the days of cell phones). Juliet fumed in frustration as she
waited for the next connecting train, freezing in her silk dress and
high heels as the wind-driven rain whipped across the platform. She
arrived at the hotel forty-five minutes late, and they consequently
had to wait over an hour for a table at the restaurant. Mr. A had
virtually nothing to say during their late dinner, not asking any
questions about her project. "I don't ask questions, but I never make
a bad decision," he informed her.

Needless to say, he did not turn out to be an investor, despite the
$650 [$1,550] Juliet had spent on the evening. The money for the
movie ended up coming mostly in bits and pieces, from friends,
colleagues, and fans. The baseball team that she felt she had vicariously fucked in Seattle came up with a few thousand dollars, as did
Nike, in return for product placement in one of the fantasy scenarios.

Then, of course, the movie needed a star. None of her erstwhile
co-stars suited her needs. She advertised, but after a couple of
months had not yet found one to her liking. Then, while grocery
shopping one day at the Berkeley Bowl, she met a young man who
recognized her. He told her his girlfriend had a lifelong dream of
being a porn star. Juliet gave him her card. She was used to such
stories; they usually turned out to be the boyfriends' wet dreams.

But twenty-four-year-old Mitzi Landis was for real. A nursing
student at San Francisco State, she was planning to become a mid-
wife, but had fantasized about getting into porn since she was in her
teens. In fact, she was working her way through school as a stripper
at the O'Farrell Theatre. When her boyfriend returned from grocery
shopping with Juliet's card, Mitzi had him take some erotic photos of
her, and she mailed them to Juliet with a cover letter. Four days later,

she was walking up the steps of the Richmond Boulevard house Juliet shared with her three roommates, for an interview.

The two hit it off immediately. Juliet was impressed with Mitzi's intelligence, her work ethic and lack of any substance abuse issues—virtues not always easy to find among porn actors. Juliet and Mitzi spent several days going over the script, with Juliet coaching; she had very exact ideas about how lines should be delivered, and what poses and facial expressions Mitzi should use. Before long, she brought in the other actors: Karen Summer, Mike Horner, Billy Dee, Lili Marlene, Nick Niter, Dan T. Mann, and Aaron Stuart. and they did some brief rehearsals. Juliet paid the major actors by the hour, just as she had been paid as an actress herself: $500 [$1,150] per twelve-hour day with $41.50 [$95] per hour overtime. Ironically, considering Juliet's recriminations against the industry, she did not offer any royalties to the actors, although admittedly, tracking the sales and calculating payments would have been a monumentally complex undertaking.

Juliet rented space in Bob Vosse's San Francisco studio, Vosse-land; the few outdoor scenes were shot separately. They started filming as soon as Juliet could coordinate everyone's schedules, in early April 1984, just a few weeks after her first meeting with Mitzi. Technical crew were fairly minimal: a cameraman, a monitor, a few lighting technicians, a production assistant, a gofer. Juliet assisted with makeup for those who needed it, and helped track down costumes. For sets they used what was available at the studio.

It was an intense long weekend of filming. Everything had to be done in these few short days; studio time was expensive.

But the product was well worth the effort. *Educating Nina* was ground-breaking—more true-to-life and complex than what Juliet termed the "jackhammer" approach of the male-directed films of the time, with more focus on women's needs, while still appealing to men.

Indeed, *Educating Nina* was clearly designed to cater more to a couples audience than to a male-only one. While the mandatory "money" (cum) shots were included to satisfy the male need for orgasm verification, the scenarios themselves were staged to appeal more to women. Entire sex scenes were acted out, from proposition and seduction all the way through to after-sex talk and cuddling, and the pacing was slower and more measured than in the standard porn films of the time, which tended to show only the hard-core sex acts and to focus on male virility. There were many more facial shots, more realistic dialog and banter among the actors, plentiful clitoral stimulation and female orgasms, and more female-only genital shots (no cock involved).

Under Juliet's direction, the young actors performed with a refreshing genuineness. Billy Dee, Juliet's old fuck buddy from 1978, delivered a stunning performance as a male stripper, topped with a short dance routine and torrid coupling with Nina (Mitzi); both were skilled in the art of seductive moves. Lili and Karen played their assertive-women roles convincingly, without being domineering. In fact, there was no suggestion of exploitation in any of the scenes; no one needed to prove themselves by over-powering or manipulating anyone else. The tiresome "no, but I really mean yes" routine—so common in straight-male-oriented porn films—was completely absent from the script.

Juliet's influence is pervasive in the film, and obvious to anyone who knows her background and approach. The first scenario, for example, involves a maid (Karen Summer, dressed in a costume identical to the one Juliet wore in *Pretty Peaches*) who jumps up on the bed and starts eating Nina Hartley's pussy while the husband (Aaron Stuart) looks on. There are plentiful examples of women taking initiative, including asking for what they want (even requesting at times—perish the thought!—that the man slow down) or directly propositioning the man, as in the locker-room scene with Karen Summer and Dan T. Mann.

Not that the men's needs are neglected. They get plenty of female attention, and Juliet clearly encouraged the women to praise the males' bodies and performances. Juliet herself, in the one scene she participates in—the phone-sex customer's fantasy—freely plays out the role she loved best: enjoying herself immensely while being sure to include her fellow participants. After engaging with Lili, giving and receiving pleasure as the customer (Dan) watches, Juliet literally reaches out to him with her free hand, fondling his inner thigh even though she cannot reach his cock, inviting him to join in. And when she gets the opportunity to suck his cock, she raves about how good it tastes.

The film included a sex-education slant, too. The manual and oral stimulation techniques performed on the female actors—filmed in close-up detail—could serve as good demonstrations for any straight man who cares to pay attention. And the film ends with Nina and her friends sitting together and talking about what they learned about themselves and their sexuality from their participation in the fantasy scenarios.

This film was, indeed, the fulfillment of Juliet's dream. A real, true-to-life story line, respectful treatment of intimacy, genuine dialog, explicit but not exploitative sex, and a demonstration of how both women and men can freely engage in mutual pleasure. While not a masterpiece, it was certainly a promising beginning to what Juliet hoped would be a long career in producing erotic films. With the money she hoped to earn from it, she could go on to produce better and more elaborate films, bringing her message of true sexual liberation to a wide audience and making a name for herself as a writer and director.

The most time-consuming work, of course, was the editing, after the filming was done. Juliet did almost all this work herself, renting editing equipment from Bob Vosse. It was late summer before the finished product was ready.

The release party was a hit. Held at Juliet's Oakland house, it was attended by the investors, the cast, the crew, and many of Juliet's old friends in the business. The *Educating Nina* video was playing continuously on a big-screen TV in the living room, food and drink were in abundance, and Juliet looked stunning in a long white high-bodiced dress, her hair done up in a Grecian style. She was reminded of her high-school performance as queen at the Latin banquet, and realized how far she had come toward realizing her teenage dreams of becoming an artist, an actress and a successful business person. And although the party was costing her a pretty penny, it was money well spent, she felt—unlike the disastrous courting of potential investor "Mr. A" the previous October.

The only minor glitch was that Mitzi, while attempting to negotiate her way through the crowded living room, accidentally backed into Juliet, causing her to spill red wine all down the front of her

lovely white dress. Mitzi truly appreciated Juliet's graciousness over the matter, as Juliet assured her that it was just one of those things that can happen to anyone, and excused herself to go change. Unbelievably, the same mishap occurred again an hour or so later, when everyone was getting tired and tipsy; Juliet was equally gracious.

This minor misfortune, though, was not enough to throw cold water on the day; Juliet felt that the project and the party had both been a wonderful success, and fell into bed that night feeling more at peace than she had in many years.

Not that the work on *Educating Nina* was over. The video still needed to be distributed and sold before she and her investors would recoup their money and turn a profit. After seeking advice from several of her contacts in the business, she selected Atom Home Video, owned by Larry Carr (no relation) as distributor; she signed a contract with him in the fall of 1984.

Once her work on the movie was finished, Juliet continued in her various jobs—assistant to Paul Johnson, phone sex, live stage shows, and occasional escort work. And acting. The movies she performed in during 1984 and 1985 included *Dirty Pictures, Physical 2, With Love Annette,* and *San Fernando Valley Girls.*

By late 1984, *Educating Nina* was available in adult stores, and Juliet was expecting some income from the video. Yet no checks showed up in the mail, and Larry Carr was not returning her phone calls. When she did chance to get hold of him directly, he gave her the run-around, explaining that he still had not recouped his own reproduction costs. By January 1985, though, it was clear that Larry had essentially stolen the movie.

Juliet's first reaction was disbelief, her second, heartbreak. *Educating Nina* was an expression of who she was; it was her coming-out party as a director. To have it ripped away from her felt like having her heart torn out and trampled on. She alternated between pain and numbness.

And, still, she dared to hope. Surely there was something she could do. After all, stealing was illegal. She again consulted her contacts in the business—other directors and producers. Only then did she realize that they did not really have her back. None of her successful male colleagues was going to come to her aid in any way. She had done the unthinkable: intrude into their territory. She was not going to be accepted as one of them, no matter how professional she was or what she produced. Financial success in this industry depended, most of all, on having enough clout to strong-arm people, and that required being connected to the insiders who controlled the business. Up-starts need not apply.

Juliet began to feel the ground giving way under her feet. She had felt, as early as 1979, that being a porn star was only the means to something more lucrative, more fulfilling, and she thought she had found that something in directing and producing her own film. To find this road now blocked left her bereft of a future and almost in shock.

She engaged a lawyer, even though she knew her chances were slim. Although the Mitchell Brothers had established, in their 1979 lawsuit, that pornography was copyrightable, the courts still did not look kindly on the art form. This was still the case even as late as 2000, when another director, Andrew Blake, was cheated in a situation similar to Juliet's, winning his case but being awarded only one dollar in damages.

Juliet floundered in heartbreak, disbelief, and confusion. While she clung to the hope of recouping some of her losses through the courts, it would be a long time before that happened, if it ever did. Meantime, she had to support herself, and to find another direction for the rest of her life. Her future as a writer, director and producer was obviously dead. And she was aging, now forty-six.

She could continue her other work in the sex business, of course. (Contrary to popular perception, there is actually a substantial demand for older women—in the more private venues of prostitution and phone sex, if not in the more public ones such as stripping and films.) But the porn scene had a bitter taste now. Juliet felt humiliated and abandoned by the subculture that had brought her so much adulation.

This was one of those times in Juliet's life, as in 1976 when she was preparing to leave Finland, when she railed against the necessity of supporting herself financially. If only she could be independently wealthy, or find a man to support her, she would not be faced with this pressure and could devote her life to art, as she was surely born to do. Life was monumentally unfair.

One night in February, as she struggled with insomnia, she had another of her epiphanies. She suddenly realized how burned out she was on the entire porn industry, how much of a drain it had been on her, even while she reveled in its intensity. She needed to leave the business, and find some other way to support herself while she waited for a sign from God about what she was to do with the rest of her life. She knew she had gifts to offer, but the specific means by which she was to offer them were unclear right now. Like all great seers, she would retreat from the world and devote herself to self-examination and spirituality. That process would surely lead her to an answer.

The next day, Juliet went to Tilden Park in the Oakland hills and performed a ritual to mark her decision. Taking along a small shovel and a copy of the movie poster from *Aunt Peg Goes Hollywood*, she dug a shallow hole, tore up the poster into small pieces and buried it, affirming her resolve with a declaration: "I now release my Juliet Anderson persona and open myself to a new way of life." She would go back to using her birth name, Judith Carr.

But how, specifically, would she support herself? The only other professional work she had done was journalism. But she had no recent experience, and no connections in that business, and competition was fierce. Clerical work was a possibility, but she hated fixed hours and tedium, and the pay would be too low to meet her needs. Besides, working at a regular job would require staying in the city, with its stresses and constant reminders of pain and humiliation. She wanted to get away, to regain her balance. Her first choice would have been to "run away to a foreign country" again, but there was no sugar daddy now to whisk her away, no man whose life she could piggyback on. Low on resources—economic, emotional and social— she had to escape on the cheap.

The next logical place to turn was rural California. She had, after all, always loved being in the country; it was what she missed most about Finland. She remembered, now, her vow on returning from the visit to Greece in 1978: "I must move to the country, have a garden, a few animals, a fireplace, a lover or two. I must now pursue whatever means necessary to reach that goal—soon." Why had she let almost seven years slip away?

Well, the nearest rural area where she might actually find work was in the Sierra foothills. She had often stopped in Placerville on her ski trips to Lake Tahoe, and knew that the town was a retreat for the well-to-do. She might even work in one of the bed and breakfast inns there, or round up some house-cleaning jobs. She looked in the want ads in the *Sacramento Bee*, and found out that Blair House bed and breakfast would be needing a new housekeeper in June. Juliet went for an interview and immediately hit it off with the owner, Patsy Thompson, who agreed to hire her in return for room and breakfast, along with a supplemental wage of $3.35 [$7.50] per hour; she would have to get her other meals for herself, but could use the house kitchen, including the refrigerator. Juliet assured Patsy that she expected the arrangement to last only a few months, until she could find more permanent employment; she was not sure she really wanted to settle in Placerville, but was looking around for a new home and direction in life. She did not reveal to Patsy what kind of work she was retreating from. It was not uncommon, after all, for middle-aged middle-class professionals to get burned out on city life and start seeking more creative venues.

Juliet was also able to line up some housekeeping and yard work at a small farm near Placerville, albeit at a piddling wage—$4.50 [$10] an hour. Still, it was a start, and would supplement the bed-and-breakfast arrangement.

The employment question at least partially settled, Juliet went about tying up her loose ends in Oakland. She continued doing phone sex and stage shows when she could, and working for Paul Johnson. It was enough to get by on. She sorted through her belongings, and held a garage sale in March to sell off much—although not all—of her sex-work attire and accessories. In early June she made a sort of trial run up to the Sierra foothills, attending a Women's Alliance Camp in Nevada City, a much more isolated and rural town than Placerville. She loved the peace, quiet and simplicity of the small-town atmosphere.

The crash from *Educating Nina* had been intense, a fitting end to an intense way of life. Now she was coasting down the end phase of that fall, letting go of one thing after another—her film-star life, her sex-worker social circle, the house on Richmond Boulevard, her sexy wardrobe, city life with all of its cultural opportunities but also its stresses. And most of all, she was letting go of a part of her very identity. What would be left?

17
Getting Away

Juliet was tired. Tired of filming. Tired of traveling. Tired of publicity. Tired of getting herself psyched up only to be put down. Tired of hassling with incompetent, disrespectful, or just plain clueless people. Tired of being lonely. Tired of the city. Tired, most of all, of being Juliet Anderson, the porn star, the golden goddess, the fun-loving cut-up.

It was time to withdraw—from the sex business, from the city, from the social circle she had been a part of for seven years. Time to retreat from the hurry and stress, and get away to the countryside, to quiet, to nature. Time, she hoped, to find a new path in life.

It was Sunday, the 30th of June, 1985, and although she had no hard and fast deadline, Juliet wanted to get on the road in time to arrive in Placerville before dark. She had been sorting, packing up, and storing her stuff for the past several weeks, but was still left with those numerous last-minute trivial tasks and decisions that always characterize a move—what to do with the cleaning supplies, whether to take the vase of dried flowers on the dresser, what items to put loose in the car for the trip up to the mountains. "Running on adrenalin, exhausted, sad, hurting, but pushing to get out of Oakland by 5 p.m."

Her cat Snuggles, by contrast, was calm, watching quietly from her perch on the windowsill, confident that her mistress would need her, as she always did, as soon as she finished her frenetic chasing around. And at last it *was* time: Juliet picked up Snuggles, put her into the carrier and set it on the front passenger seat of the car. Then she settled herself into the driver's seat, started the engine, and pulled out into the late afternoon traffic, headed for the mountains.

Not that everything was settled. Certainly not Juliet's emotions. She was still reeling from feelings of betrayal and loss. Most of the people she had invited to her March going-away party had been no-shows; only three women had come, all of them strippers she knew only casually. After they left, having bought very few of the sale items, Juliet had sat sobbing on the dining-room floor, blindly

234

throwing dishes, vases, candlesticks and stage memorabilia—symbols of her life as Juliet Anderson—into boxes to be taken to Goodwill. Most of the lovingly prepared, expensive food had gone to waste as well. Juliet had stumbled numbly through the following two months, wrapping up loose ends, trying to focus on the future but mostly floundering in confusion. And now, to top it all off, she could not find the key to the trunk where she had packed most of her clothes and the other belongings she was taking with her.

She was in physical pain, too; her back hurt so much she couldn't afford to think about it; she had to drive. And she still had freeway traffic to get through, on her way out of the Bay Area, through the valley and past Sacramento, before she could turn off onto U.S. Highway 50, and begin to ascend into the rolling hills carpeted with wild oat grass, golden in midsummer, dotted here and there with the rich dark green leaves and deep reddish brown bark of manzanita, or with majestic live oak trees, some of their crazily twisted branches reaching toward the sky and others sweeping down to the ground. She summoned up her last bit of energy, urging the car on toward the snow-capped mountains reflecting the late afternoon sunlight, toward, hopefully, peace and quiet, a new home—and a new identity, whatever that might turn out to be.

Juliet had chosen Placerville for her escape from urban life in the same way she made most of her decisions: impulsively, with little thought to the long-term ramifications. Far from being the quiet, rural community Juliet envisioned, Placerville sits directly on Route 50, the main highway from Sacramento to Lake Tahoe. Main Street roughly parallels the busy highway, two short blocks away, with only narrow Placer Creek as a buffer. Now little more than a gateway community, Placerville was settled during the California Gold Rush; it was a stopover along the way to the gold country, a wintering place for prospective miners, chosen for its convenience and relatively mild climate. It sits in the ravine created by the creek, sheltered from the worst of the winter storms. In its heyday, of course, it was a wild place—it still proudly advertises its nickname, Hangtown—but it is now the seat of aptly named El Dorado County. And, like innumerable small Western towns, it has morphed into a tourist stop, the long-time locals mixing uneasily with the newly escaped urbanites.

Downtown Placerville. Left: the Bell Tower; Right: Main Street, looking east.
Photos by Marian Rhys.

The residential areas branch off Main Street, with its many restored old buildings, and climb into the rapidly rising hills, with no
insulation from traffic noise. While commerce is dominated by restaurants and boutiques, more practical businesses also thrive, serving
the day-to-day needs of the residents. Placerville Hardware claims to
be the oldest hardware store west of the Rockies (it retains its old
wooden floors). Less than fifty feet from its front door looms the old
Bell Tower, originally erected as a fire alarm. As the county seat,
Placerville also hosts a few government buildings—courthouse,
sheriff's office, and of course City Hall—as well as a law library.

The James Blair House, where Juliet was to live, was an imposing, three-story gingerbread-trimmed Victorian built into one of
the hills, facing west, enclosed by the stereotypical white picket
fence, brick steps leading up through an archway to the front veranda. Juliet's room was a converted sun porch on the south side of
the house, with windows reaching two-thirds of the way down from
the ceiling. While a mixture of evergreen and deciduous trees sheltered much of the building, the southwestern exposure was open,
and a few lingering rays of early evening sunlight warmed the hard-

wood floor and Juliet's white-painted iron bed made up with tulip-patterned sheets.

The James Blair House. Juliet's room was on the right, hidden by trees here. Photo by Marian Rhys.

Chris, Bob and Monica awaited her, to help her unload the car and begin to get settled in her new place. Their presence helped ground her, and she was glad she had asked them to meet her there.

The Pettits had taken a guest room. After unloading the car, traipsing up and down the slope with box after box (and the inaccessible trunk), and getting Snuggles settled in the sun room, everyone showered and went out for dinner at one of the quaint touristy restaurants that lined Placerville's Main Street. Juliet fell into bed that night, exhausted but relieved, with her fourteen-year-old niece Monica by her side and Snuggles purring between them.

Juliet had placed the bed facing south, and had opened the curtains on this first night, so that light from the almost-full moon streamed onto her bed. "[I can] sleep in beams of moonlight ... Aradia, Daughter of the Moon, I am here and you are full[23] and

---

[23] Although Juliet often wrote in her journal about the full moon, it is obvious that her perception of the full moon was any phase between gibbous and disseminating. She did not appear to understand that there was actually an event, the full moon, that occurred only one night a month.

bright on my left as the brilliant pink and purple sky, passionate and fiery, dies on my right. A remarkable omen to herald a new beginning." (Actually, since the hill behind and to the east of the house blocked the rising moon until about eleven p.m.—well past sunset even at the summer solstice—this ode was probably more fantasy than reality.) The little sun porch reminded her of her room in the Greek villa by the Mediterranean Sea, another romantic interval in her life, now long gone.

Juliet awoke early, as she always did unless recovering from late hours, and stepped out of bed onto the small carpet woven into the likeness of a cat. Indirect light from the rising sun illuminated the clump of trees just southeast of her room. In the early morning, before the incessant traffic noise ratcheted up, this new home felt peaceful and sheltered compared to the hectic Oakland house, as if she were just on a short vacation to the mountains, rather than living here. "I don't have to lock my door, wear makeup, wake up to an alarm, hide my purse... what freedom." The smells of summer in the mountains—tree resin, wildflowers, the good California dirt— reminded her of the cabin in Wrightwood when she was a child. She also loved being surrounded by elegant furnishings, in a house that still exuded the aristocratic ambiance of its original inhabitants.

After breakfast with her family and the other guests, Juliet and the Pettits piled into the car for a short jaunt out to the nearby farm where Juliet would be cleaning and doing light yard work on weekends. Even her interactions with Chris were calm; Juliet felt that her sister was mellowing out in middle age, although more likely it was Juliet herself who was changing.

The Pettits left that day, and Juliet tried to settle into her new life. The loss of the key to the trunk did not prey on her so much now; she took it in stride. "I can learn a lot from Snuggles; she is secure and calm, sits like a sphinx." Juliet unpacked as much as she could and made her new little porch room into a home.

Her job at Blair House included cleaning and other housework, helping with breakfast, and occasionally serving as hostess when owners Patsy and Richard were away. She was finding her new mundane identity a great relief after the pressure and intensity of the past seven years. "I feel not in the least like a film star. I get grubby, wear yesteryear's shorts, T-shirts and Birkenstocks. Window washing and watering is like a Zen meditation," Juliet noted—although she still wore makeup for social occasions. On the Fourth of July, the bed and breakfast was full for the holiday, and Juliet loved chatting with the guests. She was a natural here, her ebullient personality and wide-ranging interests enlivening the conversations. Patsy made homemade boysenberry ice cream —a novel treat for Juliet, who sat on the patio with goo all over her face and hands and arms, licking the leavings out of the churn.

Street leading from Blair House to Placerville's Main Street, only about a block from this location. Photo by Marian Rhys.

The price of these indulgences was a lot of hard physical labor. Sometimes Juliet was reminded of the ordeal of being a Japanese housewife so long ago. "Up at 5:30 to fix breakfast for river rafters at 7. Then cleaned rooms, went to the farm and worked 5 hours. Did three loads of laundry, hung them on the line, took them in and folded them, mopped the kitchen floor, fixed up three rooms and two baths, vacuumed, dusted, and watered plants." Only now she was forty-seven instead of twenty-two. And the heat was fierce, even in Placerville; the mercury often pushed past a hundred degrees and physical work became impossible as the day progressed. Juliet had to finish her work in the mornings, napping or reading on these hot summer afternoons.

In addition to the hot-weather stress, life in Placerville was not quite as idyllic as her full-moon rhapsodies had made it out to be. It was definitely a town—more a miniature urban center plunked down in the country than a truly rural area. Light pollution outshone the bright moonlight she loved. Traffic noise from Highway 50 was constant during the day, as Blair House sat only about a block south of Main Street. A dog across the street barked incessantly; Juliet fantasized about poisoning it. The high-pitched whine of neighbors' power tools often interrupted the placid summer afternoons. "Oh, to be really in the country!" Sometimes she escaped to the nearby mountains, but even in these more remote areas there were signs of human stupidity, like the litter she found along the banks of the American River.

Juliet had not completely cut her ties to the Bay Area; she made frequent trips back there for the first several months, retrieving some of her possessions from the Oakland house, picking up a little extra money with a few tricks here and there, from faithful old clients, and often staying overnight with various friends from the days. Some of these women were heavy into the S & M scene, and their apartments were decorated with the expected trappings: handcuffs, dildo harnesses, black leather collars studded with steel spikes, cages and nets, whips and riding crops, as well as closets filled with black leather halter tops, corsets, tight shorts, boots with spike heels, chaps, etc. These were familiar to Juliet, but triggered no particular response in her now: "Strange how these women still figure in my life when I don't have any interest in that game." And although visiting some of her old haunts brought up memories, the nostalgia was becoming less gut-wrenching; her feelings were softening as time went on.

In mid-July, Juliet finally found the lost trunk key, back at the Oakland house. To celebrate this accomplishment, as well as her birthday, she indulged herself by buying $100 [$220] worth of new summer clothes, and then made up another one of her lists of wants (good health, living in the quiet countryside, regular skin contact, good food, good books, good music, time to write, a few real friends, intimate partner, financial security, and making "a beautiful, intimate, enduring erotic film") and don't-wants (fame, having to dress up, having to associate with low-consciousness people, having to work at a job I hate, having to live up to expectations, having a predictable life).

While at first the effort of adjusting to a new environment was a full-time job, she soon had enough free time and energy to become aware of an empty space in her life: her all-important need for intimate social connections was going unmet. "There isn't a single person I can think of I want to visit me. So many people I know are now part of my past. It makes me sad, but it is reality. I am moving on and they aren't... or if they are, it's on different paths." Even Mirja was not a support; Juliet felt alienated from her old friend's current pursuit of material success as a real estate agent. Carolyn Elderberry came closest to being an intimate friend, but Carolyn was going through a messy breakup with Paul Johnson, who would "always be compulsive, needy and childish."

Yet, little by little, Juliet was beginning to build a new life for herself in Placerville, settling into new routines, making new acquaintances, and becoming a member of the community. For while the physical environment of Placerville was primarily suburban, its social environment was definitely small town, and any newcomer had to carve out a place for herself in that environment. At the El Dorado County Fair Juliet served coffee at the baked goods judging stand, dressed up in turn-of-the-century finery from Blair House. "So feminine, lovely, [and] fragile in my long white lace-trimmed dress with pink-embroidered skirt and sash, pink full-brimmed hat with flowers and black veil. Mrs. James Blair wore these in the late 1800s. I felt comfortable and accepted... There is so much artistic skill in this area. No wonder the Goddess steered me here." Juliet was finally finding women friends, some of whom, like herself, had left professional careers to support themselves with mundane work. She enjoyed socializing with these women, going to movies, visiting each other's homes, sharing ice cream sundaes at the cute downtown eateries. She felt like a teenager out with her girlfriends, a part of life she had missed because of her childhood illnesses.

Perhaps that resurrection of her inner teenager helped her connect better with her niece Monica, now fourteen, who had come up to spend a few days with Juliet in August, before school started. Deep into the emotional upheaval that accompanies adolescence, Monica was often in pain over her relationship with her father; they simply had incompatible personalities, and their conflicts often drove Monica to tears. After listening to Monica's litany of complaints, Juliet, in one of her rare moments of detached insight, advised her niece, "You don't have to like your father. Maybe you never will. But you can love him just the same." Monica was caught up short; it had never occurred to her to separate the two emotions. (In fact, it never occurs to most people.) It was the best advice her Aunt Judy ever gave her. Ironically, it was the same piece of advice that Monica would learn to apply to Juliet herself, years later.

Other social events in Juliet's life were less satisfying. A rafting trip with Paul and Carolyn turned into what would be one of a number of disastrous Sierra Nevada outings. Paul overslept, and Juliet and Carolyn had to wait three and a half hours at the crowded, noisy raft rental shop until he showed up; then he and Carolyn spent a good part of the trip screaming at each other, until even Juliet finally exploded, despite her attempt to remain aloof from the conflict. Not to mention the other rafters, "groups of beer-drinking, can-tossing pigs." So much for the great outdoors.

Physical activity, though, was a must. Whatever her ultimate relationship to sex work, Juliet lived in her body. She always had, and she always would. Yet that body was clearly aging now. As this fact took hold in her consciousness, she embarked on a wide-ranging program of exercise and health care. Whenever she had time and the weather permitted, she took early morning walks, usually with Snuggles. She supplemented her yoga workouts with Chinese wand exercises, and added regular acupuncture, chiropractic and massage treatments.

As for that other major area of life, eating, Juliet continued the pattern she had set during her sex-work days, vowing to stick to a healthful, mainly vegetarian diet, but frequently falling off the wagon, bingeing (she often comforted herself, or celebrated some accomplishment, by consuming a full pint of Häagen Dazs ice cream in one sitting) and then purging with fruit-juice-and-water fasts. Hence she managed to maintain her slender build, if not the health of her digestive system.

In mid-August Juliet was hit with a series of physical stresses. The day before she embarked on one of her fasts, she fell down a short flight of concrete steps and injured her leg. Then, a few days later, on another rafting trip (sans Paul and Carolyn), she fell out of the raft as it was zooming backwards over a particularly rough rapid, badly bruising the same leg again. Weakened both by these injuries and by lack of food, she found her rigorous physical chores even more of an ordeal than usual. The pain reached its zenith after a day of washing windows in the rain at the farm. She came home and collapsed, sleeping until noon the next day, but finally woke up pain-free and decided to break her fast with a hearty breakfast and strong hot coffee.

Underneath all of her new hopes, plans, and social life, there were times when Juliet was seized by a cold panic, feeling as ungrounded as she had in those first few days after the *Pretty Peaches* filming but without the euphoria. "For the first six months in Placerville, every night I went to sleep certain that I wouldn't be alive the next morning," she wrote to a friend several years later. Major life changes were getting more difficult as she grew older, draining her emotional energy more than inspiring her. It was going to take time, this transition from intensity to ordinariness.

Finances were an ongoing issue, as they had been for most of her adult life, at least when she did not have a man supporting her. She had originally planned to stay only two months at Blair House, but she was beginning to think of Placerville as a new permanent home. But how to swing that financially? She had a little less than $3,800 [$8,400] in savings, and while her Blair House job included free housing and breakfast, her additional income amounted to only about $200 [$445] a month. She knew she could get some additional house cleaning work at $10 [$22] per hour, but when would she find time? Clearly, she needed to phase out the work at the farm, for a start. She made a pitch to Patsy and Richard to see if they had more work for her, at an hourly wage, but they did not. After all, managing the bed and breakfast was their vocation.

There seemed to be nowhere she could turn. "[T]his time there is no one from whom I can borrow money," she wrote to her parents in October (perhaps hoping they would jump in and offer). "It is a very frightening and humiliating situation." Evidently, she did not consider borrowing money itself to be humiliating.

Juliet was still pursuing legal action against Larry Carr and Atom Home Video, hoping to collect at least some of the royalty money from *Educating Nina*, but that was a very iffy proposition. Later, she would realize that her lawyers had no more integrity than Larry. She did manage to land a contract to write a promotional brochure on Gold Country bed and breakfast inns for the El Dorado County Tourist Board, bringing in $1,000 [$2,200], which helped for a short time. She also procured a home-care job, taking care of 79-year-old Harry ("a special friend... the grandfather I never had"), cooking and cleaning for him. She would go over once or twice a week, prepare several meals and leave them in the freezer for him to re-heat later. Opportunely, her chiropractor ended up being a new source of income for her; she did grocery shopping and cooking for her and her husband, first as trade and then as a regular $50 [$110]-a-week job. Later, she started doing after-school day care three days a week for their daughter Robyn, a "bright and psychically gifted child."

Juliet performing her employment activities: left, housekeeping; right: staging a phone-sex call for the camera. Photos: Carr/Pettit family collection.

And she went back to work for the phone-sex company, doing calls after hours in her small porch room, which was isolated enough from the main house to afford the necessary privacy. Like any highly intelligent, observant phone-sex operator, Juliet took the work very seriously, understanding that with many clients it was more counseling than sex work. Yet, on another level she was less than professional, clearly violating the terms of agreement with the phone-sex company, as she had direct contact with several of the regular clients —a major no-no for any employee who works through an agency. She sold pornographic photos of herself (new ones she had taken by Paul Johnson or other photographers she knew) to many of her regulars, and, as time went on, she even met some of them in person. Her most dedicated clients tended to be submissives and cross-dressers, always the mainstay of the phone-sex business. The people with secrets.

In July, she got an offer for a modeling job with Cabriolet Limousines, in Sacramento, with a ten-percent commission for any other model she could bring in. After several months of frustrating miscommunications, though, this offer turned out to be a fraud. The manager, Buddy Griffin, was a con artist and the modeling job was only a cover for meeting X-rated actresses. Juliet's friend Crystal said he'd been making obscene phone calls to her, and had requested a nude photo of another woman who had signed up to model. Although such incidents were not a total surprise to Juliet, it was nevertheless a disappointment, as she was still living on a shoestring, even with all of the part-time work she had cobbled together.

Sun-Dried Laundry

Sweet-smelling sheets flapping against my legs,
spilling over my tanned arms, gathering in the billows
of cotton clouds strung across the yard, a brown
checkered pioneer sunbonnet protecting my fair
complexion from the ruthless rays of the hot El Dorado
sun.

Sniffing panties, inhaling socks, perverted pleasures of
a line-dry laundry freak. Fluffy towels; I inhale their
fragrance before stacking them in the linen closet.

In the cool guest rooms I smooth the still-warm sheets
on the heirloom canopied bed, wondering what erotic
fantasies will be acted out tonight.

-- Juliet Carr

And, despite her withdrawal from the film business, Juliet tried to continue her stage shows, traveling to New York for this purpose in early January 1986. Jumping back into the sleazy sex world was a shock. She stayed with Spider, a drug addict and compulsive hoarder, whose apartment was chaotic and dirty, with Spider's fellow addicts drifting in and out at all hours of the day and night, indulging in drugs and indiscriminate sex. Juliet only kept her sanity by meditating every morning. And this attempt to restart her sex performance work ultimately fizzled. Her Helen the Housewife routine

bombed, and the follow-up tour she had hoped for fell through, for
reasons she did not elaborate upon in her writings. She did do a
photo shoot for *High Society*, but at below-market rates, as they were
"no pink" (no pussy) shots.

Through all these physical and financial ordeals, though, Juliet's
libido was not slumbering. One morning before she was even fully
awake, lying in her bed and dreamily watching the dawn light
creeping across the lawn, she could hear the handsome young guest,
Rich, from Wyoming, showering in the bathroom. Just imagining
him nude, drying himself after his shower, got her hot. "Oh how I
miss a nice, smooth-skinned tender man in my bed!"

She got a small taste of sensuality when a male friend from her
sex-work days, Bob Grundy, stopped by for a visit during one of
Patsy and Richard's vacations. He and Juliet spent the night in one of
the empty rooms in the house, cuddling and stroking each other non-
sexually. The next day, after an elegant breakfast and some cooperative housekeeping chores, they spent several hours editing his
collection of pornographic poems. This taste of sensuality only made
her hungry for more, though. "Oh, it's time for me to have a relationship." Actually, it wasn't, and, truth be told, it never really would be
time.

On a happier note, Juliet was also finding some getaways—quiet,
peaceful places where she could walk with Snuggles, or lie—sometimes naked—in the grass, listening to the wind and the birdsong,
letting the sunshine warm her body, feeling utterly safe. Apple Hill
and Empire State Park were two of her mountain-home sanctuaries.
Later, as she expanded her social circle, she would take up serious
hiking and begin to go on short backpacking trips into the Sierras
with some of her new acquaintances. She continued as well to make
regular trips to Wilbur Hot Springs, either to attend workshops there
or simply to relax for a few days.

Juliet also continued to visit Raamwood, her friend Shirley's farm
in Mendocino County. Returning from a short vacation there in early
May 1986, she wrote to her sister Chris:

> It was a working vacation, my hard labor for partial
> room and board... I pulled weeds from a steep hillside
> and raked and hauled it, cut back blackberry bushes
> [Himalayan blackberry, the invasive weed that plagues

> the entire west coast of the U.S.], ripped up tons of
> wild morning glories that were strangling [other]
> plants, prepared garden beds, transplanted veggies
> and groomed the burros. The earth is so clean up
> there, the air and water fresh... Shirley is a fabulous
> cook and pampered me with 3 great vegetarian meals
> a day, catering to my special dietary needs... I read,
> wrote, and had lovely candlelit conversations with
> Shirley before falling into a deep sleep (with her cats
> by my side).

Indeed, one of Juliet's dreams at this time was to make enough money to buy out the other remaining owners' shares of Raamwood and move there permanently—a dream that never came to fruition.

Gradually, Juliet was beginning to develop some emotional distance from her "high-society" life. The hours she spent in meditation and outdoors, in nature, were bringing her insights she had not been able to afford when she was immersed in the porn scene; she came to realize how much of an ego trip those seven years had been, that what had drawn her to and kept her in the business was her insatiable need for attention and adulation.

> The X biz was a crafty, passionate beast that seduced
> me with sex, power, fame and riches. It fed on my
> desire to be loved [and] admired and gave me a chance
> to indulge in exhibitionism and glamor. It almost stole
> my spirit, but I broke free. With this new insight it'll
> be fascinating to see how I write my memoirs. I was so
> 'pro-porno', an eloquent and convincing advocate.
> What will I say now? I'm certainly having to re-make
> my map!

She would spend the next five years answering that question: reassessing her attitudes, seeking a better place for herself in the world of sensuality, and threshing out what was real and genuine from what was merely self-aggrandizing. While she may have been done with the porn film industry, she was not done with sex work. Sex and sensuality—living in the body—were at the core of her being, and she had to find a way to take that gift out into the world again.

18

Some Mistakes Are Expensive

Ever since Juliet had visited her ex-husband Bob Watt in April 1975, on her vacation back to the States from Finland, she had kept a special place in her heart for him. And even though her short stay with him in October 1978 made her realize how poor a match he was for her, he was still her first serious love, someone with whom she had been intimate and whose life she had briefly shared. They kept in touch from time to time, and his mounting troubles still evoked her compassion.

At the time of Juliet's 1978 visit, Bob had recently split up from his second wife, Susan, who had a major alcohol abuse problem. He had retained their house in Westbury, where he lived with his then-twelve-year-old daughter Laura. After retiring from the navy in 1979, Bob held down a couple of restaurant-manager jobs and then started working at the post office—an easy job for a veteran to land, with the bonus civil service points given to vets.

He led a quiet life, working at his relatively mundane job, maintaining his house and grounds (he had always been an avid gardener), socializing with both men and women friends, and generally living a typical suburban lifestyle, although he evidently had at least a moderate substance abuse problem with both alcohol and cocaine.

While after two divorces Bob was not inclined to marry again, in 1980 he started keeping company with Joan Turk, whom he had met through her daughter, a young woman he knew at work. Joan had four adult children, two sons and two daughters, the younger of whom was the same age as Laura. Joan had led a somewhat tragic life, having had her eleven-year affair with a married cop recently ended by his untimely death from cancer.

About two years into Bob's and Joan's relationship, she started pushing for more security—in other words, marriage. Bob was up-front with her about his lack of interest in a third marriage and his inability to maintain a monogamous relationship. He wanted to continue his unencumbered lifestyle, keeping irregular hours and maintaining an independent social life. Although Joan claimed to be comfortable with this arrangement, in reality she had other ideas, probably thinking, as many women do in such circumstances, that she could bring him around. They were married in the spring of 1982, and Joan moved into Bob's house. Joan's youngest son Marc continued to live with them; he was just out of high school, holding down odd jobs here and there and still trying to figure out what to do with his life.

To Bob it was a useful arrangement. He had a regular sexual partner who helped pay the mortgage and who took care of the cooking and cleaning while he managed the minor house repairs and puttered in the garden. If marriage was required to keep Joan with him, it was a small price to pay. Or so it seemed.

By early 1982, Bob had taken up with another Judy, and he began spending more and more time with her and away from home. Judy was a widow with no interest in remarrying, and was much more suited to Bob's needs at the time. They had essentially a sexual friendship: going out, listening to music, making lazy love and sometimes traveling together. Joan seemed to accept the situation. In May of 1984, though, after Bob's return from a Florida vacation with Judy, Joan blew up at him. They had a fierce fight, and Bob effectively moved out and moved in with Judy. Still, the Westbury house belonged to him (although he had voluntarily given Joan a legal share in it), and it continued to be listed as his official residence. He stopped by almost daily, especially to care for his beloved orchids, which needed almost constant attention.

Bob and Joan began to talk of separating. Basically, Joan needed an affordable place to move to, and they needed to determine how to split up the credit-card debt. Bob managed to get a loan to pay off the bills, with about $5,000 [$11,450] left over to help Joan establish herself in a new place; she would be able to repay this advance out of her share of the house proceeds.

On Friday, July 27th, Bob went by the house and gave Joan $500 [$1,145] to pay some of the household bills. He picked up some of the remaining clothes he still kept there and left. When he returned on Saturday afternoon to water the plants, he and Joan got into a furious fight, outside the house and loud enough to be taken note of by their next-door neighbor. Early Sunday morning, July 29th, Bob made a trip to nearby Captree State Park, dug up two pine saplings, brought them back to his girlfriend Judy's residence and transplanted them in her back yard. Later, in the early evening, he went back to his house (Joan's residence) to pick up some more of his things, and made a quick phone call while he was there. Joan's son Marc and his seventeen-year-old girlfriend were in one of the bedrooms, but Bob did not interact with either of them, as he was in a hurry and it was clear they were preoccupied. Joan was at work; she had a swing-shift nursing job. Bob left her a note, suggesting some terms of a divorce settlement—including an offer to pay off the credit-card debt, and asking her to get moving on finding a new place to live so that he could return to living in the house (presumably with Judy) until it was sold. The note did not conclude on a friendly tone: he called her a cunt for giving away one of his prized plants, a staghorn fern. Bob left around 9:30 or ten p.m., inadvertently leaving a pack of cigarettes and his lighter in the livingroom, and returned to Judy's place. He and Judy retired about 11:30 p.m., so that he had only a few hours sleep before getting up at 2:30 Monday morning to go to his grave-yard-shift job at the post office. Judy drove him, and they stopped at Dunkin' Donuts on the way.

Joan's son Marc, spending his first night on a new graveyard-shift job as a gas-station attendant, called his mother at about one o'clock "to see how she was." This was rather strange behavior, but he may only have been lonely at his all-night job. Joan had not been home long, as she often stopped off for a drink on her way back. She may also have had a companion with her, as, despite her recrim-inations against Bob, it was not unusual for her to pick up a man at the bar. (As it turned out later, she was also having an affair herself.)

Around 1:45 on Monday morning, July 30th, Joan's next-door neighbor, Barbara Koch, was awakened by Joan's hair-raising screams. Mrs. Koch was too far away to make out any definite words or phrases, other than perhaps repeated calls of "Stop!" She called the police (the 911 system was not yet fully implemented) at 1:52 a.m. The screams stopped before the sirens started.

Officer J. Gibbons responded to the call, arriving at the totally dark house at 1:59 a.m. He knocked on the front door, but receiving no response, proceeded to the back yard, flashlight in hand. He heard footsteps running away but could see no one, although he shone his light over the yard and the back fence, in which there was a two-foot-wide opening. Mrs. Koch called out to him from next door, informing him that she was the one who had called the police. She said she would call the house number. Officer Gibbons could hear the phone ringing in the house as he approached it. Another police car arrived, with Officers Campo and Rochester. The three cops entered the house through the sliding glass door from the back patio, already open. (That the door had not been forced was not significant; it was Bob and Joan's habit never to lock any of the doors.) There were numerous large splotches of blood on the ground outside and on the floor and walls of the house. When they reached the living room they found Joan's body lying on the floor in front of the fireplace, face down, broken and bloody. She had been stabbed, strangled and severely beaten with the fireplace poker and shovel, and had died from multiple skull fractures.

There had obviously been a physical struggle in the room: there was furniture damage, and a reel-to-reel tape recorder had been thrown or dragged down onto the floor. An opened pack of cigarettes and a lighter also lay on the floor nearby. Both belonged to Bob.

A small awl was found lying in a neighboring yard; it had evidently been used to punch Joan repeatedly, as she had numerous shallow (quarter-inch) stab wounds. No fingerprints were found on the awl, whose blade had also been wiped clean of blood, although some of Joan's blood was found on the handle. The murder weapons —the fireplace poker and shovel—likewise held no fingerprints. In fact, the only fingerprints the police found at the scene were on the telephone, and these belonged to Joan's son Marc.

Nevertheless, Bob was an immediate suspect, and the police came by the post office at about 5:15 a.m. to pick him up for questioning. Bob, along with four or five of his co-workers, was taking a break, lying on the loading dock, smoking. Two plainclothes police officers walked up to the dock and asked for him. When Bob stood up and identified himself they informed him that they were police and asked him to come with them. "Why?" Bob asked. "What's happened?" fearing that it must be bad news about a family member. "Your wife is dead," they replied. Stunned and confused, Bob asked for details. They responded that they would only discuss it at the station and asked him to come with them. After getting permission from his supervisor, Bob got into the car. Although he continued to press them for more information on the way to the station, it was not until they got him into the interrogation room that they informed him of the murder.

Thus began a twenty-one-hour ordeal. Without informing him of his right to counsel or to remain silent, they grilled him: "How many times did you hit her? Stab her?" They wrote up a confession for him to sign; he of course refused. In addition to fingerprints, they took hair samples, dental impressions, and photographs of some areas of his body, and gave him a polygraph test. Bob had sustained several minor cuts and bruises during his earlier gardening work. These were taken as evidence that he had engaged in a physical struggle with someone (e.g., Joan). In fact, however, these minor wounds were clearly more than a few hours old, as the cuts had already begun to heal. Furthermore, later DNA testing found no trace of Bob's blood or skin under Joan's nails—only her own blood—debunking the police claim that Joan had scratched him in her fight for her life.

At one o'clock on Tuesday morning the cops took Bob, at his request, out to Captree Park so that he could show them the holes where he had dug up the saplings. But, exhausted and confused as he was, Bob could not find these, especially since it was fully dark and he did not remember exactly where along the seven-mile stretch he had stopped.

He was finally driven to his girlfriend Judy's home and dropped off. It was now early Tuesday morning. Physically and emotionally exhausted, Bob fell into a deep sleep.

No charges were brought against Bob at this time, there being no real evidence against him. However, his girlfriend Judy thought he should get a lawyer, and helped him find one from the Navy—much cheaper than hiring a private attorney. It did not seem important to either Judy or Bob that the attorney, William Pries, had no experience in criminal defense. This was their first major mistake.

It was a couple of months after the tragic incident that Bob made his second major mistake. He owned a small handgun, a .22-caliber, that a friend had given him back in 1969. As he had never had any use for it, and indeed had never even registered it, he decided this would be a good time to get rid of it. Unsure of what to do with the gun, he asked his attorney for advice. The obviously incompetent lawyer advised him to turn it in to law enforcement, who would know how to dispose of it safely. While this might have been good advice under ordinary circumstances, it was clearly a bad idea for someone still under suspicion for a brutal murder. Bob chose to give the gun to his erstwhile friend and next-door neighbor, the husband of Barbara Koch (who had called the police the night of the murder); Koch was a state trooper. For some reason, however, Koch had evidently taken an extreme dislike to Bob, and promptly turned him in for possessing an unregistered weapon. Although there was no connection whatsoever between the gun and Joan's murder, this incident certainly did nothing to elevate Bob's character in the eyes of the local criminal justice system. It took over six months to get the case dismissed.

By November 1985, more than a year had passed since Joan's murder. Bob and Judy had moved into the house where Joan had been murdered. Life went on, uneventfully. But the district attorney was getting desperate. No suspect had been found, and it did not look good for him to have a brutal unsolved murder on his hands. Something must be done. Although there was no hard evidence against Bob, there was circumstantial evidence, and plenty of material to attack his character. Bob was finally arrested and charged.

After spending twenty-seven days in jail, he was released on $50,000 [$104,500] bail. It was a year and a half later before the trial began—near the end of May 1987—during which time Bob was free and continued working at the post office.

Bob, naively trusting in the criminal justice system, was not too concerned about his attorney's lack of criminal defense experience. After all, he was innocent, and as we all know innocent people never get convicted.

The prosecutor, Assistant District Attorney Littman, built his case primarily on character assassination, not just of Bob but of his witnesses. Bob was a philanderer, and a drug user with a $3,000 [$6,270]-a-month habit.[24]

---

[24] Bob admitted to occasionally taking as much as one gram of cocaine in one day. This was extrapolated to mean that he took one gram every day (not at all what he had admitted), and the "official" local street price for one gram of cocaine was set at $100 [$210]. In fact, the monthly amount was originally stated as $30,000 due to a misplaced decimal point; this at least was corrected at the trial.

Bob's inexperienced attorney made numerous blunders. Jurors mingled with the victim's family members in the hallways and restrooms; the attorney made no request for sequestration or separate facilities for jurors. The failure of the police to read Bob his Miranda rights was not brought up. The defense called no expert witnesses, only character witnesses. None of Bob's financial statements—documents that would have debunked the "$3,000-per-month cocaine habit" claim, or his supposed motive of wanting to keep the house for himself—were entered into evidence. Neighbor Barbara Koch changed her story from her original statement, claiming at the trial that she had definitely heard Joan utter several distinct words and phrases: "Oh my God... stop, Bob, stop... somebody help me... he's killing me," rather than admitting, as she did originally, that she had heard, at best, only "Stop! Stop! Stop!"; this inconsistency was not challenged. And the DA frequently harassed defense witnesses, with no objection from defense council.

All of Bob's character witnesses, especially Juliet, who voluntarily flew out to New York to appear, were discredited. The other witnesses included his mother ("Of course, any mother will defend her son"), his girlfriend Judy ("What kind of a woman would have an affair with a married man?") and a long-time friend Bob had known since his Navy days (the DA ignored this man's record as a veteran, good husband and father, focusing instead on a minor shoplifting conviction in his youth). Juliet, of course, was the crowning jewel in the DA's cap, and Bob's acceptance of her offer to testify was his third major mistake. The most helpful thing Juliet could have done for Bob was to lay low and hope the prosecutor did not find out about her. As Bob's attorney ought to have expected, she was harassed and humiliated more than any other defense witness.

DA: "What is your present occupation?"

Juliet: "I'm a manager of a bed and breakfast." [This under oath; Juliet was a housekeeper, not a manager.]

DA: "And before that?"

Juliet: "I was an erotic film actress." [Then, obviously trying to divert attention:] "Before that, I was a school teacher, and a radio producer, and held other jobs."

DA: "You are too modest. Weren't you in fact a major star in adult films, erotic films?"

Juliet: "For about six years, yes, until late 1984/1985."

DA: "And you went by the name Aunt Peg?"

Juliet: "No, I went by Juliet Anderson."

DA: "Approximately how many adult erotic films were you in?"

Juliet: "Fifty or sixty, between 1978 and 1984." [Again, trying to divert attention:] "I change professions about every seven years. Right now I'm studying."

Juliet left the stand feeling humiliated. And of course the DA trashed her in his closing statement as well: "A porn star['s] ... idea of a warm and sensitive guy may not be the same as you good people['s]." In fact Juliet had never used the words "warm and sensitive guy," stating only that Bob was not a violent man. Yet both her and Bob's inability to anticipate this bashing is a testament to their naive trust in the criminal justice system. That Bob's attorney did not anticipate it is inexcusable.

Bob did not testify in his own defense. He was terrified of public speaking, and worried that his nervousness would damage his credibility.

For Juliet, this third traumatic experience with the legal system (following on her 1982 Chicago arrest and her 1984 betrayal by the unscrupulous Larry Carr) was the last straw. The so-called justice system had not only turned its back on her; it had now dragged her down, publicly, to the level of "fallen woman," someone to be scorned, not even worth listening to. This mistreatment by official authority figures brought back some of the rage and helplessness she had felt in the hospital as a child, re-opening wounds that she had spent years trying to heal.

As for Bob, in addition to the negative DNA evidence (which was not available in 1987 but was determined later), other factors favored his innocence.

• He had no motive. He and Joan were already in the process of separating, and he had just taken out a loan to pay off their debts, and had agreed to sell the house and share the proceeds with her. While they had some debts, these were not overwhelming and could easily be paid out of his share of the house proceeds, and he had a decent income from his navy pension and his post-office employment.

• Bob, aged forty-six at the time of the crime, had no history of physical violence, domestic or otherwise, nor any brain trauma that would have caused such a personality change. In fact, a psychological evaluation of Bob had stated that he "does not...show indications of having poor impulse control or any tendency to resort to violence under stress." (Joan, however, did have a history of interpersonal violence, although not against Bob.) Bob also had no criminal record.

• Bob was emaciated from his cocaine habit, with only a hundred fifty pounds on his 5′10″ frame; Joan, 5′8″ and overweight from her drinking, outweighed him by twenty-five pounds.

• Even the expert medical witness for the prosecution (the Nassau County Medical Examiner) admitted that the scratches on Bob's arm and the cut on his finger, which were photographed at his interrogation, were at least twenty-four hours old, whereas the crime had taken place less than twelve hours earlier.

• If Bob had been the perpetrator, either his car would have still been parked at the house, or, if he had been driving away, he would not have been able to escape detection; the police arrived too quickly. Furthermore, there was no way he would have had time, between 1:55 a.m., the time of Joan's death, and 2:30 a.m., when he set off for work, to drive back to Judy's house, clean all the blood off himself and his car, either destroy or dispose of his bloody clothing, and leave no traces in Judy's house. (Both the car and the house were searched by the police on the night of the crime. The car, in fact, was still dirty from the trip to Captree State Park, and there was even some spilled soup residue on the inside of the passenger-side door, from a fast-food run Bob had made the day before; the car had clearly not been cleaned.)

If Bob had traveled to and from the house on foot, it would have taken him at least ten minutes if he had gone at a fast run (an action that would have drawn police attention), and close to half an hour at a walk, to return to Judy's house, arriving just in time to set off for work at 2:30; again, he would not have had sufficient time for clean-up.

The guilty verdict, returned on 10 June 1987, took Bob—and Juliet—completely by surprise. The jury appeared stressed as well; eight of them—all of the women—were openly weeping. Yet the defense attorney did not request that they be polled. Bob started serving his term of twenty-five years to life, in Sing Sing Prison, a few weeks later.

Although Juliet had long ago moved on from her early relationship with Bob, his trial, and particularly the guilty verdict, did trigger in her a deep compassion and an aching sadness for this first love of her adult life. "You fair-haired lover and friend who polished the mirror of my innocence to reveal the woman beneath the child... It matters to me that you are in Sing Sing for life and that I'll never see you again, my first and dearest love," she wrote in her journal. Yet she vacillated, sometimes railing against him: he was "not guilty of the crime you were charged with but guilty of the crime of breaking my heart, killing my love for you." Juliet could carry a grudge for a long time.

She would continue expressing these mixed feelings for two more decades. In the last two years of her life, she started mentioning Bob's situation at odd moments, with friends and acquaintances, even referring to it in her interview for *Golden Goddesses*. The injustice preyed on her mind, and she grieved that someone who had, after all, given something of himself to her, was living, unjustly, in pain and deprivation, in prison for a murder he did not commit.

19
New Directions, New Losses

If there was one focus to Juliet's life during this time of withdrawal and reflection, it was self searching—an activity she threw herself into with the same intensity with which she had pursued all of her other major life projects: surviving childhood illnesses, discovering sex, living in foreign cultures, manipulating rich men, being a porn star. She continued psychotherapy; devoured self-help books; attended workshops, retreats, and twelve-step programs; took psychedelic drugs; joined all kinds of spiritual groups—from the Episcopal church to Native American rituals to Goddess worship; meditated; received Tarot card readings; experienced past-life regressions; took classes in psychological and sociological subjects; took private voice lessons; sought out various alternative health treatments, including psychic healing and the use of crystals, magnets, herbs and essential oils; joined the local health club for workouts and swimming; practiced Yoga and Qigong; and, of course, journaled. Aside from a short interlude in 1983, she had taken a break from personal writing after 1980, knowing that she could not survive the sleazy aspects of the porn business if she had to put her real feelings and perceptions down on paper. But now she wrote voraciously, recording incidents both mundane and profound, letting her emotions run freely out through her pen. "Writing is medicine to exorcise the demons and fairies, muses and monsters—liberate them on paper."

For the first time in her life, Juliet was actually doing some serious self-reflection, trying to find out who she really was and what she wanted to do with her life, now that her porn career had crashed. How much of that persona was really her, and how much was just a means of financial survival and of getting the attention she craved? What was her true mission in life? What work was she drawn to, that would sustain her financially while helping her fulfill this mission? How had her early family life affected who she was today? What were her real values, especially spiritual and interpersonal? What people did she want in her life, and whom did she want to let go of?

These questions would absorb her for the next several years, and she worked hard at finding the answers. After all, she would soon be moving into her fifties, and whatever she was going to do with the rest of her life, she had better get started on it. True to form, she was starting this self-reflection work about ten or fifteen years later than most people do. "[I] recognize how I procrastinated in solving the problem of my dissatisfaction with the porn biz. I wasted so much time!... I'm such an action-oriented, over-achieving person... I have never come to terms with suffering, did not acknowledge my sorrow or pain, did not express it. Instead I bravely pushed forward, suppressing my fears, my hurt. I hope it isn't too late to learn."

Her first step was to embark on an ambitious reading program, delving into popular self-help and new-age books, starting with M. Scott Peck's *The Road Less Traveled*. This reading, along with her meditation and yoga practice, led her to a more serious search for a spiritual practice. In April 1986 she participated in a ten-day silent Vipassana Insight Meditation Retreat in Yucca Valley (although it is hard to imagine Juliet being silent for ten days). Over the next several years, she would attend a number of similar programs, at various venues. She also turned her attention, not surprisingly, to the New Age and pagan religions, which she had been exposed to by some of the self-appointed sex goddesses she had met during her porn years. She soon found an informal spiritual group in Placerville, and these people, primarily women, became her main circle of friends in the mountain community.

Along with her focus on emotional and spiritual health, Juliet reconnected with her body in non-sexual ways. She started getting regular massage, acupuncture and chiropractic treatments, joined a local health club, was diligent in her yoga practice, and walked and hiked in the Sierra foothills. Although this body connection helped ground her somewhat, her emotions were still in turmoil a good part of the time. An Adult Children of Alcoholics conference in Sacramento set her off on a crying jag, grieving not only her own "lost, lonely [inner] child" but her parents' as well. In fact, over the next several years, she would sometimes relive her mother's painful childhood events—as she perceived them—rather than her own.

Unfortunately, though, this empathy did not bring her and her mother closer together, as Dorothy was not doing any emotional work on herself; rather, her depression and alcoholism spiraled downward. Dorothy was even hospitalized several times. At Chris's urging, Fred and Dorothy had moved from San Diego to Thousand Oaks in 1984. Chris herself had moved back to the U.S., in order to live nearer to her parents as they aged. They were now in their early seventies, retired, and, freed from the pressures of earning a living, able to freely indulge their emotional dysfunctions. Juliet's attitude toward them during these years revolved through cycles of empathy, recrimination and acceptance. She spent a great deal of her time in therapy talking about, and acting out through child-therapy-style sand-box play, her early relationships with her family and how these continued to affect her. Then, armed with new insights, she challenged her parents and sister, through letters and phone calls, and during her occasional visits, to confront their problems and change their behaviors. When these efforts not only failed but backfired, she reacted with alternate anger and acceptance, struggling to be loving but still primarily self-focused and resentful. She longed for a peaceful resolution of her issues with her family, but sought it from them rather than from herself. And, no matter how much therapy she went through, she was never able to let go of her anger at not being allowed to be a child actress; she obsessed about this issue for the rest of her life. "[I have put on so many] performances: geisha, playgirl, model, wife, radio personality, X-film actress, stage performer. It would have been better to have been allowed to be an actress, singer, painter, dancer, etc." In other words, it was obviously her parents' fault that all of her meanderings in the attempt to achieve her life dreams had come to dead ends.

Nor was Juliet's inclination to critique others and proffer unsolicited advice limited to her family. In November 1985, when Bob Watt was arrested for his wife Joan's murder, she wrote a letter to him and his girlfriend Judy, full of New Age dogma. "There are no 'problems,' just challenges to work through... no one else but YOU can come to terms with it... I encourage you to turn to inspirational writings... Remember, there are no 'accidents' or mistakes. You are exactly where you are suppose[d] to be. How are you going to work it out?... Love, Juliet."

Despite her emotional ups and downs, though, life went on, and Juliet was always someone who lived in the moment; her attention

never really wandered far from daily joys and struggles. And sometimes these mundane days brought unexpected events of real significance.

Her second summer in Placerville, in 1986, was as hot and miserable as the first. She returned from her short working vacation at
Raamwood to hundred-degree midsummer heat. By this time, a year
after her escape from the Bay Area, Juliet was longing to leave her
Blair House job and seek more isolated living quarters. Yet the bed
and breakfast was to give her an unexpected gift.

One afternoon, as she lay on her bed reading, trying to escape the
stifling heat, she heard a pitiful crying, which proved upon investigation to be emanating from high up in the tall redwood tree in the
back yard. Juliet, gazing up through the branches, could see a small
black spot huddled there, clearly a cat. Passionate feline lover that
she was, her heart went out to the hapless creature, and over the next
several days she tried, to no avail, to coax the creature down with
sweet talk and food. Richard, meanwhile, distraught over the annoyance the crying was causing his paying guests, threatened to
shoot it.

The days dragged on. The crying became more plaintive. Juliet
was anguished; she dreaded being at home. Richard ranted, setting a
deadline for the "execution," as Juliet referred to it. On the eve of the
dreaded day, Juliet stood at the base of the tree and sent a telepathic
message to the terrified cat: "If you come down I promise I'll always
take care of you."

The next morning, Juliet, climbing up the front steps to the house
on her return from an early errand, saw a black blur streak across her
path. Although at first just startled, she quickly realized it was the
cat. She spent the rest of the day wandering the grounds, calling
"Here kitty, kitty, kitty!" but there was no sign of the creature. She
worried that he might be injured, as it would have been a long fall
from the tree, and she knew that cats are not able to dig their claws
into redwood bark. But as she was hanging out laundry the next
morning, she caught a glimpse of two luminous spots in the crawl
space leading into the cellar. She froze, closed her eyes, centered
herself, breathed gently and then slowly squatted on the gravel. She
inched her hand out, palm up, and started softly singing a lullaby.
The eyes became a head, then a body. A skinny black fur ball

attached to four legs cautiously crept toward her. Their eyes locked. The cat paused, then leapt onto Juliet's knees, put his forelegs around her neck and rubbed his muzzle under her chin, trembling and purring simultaneously. Juliet continued singing as she stroked his thin body. When she stood up, though, he darted for the safety of the cellar. Juliet returned to the house and brought back food and water, placed it near his cave and returned to her room. The repast was devoured immediately.

For a week the cat laid low and only came out at night when Juliet called him. She sneaked him food and said nothing about him to either Patsy or Richard, who were probably too relieved at the cessation of the pitiable crying to think about what might have happened to the cat.

But Juliet had to figure out how to honor her vow to the rescue victim—a vow that she took more seriously than one she might have made to a human being. The first problem was Snuggles: how would her "only child" of many years take to the orphan? Juliet had a long talk with Snuggles, holding her, meditating, sending Snuggles visualizations of the three of them as a happy family. And when the new cat finally agreed to enter the little porch room, Snuggles was amazingly receptive: it was the first other cat that didn't provoke her jealousy. She was only curious. The orphan evidently brought out her maternal instincts. Juliet aptly named her new son Lucky. After about a week, Lucky filled out into a sleek, beautiful, coal-black feline. "The other half of my psyche," Juliet mused; "he and Snuggles represent my dark and light sides." Indeed, his playfulness contrasted with Snuggles's regality.

It was not too long after the Lucky incident that Juliet and Carolyn Elderberry decided to train as massage therapists. It was a natural step for both of them. They both loved and celebrated sexuality, and they had both experienced pain and healing in their own bodies; why not put these two aspects of their lives together? They took a two-week crash course at a massage school in Sacramento, getting their certificates in September. It was a propitious time for Juliet to seek a new income source, as her elder-care client, Harry, died on August 30th. And, having managed to get her bed-and-breakfast work hours reduced from twenty per week to fifteen, she had both the time and the energy to devote to building up a practice with Carolyn.

Their intention, from the beginning, was to combine regular massage with sex work, although they saw themselves as higher class than those who worked the common massage parlor trade. As they were, of course. In addition to giving the client a good massage and sexual release, their services were performed in a comfortable and respectable private venue: Carolyn's Oakland house (she had since moved out of the Richmond Boulevard house she and Juliet had shared). In the separate room Carolyn had set aside for seeing clients, both women worked, sometimes singly and sometimes doing doubles. Juliet soon built up enough regular clientele to start scheduling one week per month there, paying Carolyn 25% of her fees for use of the space.

Ex-husband Bob Watt's murder trial was scheduled for the end of May 1987, and Juliet decided to combine her trip back to New York state, where she would testify in his behalf, with another stage-show tour on the East Coast. She did the shows before the trial—60 altogether, finishing up at Show World Center in New York City. This netted her about $1,700 [$3,550] and gave a needed boost to her ego. "[The] shows are dynamite; sexual energy [is] high in [the] audience. I move very beautifully, they are mesmerized." The Q & A sessions went well, too, and she was starting to bring spirituality into the discussions. She also turned some tricks at the Live-Sex Theatre, and it was thus that she met Dennis, an ex-fan from her film days who was of course thrilled to have an in-person session with her. Feeling that they had a deep personal connection, she gave him her address and phone number in California and invited him to keep in touch.

She had enough leisure time to enjoy the perks of the city—plays, operas, and social time with her friend Annie Sprinkle, who put her up, even giving her a room to herself this time—a vast improvement over the accommodations she had provided during the height of Juliet's show career. Juliet also managed some quiet, meditative time in a church on 42nd Avenue, a needed respite from the intensity of performing and the degradation in New York—the filth, the constant loud music in the performance venues, being around so many "low conscious people...a city of escapists, smokers, drinkers. Sirens, many street cops, panhandlers, street people... How can anyone *live* here?!"

The show schedule taxed her to the utmost; her last show started at one a.m., and she was exhausted beyond thinking by the end of her work day.

After the tour she went on to Westbury to testify as a character witness at the trial. The prosecuting attorney's successful attempt to discredit her was a painful reminder of how little the more conservative element of American society understood of who she was and what she had to offer the world.

Back home after that trauma, Juliet turned her attention to building up her massage practice, and by the fall of 1987 was finally beginning to experience some financial stability. In mid-September, she drew on her modest reserves to take a five-day vacation to Big Sur, where she stayed at the Immaculate Heart Hermitage (now the New Camaldoli) in the Santa Lucia Mountains.

While this was ostensibly to be a period of withdrawal and reflection, she in fact spent much of the time caught up in her usual emotional turmoil. She started out well, awakening early on Wednesday morning, September 16, from her first night of pain-free sleep in three weeks, to a mountain bathed in fog and silence. Dressing quickly in the chill cabin, she fixed herself a cup of hot tea and sat by the window watching the thick fog turn to wisps of drifting white, her cold hands wrapped around the hot mug. At 6 a.m. the muffled sound of prayer bells drifted through the fog, as the brothers made their way to the chapel. She joined them, and "could feel their love, sincerity, faith and humility." Later, after a midday drive down the coast, a walk on the beach ("feeling the healing sand beneath my feet, cries of birds, barking of seals, sound and feel of wind, water and waves—unrivaled bliss! Memories of childhood summers") and lunch, she returned to nap, read the Bible and pray; then she sat again by the window, writing in her journal and watching the sun set behind the western hills and the stars come out in the clear autumn sky.

By the second day, though, she was off down the coast to visit Tom, an acquaintance from her sex-work days, who had been a holdout from her charms: "I was exuding my sexual energy [then] which attracted and mesmerized many others but not Tom...[but now we can] let our long friendship be the foundation, then explore intimacy." Although they did not engage in any overtly sexual acts, their touching was sensuous and intimate—enough to draw Juliet into her emotional dependence pattern. She chose to ignore obvious signs of Tom's dysfunction, such as his dirty unkempt house, the pervasive smell of marijuana smoke, and the lack of any nutritious food in the house. She spent most of the next two days with him, walking on the beach at Big Sur or along the cliffs of Point Lobos, eating at quaint restaurants, and visiting the Monterey Bay Aquarium. And of course she managed to find time to engage in her third favorite activity— shopping for clothes. She had to indulge her inner child, little Judy.

Eschewing the simple but expensive cabin she had paid for back at the Hermitage, she spent Wednesday and Thursday nights sleeping on Tom's living room floor; the second night was so miserable she only got about five hours of sleep. This was a little too high a price even for a romance addict, and she returned to the hermitage on Friday, where, after reading from *Drama of the Gifted Child*, she was overwhelmed by intense feelings of loneliness and loss. She fell into a troubled sleep at eight p.m., and rose at 2:30 Saturday morning to drive down the coast, through the fog, to Esalen, where she soaked in the hot baths. Back by five o'clock in the morning, she read herself back to sleep, waking again at seven. The rest of the day she spent reading, napping, obsessing about her emotional problems, writing letters and chronicling the weekend in her journal.

One of the letters she wrote was to Dennis, the man she had connected with at the Live-Sex Theatre in New York back in May, in response to his last-minute cancellation of a planned visit to her in August. Never mind, it was for the best, she assured him, and no worry about any emotional involvement between him and her; she was a free spirit, into non-possessive, divine love, letting it flow through her without personal attachments. She cited her liaison with Tom as a shining example. If she and Dennis had further encounters, they would follow that pattern as well. In her enlightened spirit of openness, she addressed this letter to both Dennis and his partner Amy, and encouraged Amy to express her opinions on the matter.

On Sunday, after a deeply restful sleep, Juliet rose early and joined the brothers for morning prayers and breakfast, before departing for the long but pleasant drive home. The five-day sojourn had reminded her of the 1976 vacation at the summer cottage in Finland, complete with an unsatisfying sexual encounter, although without the physical labor.

In October, Juliet moved to Pollock Pines, near Jenkinson Lake, renting the guest cottage behind a house owned by an elderly couple, Norm and Rae. She paid part of her rent in labor, cleaning their house once a week and doing light yard work. The property was accessed via an unpaved driveway: the real "out in the country" habitat she had always envisioned. She had to manipulate her new landlord into accepting Lucky, as he had insisted on only one cat. Unfortunately, Lucky was somewhat of a nuisance, even to Juliet. He was an inveterate climber; he seemed to love high places—the inclination that had led him to the crisis in the redwood tree—and the cottage roof was one of his favorite hangouts, to Norm's great annoyance.

But Juliet settled into her new home, glad to have a little more space, and surrounded herself with the things she loved: in the kitchen, the white-ducks-on-blue-background tablecloth, the teapot wrapped in a black-cat cozy, and a dinner bell in the shape of a troll; in the main room her light blue velveteen chair with a small brocaded vanity stool for a footrest, her cat rug, a tall white bookcase, a new brass floor lamp, two steamer trunks, a door set atop two filing cabinets for a desk, an altar honoring the goddess, and of course cat perches in the windows. The place was heated by a wood-burning stove, and the indoor woodpile added a rustic air to the main room. And everywhere there were arts and crafts decorations, and memorabilia from her past lives: raku pottery, peacock feathers in a black champagne bottle, purple satin bears hanging from a curtain rod, a heart crystal over the desk, earring and necklace trees, a match container from Mycanos, a chicken whistle from Finland, a Japanese paper lantern, a honey bear—a gift from her elder-care client Harry; and on the walls, photographs and posters of various subjects, from Juliet herself to sunrise over the San Diego harbor to a poster of Higher Power from her twelve-step ventures, along with a Farside calendar. On summer evenings, she could leave the windows open and listen to the frogs singing and crickets chirping as she drifted off to sleep; in the winter, she could sit in the big chair wrapped in a blue hand-crocheted shawl, her feet on the sheepskin rug or propped up on the footstool, basking and dreaming as the winter sun streamed in through the large window. This was to be her retreat, although it would also be a place to entertain clients from time to time.

Despite Juliet's claim that she had never owned a television, she did actually acquire one at this time, although her viewing was almost entirely limited to public television, or to watching videos. Something to ease the isolation of rural life.

It was in this fall of 1987, too, that Juliet started on two new healing modalities. The first was ortho-bionomy, a gentle bodywork technique used to relieve pain and stress. Juliet had great hopes for this treatment, as it was specifically promoted for pain relief. Sometimes it worked very well for her and sometimes it did not work at all. Eventually, she took training in ortho-bionomy herself and incorporated it into her bodywork practice.

She also started to work with a new healer, John Sibbett, who seemed to practice a combination of acupuncture, body work, and herbal remedies, with a few miscellaneous fads thrown into the mix as well, such as past-life regression and reliving one's birth. Juliet was very impressed with his work, and was soon visiting him almost every week. She rarely left a session without having purchased a bottle of Bach flower remedy; surprisingly, she seemed to need a different remedy every time, and they were expensive.

December, beginning with another short visit to the Hermitage (including another liaison with Tom), was a whirlwind of social activity, some of it disastrous. Her hot date in San Francisco fizzled; Juliet had attired herself in a flimsy dress and high heels, but she and her date had to walk six blocks uphill to the Fairmont Hotel (after driving around for half an hour looking for a closer parking place); her date was determined to impress her with his personal acquaintance with the owners. Then they got lost going home. A three-day visit with Carolyn and Paul turned into a long screaming and yelling session because of various miscommunications about who would sleep with whom, when. Later in the month she had a better time with Paul alone, with Chinese take-out food, good sex in front of the fireplace, and a visit to the Unity Church. The next day she went to a Christmas concert at Davies Hall with some women friends, including Carolyn. She came back home the next day, attending a metaphysical Christmas party where she dressed sexily in a red jumpsuit and high heels, and to her surprise ran into Barbara Bills (Henderson), her co-star in *Summer Heat*; unbeknownst to Juliet, Barbara had been living in Placerville for the past four years. On the 23rd, Juliet went to a solstice gathering with friends from her women's spirituality circle. The last two days of December brought a major storm; she was snowed in for several days.

Juliet celebrated the New Year of 1988 with what would become a tradition: several days at a cabin in Mendocino with Carolyn, high most of the time on ecstasy, their newest drug of choice. A couple of weeks later she attended a ten-day conference, "Companions on the Inner Way," led by Jack Kornfield, on Mount Tamalpais in Marin County. This was a heavily Christian, although liberal, event, with Eucharist every morning; Juliet partook enthusiastically. There were also interesting lectures (Christianity and healing, missionary work in Lebanon, women and patriarchy), and long sessions of interpersonal sharing. Juliet was torn when it came to talking about her sex work, especially her film career, either feeling too vulnerable or worried she'd be bragging too much. Yet after hearing some heart-rending stories of pain, loss and grief, she did decide to share her own story. To her surprise, she met with amazing acceptance and a total lack of prurience.

Sometimes she found the twelve hours per day of interpersonal interaction exhausting. She took several long breaks, going to the movie *Good Morning Vietnam* with her friend Becky, and hiking on Mount Tam and around Phoenix Lake, where she took a long nap on an inflatable mattress she'd brought along. The conference venue had some physical challenges for her; it was three days before she found a chair she could sit in without pain, and the slow walking meditation they were supposed to do was so hard on her back that she finally abandoned the attempt. The food, surprisingly, was not only good but digestible; she had no IBS episodes. Of course she met a man she was attracted to, although he was currently in a relationship and they did not connect sexually.

All in all, the conference was good for her. Long enough to thoroughly process some issues and to share with her fellow attenders some of the complexities of their lives. "People like me even tho I'm different, and maybe I'm not that different. My energy and enthusiasm are appreciated... I have a lot to offer people who are in pain...

Finally my life is making sense." She felt a renewed sense of spirituality, confirming that she really did need to bring more God—however she might define that—into her life. She took another momentous step after this conference: removing from her finger the friendship ring that Nikolas had given her twenty years earlier. She still kept the ring, but no longer wore it.

Despite her newfound optimism about changing her life, Juliet still suffered a fair amount of physical pain. The health problems she had struggled with all her life were plaguing her more as she began to age. Along with the chronic irritable bowel syndrome problems— diarrhea, constipation, intestinal cramps—she endured indigestion and gas pains, severe menstrual cramps, and skin inflammations. Her arthritis often flared up, and she suffered pains in her neck, back and legs. She tried everything to deal with these various issues, from allopathic remedies to mind-over-body techniques: pain pills, anti- inflammatory drugs, herbal remedies (including marijuana brown- ies), body work of various types, chiropractic treatments, acupunc- ture and acupressure, exercise, hot towels, hot showers, magnets, crystals, stones, meditation and prayer, surrendering to God, sur- rendering to the pain, self talk, sitting in visualized white light under the trees, holding or rubbing energy points, listening to inspirational tapes, laying on of hands, and just plain diversions. She made a sin- cere effort to accept the pain, to convince herself that it was in her life for a reason and that as soon as she understood what that reason was, she would be able to deal with it. "I'm trusting in Divine Guid- ance and know I'm being taken care of, but my body isn't buying it... I'm getting healthier, but it's a roller coaster ride... I have lots of fear around money [and] security, [and] it shows up in my body. Sickness is caused partly by not integrating the shadow part of ourselves." Whenever an incident triggered some old hurt and pain from "the JA vamp days, I take it into my body with physical pain."

"What if you just surrender to the pain?" her therapist asked her once. "I'm afraid of feeling helpless, *out of control*, unlovable, depen- dent, different. Of course I need to go there, accept the pain, own it and forgive myself. I don't yet know how to have a relationship with chronic pain, how not to let it own me."

And she did sincerely try to accept responsibility for her pain. "The anger has kept me in pain. I need to get over this. *I'll keep doing*

new things until I find a way. I'll try telling it I don't need it any more."
She also noted, "Pain is such an exquisite teacher for me... Physical
pain brings me to center." Yet the only remedy that had ever really
released her from pain was sex: "Sex was the miracle drug." And she
wasn't going there again, at least not in the all-out, devil-take-the-
hindmost way she had lived during her years as a porn star. She was
determined not to use pure physical sex as a pain killer any more.

Transcription of 140 pages of taped "confessions" *2* (X pages per hour @ $10/hour	$470.00
Everytime you said incredible or amazing @ 5¢/word	35.50
Everytime you mixed who/which or he/she @ 5¢/word	86.05
Asprin for my headache	3.75
The nervous breakdown of my typewriter (example, this typed line...it truly is broken and must be replaced as it can't be repaired)	335000
Everytime you yawned, burped, mumbled @20¢ each	125.40
For every bang, crash and unintelligible garbles @20¢ ea.	~~442200~~ 44 ⅔
For the carpet cleaner for all the vomit on the rug	6.32
The toilet paper for my diarrhea	4.56
Batteries for my vibrator when I got turned on	2.70
Eventual loss of libido	600.00
Everytime you said "fucked up the ass" @ $40 each	800.00
Massage therapy for my stiff neck @ $30/hour	300.00
Verbal therapy for my sanity @ $60/hour	180.00
Vacation to unwind and regain my sanity	487.24
Transcriber rental (3 weeks)	64.20
Typing paper, ribbon etc.	8.50
Proof-reading - 1 hour	10.00
Hysteria resulting there-from and treatment of	269.13
SUB-TOTAL	$3,832.55
Professional discount	~~2,800.55~~ 2,932.00
	932.00
Paid in advance	200.00
TOTAL DUE	~~$832.00~~ 732.00

Sarcastic invoice Juliet sent to Michele Capozzi, for transcribing his
autobiography

For all her alternative therapies, dieting and spiritual practices,
though, there was one very stressful, unhealthful activity that Juliet
she spent an inordinate amount of time doing, during these years:
driving. To Sacramento, to Oakland, to Marin and Mendocino counties, to Wilbur Hot Springs, southwest to the Monterey Bay, east and
north to various mountain getaways; even the short trip between
Pollock Pines and Placerville was a twenty-minute drive. She went

through three cars during her years in El Dorado County. While she tried to make good use of this driving time, listening to inspirational tapes and audio books, driving was still driving, with all the attention it requires and the stress it puts on the human body and mind. Her withdrawal from urban life required her to spend many of her waking hours virtually immobilized inside a glass and steel contraption, unable to smell the mountain air or feel it on her skin, or to hear the subtle mountain sounds. Country living in the late twentieth century demanded considerably more traveling than urban life, all of it via this most stressful mode of transportation.

Juliet was now into her third winter in Placerville, and feeling settled in. She had her cottage in the country, her New Age friends and activities, and several steady sources of income: massage, phone sex, and her cleaning and yard work. She went cross-country skiing in the winter and hiking in the summer. She rose early almost every morning and took her cats for a walk, often on the shores of Jenkinson Lake. She was still processing her life, searching for her true nature and life's work. While she was done with being a porn star and spokesperson, she felt in her bones that she was deeply connected with sex, erotica and sensuality. "I haven't finished with sex, as an expression of wholeness, to have my views expressed on film, video, written or spoken word, who knows." She toyed with the idea of an *Ask Aunt Peg* book—questions and answers about sex, pornography, etc. She also considered renting an apartment in Sacramento, for doing erotic massage; it would not require traveling all the way to Oakland and paying Carolyn 25% of her income. But she abandoned this idea after researching the sex-work scene in Sacramento; the vice squad there was overly vigilant.

In February, she took on a new short-term project: transcribing, on her old manual typewriter from Finland (Juliet, technologically challenged, would not have gone near a computer at this point in her life) audio tapes for Michele Capozzi, an Italian immigrant friend of Annie Sprinkle's who was writing his autobiography, and whom Juliet had met and had a brief fling with, on one of her trips to New York. This turned out to be grueling work; Michele meandered through his material, his heavy accent made his words difficult to make out, his narrative was peppered with obscenities and invectives, and to tell the truth, his life story was boring. Still, Juliet plodded doggedly through the work, determined to keep her commitment even as her resentment grew. Besides, she needed the money. She finished with the tapes in April, sending him a creatively sarcastic invoice, relieved beyond words to be done with the project.

Juliet hiking in the Sierras, and taste-testing the camping dinner while her (unidentified) friend checks out the wine bottle. Photos: Carr/Pettit family collection.

March was an intense month. Juliet spent a weekend in the Bay Area baby-sitting both Robyn, her regular charge, and a school-aged brother and sister whose parents were on a weekend getaway. It was a weekend from hell: the children were undisciplined and seriously acting out; Juliet had to guard her purse, as the brother and sister had both been known to steal from their parents; and the boy was into playing with matches. On top of this stress were several others: her car broke down on the Bay Bridge, she had terrible diarrhea the entire weekend, an earlier sexual liaison with Paul Johnson had triggered vaginitis, and a phone call to her parents revealed them to be under serious stress, with her father suffering from heart problems and her mother on a crying jag. Indeed, a few weeks later Chris called to say that Dorothy had been admitted to the addiction ward of the hospital.

By the time Easter came, on April third, Juliet was in a very vulnerable place. The New Age Easter ritual she attended touched her
deeply, with its themes of death and renewal, temptation, betrayal,
crucifixion, suffering, and resurrection. "What is growing inside me
waiting to be born? Who are my Judas, Caesar and Peter? [answer:]
My ego, the ignorant public, my lack of faith... I still have lots of
inner work to do." Later she hiked in the Sutter Buttes; the mountains were resplendent in springtime: "butterflies, hares, snakes,
hawks, turkey vultures, song birds, squirrels, insects, wild-flowers,
unclouded blue sky, utter tranquility." She felt more release several
days later in a session with John Sibbett, reliving her birth and some
of the trauma of being hospitalized as a child, finally claiming her
innocence in that situation.

In mid-April, Dennis, the client she had connected with so deeply
during her trip to New York in May 1987, called to tell her he was
coming to Lake Tahoe on a business trip, and this time he definitely
wanted to see her. Although Juliet had set him aside in her mind, the
thought of seeing him again re-awakened her passion, and she eagerly accepted an invitation to join him for dinner and a stage show at
the plush Harrah's hotel and casino. Arraying herself in a sexy black
strapless mini dress, black hose and heels, decorated with silver
jewelry and a fur shawl, she set out with her friends Paula and Lin-
da. They took a few hits on the drive over; Juliet needed only two to
get thoroughly stoned, and to start feeling insecure. Not only was
she nervous about seeing Dennis, but she felt out of her element.
"Juliet Anderson knows how to be sexy but Judy Carr doesn't, and I
don't want to be Juliet Anderson any more... this was the first time in
28 years (since first meeting Bob) [interestingly, Nikolas didn't count]
that I had allowed myself to be open to intimacy and emotional vulnerability with a man... I was like a virgin, awkward and unsure of
myself. I was entering uncharted areas of my inner being, terrified,
but I refused to pull out all the old tricks to hide the real me."

Arriving at the hotel, they parked the car and made their way to
the lobby. And there he was, handsome and smiling, looking elegant
and poised in his suit and tie. Juliet relaxed, feeling safe in the
warmth of his presence. "I felt an immense love that engulfed my
whole being." It felt more like love than lust.

Dennis had a pass for the show, and they went to the head of the line and were given a reserved table, front and center. While the show itself was excellent, what it evoked most in Juliet was a longing to be back on stage herself, to experience the high she got from being in front of an adoring crowd. Yet she recognized that there was an addictive element to that high. "I need to find a healthy outlet for my talents."

Dennis and Juliet returned to her Pollock Pines cottage in his rented car and lost no time in renewing their intimacy. "It was a passionate coming together; I have never felt anything like it. We love each other very much; each answers a need the other has. His coming into me was like nothing I have ever experienced. I had forgotten what a beautiful body and cock he has and how perfectly we fit together." They spent three hours in sensuous ecstasy, finally falling into a sound sleep at seven in the morning.

Awakening a few hours later they felt almost shy of each other, as they showered and ate the simple breakfast Juliet prepared. Dennis took her to pick up her car, which she had left at Paula's the night before; they made a few short side trips to show Dennis some of the sights. Back at the cottage after lunch, they made love again for hours. Juliet was in an altered state. "In the past I have been touched by God thru passion when I am so open, where my boundaries dissolve and my heart, body and soul blend in harmony with the Divine Lover. Here it was again." On this last night together they slept well but set the alarm for 6:30 so that they could indulge in a half hour of love-making before arising.

Dennis drove himself to the airport and Juliet was left alone to process the fallout from the intimacy. On Tuesday she worked with her Sacramento therapist, Sean, and gained more insight into her feelings of deep connection with Dennis. He reminded her in many ways of her beloved father—indeed, Juliet had earlier noticed that she and Dennis shared a physical resemblance; she had even referred to him in her private writings as her twin brother. But the two men shared an emotional resemblance as well—sensitivity and an artistic temperament. In some way, Dennis represented an archetype for Juliet. "It's not Dennis that I love, it's the physical embodiment of love. God has shown me thru the flesh, thru sex with this beautiful young man the *feeling* of true love. I now understand the love I am capable of. It may not even be for one man; perhaps it will be in the work I do. Perhaps my only love will be with the Divine Lover. I must admit I am still attached to the idea of a real man, but another, wiser part of me tells me to be patient, that now that I know what love is it will always be with me. I know for sure that I don't want casual sex any more." Yet, despite these insights, an emptiness came with Dennis's absence. "I don't miss Dennis but I miss the feeling I had with him and it hurts... I am living in the middle of the pain." For all her intense feelings of love and connection, Juliet was alone again.

And within a week, despite her new resolution, she was enjoying a casual sexual liaison, with Bill, a former massage client. She rationalized that she had made the arrangement before she had found out about Dennis's impending visit and therefore felt obligated to keep the agreement. It was just sex—good sex, but just sex. Juliet quickly got bored but appreciated the touching. Just as Bill was finger-fucking her, Chris called to tell her that Dorothy was being held in restraints at the hospital and Fred was devastated; Chris was staying with him to try to keep him calm. Difficult news to focus on while being penetrated.

A few days later Juliet received a warm letter from Amy, Dennis's girlfriend, thanking her for the erotic massage treatment she had given Dennis; it had improved their relationship. Amy's thoughtful note, along with her apparent ignorance of the deeper sexual encounter, allowed Juliet to think of her not as a rival, but as a person in her own right. Juliet remarked to herself, "What a remarkable and intelligent woman Amy is!" She looked forward to meeting Amy on her next trip to New York, although she was not without a certain amount of anxiety about it as well. Despite her protestations, she knew on some level that seeing the Dennis and Amy together would trigger jealousy and feelings of deprivation in her.

The last weekend of April brought Juliet another intense experience to distract her: a trick with Carolyn at the plush East Brother Lighthouse Bed and Breakfast with a well-to-do client, "Max," later to be her co-star in her video *Ageless Desire*. The room, with its view of the ocean, was well appointed, the gourmet meals excellent, the sex great. She and Carolyn made $200 [$400] apiece in addition to their room and board. Back home, she received an intriguing invitation: John Sibbett wanted to train some hand-picked people in his healing techniques, and invited Juliet, along with eleven others. She was both flattered and fascinated, and of course she signed up. The training was to consist of thirty-two sessions over sixteen months—for a substantial fee, naturally.

After a fairly uneventful May, June brought new dramas. Juliet finally fired her attorney handling the case against Larry Carr—who, it turned out, had just filed for bankruptcy anyway. Then Robyn's mother fired her as caretaker, following a series of mutual misunderstandings and verbal recriminations, largely resulting from the disastrous weekend in March when she had looked after Robyn and the two other children. Juliet and Carolyn started advertising in the *San Francisco Chronicle*, but the clients they garnered there were mostly losers—no-shows, under-payers, non-performers, or requiring an excessive amount of pre-appointment telephone time. The two friends also became aware of how their approaches to this work differed. Carolyn was primarily nurturing, while Juliet was adventurous, wanting her clients to experience new sensations. Carolyn felt that Juliet was too aggressive in their double sessions, seizing control rather than following Carolyn's lead. (Whether the reverse might have been true did not seem to occur to her.) This confrontation felt at first like rejection to Juliet, as well as threatening to her livelihood, but she soon realized that she needed to break out on her own more and develop an independent practice. She set herself a goal, and took the plunge, in September, of setting up a practice in Placerville, joining with two other women in a venue they named Pathways. Given the cultural atmosphere in the small town, her work there would not include any sexual massage and hence would have to be offered at a lower rate—only $30 [$60] per session. Still, it would be some additional income, and it would also give her more independence from Carolyn. Juliet was in fact very proud of this accomplishment—setting up an official public office for her touching and healing work.

An early June visit from her mother and sister, though, marked a low point. Despite Juliet's good intentions, she reverted to her usual family role of the angry, combative child. Dorothy spent most of the time crying and sulking, and of course there was plenty of drinking. Directly after the visit, Juliet wrote her most critical letter to her family ever, detailing all their dysfunctions and how these had affected both her and them, and put out an ultimatum: she would have nothing to do with them unless they got into recovery from alcoholism and co-dependency. "That may be a long time or never again," Chris admonished her. "You can't just abandon the family." Fred took the criticisms more in stride, writing a short letter in return. "That was *some* letter you composed. You couldn't have written it more succinctly or in better taste. I agree with you 100%!," ending with a plea similar to Chris's: "I love you and think of you often. Please don't throw us away... Your loving Father."

"At least," Juliet concluded, "we were all able to admit that we did not have a good time but that we love each other." But still she was torn. She wanted to give up on her family of origin and create a new one with her more enlightened friends, and yet she grieved deeply over the potential loss.

A trip to New York City was a good distraction from the trauma. She felt as though she were part of a sisterhood there, and accepted the nurturing of entertainment, trips to the hot baths, and of course admiration for her mature sexiness. A side trip to Philadelphia, including a long visit with Dennis and Amy, ended in her resolve to abandon her relationship with him; he was too immature and emotionally unavailable. Yet she would always appreciate his opening her up to intimacy and vulnerability, so that she could move on and find her true soul mate. At least, that was the story she told herself.

Juliet celebrated her fiftieth birthday with a short backpacking trip into the Sierras with Carolyn and their artist friend Roger Franke (no relation to her friend and hairdresser Greg), a "passive and self-negating" man trapped in a twenty-year loveless marriage. Although Carolyn showed up two hours late, as usual, they enjoyed a pleasant hike to 7,000-foot Loch Leven, a small sun-warmed lake (an unusual phenomenon in the high Sierras, where chilly nights negate any daytime warming of the normally frigid water, even in summer). The lake was so secluded that they were able to spend most of the time nude—one of Juliet's favorite pleasures in the outdoors.

Juliet professed to feeling good about being fifty; she still had a wonderful, relatively healthy body, aside from her chronic pain and digestive problems. "50 does not feel old to me," she wrote to her family. "I am just embarking on the most exciting period of my life." Back in Placerville, she indulged herself in a

Juliet enjoying one of her favorite activities in the Sierra Nevada mountains. Photo: Carr/Pettit family collection.

cheeseburger and a peach milkshake, and delighted in birthday phone calls, cards and presents: a white jumpsuit from her mother, a gold inscribed necklace and two Far Side books from a gentleman friend, and a humorous present from Chris: toilet-plunger earrings.

The following weekend, July 29th to 31st, a women's spirituality full-moon gathering ended early because Carolyn never showed up and Juliet, as well as several others, were worried about her, even filing a missing person report. It turned out she had gotten lost on the way there and had decided to go elsewhere with another woman she had met up with. It had never occurred to her that the others might be worried about her, enough to cut their own trip short out of concern.

In August Juliet participated in the summer El Dorado County Fair in Placerville, helping staff the booth for the Foothills Holistic Practitioners Guild, which she had recently helped found. She administered mini-massages at the fair booth, and was pleased with some of the potential clients she found there, like the buff male bicyclist in his skin-hugging spandex. She was also still pursuing some legal action against both Larry Carr and the attorney who had handled her case. Her suit against Larry was dead, but she might be able to turn him in for tax evasion, and she could file an ethics complaint against her former lawyer.

The most intense event of 1988, though, was the "reading" she received from David, an intuitive she had found through her acupuncturist.[25] He pegged her very well: she was impulsive and inconsistent; pushed herself too much and then collapsed; had a tendency to throw herself, body and soul, into new projects after initially holding back from them; and her high intellectual capabilities were frustrated by her inability to stay focused. He advised her to stop and think before making major decisions, asking for feedback from people she trusted, to intersperse her frenetic activities with frequent rest periods, and to give up meditating; her meditation was life itself, her ability to immerse herself in the moment. He also urged her to develop friendships rather than sexual relationships; they would serve her needs better in the long run. Juliet liked to quote David's advice in future years, but only the parts she agreed with, primarily his opening statement: "You are a very rebellious woman." That fit her self image very well. Although she did make up a list of do's and don'ts from this reading, she rarely looked at it, much less followed it. After leaving this intense reading session, Juliet indulged in her usual comfort foods and then went over to Carolyn's for a nap and conversation; Carolyn—no surprise—talked almost non-stop the entire time.

In September, Juliet, as part of her campaign for self-revelation, decided to take a class in "Women's Psychology and Feminist Theory" at Sacramento State College. One more bandwagon to jump on—militant feminism—and another whipping boy to blame for all her problems: sexism. She soaked up the party line, writing a paper detailing how the patriarchy had abused her. Some of her points were well taken, especially her thoughts on her childhood experiences in the hospital. But others were grasping at straws, like accusing her parents of being sexist because they had hoped for a boy when her sister Chris was born; most likely they had just wanted some gender balance in the family. The porn business also came in for some scathing remarks, of course, although her criticisms were only of some individuals and situations, not a rejection of the entire industry.

---

[25] See Appendix E for full text.

In November, Juliet accepted an invitation from Roger Franke—with whom she had taken the backpacking trip in July—to accompany him on a camping trip to Hawaii. This turned out to be a train wreck. It rained most of the time, the mosquitoes (one of those invasive species introduced by European explorers) were fierce, the rented car broke down, and it was hard to find decent campgrounds with available spaces. At least the whole trip was on Roger's tab.

Aside from the Hawaiian vacation, though, the last four months of 1988 were blessedly uneventful, and Juliet and Carolyn again spent the New Year transition at the cabin in Mendocino, tripping on ecstasy. While she was still very attached to Carolyn, Juliet was beginning to see characteristics in her friend that gave her some pause: excessive loquaciousness and physical coldness. "I realized something new about Carolyn," Juliet wrote in her journal. "She doesn't like touching; doesn't even hug new acquaintances." A rather strange quality in a massage therapist.

Juliet had now spent three and a half years in El Dorado County, seeking a new direction for her life. And she was finding it, slowly. She had a new career—massage, and was beginning to see herself as a healer. She was concentrating on those aspects of the sex business that she still enjoyed and felt drawn to—erotic massage, phone sex, live shows. She was finding some financial stability. Yet she still did not have a clear picture of her future, and had not really finished processing her past losses and pains. "My life is a book whose loose pages have been scattered."

The new year brought another challenge as well; physical pain was starting to plague her more and more, and in mid-January she was diagnosed with both an inguinal hernia and fibroid uterine tumors. After some success at wearing a truss for the hernia, she decided to undergo surgery in early March, with some trepidation because of her unpleasant experience in Yokosuka in 1962. Yet it was relatively uneventful, and she was up and about the next day, eating ice cream. The uterine problem would continue to plague her throughout the summer. Although she was not opposed to having a hysterectomy, she preferred to try some of her alternative healing techniques, and the discomfort came and went over the first half of the year.

Massage, both erotic and "straight," was taking up more and more of Juliet's energy. And what a difference there was between the two modalities! Although the regular massage that she did in Placerville was often physically stressful—she had some serious bouts of pain in her thumbs—it was the Oakland erotic massage work that took the most out of her, because of its emotional nature. The need to be present, to be attentive to the client's intimate needs, to be "up" all the time, was draining. And there were the usual stresses of self-employment—bad clients, last-minute cancellations, the erratic nature of any business. One day, when the air pressure dropped rapidly, five clients canceled—all of them after being confirmed the day before. (And they say men don't have bio-rhythms?) There was a reason why the sex business paid more, and it was not just because of its legal ambiguity.

Phone sex was also becoming more draining, although in a different way. The truth is, business was dropping off. The proliferation of phone-sex services had reduced the market share for individual providers, and there were simply fewer calls. Many were the days when Juliet would be on call for hours and receive no business at all. She disliked the constraint of waiting by the phone, and having to be always "up" for her few callers, and she began to consider quitting.

Other stresses began to pile up as well. Although her mother was back home from the hospital, both of Juliet's parents were drinking again. Her idyllic cottage was not so idyllic, as a nearby rooster's insistent crowing woke her every morning, neighborhood dogs were driving away the small wildlife she loved to watch and listen to, and the huge fir tree that had shaded the cottage became diseased and had to be cut down. In summer, the constant drip, drip, drip of the swamp cooler on the roof drove her to distraction; she placed a few stones in it to muffle the noise, unaware that these would break the floater valve. There was more friction with her landlords, as her work took her away from home for long periods of time and she fell behind in her cleaning duties.

Her time in Oakland, lucrative as it was, also had its down side. There were territorial issues; it was, after all, Carolyn's space, and she consequently got to set all the rules, but her frequent changes of mind and mood were hard to keep up with. Carolyn had also taken up piano lessons, and her practicing, sometimes starting as early as five a.m., grated on Juliet's sensitive ears—this was not the way she wanted to be awakened in the morning, especially since her sleeping quarters were the living room couch. She had only the massage-room closet for storing her belongings, and no real space to call her own. On top of all this was the general stress of being in the city, away from her mountain getaway and her feline companions.

One exciting break from the daily grind arrived in the form of a long-time phone-sex customer, cross dresser Walter (not his real name). He traveled from New York—at her invitation—to see her, and they spent a pleasant week together in early April. They got along well, although Walter clearly had a drinking problem. For Walter, it was a thrill to meet his idol Juliet Anderson; for Juliet, their sexual encounters were pleasant but not intense. She got to indulge in her favorite activities—lots of skin contact and cock sucking—but the two of them refrained from actual intercourse. Walter had a fetish for backs; he came on hers, and asked if she had ever noticed how many scenes in her films included cutaways to her back (she had not). The only down side of the sexual play was Juliet's sore pussy; she was not up for much cunnilingus. After two days at the cottage, Juliet and Walter traveled to the Mendocino hideaway where Juliet and Carolyn spent their New Year vacations, stopping in at Raamwood on the way back home. Overall, she was happy with the visit. "I think it was the best week I ever spent with a man." A sad comment, if it was true, considering all of her relationships over the years.

Following Walter's visit, Juliet had an exceptionally busy and intense week at Carolyn's. On one of the days, all their appointments fell through, but four last-minute clients filled the gap; one of them had an elaborate fantasy he wanted them to play out with him. Another day, one of Juliet's favorite regulars actually gave *her* a massage—a good one, too. And a first-timer was so moved that he went into an altered state of consciousness, vibrating all over. After he recovered he stayed for dinner.

Carolyn and Juliet took a two-day trip to rural Marin County after this intense week, clambering down cliffs to walk on the beach, riding horseback from Five Brooks Stable (the departure point for the disastrous erotic filming expedition in 1979), playing nude frisbee in a friend's back yard, enjoying fabulous food at some of Point Reyes

Station's touristy restaurants, and being lulled to sleep by the sound of the surf. Juliet "felt tears of gratitude for this beautiful earth and my many blessings." She returned to a foot of snow in Pollock Pines: California, the land of diversity.

Meantime, John Sibbett was beginning to show his true colors—and poor boundaries. He spent class time enumerating his personal problems: his marriage was falling apart and he was in love with another woman. At Juliet's next private session with him, he spent the entire hour and a half talking to her as she lay nude on the massage table wrapped in the customary sheet. Juliet sympathized with his situation, of course; nothing like a story of true love to engage her attention. She was clear that the new woman was right for him and his marriage was a mistake. Disappointingly, in July he reversed his position and returned to his wife, who, alas, had moved on by then.

Actually, Juliet's reliance on alternative healing technologies in general was beginning to seem ill-advised. By early June, her fibroid uterine tumors were worsening, and her doctor recommended surgery. With some trepidation, she scheduled a hysterectomy for late August.

Juliet was also feeling some conciliation toward her family, relenting on her ultimatum—recovery or no contact—only requesting that her family refrain from drinking during her visits with them. She later dropped this request as well, realizing that she could choose to absent herself, at least temporarily, from uncomfortable situations. In early May, a short visit from Chris and Monica—who were on a college investigation trip—went well. The sisters were able to set aside their differences and focus on immediate problems and situations.

In mid-May, Juliet attended another Jack Kornfield workshop in Marin County, but a bad cold prevented her from getting much out of it. She came home and collapsed into bed, congested, coughing and feverish. A few days later a four-person backpacking trip to Sutter Buttes, scheduled to coincide with the full moon on May 20th, did little to improve Juliet's mood. The party separated, as Carolyn, high on ecstasy, wandered off to a more secluded spot. Relatively ignorant mountain hikers, the group had injudiciously chosen to set up camp on a ridge top, exposed to the frigid spring winds. So much for the planned drumming and dancing; just sitting and watching the moon rise was a challenge, especially for Juliet, who was still recovering from her severe cold. She did manage to find the one flat spot on the ridge, and spent the night huddled in her sleeping bag, even her head drawn in against the cold, the howling of the wind penetrating her sleep. Although the sunrise, glimpsed through the morning fog drifting up from the valley, was stunning, Juliet was relieved to get home to junk food, a hot shower, and a nap with the cats. She fell asleep listening to a tape of John Zaradin's classical guitar music. ("I wonder whatever happened to him.")

Luckily, a pleasanter vacation was in the offing. Phone-sex client Walter had invited her to New York for five days in early June. This triggered an argument with Juliet's landlady, who asked her to be around to help with household chores during her own surgery, on her hand. But of course recreation, especially a sexual liaison, came before duty for Juliet; God forbid she would ever consider changing her own plans. This incident, along with her landlord's discovery of the swamp cooler damage, sealed her fate at the cottage: an eviction notice followed. Juliet managed to get this postponed, only until after her surgery and recovery at first, but later, to the end of the year.

Her trip to New York, while not a high point, was relatively pleasant. She saw Annie Sprinkle's show, and Michele Capozzi, the Italian immigrant whose autobiography she had transcribed, took her around to some of the Italian hangouts. The highlight of the trip was finally meeting Joseph Kramer, who was there visiting Annie. He and Juliet connected immediately, and he urged her to consider teaching a class in sensual massage at The Body Electric in Berkeley.

Staying at Walter's dirty ill-kept apartment was more of a challenge, as was listening to his litany of personal problems, but the low-key sexual encounters were pleasant enough. Juliet visited art galleries and of course shopped for clothing, to assuage her discomfort with the dirt, noise, misery and "low-conscious" New Yorkers. A tour of the Bronx was a mistake, leaving her depressed and disgusted. Good to get home to civilized California.

On returning home, Juliet switched therapists, returning to Maureen Namen in Oakland, whom she and Carolyn had gone to back in 1984. She continued, though, with both the same techniques —sand tray work and visualizations in addition to talk therapy, and the same issues—giving up her victimhood and finding her power, getting over her anger at her parents for stifling her creativity and for using her illnesses to avoid dealing with the real family problems. While Juliet acquired many insights and developed many counter-affirmations over the years, she continued obsessing about these same themes, visiting them again and again.

The big event at the end of the summer was Juliet's hysterectomy, scheduled for Wednesday, August 30th. She prepared herself emotionally as well as physically, meeting ahead of time with the doctor and anesthesiologist to get her questions answered and discuss details of the procedures at the hospital, and engaging in a ritual with her supportive women friends. They sat in a circle, running a long length of red yarn between them—a symbol of menstrual blood, passing around an egg—a symbol of fertility, and chanting Goddess rhymes: "I am the flow, I am the ebb, I am the weaver, I am the web." Juliet kept some of the yarn, entwining it into her MedicAlert bracelet. The women also gave her crystals—two carnelian, two aventurine and a tourmaline—which she put into in a pouch that she hung around her neck; she even wore this into the operating room. Later there was a tampon-burning ceremony.

Juliet spent the night before the surgery at a friend's house, awakening at 5:30, in an anxiety that all her preparations had not been able to completely assuage. At dawn she walked to the hospital. She was shown to her room and the anesthesiologist came in to talk with her. At 7:30 she was wheeled into the operating room, fully awake. The nurses were personable and friendly, dressed in blue with flowered caps. The IV was put into her left forearm; it would stay in place for two days. Soon the relaxant kicked in and the anesthesiologist gave her the epidural shot. Juliet drifted off into numbness, and the surgery commenced. Only once during the two-hour procedure did she experience any discomfort—some cramps. The anesthesiologist offered to put her under but she declined, opting instead for an additional epidural shot. The doctors waited patiently for the twenty minutes that it took to completely kick in, the anesthesiologist stroking her cheek and speaking softly to distract her. When the operation was over and she was to be moved to recovery, the nurses asked her if she wanted to see her removed uterus. She assented; it seemed to be about the size of a Crenshaw melon. Both the surgeons spoke to her kindly before taking their leave.

The next few hours in the recovery room were dreadful. Juliet was in tremendous pain, her jaw locked and her muscles weak, and she was trembling violently. Her cries of agony brought the nurses, who massaged her neck and put warm towels on it. Unfortunately, although her lips were parched and she was ravenously thirsty, the lingering effects of the anesthesia restricted palliative measures to a damp cloth to moisten her mouth. The agony seemed to go on forever, but the staff were kind and attentive; the anesthesiologist came by several times, comforting her and apologizing for her pain; it was an unexpected aftereffect that occasionally occurred.

Back in her hospital room the next day, she found that the pain had shifted. Her neck felt fine now, but abdominal, back, leg and arm pain had started up—partly a result, she found out later, of her arthritis, which can be activated by surgery. Still, she could at least sip water and lie on her side, and—blessing of blessings—scratch herself; one of the aftereffects of the anesthesia was itching. She also taped four magnets onto her bandage, a treatment from her arsenal of alternative healing regimes. And, eschewing most of the "atrocious" hospital cuisine, Juliet had brought her own food. She was the talk of the first-floor staff: "That lady in 1142 with the stones, magnets and health food."

One final trauma was her roommate in the hospital, a seriously injured biker recovering from a traffic crash in which five of her friends had died. Between those losses and having to endure questioning by the California Highway Patrol, the unfortunate woman was in so much shock that she moaned and ranted much of the time. She was finally moved to another room and assigned a crisis worker.

That stress relieved, Juliet could relax and start to focus on healing. Not one to turn her back completely on allopathic medicine, she accepted two pain shots and later occasional pain pills, supplementing these, of course, with another alternative remedy—marijuana brownies. The resulting haze made the entire hospital experience much more tolerable.

Letter from Friend before Hysterectomy Surgery

Dear Judith,

Thought I would drop a little note to you before your surgery on August 31. Want to let you know that my prayers will be with you as always as you undergo this operation. May the Lord be with you during the surgery, and God speed a quick and healthy recovery.

Hard to imagine that the photo layout in 40+ was taken nearly eleven years ago. Your beauty has been well maintained, for you look just as good now, perhaps even better, than you did back then.

I know that the persona of Judith is a far cry from that of "Aunt Peg" or Juliet Anderson, but it is somewhat mystifying to me why you should talk of your past personas as being the "sexy" part of your life, about how "she" gave so many pleasures, and that via that persona, "she" still does.

If it is meant that those personas were strictly used to elicit emotions to and from those who sought enjoyment from them, then I think you underestimate the woman inside those personas. Sure Aunt Peg and Juliet Anderson were "roles" that you played as an actress, and yes those characteristics demanded sultry, sexy, and often prurient emotions, but to many it was not the character who elicited those emotions, but it was the woman behind the character.

Aunt Peg / Juliet Anderson could not have been so emotionally charged, so full of that vitality, if the person portraying the personas did not have those same emotional capacities built up within herself. This is not to say that the roles and the person were one and the same. I'm quite sure that off screen you did not run out looking for the nearest man and bedroom. But you have the personal capacity for those emotions, and I think it would be a tragedy to declare them void in your life.

How many times have I heard you mention a search for a soul mate to share your life with. That emotional desire, that capacity for love, is part of you, Judith Cathleen Carr, not merely that of Aunt Peg or Juliet Anderson. Yes, now those emotions have taken on a different form, that of personal love and a belief in inner peace, but they are still there, for they grow, just as we grow, and while the form may change, the being remains.

Yes, the old personas served you well. But the new persona, the person you are and desire to be still can be served by allowing those emotions, that capacity to love, to be allowed to see the sunlight, to breathe the air, to live.

But enough already. My best to the cats, my prayers and love to you.

Love, John

All in all, though, the project was a success, a far cry from "the cold, sterile, frightening wards of my youth," imbued as those were with feelings of loneliness and abandonment. She had asserted her needs, asked for information ahead of time, taken care of herself as much as she could, and received warmth, nurturing and acceptance from the staff. One thing she neglected to assert was that she did not want her ovaries removed, probably because it did not occur to her. There was no need to remove them, but to the still-male-dominated medical establishment of the time it was standard procedure to do so. After all, you can't see them, and what good are they anyway? Well, they happen to be the primary source of a woman's libido. It was many months before Juliet realized the effect their removal had on her. While it was true that she was near menopausal age anyway, that transition was made more abrupt than it would have been with her ovaries still in place.

The next several weeks were peaceful, as Juliet took it easy and relied on her friends, especially women, to help and support her. She spent the first two nights out of the hospital with the same friend who had put her up the night before the operation, and continued to accept food and errand-running help for the next week or so.

In September, she got another health scare when a cyst was found in her breast. It was minor, though, and no cause for alarm. By the time the women's spirituality group gathered for their equinox ritual near the end of the month, Juliet's health had settled down, and she was relatively pain-free and able to focus on her life again. It was about this time that she took on another part-time job facilitating a cancer support group.

Other stresses began to add up, though. Her mother was drinking more and having emotional breakdowns; Chris had her committed to the state hospital again. Her father's heart problems seemed to be worsening. The October 17th Loma Prieta earthquake, while it did not affect her directly, upset both animals and humans. The cats were restless and frightened, and the erotic massage business took a dive. Chris wanted Juliet to come down to southern California to stay with their parents while she herself took a trip to England with her husband. Juliet agreed at first, out of guilt, then declined after talking it over with her therapist and some of her friends. Despite her mother's deteriorating mental state and her father's despair over her, they were after all adults and could manage by themselves. And they did.

Anonymous letter from client, 1989

Juliet:

I don't know if I will ever see you again. It was a magical moment. It was more than just the touching, feeling, embracing, and kissing (although the kissing was mind-blowing). I think it was just you!

There is something unique and incredible about you. Maybe it's because you are 51; like aging wine. I recall expressing my surprise, and your rejoinder being "It really is amazing." But I was truly impressed that sensuality and spirituality flowed through you without contradiction; sort of like being of this world and other-worldly at the same time.

I can feel and smell you as I write. You were a beautiful experience; like feeling the world was really good, ecstatically so.

Only an hour, but I feel I know you in some unknown way. In fact, I may never know you any better than now.

I believe there are cracks in the universe. Occasionally, one comes across such a crack and gets a glimpse of something Extraordinary. Maybe in that one hour I experienced one of those cracks.

You may wonder why this is unsigned. For one thing, you don't know me. I suspect I am just an unknown face in the crowd. If, however, you experienced something in that hour also, then you will know who I am.

As I read the above, I see angels with tears running down their faces, bent over, holding their stomachs in a paroxysm of laughter.

In early October, Joseph Kramer called to formally offer Juliet a position at The Body Electric, teaching sensual erotic massage for women, for two weekends early in 1990. They would negotiate her exact payment, but it would be between $500 [$900] and $1,000 [$1,800] for each class. At first she thought she and Carolyn might lead it together, but Carolyn declined and Juliet realized this was a signal to her to step out on her own more. This was to be the first such offering in the Bay Area. "I'm blazing a new trail again."

Only a few days later, Carolyn called with an even more exciting proposition: a client had offered her the use of his condo in Hawaii for a week, as payment for a long weekend trick. Would Juliet like to come along? Carolyn called at 10 a.m.; they needed to make a decision by one p.m. Juliet gave it about twenty minutes before calling her back to accept, putting aside her cleaning work and a few health-care appointments she had scheduled. So off they went.

The trip turned out well, as their schedules were complementary. Juliet was a morning person; she would rise early, do her exercises, make coffee and bring a cup to Carolyn in bed, then go out for a walk; Carolyn would rise at her leisure after reading in bed. When Juliet returned they would go out for the day together. They had a pleasant time and managed not to get into any major altercations. It was certainly a contrast to Juliet's trip with Roger almost a year earlier, and gave her a much more positive view of Hawaii; she returned several times for vacations over the years.

In November, in accordance with her agreement with her landlords, Juliet found another cottage to rent, back in Placerville; she planned to move within a few weeks, but ended up delaying until January, giving her time to spiff up the new place more to her liking, putting up more shelving and painting the walls pink. The autumn was beautiful—warm and sunny; the rains were late this year. She spent a quiet Thanksgiving alone, making lists of things she was grateful for.

The warm weather gave Juliet a chance to experience another New Age ritual: being buried up to her neck in a friend's back yard. A small group of both women and men helped her dig the shallow "grave" and line it with a foam pad and sleeping bag. Juliet lay down in the depression and the others covered her with rich damp earth, placed a flat piece of obsidian over her heart and lighted candles on top of it. She lay there in the warm November sun under the almost-bare branches of an oak tree, for two and a half hours, watching the falling leaves and the hawks soaring overhead, listening to birdsong and the buzzing of insects. "It was humbling to view life at that low level," she wrote in her journal. "I felt great peace and connectedness with all living and dying things."

In early December, Juliet spent eight straight days in Oakland, staying in Carolyn's house while Carolyn herself was gone. It was the most financially successful week she had ever had, netting $3,600 [$6,900]. She also experimented with a new erotic massage style, working on the floor on a fur rug and using a light rhythmic touching; it felt deeply powerful to both her and her clients. Staying and working at the house by herself made her realize how stressful sharing it with Carolyn always was, and she determined to find her own space. Her thought was to buy her own house in Oakland; she could sublet it to other massage therapists, and even hold classes there.

She had a good visit with Mirjia as well, even lending her money, for a switch; it felt powerful. Mirja had gotten into therapy and Juliet felt she was making some positive changes. They walked on the Marina Green in Berkeley together, and drove through the area of Oakland that had been damaged by the earthquake; Juliet declared it "not too bad." The neighbors there, primarily low-income families of color, might have had a different take on it.

Heading back home afterward, she stopped for an appointment with John Sibbett and did a past-life regression in which she had been martyred by the Puritans. Wonderful material for a drama queen, and for a new affirmation: "In expressing my Divine Purpose, I now openly express myself and my heart and love!" By the time Monica arrived for a short visit, Juliet was in fine form, advising her niece to listen to her inner voice, be aware of the potential destructive power of her beauty, and guard against being a manipulator. She also took her along to a medicine wheel celebration.

After a short trip to Raamwood, where she was beginning to feel exploited now that the romance of the rustic unheated sleeping quarters was wearing thin, and then on to the more luxurious Wilbur Hot Springs, Juliet spent the last two weeks of December saying good-bye to the Pollock Pines cottage, sorting through her belongings and discarding things—even the bright yellow telephone that had gotten her arrested in Chicago; she gave it to a battered women's shelter as a toy for the children. She also got rid of the last of her show clothing. "I feel so much lighter. It's part of my past, not my current life."

Still, she was her old narcissistic self at a Christmas get-together. Although she realized she was being controlling and sarcastic, "I can't stop myself even though I know it's obnoxious. I'm ashamed of myself. I won't have any friends if I keep this up." She also followed her old pattern of using sex as a distraction, inviting an old fuck buddy, Per, to visit her. A Trager therapist had advised her that rocking and thrusting motions have a healing value for whole body; they loosen the spine and neck. A great rationalization.

Juliet returned to Carolyn's house on Christmas night and they did four days of doubles together before setting out for Mendocino for their traditional end-of-year ecstasy retreat. She and Carolyn got along much better than usual. Carolyn was sure that it was because they were no longer competing. Juliet was dubious, "I never felt any competition before," but kept her reservations to herself.

After returning home they went to a show at the Market Street Cinema to see a stripper friend, Crystal, perform. Although they arrived too late to see the performance they hung out in the lobby; Juliet even stripped off her upper-body clothing and did a photo shoot with an old fan, who was thrilled. The incident reminded her of how much she loved performing live, despite her new resolutions. Carolyn encouraged her to find a way of doing it occasionally.

Juliet enumerated 1989's accomplishments. Her handling of the surgery was a major breakthrough. She had learned to be assertive with health professionals but also to admit her vulnerability and to ask for help. And, "I can now accept the wearing down of my body and don't feel a failure because my health isn't perfect." She had clarified her approach to her family, finding a good balance, she felt, between co-dependency and abandonment. She was leaving what had become a toxic living environment, and had discovered a new bodywork style. "1989 was a culmination of four to five years of hard work and inner growth." The final year of the penultimate decade of the twentieth century, however, would bring changes that she could not foresee.

20

Wherever You Go,
There You Are

Juliet celebrated the new year of 1990 with a twenty-guest dinner party at her Pollock Pines cottage on January 8th, a last sendoff before her move back into Placerville. The meal was partly an opportunity to offer her guests real food—homemade ratatouille, polenta, and lemon mousse; one of her frequent complaints about the potlucks so popular with the New Age crowd was their consistently unimaginative culinary offerings—crackers, bread, cold cuts, vegetables and dip, fresh fruit and cheese. "Cooking is a way I share myself with others." A good time was had by all, and everyone even left on time at nine p.m.

Three days later, Juliet rented a U-Haul and hired two strapping young men to help with the move. After another day spent emptying and cleaning out the Pollock Pines cottage, she slid into a mild post-moving depression. She had not yet built her new nest, and the Placerville cottage, shaded on all sides by tall trees, felt dismal compared to the light-filled rooms of the Pollock Pines home she had left. The cats were not happy, either; Snuggles stayed indoors most of the time, and Lucky was injured in a fight with a neighborhood cat, requiring an expensive vet call. In an attempt to make the new cottage more livable, Juliet went shopping in Oakland, spending $900 [over $1,640] mostly on accessories for her new home. She almost had an anxiety attack after adding up all the bills. And despite these purchases, she was not enjoying the process of settling in. She was also disappointed in her declining libido and the physical pain she now experienced during sexual intercourse; even hormone replacement therapy did not restore her to her former state of nubility. The weather was dismal as well, with heavy snows in February preventing her from getting back to the cottage after one of her working trips to Oakland.

The next few weeks were a little better, as Juliet settled back into Placerville and started up her usual round of socializing, obsessing about men, and practicing various New Age therapies. Naturally, she also managed to create enough negative experiences to keep up her usual drama. She wrote a confrontational letter to her friend Shirley, owner of Raamwood, about her feelings of being exploited there; Shirley replied with anger, hurt and resentment. A few days later, attending a fund-raising event for a local non-profit, dressing up despite the frigid weather in flimsy dress, hose and high heels, Juliet made one of her grand entrances—slipping twice on the icy walkway and finally falling. Undeterred, she did not hesitate to advise the hostess on how to improve her presentation, which Juliet felt was woefully inadequate.

Still, despite the continuation of many of her old patterns, the past year had brought some subtle shifts in her consciousness. The primary one was around housing. The eviction from the Pollock Pines cottage and the move back to town felt like a such a defeat that she needed to counteract it. She was tired of—as she put it—fixing places up and then getting evicted, although of course her idea of fixing a place up consisted of changing it to suit herself, not necessarily adding any value for the owner. Her frustrations, at any rate, were a great rationalization for the "American Dream" of buying a house; surely she was just as entitled to owning her own home as anyone else was. And the Universe was sure to agree: "I don't know how I'm going to manifest it, but not to worry... when I set my mind to something that is RIGHT for me it all falls into place." She determined to start shopping for property in El Dorado County.

She had big ideas. She would find a two-bedroom house to rent with an option to buy, purchase it, fix it up, sell it for a profit and then move on to a large property on which she would build a main house and several smaller cottages, making it into not only a home for herself but also a retreat center. She was sure she could find one or two partners for this project, among her New Age friends; several had expressed similar desires.

Yet even while she focused on moving into the foothills permanently, she was spending more and more time in Oakland and San Francisco. In addition to her continuing work with Carolyn, there was the invitation from the O'Farrell Theatre to do some stage shows for the new "Star Stage" they were building. Juliet was tempted, despite her resolution of just a few weeks earlier. She also fantasized

about creating workshops and educational films that would teach
women how to empower themselves sexually. Best of all would be to
have her own theater, if she could find a way to swing that.

Thus, along with her dreams around housing and work space,
she was beginning to feel a shift in identity, although in a more
positive way than when she had fled the city in 1985. This time, she
was turning toward something rather than turning away, and thinking about reclaiming those parts of her sex-worker persona that still
fit. "I'm liking the Juliet name better than Judith; she is more
vibrant." But not "Juliet Anderson;" she was gone. The new Juliet
would incorporate the sex star's spontaneity, creativity and sensuality, but without her egotism or drama. "I've noticed I'm quieter, more
centered, sexy but in a lovely, powerful, deep way. My style continues to take form."

Exactly where or in what way this new Juliet would live and
practice her craft was not clear. Mundane details like that were
unworthy of a free spirit. No contradiction entered her mind, for
example, between her plans for permanent residence in the Sierra
foothills and her increasing dependence on the Bay Area for her
livelihood. She was steeped in the New Age dogma of self fulfillment
and the 1980s mentality of "having it all." Although she had very
little money saved up, and no clear plan about how to accomplish
her new goals, a few affirmations would surely do the trick: "I'm
divinely guided in all I do, so it will all be OK... I am easily going to
get the money I need for this house and other things!" For all her
rebelliousness, Juliet was still driven by many mainstream American
values, albeit couched in new terminology.

First on the agenda was to get out of Carolyn's space and find her
own workplace. Juliet approached her therapist, Maureen, about
sharing office space, but when she realized that she would still need
a place she could stay overnight, she began to think more and more
about a place of her own in Oakland as well as a home in the mountains. Never one to go halfway on anything, Juliet was now fan-
tasizing about buying *two* houses, one in the city and one in the
country. She would have spaces for both living and working, and
could rent out parts of both houses for retreats or workshops.

Acting on this resolve, in March Juliet began to seriously look for
a house to buy in El Dorado County, using her friend Mirja as her

agent. At times, she could hardly believe she was actually taking this step ("Imagine—me, a homeowner!"), which to her signaled entry into true adulthood at last. She hoped to find stability and content-ment in owning property; after all, that's what everyone said would happen. The best prospect was a three-bedroom house on Ridgeway Drive in Pollock Pines—a plain-looking boxy place on a ridge just above noisy Highway 50, surrounded by tall pines but also by other houses. Ridgeway Drive was really just a typical suburban street that happened to be in the mountains, and most of the lots were only large enough for a house and perhaps a small yard. Although it was far from her ideal, the price—$90,000 [$163,800]—was within her range. "Anything under $100K [$182,000] is a steal," one broker told her. She needed $31,000 [$56,400] for a down payment, half right away and the other half in six months, and the current owner wanted to rent it back for several months, until the new house he was build-ing was finished. While this property did not fit with her vision of a small fixer-upper, it seemed good enough, and Juliet moved ahead with plans to round up the down payment amount and qualify for a loan.

It was April now, and Juliet was in the midst of tax preparation, in addition to her usual round of activities, including a Judy Fjell workshop she wanted to attend in Healdsburg in Sonoma County. Her tax bill for 1989 was higher than she had expected, eating up some of her savings, and of course her first-quarter estimated pay-ment for 1990 was due as well. The workshop was a good distrac-tion, though, as well as an ego boost, and a chance to act out her new persona: "I chose to be Juliet (the uninhibited artist) rather than Judith (the respectable matron)."

Back in Oakland, the erotic massage business continued to flourish, although it also took an emotional toll. The negatives—the no-shows, no-confirms and just plain jerks—were a real drain. And new clients were hard to get, many balking at the high price. Still, there were the occasional gems; one client called back to tell Juliet and Carolyn that it had been the most relaxing and sensual exper-ience of his life. Juliet was coming to see herself as a healer, especially in the area of sexuality. More and more of her income was coming from her city work and less and less from the regular massages in

Placerville; the market there was limited and her price per session was lower.

Her need for increased income also led Juliet to take up the offer to do some shows at the O'Farrell Theatre, and one night, as she was leaving, her old flame Frank McGrath approached her in the lobby. He was feeling bereft from the trauma of going through a painful and expensive divorce from Maggie, the woman he had left Juliet for in 1982, and had come to see her because he knew she would lift his spirits. And so she did. Although one of the issues in the divorce was Maggie's infidelity, so that Juliet could have justifiably taken a "serves you right" attitude, she was in fact all sympathy and compassion, even taking him into her bed for a "mercy fuck," as he described it later. It was just what he needed to restore his sagging ego at the time, a typical example of the warmth and caring that characterized Juliet at her best. It was a lift for her, too, in the midst of the frenetic burst of activity she was caught up in.

There were a few glitches, of course, around the anticipated house purchase. The bank wanted her house payments to come to no more than 29% of her gross income; they would in fact be 51%. Juliet resolved this problem by switching to a different bank and doctoring the income tax returns she showed them, making up a fake set that showed a higher income. One of the advantages of being self-employed: there was no employer the bank could check with, and Juliet knew it was highly unlikely that they would demand the official returns from the IRS; they did not.

Conditions in Oakland, though, were not so easy to manipulate. Therapist Maureen was beginning to weird out. She had taken up with a new boyfriend, an old gnome-like bearded hippie, a refugee from the seventies, who lived in his van and had no visible means of support. Maureen seemed to see herself as a sort of "spirit mother" to men like this. Juliet, despite her inability to see her own pattern of bad choices around men, could at least see others', and withdrew from her association with Maureen. She did, however, take on Maureen as a massage client, even doing a sensual massage session with her; Maureen wanted to experience some sexual contact with a woman.

Juliet was restless, wanting resolution on the house purchase and her new direction in business and in life. Patience had never been one of her virtues. Her characteristic ambiguity manifested now, too: "I don't want to be around people and yet I'm dissatisfied alone. Eating lots of salad and cold foods, but crave warm foods, grains and sweets." She continued her various therapies, trying to find some respite from her continual vacillations. It was also the three-year anniversary of Bob Watt's entry into prison, and she found herself thinking of him. "Bob and I are not finished. We were soul brother and sister in a previous life." But despite her frustrations, she did feel that things were about to move forward: "Yes, it's happening. I feel like I'm being tossed about on swells, waiting for the big wave to wash me up on the shore."

By early June, Juliet had scraped together enough borrowed money from family and friends to meet the down payment requirement for the house purchase. As part of her loan application she obtained her credit report, and she was shocked at some of what showed up. The report went all the way back to her early adulthood, in the 1960s. The name Juliet showed up, but fortunately not Anderson. She hoped she could cover up the porn years, using some euphemism like "performance artist." She was ready, though, to sign the papers; the closing was scheduled for Monday, June 11th.

On Thursday the 7th, Juliet was frustrated at not being able to get hold of Carolyn to confirm their double appointments on the 8th. Even Carolyn's answering machine was off. The next day, she found out why: Carolyn had been busted for prostitution and had spent the previous night in jail. Juliet went into a panic. The work with Carolyn was her primary source of income, and, to make matters worse, Juliet had also been implicated in the arrest. Yet she felt isolated and helpless. Carolyn was in Oakland, in the midst of the crisis, whereas Juliet was experiencing it from afar, deeply affected by this trauma over which she had no control. It brought back feelings from her childhood hospitalizations, when other, more powerful people had complete control over her.

A Goddess gathering on Saturday the 9th distracted her for a day, but on the 10th her anxiety returned; she sat numbly through a non-profit fundraising party at the Watterbek Winery, obsessing over her financial stresses. Nevertheless, on Monday the 11th she signed the papers on the new house. In her current emotional state, she felt no excitement. Ironically, she now had her long-dreamed-of house in the

country, but she could not live in it; she would have to move to the
city to make enough money for the mortgage payments. Juliet made
plans to rent the house out and to find living quarters in Oakland.

Juliet's house on Ridgeway Drive in Pollock Pines, and the road leading to it.
Photos by Marian Rhys.

By the end of June, she had recovered some energy and optimism. She settled into Oakland, staying with Carolyn until she could
find an apartment of her own. "My energy has shifted to this area;
Placerville is but a shadow. Once I make up my mind about anything, I simply move ahead. It's clear that I belong here and not in
the hills; my vision is much greater than what I'm allowed in a
provincial place. It's important for Juliet to be connected to Placerville, but what the extent of that connection is, is yet to be seen."

The prostitution charges against her and Carolyn had been
dropped, and the duo moved ahead with their massage business, but
with more caution. They advertised themselves simply as regular
massage therapists, while retaining the erotic clients they knew they
could trust. "What a blessing the bust was," Juliet mused. "The new
way of relating to men is deeper and more enjoyable." She would
add the sexual element for those who wanted it, after she had vetted
them sufficiently, with an increase in the price.

She soon found an apartment she liked, in Piedmont again, in a
pleasant tree-shaded neighborhood near a park. Abruptly, though,
she changed her mind, deciding instead on another place she had
looked at, on noisy Harrison Street in one of the more run-down
areas of Oakland. Why? Because the owner, Arthur, was an "amaz-

ing, dedicated and unusual man... He and I are destined to be in partnership... I know he is the catalyst for me [to] do my work." When she admitted to him the true nature of that work, he was not at first supportive, believing that it was exploitative of women. Ignoring the many red flags over her chosen new home, however, Juliet went ahead and signed the lease.

Back in El Dorado County, she had found a renter for the Pollock Pines house, getting a generous deposit and decent rent. "Getting the house was important for reasons other than to live in it," she rationalized. It would someday be a retreat center, she felt, although exactly when or how that might come about was not at all clear—par for the course for Juliet.

Hardly was the ink dry on her Oakland apartment lease when Alameda County re-instated the prostitution charges against her and Carolyn, and this time they found out the truth about the bust. Although they never did discover who the original informant had been, it was Maureen Namen's testimony that did them in. She had taken on a number of Juliet's and Carolyn's erotic massage clients as johns, for nothing more than simple sexual services—no pretense of any massage. She had been busted, and had agreed to turn state's witness against the other two women, even using information she had garnered from talk therapy sessions against them. And as for those therapy sessions, it turned out that Maureen was not a licensed therapist at all; she had no professional credentials, in fact. All of this information, Juliet and Carolyn gathered from their male clients who had been victims in the scheme. It was quite a blow. Juliet was on the verge of falling apart again: "I feel fragile, vulnerable, *very alone* and isolated." She escaped for a few days to her friends Marc and Lisa, in Woodside, and then went on to a two-day stay at Wilbur Hot Springs with Carolyn. She was also looking forward to a two-week vacation in August with the Pettits, at Lake Arrowhead in San Bernadino County, southern California—not far from Wrightwood, where she and Chris had spent so many childhood vacations.

Juliet returned from Wilbur to find the Oakland apartment still dirty. Arthur, the landlord, had not made any of the repairs he had promised. Nevertheless she remained hopeful about her new abode, hauling boxes of clothes, dishes and cooking equipment down from Placerville and saying goodbye to both people and places in her old home. She still had mixed feelings about the move, vacillating between relief at leaving "the small-town mentality...it's like a coffin, a shroud that oppresses me," and regret: "It's distressing to consider that [I'm giving up on Placerville] after working so hard to establish myself [there] for five years." But she needed to live in the Bay Area to fulfill her dreams—"here life is raw and real, hitting me full force... no more lazy days [or] tranquil nights alone in front of the fire." And she could, after all, find emotional and spiritual sustenance even within a city. "I vow to make peace and tranquility in my life in the city, to daily connect with nature in a deep way."

And she was soon so busy working on the Oakland apartment that she had no time to reflect. Fortunately, Chris came up to help her. The sisters worked their fingers to the bone fixing up the new apartment and completing the move from the Placerville cottage; they spent three days at each dwelling, stopping only briefly to eat and sleep, first at Paul's, to escape the paint fumes, and then on foam mattresses on the floor of the Oakland apartment. They wallpapered the entry of the apartment, washed the blinds, removed and polished all the brass knobs, replaced the electrical outlet plates, and painted the rooms in rosy pastel colors, working on the bathroom until midnight one night. Juliet hired someone to wash the windows inside and out. The landlord, Arthur, was so impressed with a tenant who actually cared (with most of his tenants, he was grateful if they didn't trash the place) that he pulled himself together and put in some real money, polishing and sealing the hardwood floors and buying a new refrigerator. Chris and Juliet then moved on to the Placerville part of the move, packing up the remaining items there and giving the place a thorough cleaning—this in 100° heat. By the time Juliet drove off with her last load, all she could feel was relief. "I felt light, my spirits rose, setting off for a new adventure."

Now for Lake Arrowhead. She and Chris flew to L.A. to join Bob and Monica; they traveled to the lake itself in their camper. Another couple, friends of the Pettits, met them there, and they all checked in to the Hilton, reserving the camper for daytime trips around the area.

As so often happened with her family, Juliet found this visit a mixed experience. She enjoyed their company but was critical of their lifestyles, their friends, and middle-class U.S. society in general. The Pettits had rented a suite in the hotel, and Juliet was given the master bedroom, with its sloping beamed ceiling and high four-poster bed, made up with crisp white sheets and big feather pillows. She felt nurtured and always woke well rested before going out for her usual early-morning walks. And Chris, for all of Juliet's criticism of her codependency, was a calming presence. Since Monica was now a young adult, Chris was free of child-care responsibilities, and the sisters spent most of their time together, reading, cooking, hiking, watching videos, playing Pictionary, scratching each other's backs and occasionally drinking; over the week, they finished off two bottles of champagne together. They shared what felt to Juliet like long heartfelt talks—about their lives, their relationships, their childhoods together. Juliet told Chris the details of her altercation with Nikolas in London in 1968, and felt that Chris "listened patiently and with empathy," although in fact Chris was only giving polite attention and immediately put the talk out of her mind; she retained no memory of it. She preferred not to dwell on unpleasant things, especially when they could not be fixed.

On the down side, Juliet found the public areas dismal and noisy —powerboats sputtering on the lake, lawnmowers and leaf blowers roaring as the maintenance crews went about their work, vociferous beer drinkers posturing, dogs barking, televisions and radios blaring. And, to top it all off, the indolent over-weight American tourists. The scene reminded her of her repatriation trip to Las Vegas in 1977.

And then of course she had to point out her family's flaws: Bob was drinking and watching too much TV; Chris was too much the peacemaker and was addicted to coffee and sugar; their friends were grossly overweight boorish status seekers. Juliet had looked forward to swimming in the lake, but it was not a pleasant experience with the power boats zooming around spewing gasoline fumes and stirring up heavy wakes. Juliet's tastes were far more refined than those of these uncivilized boors. She privately scoffed at such "resort vacations."

Still, for all her recriminations, Juliet was beginning to appreciate her sister's helpfulness and support. The past year had brought more stresses in her life than at any time since she had left the film business: the hysterectomy, moving back to Placerville from Pollock Pines, buying her first house, the vice bust, Maureen's betrayal, and now moving to Oakland, and "I couldn't have come thru these last

few months without Chris. She gave me [emotional] support, groun-
dedness and physical and artistic support."

Once the stress and excitement of the summer was over, Juliet
was left with real life again. By October she was settling in to the next
phase, adjusting to the city, and finding, to her surprise as usual, that
her new environment was not perfect. All the things she hated about
cities—dirt, noise, light pollution at night, low-conscious people—
were rampant in Oakland. There was no great outdoors to walk in;
her exercise was limited to going to the Y and walking around Lake
Merritt. Her landlord, who had been her major reason for choosing
the place she did, was too intrusive, even trying (incompetently) to
advise her and Carolyn about their prostitution case. And Lucky was
a major problem. He was a country cat, unlike Snuggles, who was
San Francisco born and bred; he hid in the crawl space under the
building all day to escape the constant din of traffic and the heavy
energy of Juliet's massage clients, returning nightly for food and
strokes, and then jumping up on the bed at night with Snuggles; she
fell asleep with her two feline friends by her side.

Yet even with her cats' companionship, Juliet's living quarters
did not provide the refuge she needed. Although she loved the way
she had fixed up the apartment, it was too small. The clients' needy
energy invaded her living space, making her frantic and miserable,
but she could not afford a separate work space. In order to make
ends meet, she was seeing too many clients, grabbing at new ones
whenever she could, but always afraid any one of them might be an
undercover vice cop. Her caution led her to downplay the sexual
angle, while simultaneously doing everything she could to keep each
new client entertained enough to come back for more. And the phone
work required to set up appointments was draining; only one out of
twenty-five calls netted a paying session. Then there was the paperwork, including keeping two sets of financial records (one real, and
the other for tax purposes). She was going mostly solo now; she no
longer had the energy to deal with the stress of working with Carolyn, or even seeing her socially. "[I'm] tired of hearing her complaints. Her business is down and she's started to get competitive."
Even being in Carolyn's house was annoying. Carolyn had recently
painted the walls bright pink ("she thinks it's mauve"); never mind

that Juliet had done the same for her Placerville cottage a year and a half earlier.

Meanwhile, the Pollock Pines house was up for rent again; the original tenant had not worked out. Until that was taken care of, Juliet had a mortgage to pay on top of her apartment rent. With the move into town and the additional financial demands, she had given up all her connections to her Placerville life, including the alternative health practitioners she had been seeing.

And to top it all off, she was getting genuinely fed up with the sex business. "I'm sick to death of this work, [I] feel violated... [even] experience revulsion with some clients... I certainly have empathy for the reluctant prostitute." She was especially burned out on phone sex, which was now bringing in so little money it was hardly worth being on call, yet she hung on because she needed every penny she could scrape together; her expenses came to almost $5,000 [over $9,000] per month—a totally unrealistic goal for a straight, non-sexual massage business. Although she was trying to let go and trust in God, she was in fact panicking.

There were times, indeed, when Juliet sank into real depression. Undeniably into her fifties now, she was beginning to realize—in a more concrete, direct way—that life would not go on forever, nor would the world become perfect within her lifetime. "I often ponder the futility of doing *anything*, of even living, it all seems so hopeless. Yet I know I must go on. I'm not suicidal, but I know my death would be mourned by very few, that my life is not important; none of us is important in the final scheme, that humanity will ultimately destroy ourselves and our environment. But...I must live life as if it counted."

During a therapy session, she experienced an insight that she ought to give up the sex business, but she vacillated about what exactly this meant; maybe she was only meant to give up the habit of using her sexuality to entice men, and her ego attachment to the sexy persona. She made an appointment with prominent San Francisco psychologist and sex therapist Maggie Rubenstein, one of the founders of the Institute for Advanced Study of Human Sexuality, to work on this and other questions. "I want to emphasize sensuality, not sexuality, and to empower women. How do I do this and make enough money to live on?" That was the question she had to answer, in order to give direction and meaning to the remainder of her life.

I Am Sick of Love and Lust

I'm tired of being sexy, of spreading sensual streams of bliss across naked flesh, tired of opening my heart and body to adoring gazes and transfixed longing of suppressed desires released by the erotic dance of fingertips, limbs, eyes and breath. I'm tired of carrying the chalice of passion across the parched landscape to trembling lips.

Pour the elixir of longing into *my* vessel. Let me enter the temple of my *own* body, to seek a respite from service to Aphrodite. Spread fragrant rosemary and lavender upon my bruised hands, aching breast. Let me breathe the sweet air of angels, lift me up, make a bed for me in clouds of golden light. Cover me with blossoms.

For I am sick of love and lust. I am tired of all of you, of your own fragmented feminine beneath the armor of muscles and fear, in suits of persuasion, behind the many disguises of masculinity. Let my tiredness rip away the silken veils and expose my vulnerability.

Take me away to the ocean, where the waves wash over me and I frolic in the surf with the dolphins, lie on the hot sand and follow sand crabs into the foam, with raucous gulls and squealing children to delight my ear instead of the sighs and moans of caged passion on furlough from chain gangs building plastic tract houses and concrete ribbons of speed and death.

Come dance with me! Will you feel your scarred flesh, sing with me your broken dreams, sigh with me your lost child?

Enough! Stop! Go away, leave me! I run to the hills and waters to soothe my tiredness and fragile faith. Give me respite, give me solitude, silence and sleep.

Juliet was in fact experiencing many accurate insights about herself during this time. "After the confinement of my childhood I wanted freedom, [and] went to the other extreme as a young adult. Sex gave me the experience of pleasure, that I had a body that could experience something other than pain." But "it was for me, for my pleasure, not to please 'him,' [and] as soon as a man got too close I created a scene and left." This attitude had affected all of her work:

> I had absolutely no idea of how to cooperate, work as a team, compromise. To not be in control was terrifying. I had to be the best, to do it alone, to do it perfectly. I chose professions where I could entertain, get recognition, be glamorous and work alone... What I really craved was...living larger than real life. [The sex business] gave me a chance to be an actress, satisfied my altruism, the teacher in me, and fed my ego. What it didn't give me was respect or money. I was used to being a rebel, and sex was fun. Here was another profession that made intimacy impossible. I created an elaborate facade of the virtues of porno to allow myself to stay in it. [But] all along I was looking for love, and looking for God. When the facade cracked and I got a glimpse of the Truth, I fled to the hills to discover who was really behind the masks.

These insights finally led her to the twelve-step program she most qualified for, Sex and Love Addicts Anonymous. She threw herself into it with her typical intensity, at one point attending three meetings in ten days, although she quickly found out that she needed to stick to women-only meetings, as there were too many porn addicts among the men; her presence was triggering for them, and theirs fed her ego too much.

Unfortunately, like the majority of sex and love addicts, Juliet's recovery was short-lived, for the usual reason: a new drug of choice. This one came in the form of Charles Webb, a redneck San Francisco cable-car operator and recovering alcoholic. An old porn fan turned massage client, he was smitten with Juliet, and far be it from Juliet to turn down adulation, in any form. Besides, it was a great distraction from everything else she wished weren't happening. He declared his undying love in numerous ways, showering her with love letters, original poems, and little presents, calling or showing up frequently, and of course taking her for a free cable-car ride all over the city. Juliet, desperately lonely, burdened with financial pressures, and beginning to feel time slipping away, clung to him, despite feeling no intellectual or emotional connection. She even found him physically repulsive: his long hair and beard, his heavy body hair, and especially his uncircumsized cock, were total turnoffs. Still, she tried hard to force herself to become attracted to him. She never succeeded. The result was an ironically stereotypical mismatched heterosexual relationship, with Charles trying to get more sex and Juliet trying to evade it. Aunt Peg, the great, uninhibited freewheeling porn star, acting like any sexually repressed housewife.

In November, Juliet found another escape: a new group of psychedelic drug users who got together for periodic weekend binges referred to as "family trips." They would gather in a large house, consume psilocybin, acid or ecstasy, or mixtures thereof, and hang out—often in the nude—primarily as isolated individuals, each absorbed in his or her own private world. Participants would lie around listening to music, or occasionally dance or do art work, eating only enough to sustain themselves and sleeping on and off as they needed. On one occasion, as Juliet lay on the floor under a window, bright sunlight warming her body, a gay man she knew only vaguely came over and lay down beside her. While they did not speak or touch, she loved the feeling of peace and safety he brought—quiet sensuous enjoyment of the warmth on their bodies, with a total absence of sexual energy between them. A nice break from the struggles with Charles.

On another weekend, Juliet cavorted in the back yard, rolling nude in the grass and performing a scarf dance, reveling in childlike joy, sensuous rather than seductive—sincerely feeling only pure self-pleasure, not wanting to show off. At the Sunday afternoon group wrap-up session, where all the participants got together to talk about their experiences, several people remembered her dancing and thanked her for the infectious joy of this performance; it had lifted their own spirits.

Just before Thanksgiving Juliet went to a 300-person retreat at Spirit Rock Meditation Center in rural Marin County, led by Ray Stubbs. It was during this event that Ray approached her about writing an essay for a book he was planning—real-life stories and commentary from women sex workers. She was delighted at the thought; writing was the one passion she had not really pursued, at least not since Finland.

Juliet had mixed feelings during the retreat, though. She was inspired by the peaceful rural setting, and by the participants' gentle energy. Yet she often felt lonely and inept because there were so many couples. She put off sharing in small group until the very end, but tried to tell her story straight, without drama, and several people praised her for that effort. Although this experience brought her more insights ("I must quit using my sexuality in my work, I must move to quieter living quarters, and I must address my addictions"), she sank back into depression within days of getting back home. The insights were gratifying, but how could she put them into action? She liked the title Joseph Kramer had coined for his graduates —"sacred intimate"—and his definition of work space as a temple rather than a massage parlor. Yet only "a few clients 'get' what I do— that sexual release isn't necessary or is a minor part, and they validate my work, [whereas] most clients are ruled by their sexuality." But she needed to make money—lots of it, for the first time in her life, and didn't have a clue how to do that. Maggie Rubenstein had encouraged her to start going to meetings of COYOTE,[26] the sex-worker support group founded by Margo St. James and carried on by her erstwhile partner Carol Stewart after Margo relocated to France to avoid living in an increasingly conservative U.S. culture. This outreach Juliet did not follow through on, however, until years later.

In a women's gathering in early December, Juliet was able to relax and share more openly than she had at the Spirit Rock retreat. She realized that she had one great advantage over most of the women there: she was comfortable in her body. She also felt safe enough to relive her miscarriage in Finland, although she referred to it now as an elective abortion. After intense grieving, she drew a picture: "bold, free, voluptuous in reds and purples, of my breasts, womb, vagina and heart, legs spread, giving and receiving love/sex/pleasure. From the flower of my cunt to my heart, energy flowed back and forth, a powerfully affirmative, erotic and joyful image. What a rebirth!"

Juliet spent a few days over Christmas at a friend's house in El Dorado County, trying to enjoy the silence and the pale winter

---

[26] "Call Off Your Old, Tired Ethics"

sunlight filtering through the pines, even though the house was garishly decorated ("puke green, orange, brown ochre, and the tasteless style of the 1950s") and sickeningly cluttered. She comforted herself with shopping, followed by the traditional New Year retreat with Carolyn in Mendocino. Before leaving, though, she met with a property management agent who would be able to find her a renter for the Pollock Pines house. One thing she had done right was to arrange for a house sitter in the interim, who kept the heat on enough to prevent the burst water pipes that some other residents were experiencing with the 8°F nighttime temperatures. It was good to spend a few days in the hills, even though she knew she no longer wanted to live there full-time.

The new year, 1991, started out with less hope and more trouble than the previous year had, but also with many former uncertainties at least partially settled. She had given up the last of her ties to Placerville. The agency quickly found a new tenant for the Pollock Pines house, a single mother who worked in one of the lumber mills. Juliet could now start looking for a separate office in Oakland, so that her apartment would feel more like a haven and less like an energy sink. It was April, though, before she found a back bedroom in a large house that she could rent for this purpose.

Lucky was finally becoming better adapted to life in the city, and Juliet abandoned her plans to try to find him a new home back in the country. He was now an affectionate lap cat, and was even putting on weight from lack of exercise.

Ever since Chris's help with setting up her Oakland apartment, and the Lake Arrowhead vacation of the previous summer, Juliet was also feeling a little better about her family, valuing the attachment she still felt to them and sincerely worrying about her aging parents' health—genuinely concerned now, rather than castigating them. Her father was having open heart surgery in April, and Juliet was convinced he would not survive. She grieved what she was sure was his impending death, although in fact he came through just fine. Juliet went to visit after he returned home, taking Carolyn with her. This was the first time Carolyn had met her parents, and the visit turned out very well. Carolyn's presence changed the whole dynamic between Juliet and her mother, and they were able to share some intimate talks, even delving into the topic of the erotic massage work.

"It was the best time Mom and I have ever had; we were relaxed, silly, [and] spontaneous, and talked about real things." The experience gave Juliet an entirely new perspective on her mother. She felt that they shared some core qualities: "vivaciousness, sexiness and love of adventure and glamour. I now know how thrilled she was about Juliet Anderson being a star, but couldn't share it [with me]." Unfortunately but not surprisingly, her mother's new openness did not last long; even before the visit was over she was back to drinking and histrionics.

As for her own inner work and personal change, Juliet decided to give up all but one twelve-step program—Workaholics Anonymous, obviously the least threatening to her self-concept. She figured she qualified because she spent so much time and energy on her work while accomplishing very little in the way of financial security. This decision left her free to pursue her other addictions without guilt. After all, she had a new relationship to focus on. And she did try hard, mostly to convince herself that it mattered to her in some way other than desperation. She told everyone she was in love with Charles, hoping that would make it true. She forced herself to relax her post-menopausal vagina so that sex would be less painful. She tried to focus on Charles's good points, primarily (or perhaps exclusively would be a better word) his devotion to her. Yet she knew better. "He's an alcoholic, albeit a sober one, but I don't want one in my life. When I hear 'I love you' I also hear 'Take care of me.'.. Do I want a primary partner? At this point I don't know, but Charles is not it. I'm learning a lot thru him, but it's a duty, a chore."

Then, of course, there was real life. Again. Funny how it followed her everywhere. Her new work space, while it had the virtue of being separate from her living space, had little else to recommend it. The barking of the home owner's dog disturbed her work, and the shouts of his mistress did nothing to improve the situation. As for her own property in Pollock Pines, things were beginning to fall apart. Even before the new tenant moved in, five cords of wood were stolen off the property. And then there was the tenant herself, Deanna, who seemed to be one of those jinxed people tormented by a constant black cloud. First, she suffered an injury at work and was out on worker's compensation leave, reducing her income considerably. Then she was in a fender bender, resulting in a whiplash injury. Next, the lumber mill burned down and all the workers were laid off, cutting off any future employment there, even had she recovered enough to return, thus disqualifying her from any more disability payments from that job. Juliet, never questioning whether all of these stories were true, and all too familiar herself with financial stress and bad luck, was all sympathy, even writing an entry in her journal from Deanna's point of view—how could she keep a roof over her head, feed her kids, pay her medical bills? To help her stay there, Juliet thought of using part of the house as a retreat center, thereby reducing the rent. Yet she did not in fact have the time or money to pursue this idea. Instead, she allowed Deanna's cousin to move in, hoping that would help her make ends meet, although in fact this approach did not result in any more rental payments, only more wear and tear on the house.

Then there was the stress of Juliet's family's problems. Her parents were in turmoil again, her mother in and out of the mental hospital and her father's vitality fading. He was, Juliet declared dramatically, "scared to live, scared to die. Now he'll probably waste away in a nursing home and Mom will self-destruct in alcoholism." Her grief and frustration overflowed. "I won't see them again," she resolved angrily. "It's a relief, but it hurts. I wish they were dead because to me their souls are; they're empty shells, only their bodies won't give up." Fortunately, this was just another of Juliet's overstatements.

It was Juliet herself, though, who was sliding into depression again. By the time her fifty-third birthday rolled around in July, she found herself thinking about death, even more intensely than she had the previous summer.

> For the first time in my life I am depressed to the point of thinking my life is pointless; why go on? I'm going to die anyway, why prolong this agony? I'm not so depressed as to commit suicide, but I recognize it as an option. Being brutally realistic I know my life is unimportant and my death would matter to few. Charles, Carolyn and Chris for a while, perhaps...and then they would get on with their lives. I am going to do no great things by which I am remembered, and striving to that end to leave my mark is the pursuit of a mad fool.

A far cry from her optimistic "I am just embarking on the most exciting period of my life" statement at her fiftieth birthday. Still, she had enough energy to go on, if only one day at a time. "I have touched, and will continue to touch, people's lives in small ways. I want to be satisfied and find pleasure in these 'small things.' To chop wood and carry water with reverence and joy for all of life. 'We can do no great things, only small things with great love.' (Mother Theresa). 'Almost everything you do is unimportant, but it is important that you do it anyway.' (Ghandi)." Juliet plodded onward.

One place she found relief was her journals. It was during these initial readjustment years in Oakland that Juliet wrote most prolifically—memories, remembered dreams, confessions, and often just stream-of-consciousness outbursts that sometimes screamed with anger or wailed in fear and despair. It was truly a dark night of the soul for her, and even her various therapies and alternative health practices (which she had resumed with Bay Area practitioners) could not assuage her pain and fear. She had feelings so intense they were hard to express; they felt like a tornado inside her, whirling around and around with no outlet.

She was in her mid-fifties, rudderless, still drifting on a sea of ambiguity. Perhaps even scarier was that she was beginning to lose her memory. Still cherishing the dream of writing her life story, and realizing that the details were beginning to slip away, she filled journal pages with evocative scenes from her childhood, young adulthood, and film career. She even began work on a script for a stage play of her life story. Yet the autobiography project terrified her, for reasons that she could not explain.

> I reached a wall of fear and I stopped writing... [I] don't know why I feel so inadequate, like a fraud, no talent, can't do it, won't succeed, or will succeed and have to deal with fame... [These] two tendencies have been at war within me—fear of failure combined with fear of success.

At least some of her fear around writing her memoirs may have stemmed from her realization of the effort it would take to tell it the way she wanted to present it, rather than the way it really was.

Keeping up pretenses, not only while writing but also while promoting the book, would be a monumental task; it would not be easy
to lie consistently, especially with her failing memory. Yet telling the
truth terrified her; she would be so vulnerable!

Other stresses continued to pile up as well. Reluctantly, she
started the process of eviction on the Pollock Pines tenant, who was
now $4,000 [$7,000] behind in the rent, sending her a "pay up or
else" letter, and meanwhile applying for a loan to build a carport and
storage shed on the property. She also got a scare about her own
health—a lump in her breast; she scheduled a biopsy for August 6th.
The thought of losing one of "my lovely breasts, part of my fame"
was more than she could bear. As the time approached, though, she
began to feel intuitively that the lump was benign, as indeed it
turned out to be. Juliet kept her amazing breasts for the rest of her
life, and they never seemed to age—a phenomenon that even she
herself could never explain.

Despite her bouts of depression, she did continue to have hopes
and plans. She thought of going on a lecture tour, speaking on the
subject of healthy sexuality; perhaps she and Carolyn could pair up.
She still wanted to go back on stage, and to make erotic videos—not
the simplistic jerk-off variety but something more refined, higher
quality, along the lines of *Educating Nina*. The sensual touching workshop she had led at the Body Electric stimulated her desire to do
more of this kind of work, perhaps in a different venue. Most of all,
she had come to realize that she was "*a body-centered, experiential
person*. I need to practice movement, dance, every day, followed by
silence, meditation to process it." And she realized she also did better
when working with groups or at least with a partner; the one-on-one
nature of the erotic massage business was draining. She did find a
new partner, Joy, with whom to share work space, although they did
not do doubles together.

So it was that, as summer drifted into fall, Juliet began to feel
some renewed interest in life, and hope for her future. Wanting to
bring more spirituality into her bodywork practice, she signed up for
a short course, "Religion of the Body" at the Pacific School of Religion in Berkeley.

September brought another welcome interlude as well—"a five-
day escape from the tedium and stress"—when she and Carolyn

appeared as guests on the Joan Rivers Show, as women over age fifty who were voluntarily working in the sex business. They traveled together to New York City, where they were put up in a luxurious hotel for two nights. The show itself, which took only two hours of their time, was a disappointment, as they later found out that the tag line for both of them was "Prostitute," but otherwise the trip was wonderful. "I found a New York I'd never known," Juliet wrote in her journal. In their free time they strolled through Central Park and down Sixth Avenue. They bought a delicious take-out feast, which they brought back to their hotel room and spread out on the round glass-topped table that had been draped with a full-length cloth whose soft folds fell down to the deep plush carpet. They enjoyed their repast while lounging in easy chairs, bare feet up on the beds, makeup-less in their nightshirts. Plenty of alcoholic beverages were available with which to supplement these delectables; the room was equipped with a well-stocked refrigerator and bar. Thick white monogrammed towels hung in the bathroom; fancy toiletries made bathing a sensuous experience. Juliet slept deeply and restfully both nights, in her own double bed, sinking into the huge down pillow and stretching out luxuriously between the silky sheets, covered with thick brocaded spreads, the good firm mattress supporting her tired back.

This respite was short-lived. Back home in Oakland, Juliet's poor decisions around money were about to come home to roost, and 1991 ended in much worse state than it had begun. Everything was falling apart.

It started with the huge Oakland Hills fire in October. Although the fire was several miles away, the sights, sounds and smells pervaded the entire East Bay for days. Billowing clouds of reddish-gray smoke filled the sky, airplanes and helicopters droned and clattered overhead, sirens screamed, cinders fell even in Juliet's neighborhood, incessant news reports filled the airwaves and news-papers. And always, everywhere, the acrid smell of smoke and a restless heaviness that spooked the cats and turned Juliet's thoughts to the ephemeral nature of life, plans and possessions. The smoke also brought back a scary memory from her childhood, when the hill near their Burbank house had burned and her mother, for some reason disoriented, had wandered up the hill and had almost been caught in the fire. How far would this fire spread? Would it engulf the lowlands? the Jack London house where she had lived in 1981? the University of California campus? Juliet packed up a few of her most treasured possessions, trying to imagine what it would be like to have to evacuate.

Fire on the Hillside

Summer in southern California is almost synonymous with fire; the bone-dry hills present a constant danger. On one especially hot dry evening a wildfire on a nearby hillside came dangerously close to the Carr home, and an alarmed Fred ran outside, hauled out the garden hose and started drenching the house roof, his skin turning grey from the falling ash. So intent was he on this task that he did not notice Dorothy, who, apparently unaware of the fire, was wandering up the drier side of the burning hill.

Judy, though, watched in horror. She called out to her mother, but the roar of the flames and the screaming sirens drowned her out, and even nearby Fred could not hear her small child voice. Judy ran down the street, amongst the fleeing deer and foxes, trying to scream but choking now from the smoke and silenced by her own panic. Then, suddenly, there was her mother, bounding down the hill, ghostly white but with soot streaking her face, her rich auburn hair caked on her cheeks, her summer dress clinging to her sweat-soaked body.

"Get out of here, lady! Are you stupid?!" yelled a burly firefighter, as the white stream of water from his fire hose arched against the red sky. Dorothy reached the damp lawn of a nearby house and collapsed. "I didn't know, I didn't know," she moaned, over and over again. When Judy's panic subsided enough to unfreeze her muscles, she ran to her mother, and they huddled together on the lawn, holding each other in silence for a long time, their mixed fear and relief too great for words.

It did not come to that, fortunately. But the fire left her disoriented, with another certainty in life ripped away. Then an economic downturn put a significant dent in the erotic massage business, and this at a time when Juliet was only managing to continue the work out of stark economic fear. And there was the national political situation: the Clarence Thomas Supreme Court hearings were in progress, with Anita Hill's revelations about sexual harassment in high places and the galvanization this brought to the women's movement. For Juliet, it triggered memories of the exploitative underbelly of the porn film business.

But Juliet's main stress was the Pollock Pines house. She had finally started eviction proceedings, and would soon discover that her sympathy for her tenant had been ill-placed. Deanna was in fact one of those tenants from hell. Not only had she not paid rent, she had trashed the place. Walls were gouged, the carpets reeked of dog urine, paint was peeling from the dampness, windows were cracked or broken, and there was trash everywhere. Juliet felt used, abused and violated. Where the money would come from to make repairs, she did not know; she used her credit cards, either directly or with cash advances. To cut expenses, she had to give up the separate office in Oakland, shifting her work back to the Harrison Street apartment, which she now realized she hated.

She was, not surprisingly, losing it. "I've been on an emotional tight rope ... and I feel like the tight rope is coming unravelled. Actually it broke when I started the eviction proceedings." She sought relief in writing, not just in her journals, but at a short writer's workshop in San Francisco in early December. The venue turned out to be an apartment that was just being moved into and therefore was in chaos, cluttered with children's toys (it was going to be a day care center), with no appliances, no hot water, and no food or furniture. The upstairs neighbors were beer-drinking football revelers, who clunked around on the wooden floors. It was the last straw. Juliet, dreamer that she was, couldn't understand what had gone so wrong. "What have I done to create this chaos in my life?"

Early 1992 brought some relief after she finally broke down and went to a psychiatrist, who officially diagnosed her with bipolar disorder. Juliet had mixed feelings about the diagnosis: it confirmed her greatest fear, as she foresaw herself becoming a carbon copy of her deteriorating mother, yet it offered the relief of medication, which she started immediately. She was able to function again.

First, she plowed ahead with the house repairs; she had no choice, other than giving up the house, and the $120,000 [$202,800] that the realtor assured her was all she could get for it would not recoup her losses; she needed to hang on to it and wait for better times. Forcing herself to detach and think of it as "the house" rather than "my house," she managed to get through the ordeal. It did not have to be perfect, the way she would have liked it if she were going to live there. It only needed to be livable enough to rent out again. Juliet was beginning to develop some perspective on life, albeit in small ways.

By late March, the house was rented again, for $700 [$1,185] per month, minus 10% for the management agency; it was enough to cover most of Juliet's costs. She had confidence that the new tenant would be an improvement over Deanna, and was able to put the ordeal behind her enough to attend another retreat at Spirit Rock. This was not an uplifting time, however; the feelings that came up were focused on her parents, who she felt were spiraling down into hopeless alcoholism and general mental instability, on a slow slide toward death. She grieved for the sufferings they had endured, especially as children, and for their lack of redemption from those sufferings. She imagined generations of dysfunctional ancestors preceding them, and grieved for them all, and for herself and Chris, whom she perceived as hopelessly codependent. She even brought Monica into the mix: Juliet believed her niece was already showing signs of the family dysfunction, although she was rather vague about what these signs actually were; at least drinking was *not*, stars be thanked, among them. Most of all, Juliet grieved that she would never have the perfect parents she wanted.

Following on this cheerful interlude, Juliet returned to Oakland and tried to concentrate on work and survival. And Charles. She made long lists of his faults (poor dressing habits; pockets crammed with hard, sharp objects; carries backpack; has nothing to talk about; terrible diction; limited visions for the future; poor money management skills; doesn't exercise; doesn't cook; rarely takes initiative; is groggy in the morning), and a shorter one of his virtues (genuine love and tenderness; gentle spirit; integrity; romance; accepts me as I am), deciding that he fulfilled five of her eleven requirements for a partner. Not a percentage that any rational person would consider acceptable. Still, he was there, and nobody else was.

In June, Juliet and Charles took a week's vacation to Vancouver
Island, stopping to visit cousin Pam, who was appalled that Juliet
would be with someone as mismatched to her as Charles obviously
was. Vancouver Island seemed to be somewhat of a jinx for Juliet.
While they at least had a car for getting around on this trip—no
struggles with hills or bicycle repairs—they were pressured by a
tight schedule. Furthermore, spending extended time with Charles
was stressful. She was a morning person, he a night one. She loved
revisiting the Butchart Gardens, with its variety of colors and fragrances, its waterfalls and fountains; he was bored by it. She enjoyed
meeting new people and engaging in lively conversation; he was
withdrawn and never had anything to say. And of course there was
their ongoing sexual incompatibility; she continued to be repulsed by
him, guilty though she felt.

Sending him home at the end of the week was a tremendous
relief. She stayed on alone at a Whidbey Island bed and breakfast, in
an old Finnish farmhouse, with hand-crafted stair railings and window casings, a wood-burning stove, an old organ in the living room,
and an upstairs bedroom with a view of trees and the water. She
moved the bed over to the window so that she could awaken to the
sights as well as the sounds of nature. And of course there was a
sauna; no self-respecting Finnish house would be without one. She
spent four days wandering the island at her leisure, keeping her own
hours, indulging her visual, auditory and culinary tastes with no
need to please or include anyone else.

Shortly after returning to Oakland and a brief liaison with
Charles, she headed off for a July Fourth weekend in the Sierra
foothills, staying in a cabin owned by some friends, on the Moke-
lumne River in Calaveras County, about forty miles south of Placerville. Here she had a chance to relax even more, truly away from
civilization. She lay nude on the deck, sometimes masturbating
herself to delicious orgasms, sometimes just lazing in the relentless
Sierra sun, the waves of craggy peaks rising to the south and the east
a reminder of human transience and frailty. Smelling the sandy
mountain soil and the juniper berries, listening to the hot summer
wind roaring through the tall lodgepole pines, watching the deer
pick their way among the dark reddish-brown manzanita bushes, or
the iridescent hummingbirds darting back and forth, hovering over

the feeder at the far end of the deck, ".. experiencing with all the senses the small details of ordinary life...from the heart and spirit of connection with all living things, in harmony with the rhythms of nature." And at night, reading, and writing in her journal. Only a weekend respite, but it restored her soul. She brought a small section of a manzanita branch back to decorate her Oakland apartment.

For all the positive changes in her life in 1992, though, Juliet still had no clear direction. The work she truly wanted to do—teaching both women and men how to bring together sex and sensuality, to deepen their connections to themselves and to each other—eluded her. She had a clear picture of her true calling, but the need to support herself and keep her dreams alive pressed on her, draining her energy with everyday cares and sometimes paralyzing her with fear.

The Pollock Pines house continued to be a challenge; renters never stayed long and she was burdened with the expense and worry of keeping it. She dreamed of turning it into a retreat center, but the time and energy needed to realize that hope was beyond her. Toward the end of 1992, she moved some of her own possessions into the house, making it a sort of personal retreat, and spent time there as she needed over the next two years, as a respite from the city, to keep the pipes from freezing in the winter, and to do maintenance work on the property.

And of course there was her relationship with Charles. "We're so different and both so difficult; I suspect he loves me because he's fearful no one else will because he's so eccentric. I suspect the same for me also." In other, less euphemistic, words, they stayed together because they both feared, probably rightly, that no one else would have them.

But there were comforts, too, and with advancing age her needs were becoming less intense and her expectations lower. Being on anti-depressant medication also helped immensely; her mood swings were ameliorated. While never being truly focused, she was at least able to function without being constantly overwhelmed. The internal tornado had ceased, even though some of her motivation went with it.

What Juliet needed at this point in her life was to find a way to integrate all of her life and work experience into some meaningful whole, and to spend her remaining years passing on her legacy. At the beginning of 1993, there were hopeful signs that she would be able to move in that direction.

21

A New Love

Juliet began the new year of 1993 at the Pollock Pines house, relaxing but also working: writing her essay for *Women of the Light*, getting her financial records for 1992 in order, and designing flyers to advertise both the house—as a retreat center—and potential work-shops that she planned to offer. And fixing up the house itself to be livable. Just being there, though, brought her peace of mind. Simple tasks like making a fire in the wood stove, hanging pictures, and making curtains seemed like meditations. David's 1988 reading was correct; for Juliet, everyday life was often a meditation.

At the same time she could not help being reminded of the finan-cial stress of keeping the house, even while it served as a refuge. She was often overwhelmed with fear, and longed for someone to share her burdens with. After so many years of failed relationships with men, she wondered if perhaps partnering with a woman might work better. But actually either gender would do. "I want a partner who is a wild (wo)man like me, a visionary with sweeping plans, not living on a treadmill, a person into health, environmentally and personally sensitive; someone who cooks well and dresses well, innovative and creative, likes my cats, gives me space and freedom and loves me unconditionally." That last criterion, of course, was the show stopper, and what kept her chained to Charles.

With the return of warmer weather Juliet moved back to Oakland full time, only checking on the Pollock Pines house once a month or so, but sometimes taking mini-vacations there. In May she took a real vacation, to Hawaii, alone—for the first time in her life. It was good just to relax, enjoy the sea breezes and occasional brief showers, and to sit and observe the variety of watercraft offshore—brightly colored sailboats bobbing across the waves, impressive yachts plodding along methodically, a four-decked cruise ship anchored in the bay, a freighter weathering a downpour on the distant horizon. And to people- and animal-watch. She was amused at the mating rites of pigeons:

...a horny male pursuing every female in a 25-foot
radius—puffed up, head darting up and down, wings
extended, hopping, fluttering, cooing; she is so bored,
so uninterested, with a "leave me alone; can't I go
anywhere without being propositioned" hop, skip and
flutter away. He: "How could she not be impressed
with my macho masculine charm? Oh, well, there's
another prospect... she's not interested either?...
hurumph! females... you never know what they want.
Aren't they ever horny?... Ah! there's another fine-
feathered lass!" I guess they finally do pair up 'cause
there's no decline in the pigeon population.

Good practice for an aspiring writer, who is "first of all an
observer and a listener, then a story teller." Of course, she was
disgusted as usual by the inane American tourists. The Japanese
seemed more refined and lower key.

Back home, Juliet spent most of July in Pollock Pines. Just before
her fifty-fifth birthday, she came home from a short trip to Truckee
with Charles, to find an urgent "please call back" message on her
answering machine. When she did she received heart-rending news.
Paul Johnson's daughter Becky and her husband Jimmy had been in
a horrendous traffic crash. They had been on their way to Paul's
mother's funeral, and had been pushing themselves to finish the last
leg of the trip, coming down from a cocaine run. Jimmy fell asleep at
the wheel. Becky, not wearing her seat belt, was thrown from the car
and killed instantly. She would have turned thirty-four just two
weeks after the crash. Jimmy was made quadriplegic; never again
would he walk or play the guitar, Juliet noted sadly. In fact, his
injuries were so severe that he lived only a few more years. Juliet had
known and loved both of the young people, having encountered
them at many of Paul's social events. It was Paul's third family loss
in less than half a year; his father had died about six months earlier.

The tragedy deeply affected everyone in Paul's circle of family
and friends. Juliet was almost immobilized with grief for two days
after she heard the news. Her arthritis flared up. The long trip to Mill
Valley for the memorial service was grueling, and she was grateful to
have her mountain retreat to return to. Naturally, the incident turned
her thoughts to death again. "It certainly was a critical reminder of
the uncertainty of life and how precious each day is and the import-

ance of friends and having no 'unfinished' business." She brought
her own end-of-life documents up to date.

A few days later, procrastinating on working on her essay for
Women of the Light, she decided to drop acid. Just as it was starting to
kick in the doorbell rang; it was a massage client she had forgotten
about. "How I pulled it off I'll never know." But she did such a great
job that the client "floated out" after the session and didn't even need
his chiropractic adjustment the next day. Juliet was left in such a
glow that she sat down and churned out five handwritten pages for
the *Light* article.

This writing, and her struggles with it, were a sort of practice run
for writing her autobiography. She longed to put her experiences and
insights down on paper, to share them with the world. Yet she
suffered an extreme case of writer's block. She simply could not do
it.

Part of the problem was the medium. Only longhand writing
stimulated her creativity, and with her arthritis worsening as she
aged, that was becoming impractical. She knew she would soon have
to give it up. In September 1993, she visited her friend Marc Ceniceros, who had some professional recording equipment, to tape six
and a half hours of memoirs, primarily of the porn years. She hoped
she could find someone to transcribe these for her. Yet she never
followed through with that effort, nor did she do any further
taping.[27]

She acquired a computer and made a real effort to learn to use
the word processor, reading the instruction manual, trying things
out, failing, reading again, trying again. "I hate this electronic
monster." She simply did not have the left-brained analytical mind-
set needed, and did not seek a tutor to help her. Even if she had mastered the machine, however, it might not have helped that much;
keying still required using her hands, and voice recognition software
had not yet reached the level of sophistication (not to mention afford-
ability) required to be a feasible alternative. So it was that after
mid-1992, her journal writing—never mind the more ambitious
autobiography project—became sporadic, finally ceasing altogether
in 1994, although she continued to make occasional lists—of likes,

---

[27] These tapes have been lost.

dislikes, wants, needs, losses. And without the release of pouring out her soul through her pen, she lost a vital part of her inner life—indeed, of her very identity.

The ravages of approaching old age were eroding her quality of life in many ways. Although she still looked younger than her age, internally her body was growing weary from her lifelong health challenges. Besides the pain in her hands, "this memory loss terrifies me; so does the loss of my libido," and her Crohn's disease was plaguing her again as well. For all the alternative treatments she had added to her regime, they could not forestall the aging process and its toll on her inherited physiological weaknesses. That, she would have to figure out how to live with. To be a body-centered person in a slowly deteriorating body.

Still, despite her struggles, she was beginning to develop a clearer picture of her remaining life's work. An artist, a teacher, a healer, a performer. Seminars and workshops, "hands-on, experiential, clothing optional, participatory, non-cerebral," for singles, couples and groups, all-male, all-female, mixed. Or educational videos, teaching sensual touching techniques. All-female theatrical productions, empowering women and helping them manifest their genuine sexuality. Teaching sex workers how to add sensual skills to sexual ones, and how to heal themselves from the heaviness of their work. And writing her "sexual-spiritual" autobiography, as Annie Sprinkle had done. Moreover, she could move into these arenas gradually, sustaining herself with her now firmly established massage business. While she would never realize all of these dreams, she would indeed spend her remaining years in these kinds of activities.

By the end of 1993, Juliet had finished fixing up the Pollock Pines house and was getting emotionally ready to let it go. Yet she stayed there through January 1994, partly because minor illnesses prevented her from functioning down in the city. She holed up in the house, fighting intestinal flu, laryngitis and sinus infections. And working on the *Women of the Light* piece; it needed a complete rewrite.

In February, she took another solo vacation to Hawaii. She had hoped to go scuba diving, but transportation problems prevented her from getting to the beach. She fantasized about finding a female life partner. Why not? Men hadn't worked out, although she had many men friends, some of them platonic and some of them fuck buddies.

Yet Juliet was not really a bisexual woman; she only played one in the movies. Furthermore, the root cause of her solitude was an inability to carry on a long-term intimate relationship—with anyone. The intimate female partner was another fantasy that would never come to fruition.

In fact, two of her relationships with women friends and business connections came to closure during these few days in Hawaii. Shirley Lewis, owner of Raamwood, died of a stroke; Juliet would go there for the memorial service after her return. And she had been trying to get hold of Gloria Leonard, who now lived in Hawaii but seemed to be avoiding her, not returning her phone calls. "She probably wants to forget the past," Juliet mused. This inspired an affirmation for herself: "I now know and embrace my past as part of making me who I am today and will be tomorrow."

She did enjoy a few recreations—swimming in Hanauma Bay, seeing a Japanese film at the Art Academy, visiting Wiame Valley Park, and taking a scenic bus ride along Pali Highway. Toward the end of her stay, though, her arthritis flared up; her whole left side hurt, and she had to seek emergency chiropractic treatment, which fortunately worked wonders. She awoke early on her last morning to the full moon setting over the city at dawn—a fittingly sensual ending to an inspiring trip.

Juliet returned to vacate her Pollock Pines house. She would rent it out again; even she had come to realize that the dream of using it as a retreat center was unrealizable, and she could not afford to keep it as a private refuge. The real estate market was in a slump just then, but she knew that she would be selling the place as soon as the market turned around. The loss grieved her. "I feel like a negligent mother giving up her child for adoption. The house was the symbol for the family I never had, for my unborn daughter. [Now] I feel sad and alone here, like I'm visiting a corpse in a coffin." She would finally sell the house in November 1995, for $99,000 [$154,000]—a significant loss considering all the money she had put into repairing and refurbishing it. It is not known whether she ever repaid all the money she had borrowed for the original down payment.

One development that offset this loss was the blossoming of a new friendship between Juliet and ex-porn actress Kay Parker, with whom Juliet had worked in three films (*Vista Valley PTA*, *Taboo* and

Taboo 2). They re-connected when Kay (now living in Southern California) paid a visit to the Bay Area in 1995. Now in their fifties, their porn careers far behind them, the two women suddenly "clicked," realizing that they were on a common path—sisters in spirit, integrating sexuality and spirituality into healing modalities: "We both have the gift of deep insight and a similar spiritual and professional practice." Indeed, this new-found connection with Kay was one of the major influences directing Juliet on her new path. Someone to encourage and support her, help her focus, lift her up when her energy dragged. Kay's calmer personality helped ground Juliet, and Juliet's ebullience added verve to Kay's more even temper.

I Fell in Love with My Life

I fell in love with my life one Thursday in August.

With a sigh I gazed at the red-orange sun, hovering between the clouds and distant mountain. I breathed in the cool evening air, fragrant with jasmine.

A tiring day, five clients filling my room with their sorrows, needs, frustration, reaching out to me for comfort and validation, wanting more than I would or could give.

Now sitting on the veranda facing west, still damp from the ritual shower, cleansing, refreshing, washing away clinging hopes of a better truth, wrapped in a kimono, I watch the setting sun, glad to be alive, of help to others, independent, aware of a quiet peace and longing in my heart, in touch with my vulnerability and ordinariness, like the sun, bright, then fading, hiding, sinking and rising again the next day.

-- Juliet Carr

Another connection from the past showed up unexpectedly as well. Through all the years since Juliet's international travels, her Greek ex-lover Nikolas had kept faithfully in touch, calling her several times a year and even occasionally sending letters. In September 1996, he told her he would be coming to the U.S. to attend a ceremony at the Naval Academy in Annapolis, Maryland, and asked if she would fly out to meet him; he would pay her fare and put her up in a hotel as well. She assented, although with mixed feelings.

It was a poignant meeting. They had not seen each other since 1978, and both had aged in the interval. Nikolas's once-thick curly hair had thinned, turned iron gray, and receded considerably, and although he was still fit and active, he had developed a slight middle-aged paunch. These changes were not enough, though, to prevent Juliet from feeling an instant stab of recognition, along with the aching longing he always evoked in her.

Nor was she any better able to assert her needs now, than she had been in the mid-1960s or even in 1978. Despite her resolution to eschew vaginal intercourse, she gave in to Nikolas without a murmur, having anticipated her weakness for him by bringing along an expensive lubricant one of her gay male friends had recommended. Not that Nikolas lasted any longer, or that the encounter was any more satisfying. The two nights they spent together were for Juliet a mix of unfulfilled longing and sad realization that this love had never been, and never would be, what she had dreamed of back in 1966. Yet she would also never let go emotionally.

It would be their last meeting. Nikolas did not even find out about Juliet's demise until 2014, when this writer informed him of the details.

Back in the Bay Area, Juliet put the meeting with Nikolas behind her with a whirl of social activity. The old sex crowd was glad to welcome her back to her old haunts. And she was glad to step back in. For despite her private renunciation of that lifestyle, these people were as close as she could come to finding kindred spirits, and her sex-star persona, even though it no longer fit, was the only real identity she had ever had. She needed recognition, a feeling of belonging, and emotional safety, and if she had to play the Juliet Anderson role to get that, so be it. She would retain the persona for the rest of her life, while keeping her reservations to herself. It was a workable bargain. She was, after all, an actress and a story teller.

> ## Tender Loving Touch
> ### (touch as the play, not foreplay)
>
> *What is "Tender Loving Touch?" It's difficult to describe in words a technique that is experiential and unique to each person, but I'll do my best.*
>
> *Let me start by telling you what Tender Loving Touch is NOT. It is not erotic massage; it's not a quick fix because you are horny; it's not intercourse and it's not Tantra. Tender Loving Touch focuses on slow, gentle, nurturing touch from head to toe, letting you relax into an altered state. It is a delightful, sensual/sexual experience in which we are both nude, in my bedroom, and I stroke you lightly with my whole body, not just my hands. Your genitals get special attention. You can either lie back and only receive, or reciprocate by touching me, so that you learn not only to receive, but to give erotic pleasure—pleasure that is an end in itself, not a prelude to genital sex.*
>
> *It's a chance for you to unwind, turn off your thinking mind and let your body relax into bliss. There is lots of skin-on-skin contact ... hugging, kissing, cuddling and oral sex. I will show you how to have multiple orgasms throughout your body.*
>
> *I have been sharing this unique form of touch with individuals and couples for 15 years in a personal practice and in presentations and workshops. I've been blessed with a gift of touch and a totally uninhibited and healthy attitude about sexuality. My maturity, vast life experience, sense of humor, keen intelligence and loving heart combine to make this a wonderful experience for my clients and myself.*

Besides, Juliet was finally getting some long overdue recognition for her contributions to the erotic film business. Clips from her old movies were included in some composite collections like *Legends of Porn* and *Masturbation Memoirs,* and in January 1995, she and Kelly

Nichols were inducted into the Erotic Legends Hall of Fame, traveling to Las Vegas for the ceremony—where she did not linger, as she had disliked the place ever since her 1977 stint there. She was featured twice in the porn magazine *Over 50*; in December 1995 she had a nine-page layout entitled "An Exhibitionist Like Me," and in December 1996 she was on the cover, with another nine-page layout inside: "The Notorious Aunt Peg Rides Again!" In February 1997 there was a seven-page layout of previously unpublished photos from the early 1980s, under the title "Juliet (Aunt Peg) Anderson, Classic Cum Queen," in another magazine featuring older women, *40 Plus*. And in late 1996 *Women of the Light: The New Sacred Prostitute* was finally published, containing Juliet's contribution about her life and work.

David Guy also interviewed her for his upcoming book, *The Red Thread of Passion: Spirituality and the Paradox of Sex*. More than any other published work about Juliet, this selection captured the breadth and complexity of her life and work, touching on her talents as a porn actress, her personality traits and innate aptitudes, her abilities as a teacher and a healer, and her contributions to the sex industry. Juliet comes across in this piece as the multi-faceted person she was: warm, exuberant, creative, energetic, outspoken, articulate, independent-minded, highly intelligent and thoughtful, sensitive and intuitive. Brash at times; quick to criticize but also to laugh; highly focused when she needed to be but sometimes bouncing off the walls with her excessive exuberance and offbeat sense of humor. This was Juliet at her best: knowing who she was professionally, aware of her limitations—"I'm a difficult person to be around. I know. I'm around myself all the time."—but justifiably proud of her accomplishments.

All of this attention reinforced Juliet's realization that sex work was where her bread and butter would be coming from. And she did love the work itself—performing, producing good-quality erotica, and her more direct personal work of sensual massage and education through small workshops and seminars. Most important of all, she now had more control over the kind of sex work she did, and how and where she did it. She filed two fictitious business names with Alameda County: Tender Loving Touch and Afterglow Productions. She had come to terms with her Juliet Anderson persona, accepting it as an expression of her real joy in the life of the body, and claiming the public recognition that it gave her, which she still needed for her livelihood. Hence she returned to using the given name Juliet rather than Judith, changing her legal name to Juliet Carr in June, 1994.[28]

Letter from Client, 1995

Dear Juliet,

It has taken me several days to recover enough to remember to send you a thank-you note. I've been wandering in a pink haze of delightful memories. I'm profoundly indebted to your great skill and delicious personality.

I love your enthusiasm, spontaneity and caring approach. You're a dream come true, a wish granted, a treasure found.

I flash on specific moments from time to time, but mostly I remember your presence, your voice and your touch. I was delighted that I was also allowed to give you pleasure, making my visit beyond fantasy.

My wife is pleased with my increased attention, and responds far more than I had believed possible. I can see now how much I was contributing to her depression over our relationship, by giving up. Now, I'm breaking that foolish habit, thanks to you.

Blessings and good wishes to you ...

She also left the hated Harrison Street apartment and moved to an in-law unit in the rear of a single-family house on Stuart Street in Berkeley. The apartment was a converted garage; she had the up-stairs unit, accessed by an outside stairway, with two small bed-rooms, a living room that looked out over the yard, and a small

---

[28] Although Juliet evidently filed her official name change in Alameda County in 2007, she made the change in El Dorado County in 1994, by changing her name as property owner for the house in Pollock Pines.

kitchenette. Her bedroom was on the south side, facing on the alley; the extra bedroom she used primarily for storage. A tree just east of the stairs provided shade but the sun still poured through the south- and west-facing windows; in the afternoon the place was filled with light, which Juliet loved. Charles Webb lived in the downstairs unit, the ex-garage itself (which had no kitchen), until Juliet finally dumped him; then the unit was rented to another man, who was a quiet and cordial neighbor. The main house itself was also rented, to a young straight couple. The landlady lived off-site in the Oakland hills.

It was an ideal living space for Juliet: private and quiet, compact but not cramped, where she could settle in and, she hoped, grow old. In fact, however chaotic Juliet's emotional life might be, her living spaces were always pleasant and welcoming, well organized and tastefully decorated, with paintings or posters on the walls, art objects from her various Asian and European adventures scattered about, brightly colored but never garish curtains, tablecloths, throws, bedspreads, and rugs. She claimed to have been diagnosed with Attention Deficit Hyperactivity Disorder, and she certainly exhibited those characteristics, bouncing off the walls when she was in her more manic moods. Yet the signature ADHD characteristic of dis-organized space and overwhelming clutter was never one of her symptoms. Her apartments were physically clear and functional, with furniture arranged sensibly—pleasant places to sit, read, carry on conversations and enjoy good meals. And of course partake of her wonderful massage and loving touch services.

As for Juliet's social life, it revolved mainly around the people she had known over the years—those directly in the sex business and those who patronized it. This included her friends Kat Sunlove and Layne Winklebeck, owners and publishers of *Spectator Magazine*, and Juliet soon joined a new social group loosely connected with the magazine—a motley collection of middle-aged sexual liberationists who met for lunch once a month, near the *Spectator* office in Emery-ville, to discuss various intriguing sexuality-related topics. Juliet's contributions to these discussions consisted almost entirely of relating her past achievements.

> ### *Juliet's Sensuality Workshops*
>
> #### Sensual Touch *(women only)*
>
> Our hands are some of the most versatile sexual tools
> we have. Come learn how to make sensual touching
> *the* play, not just foreplay. *Juliet Carr* aka *Juliet "Aunt
> Peg" Anderson* is a Sacred Erotic artist/teacher/healer
> who will demonstrate enhancing physical intimacy
> through touch, how to enjoy your whole body, ways to
> arouse and delight all the senses and how to achieve a
> full-body orgasm. You'll discover ways to give and
> receive erotic pleasure as an end in itself, not just a
> prelude to genital sex. What more could you ask for?
>
> #### Sensual Secrets for Sexy Seniors
>
> Whether you're in your spry 60s or your naughty 90s,
> a decrease in libido or mobility doesn't need to mean
> the end of sex. *Juliet Carr* is here to show you how to
> keep the fires of passion stoked. With tips for adapting
> to changing sexual and physical abilities, plus tricks
> for keeping encounters hot, you'll find your sex life
> getting better and better.

The group was the brain child of Don Crane, a lifelong sexual
adventurer; he defined himself as an "erologician." An old porn fan,
Don was thrilled to meet Juliet, and when Layne proposed that he
interview her for the magazine, Don jumped at the chance. So it was
that Juliet finally cut her already dwindling ties to Charles Webb and
took up with the last great love of her life.

Don Crane, born in 1947, was nine years Juliet's junior, but a twin
brother in spirit. (He actually was about the same age Juliet's brother
would have been had he lived.) His life trajectory was similar to
Juliet's—too much of a renegade to fit in anywhere, always pushing
the limits and always searching for, but never finding, his true

calling. He survived financially via a combination of menial, low-wage jobs, intermittent under-the-table work, and living with girlfriends who were willing to support him. Born and raised in Mobile, Alabama, he was one of those liberated Southern Baby Boomers who spend the rest of their lives in adolescent rebellion against the political and social conservatism of that culturally backward area of the U.S. Like Juliet before beginning her film career, Don defined himself more by what he was not than by what he was.

Don had managed to get himself kicked out of two colleges in New York state—Houghton College in the upstate area, and Nyack Missionary College in Nyack. After drifting around New York state for about ten years, he headed for that mecca of sexual liberation, the San Francisco Bay Area, where he happily settled into a life of intellectual and artistic pursuits. And of course sensuality.

Don Crane bringing Juliet a "treat." His apron reads: "First feed the face, then tell right from wrong." Photo by David Steinberg.

Like many highly intelligent, left-leaning Boomers—especially those who had grown up in relatively conservative environments—Don was intrigued with the intellectual and spiritual aspects of sex and sensuality. He read the great philosophers of both Western and Eastern traditions, and developed an appreciation for erotic art and pornography, especially the better-quality stuff that was available during the Golden Age. He saw his first porno movie, *The Devil in Miss Jones*, in 1972, was immediately hooked on the archetype of the mature, classy woman, and discovered Juliet Anderson soon after she appeared on the scene—never dreaming that years later he would connect with her in person.

Don's love of high-quality sexual experiences drew him to the Bay Area's sexual revolutionaries, and to jobs that would take him close to the porn scene. At the time Juliet met him he was working as a clerk in an adult bookstore—the type of job he had often held. (Projectionist in a porn theater had been another.) Don's life revolved around sex, just as Juliet's had during her film and stage performance days. Juliet could relate. And like Juliet, Don was often disgusted with the simplistic mentality of many of the porn customers, who "only wanted to beat off as quickly as possible." He also shared Juliet's wry sense of humor. For the lunchtime *Spectator* gatherings he made up buttons for everyone with the label "Erologician;" he did not lay exclusive claim to the title he had given himself.

> *Valentine's Day Card*
> *from Don Crane, 1997*
>
> *To find powerful yet simple words while in my awkward state of existence would be ludicrous, thus belittling the depth of feeling I wish to express to you on this Valentine's Day. Your spirit, your humanity, your intellect, and your sensual soul has brightened and enlightened the core of my BEING. Your daily friendship has nourished a sometimes empty heart and sad soul. There are tears of joy mixed with this ink as I reflect on all we have said and done in the short time we have known each other.*
>
> *You have my Eternal Love.*

Of all the men Juliet was involved with over the years—with the possible exception of Frank McGrath—Don was probably the best suited to her. He was her equal in intelligence and sensuality. His calm personality and laid-back manner offset her frenetic impulsiveness. They could share their intellectual passions as well as their sensuous ones. He was devoted to her—just what Juliet needed to be swept off her feet. Soon after he interviewed her for the *Spectator*, they became companions and lovers, spending long hours in conversation as well as love-making, attending and critiquing plays and concerts, and socializing with the sexually enlightened crowd.

Although they never lived together, they spent frequent overnights at each other's homes, mostly at Juliet's place, as it was more livable. Juliet also joined the long line of women who helped financially support Don, sometimes paying him for simple chores like running errands or doing her laundry.

Juliet's massage business was robust enough to sustain her now, especially without the excessive travel costs she had borne while living in El Dorado County and working in Oakland. She now had enough time and energy to devote to making a go of some of her dreams. In early 1995, she formed the Wild Women Theatre Company, with hopes of producing plays and dances that would depict women's sexuality as powerful and life-affirming, also including humor and lightness where appropriate. Juliet had always loved live performing and longed to return to it. She got together a group of fifteen women and started tossing around script ideas. Their first planned production was to be "Lies Our Mothers Told Us About Sex." Other ideas included "Sluts, Wild Women, Femme Fatales and Porno Queens," "A Consumer's Guide to Sex Toys," and "Church of the Divine Harlot."

Carol Queen offered to be involved, as performer, and if necessary as publicist, but primarily to support Juliet in her venture. Carol was too busy with other projects to participate full-time, but she whole-heartedly approved of the idea. Whether any of these scripts actually reached production, however, is not clear.

Don enthusiastically joined Juliet in her pursuit of performance art, floating ideas and sometimes even writing scripts himself. Or at least starting on them; none of them were ever finished. One of his brainstorms was a television talk show that would interview porn stars and other sex workers, but rather than trying to discount them or to sensationalize their work, the show would focus on their thoughts on social, political and philosophical topics. A tantalizing idea with probably little market value. Don, like Juliet, was a dreamer, although Juliet at least had enough practical sense not to throw good money after bad in the pursuit of lost causes.

Don also wrote several papers along the theme of enlightened sexuality: "A Pornographer's Manifesto," "In Praise of Older Women, Wolves and Underwear" and "The Ghosts of Eros: Religious Dogma, History and Sexuality"—this last being one of those typical rants about how mainstream Christianity has suppressed sexuality over the centuries. Don's mastery of classical Western literature and philosophy comes through clearly in these writings, which were liberally sprinkled with references to, and quotes from, such luminaries as Plato, Socrates, Nietzsche, and St. Augustine.

One project that got a little further than the dreaming stage was a screen play, *Coming of Age*, on which Juliet and Don collaborated with another writer friend, Jeremy Slade. It was probably intended to be the story of a middle-aged woman's discovery of hot sex. The opening scene depicts a forty-something widow conversing with a female relative just after her husband's funeral. The script, however, got no further than this opening scene.

The Juliet-Don collaboration that did come to fruition was *Ageless Desire*, a primarily educational video demonstrating how heterosexual couples over the age of fifty can keep their sex lives hot. This was Juliet's most ambitious project since *Educating Nina*. Again, she had to round up financial backing, hire photographers, rent equipment, find appropriate settings and of course actors. Profits were to be split three ways—40% to herself and 30% each to Don and to Ray Glass, cameraman and director of photography, who also helped with editing.

It had been Juliet's greatest dream, ever since her initiation into the sex business, "to make high-quality, dynamic, non-formula videos featuring REAL people (not the typical Hollywood, plastic, buffed hard bodies) who are comfortable with their sexuality and have a genuine love and passion for their partner which they uninhibitedly demonstrate... an alternative to the predictable, usually boring jack-hammer sex of mainstream porno, soft-core fluff and amateur videos." Now she had the support she needed to embark on such a project: someone else with energy and enthusiasm and connections, who shared her vision.

Yet developing compelling scenarios and finding appropriate actors was a serious challenge. She envisioned three scenarios for the film, all of them involving couples who were either married or had been together long-term. The first was to be about how to create a romantic setting at home, starting out with some expressions of mutual appreciation, moving on to a candlelit dinner with wine and music, and culminating in hot sex; the second, about ways of coping with, and compensating for, the declining physical abilities that sometimes come with age; the third with a double theme: how to attract the interest and attention of a reluctant or distracted partner, and how to add variety to one's sex life by trying out some alternate positions, including anal sex.

For the first scenario—the only fictional one—she cast herself, choosing as her partner a client and erstwhile lover who took the stage name Max for the production. This was a most unfortunate selection, as Max had no performance ability whatsoever in front of the camera, either as an actor or as a sexual partner. Even Juliet's talents were insufficient to overcome his camera shyness and his inability to express any genuine emotion, as is painfully obvious in the released production. (Ironically, his non-performance created some serious fallout with his wife, who evidently had not been informed of his relationship with Juliet; she divorced Max not long after the film's release.) Why Juliet chose this inadequate partner is not clear, although it may not have been easy to find a willing older man with a reasonably attractive physique; whatever Max's shortcomings, he was tall, slender and relatively good-looking, without the standard middle-aged paunch. His body type, in fact, was a good match for Juliet's.

For the third scenario she recruited a nearby neighbor couple, personal friends Kim and Stuart Greene, whose performance should have been entitled something along the lines of "fifty ways to fuck your lover," as it consisted almost entirely of a series of heterosexual intercourse positions, with no emotional energy at all, at least on Stuart's part. While Kim did have some acting ability, and made a valiant attempt to bring spontaneity and liveliness to the scene, her husband performed like an automaton. But at least he did perform, which was more than one could say for Max, who never managed to get it up for the camera, even with a cock ring.

The real gem in this production, though, was the middle scenario, presenting a wonderful older couple, Shell and Richard Freye-Byrnes, who shared some truly intimate moments in the process of demonstrating tips on how to deal with erectile dysfunction; their performance, along with Juliet's own attempt to salvage the scene between herself and Max, rescued the entire video, which would otherwise have been pathetic.

Don was a constant support and participant in this project, help-ing with both directing and editing. Juliet's scene with Max was filmed at the lovely Rockridge home of her friend and hairdresser Greg Franke and his partner Lee, with the sex scene taking place on their opium bed. Juliet's cousin Pam was present for the rehearsal of this scene and was impressed with Juliet's directing talents. Planning for the project started in early 1997, production ran through the sum-mer of 1998, and the video was released in 1999. Some of the delay in completing the project was, as usual, finding the financing. Juliet made numerous appeals to fans, friends, family and previous investors; the money trickled in over these three years.

Along with all these positive developments in her life, though, Juliet suffered some significant losses during these early years back in the city. First was the death of her beloved father in the summer of 1994, from heart failure. Fortunately, Juliet had been preparing for this for a long time, grieving for several years before the actual event. Still it was a loss; the world was a different place without him. It was two years later, in November 1996, that she lost Snuggles, the feline companion she had acquired from the SPCA in 1977. The absence of that calm regal presence left an emptiness in her home and in her life. Lucky brought her some comfort, but he passed on himself in May 1997. Never one to be catless, Juliet soon acquired another compan-ion, Angel, but all the losses affected her deeply. One of the stresses of growing older.

Juliet was also beginning to suffer more with physical ailments than she had in years. Age and lifelong health challenges were catching up with her. She was in frequent pain from her arthritis, back spasms, and repetitive strain injury from using the computer, which she had finally mastered enough to start turning out a regular newsletter for her fans.

This regular communique was actually the result of joining a website, pornlegends.com, run by a company called 5K Sales, and it progressed through the titles "Juliet 'Aunt Peg' Anderson" and "Juliet Anderson Update" before finally settling on "Aunt Peg's Update." This foray into the online world led Juliet to realize that she actually needed her own website, and in 1996 she stopped in at a technical conference, with the intention of finding someone who could set one up for her. There she met Tom Tilton, a boomer-aged techie with several decades of experience in IT. With some trepidation, she asked him whether he would be willing to set up a website with some explicit sexual content. Tom responded that he was neutral to the idea; he was a technician and was not concerned with the subject matter of the websites he developed.

Photo: Carr/Pettit family collection

By the summer of 1997, Tom had built the basic site, auntpeg.com, and had taken care of the technical and administrative details required to maintain it. He advised her, though, to find someone else to handle the ongoing maintenance, as he was too busy with other projects. Besides, Juliet needed someone who would take on the job in trade for erotic massage work, an arrangement Tom was not comfort-able with. She had no trouble finding another techno-savvy client to step up. Juliet and Tom remained casual friends, though, seeing each other socially from time to time, for the rest of her life.

With all her irons in the fire—her massage business, *Ageless Desire*, her newsletter, website, Wild Woman Theatre Company, and her workshops on Tender Loving Touch, she was looking forward to the International Conference on Prostitution, to be held in the Los Angeles area in March 1997. While there, she would be promoting her contribution to *Women of the Light*. The book had finally been published, and Juliet hoped to use this opportunity to get publicity for her workshops, seminars and new video as well.

22
A Gathering of Whores

Prostitution. The very word is loaded. It is often used in public discourse as a synonym for decadence or degradation, or to refer to the selling of one's integrity for base motives. Almost everyone has an opinion about it. Very few people know much about it from direct experience, even though many millions of people have been involved in it, one way or another—as providers, as consumers, or as law-enforcement personnel.

For more than a century, prostitution has also had an academic following of sorts: researchers who are interested in studying it as a social phenomenon. And, beginning with the so-called sexual revolution of the 1960s, prostitution has had its advocates outside academia as well—many of them sex workers themselves. Why, then, not bring these two groups together, to share their knowledge and their visions, and begin building a base of mutual support? Maybe such a coalition could develop strategies for reforming the laws around sex work.

This was the vision of Bonnie and Vern Bullough, eminent researchers and historians, whose 1987 book *Women and Prostitution: A Social History* was one of the most comprehensive studies of the subject. The Bulloughs also formed the Center for Sex Research within California State University at Northridge, in the San Fernando Valley north of Los Angeles (where Juliet had grown up). Along with the Society for the Scientific Study of Sexuality (of which Vern Bullough was past president), the American Association of Sex Educators and Counselors, the Network of Sex Work Projects, and a few more informal organizations like COYOTE (Call Off Your Old Tired Ethics, founded in San Francisco by Margo St. James), the Bulloughs organized a four-day event, the 1997 International Conference on Prostitution, to be held 13 to 16 March, at the Airtel Plaza Hotel in Van Nuys, California; the venue abutted the Van Nuys Airport (a private airport with no commercial flight service). The first day, open to sex workers only, was to be a time for front-line workers to gather, share their stories, and propose a few additional workshops. The formal conference began on Friday the 14th; the format was primarily panel discussions with four or five presenters each followed by Q & A, formal conference-wide opening and closing sessions, a keynote speaker—former U.S. Surgeon General Joycelyn Elders, an art show, a video room for showing films, a performance night, and the grande finale, a hooker's ball. Bonnie Bullough, sadly, passed away before the conference came to fruition; it was dedicated to her.

The conference drew over five hundred attenders, and was truly international, with a wide variety of countries represented—the U.S. of course, the United Kingdom, all three Scandinavian countries, the Netherlands, France, Germany, Italy, Spain, New Zealand, Australia, Canada, China, India, Japan, and several Central and South American, African, and southeast Asian countries. One delegate from Thailand arrived but quickly left because the interpreter she had been promised had not been procured.

That oversight was characteristic of the chaotic nature of some of the logistics planning. Miscommunications among the conference organizers, while not frequent, were highly disruptive when they did occur. The first issue was around the handling of money. The academics, being mainstream and middle-class, tended toward long-term planning, to-the-penny accounting, and electronic financial tracking, while the more free-wheeling sex-workers had a shorter-term, more cash-based, laissez-faire approach: don't be concerned with messy details, just scramble around and try to pull everything together at the last minute. The result appeared to be a shortage of money for Joycelyn Elders's speaker fee and for subsidies for the international sex-worker delegates. While these might have been worked out with better communications among the conference organizers, hotel staff, and the University accounting personnel, the shortages were in fact covered, in typical sex-worker fashion, by on-the-spot fundraising, some of it from a rich john who came up with some quick cash. (Donors were later reimbursed from the official conference coffers.)

Despite this rough beginning, and some sporadic glitches throughout the four days, the conference was overall a success. Participants were for the most part respectful of each other's needs, time, and talents. Translators helped everyone communicate. The major problem around translation came from the Americans (the

U.S.-ers)—at least, the formal speakers, who absolutely could not remember to slow down their speaking, punctuating it with pauses, to allow the translators time to translate. The other English speakers could do so—the British, the Canadians, the Australians, the New Zealanders, and the South Africans—but not those from the U.S., despite several requests and reminders.

Probably the most heartfelt sharing came in the small-group session for sex workers only, on Thursday afternoon. About twenty persons gathered in the partitioned-off half of the main ballroom where the large events were to take place later on. Sex workers talked about their lives, their work, the challenges and struggles they faced, their perceptions of themselves, their customers, and the larger society they had to deal with. Whenever a non-English-speaker spoke, the translator translated her or his words into English, and then the translators for the non-English-speaking listeners translated the English into languages they understood. Those who already understood what was being said, either in the original language or in English, waited with the utmost patience for the whole process to be finished, before responding to the original speaker. When an English speaker spoke, the process was the same, only without the first step of translating into English.

Throughout this session, there was a deep quiet in the room, and an atmosphere of compassion and respect. Perhaps the slow pace forced participants to really listen to each other. Perhaps there was a realization, on a deep level, of the shared experience of living outside the formal, accepted rules of society—on the *real* inside of society, immersed in the powerful emotions that drive all human behavior—looking out. The differences in language and culture were trivial compared to that shared human experience of relating to other people on an animal level—the purely physical experience of sex, stripped of any pretense of long-term intimacy.

There were moments of humor too, of course, as there always are when people get together. One very young Japanese woman offered her perception that many clients are looking for a nurturing mother rather than just a whore, and one of the Central American women responded that if a man wants a mother, he should go back to his own, not turn to a whore. That remark brought laughter and cheers.

The 1997 International Conference On Prostitution

An Interface: Cultural, Legal and Social Issues

MARCH 13 - 16, 1997

AT THE Airtel Plaza Hotel Van Nuys, California

ICOP'97

Presented by
The Center for Sex Research,
California State University Northridge
and COYOTE LA
Co-Sponsored by
The Society for the Scientific Study of Sexuality,
American Association of Sex Educators and Counselors
Network of Sex Work Projects and Affiliated Sex Worker Organizations

But there were heart-breaking stories as well. One of the strongest personalities present was a middle-aged Indian woman who had been sold into sexual slavery at the age of twelve. She talked of how most of her fellow prostitutes advised her to simply accept her lot in life and make the best of it. Yet she always had a rebellious spirit, and even though there were many times when she despaired, she persisted, finally managing to free herself in her mid-thirties. She now worked for a non-profit specializing in AIDS education for sex workers in India. That she actually lived long enough to reach that point in her life was every bit as amazing as that she had finally escaped prostitution, since many of her fellow workers died young from disease, drug use, or harsh conditions.

Another tragedy was the recent violent death of a street hooker from Central America; this had occurred only a few weeks prior to the conference. Her comrades had put on a public memorial for her, marching through the streets with banners and colorful costumes, demanding more safety for sex workers; they brought slides of this march to show at the conference.

The middle-class, educated Americans and Europeans had little to say during the session, but listened respectfully. None of the high-profile self-appointed sex goddesses attended, nor did Juliet, and that was just as well, as their narcissism might have disturbed the communal atmosphere.

The formal conference started off with a bang—Thursday evening's stage performances—the "Whore Carnival." While some presentations were pretty lame, such as a black-and-white film on female ejaculation (who cares?), some were quite good, showcasing real talents. The best performance was Carol Queen's spoof of life as a peep-booth worker. Using the technique developed by Ruth Draper and later adopted by Bob Newhart, Carol used her own monologue to imply dialog between her and the customer; for example, "OK, you tell me where my clit is." Pause; then (with a mischievous smile): "What do *I* get if you're wrong?" And, after licking and sucking on the head of a dildo, "This is actually the most sensitive part of the penis—the head, not the base"—a dig at the deep throaters. This whole routine, not surprisingly, went completely over the heads of most of the audience, especially the johns who were present; they crudely hooted and hollered at some of her more explicit moves. They never got that she was ridiculing them.

The official conference began on Friday morning with opening remarks by the three main conference organizers: Vern Bullough and James Elias of the Center for Sex Research, and Norma Jean Almodovar, director of COYOTE Los Angeles. The rest of the day, as well as all day Saturday and part of Sunday, was devoted primarily to workshops, with a special luncheon on Saturday, featuring keynote speaker Joycelyn Elders. Friday also included a special session, just after lunch, "After the Headlines Cease: The Lives of Women Beyond the Arrest/Scandal/Notoriety in High-Profile Prostitution Cases," with scheduled speakers Xaviera Hollander (*The Happy Hooker*), Sydney Barrows (the "Mayflower Madam"), Margo St. James, Norma Jean Almodovar (*Cop to Call Girl*), Dolores French from Atlanta, Coral Velisek from Florida, and Helen Buckingham and Cynthia Payne from London. Several of these women had suffered severe consequences from their arrests and prosecutions, losing not only friends and family connections but often their homes or even their life savings. High-profile prostitution is automatically assumed, by prosecuting entities, to be organized crime (you're guilty of this before you have a chance to make a case in court) and can therefore be subject to the Racketeering Influence and Corrupt Organizations (RICO) Act, allowing the government to seize all of the accused's assets—house, car, all of their bank accounts. Sydney Barrows had been so destitute at one point that she only managed to eat by attending parties thrown in her honor; she had been left literally penniless. All of her old friends had abandoned her. During the height of the hoopla, her attorney had advised her not to speak to the press, and enterprising reporters, desperate for stories, simply made them up; she had been helpless to refute any of them. Sydney was still recovering in 1997, trying to put her life back together, surviving on jewelry making. She had no further interest in being involved in the sex business.

Aside from the special presentations, there were a wide variety of panel discussions and speakers: on various legal issues, trafficking and the global sex trade, STD prevention and treatment, research on sex and sex work, sex-worker advocacy and support, historical perspectives, and spirituality and how it relates to sex work, along with a few miscellaneous but fascinating topics: "Sex Work and the Disabled," "The Transgendered Community and Prostitution," "The Dominatrix as Sex Worker," "Male Sex Work," "Sex Workers as Real People: The Non-work Lives of Sex Workers," "Porn Stars Discuss Their Work, The Law and Society" (although Nina Hartley spoke on this panel, Juliet did not), and "Exotic Dancers Alliance: Unionizing Dancers," led by stripper and labor organizer Daisy Anarchy. Juliet, along with her friend Carolyn Elderberry, presented at only one panel, promoting the recently published book *Women of the Light: The*

New Sacred Prostitute, a collection of articles written by women sex workers, edited by Kenneth Ray Stubbs, to which both women had contributed essays.

Individual presentations within the panel discussions included "Working with Male Sex Workers in Calcutta, India," "Sex Surrogacy for the Disabled," "Whores and Other Feminists," "She-Male Prostitutes: Who Are They, What Do They Do, and Why Do They Do It?" "Coping with Mistress Burnout," "Female Footsuckers: Feminist Theories of the Fetish Meet the Sex-Positive Whore," "Sex Work as Emotional Labor," "Sex Workers and the Elderly Male Client," and "Who Says the Oppressed Can't Speak? Feminist Theory and the Silencing of Women" (an excellent rejoinder to Catherine McKennon's and Andrea Dworkin's work). Presenters included all the usual suspects: Carol Leigh, a.k.a. Scarlot Harlot, founder of BaySWAN (Bay Area Sex Workers' Action Network); Joseph Kramer, founder and former director of The Body Electric in Berkeley; Melissa Blake from PONY (Prostitutes of New York); Teri Goodson from COYOTE San Francisco, later to found the Cyprian Guild; Maggie Rubenstein of the Institute for Advanced Study of Human Sexuality in San Francisco; Carol Queen, one of the most creative, thoughtful and multi-dimensional people—besides Juliet—ever to enter the business; Richard Shapiro of the California Institute of Integral Studies; Annie Sprinkle, of course—she (like Juliet) would never miss an opportunity to be the center of attention; and porn stars Mike Horner (with whom Juliet had worked), Christi Lake and Stacy Valentine—in addition to all those already mentioned. There were also representatives from the law enforcement community, as well as a few johns who wanted to jump on the bandwagon.

Actually, there were a number of law enforcement personnel already on the premises when the official conference began on Friday, as a DARE drug war conference was going on at the hotel at the same time as ICOP. Partly because of this presence and partly to protect the sex workers from being hustled by potential customers who thought they might get a bargain, none of the signs directing attenders to the conference area included the words "prostitution" or "sex"; they read simply "ICOP."

Yet despite this careful consideration to detail on some levels, there were undercurrents of competition and resentment on other levels. In the lounge set up for films and videos, there were arguments about whose works should run, when, and how often. (Although these had been scheduled as a continuous loop, technical glitches interfered.) There was jostling among participants about who would get to be interviewed by the carefully selected press personnel. By the time Joycelyn Elders arrived on Saturday to give her keynote address, energy was high but so were tensions. Because the luncheon carried an extra cost, some participants—especially those from developing countries—were unable to attend; insufficient attention had been given to providing them with needed subsidies. Nevertheless, Dr. Elders gave an inspiring speech in support of decriminalizing sex work and honoring some of the services sex workers perform—working with customers with disabilities, for example.

One of the purposes of the luncheon was to give Margo St. James an award for her contributions to the field of sexuality and sex work. St. James's contributions were primarily in the political realm, for she had convened the San Francisco Task Force on Prostitution, promoting decriminalization; she herself was, contrary to popular opinion, never actually a sex worker. She had run for supervisor of the city and county of San Francisco the preceding year, coming in a close seventh for one of the six open seats; many of her sex-worker friends had campaigned for her, including phone banking from Tony Serra's law offices on the Embarcadero. (Sex workers are great on the phone; it used to be how they got their business, before the Internet).

The conference ended, unfortunately but probably not surprisingly, on a sour note. The final two sets of workshops were on Sunday morning, from 9:00 to 10:30 and from 10:30 to noon; the all-conference closing session was to begin at noon. While the latter had originally been scheduled to take place in a room not being used for a morning workshop, it was for some reason switched to the room where the "Sex Worker Outreach/Organizations in Central and South America" session was being held (in Spanish, of course). The room itself was a double one, that could be split into two with an accordion-style movable partition, and the workshop was in the back half—the partitioned-off part of the room. For the final session, the partition needed to be pushed back to make one large room, and chairs had to be set up for the audience. But the Latinos' workshop ran overtime, as workshops tend to do, and the attenders refused to disperse. Partly because of communication difficulties (although translators were present in the workshop, and tried to help) and partly because they were sex workers, with the usual emotional challenges, the workshop attenders became irate, insisting that they were being shut down unfairly, discriminated against because of their ethnicity, etc. After ranting for nearly half an hour, they agreed to move back the partition but staged a protest by marching into the front half of the room, chanting slogans, raising fists, and generally creating as much chaos as they could.

It is sad that the blame for this unfortunate scene was placed entirely on Vern Bullough. Of course it's true that booking the same room for two events, with absolutely no break time in between, was a mistake; some other arrangements should have been made. Anyone who has ever attended a convention knows that workshops always run overtime; that's why you allow break time between events scheduled into the same room. And in this case the problem was exacerbated by the nature of this particular group—a non-English-speaking minority. Organizers would have been wise to go out of their way to accommodate this group's needs. On the other hand, it was the very end of the conference, and the organizers were no doubt exhausted and did not have the energy to run around at the last minute trying to find a better room for the Latinos' workshop, or to switch in another group who might have been better able to deal with the double booking. Human beings make mistakes, and this unfortunate scene was one of the expensive ones.

As it was, the disruption affected not only the Latino protesters and conference organizers, but all the other attenders who deserved to experience a sense of completion for the conference. And, contrary to some reports, never did Vern Bullough make any derogatory remarks either to or about the protesters. He made a valiant effort to restore some order, and the ranters did eventually quiet down enough to allow the passage of a resolution urging the decriminalization of prostitution, but there was no closure to the conference. It was a sad but not atypical ending to a gathering of whores.

Considering that it was a coming together (yes!) of two very different subcultures—sex workers and mainstream academics—the first (and so far last) International Conference on Prostitution was a rousing success. The contentions that surfaced here and there were primarily the result of these two different approaches to social and economic life, and aptly referenced in the title of the event itself: a *conference* on *prostitution*? The format was that of a standard conference—workshops from nine a.m. to five-thirty p.m., early evening events, side rooms for the display of creative works, a press room for interviews; the content included panel discussions, performance events, a formal luncheon, and featured speakers, with some informal down time. Prostitutes, however, tend to lead a less scheduled and more spontaneous life, primarily during the night hours; few are early risers (Juliet was always a glaring exception to this pattern). The conference organizers did an excellent job of pulling together a diverse group of people and topics, obtaining the venue, handling the finances, developing the schedule, and supplying equipment. The sex workers brought their passion, spontaneity, and sometimes pathos. That the event came off as well as it did is a tribute to all who participated.

As for Juliet, the trip at least provided her the chance to visit with her friend Kay Parker; she spent the following Monday and Tuesday unwinding at Kay's. Throughout the conference itself, though, she was miserable (a fact of which "best friend" Carolyn was completely unaware). She had been anticipating being lauded as a star and having more opportunity to promote her new persona as sexual healer and educator. Yet she had so many fellow narcissists to compete with that she felt totally ignored and unappreciated, referring to the whole experience, in her private writings, as "the horror of ICOP." Nineteen ninety-seven was, in fact, to be one of her most tumultuous years.

23
Picking Up the Pieces

Back home after ICOP, Juliet continued work on *Ageless Desire* while she kept her massage business going. Life was rough going, in many ways. Health problems still plagued her—anemia (resulting in lethargy), dental problems, a bite from a feral cat she had befriended. Her Crohn's disease was flaring up again, and she scheduled her first colonoscopy for October.

In late August, the Bay Area was hit with unseasonable rains (it would be an El Niño winter), and her kitchen ceiling started dripping. After a few days, the drip became a constant stream whenever it rained. Juliet was not at first able to convince her landlady there was a problem; she thought Juliet was exaggerating, and took steps to have it repaired only after that section of the ceiling literally collapsed. Then the repairmen accidentally cut Juliet's business phone line, and it was out for several days until a friend was able to come over and fix it.

The rains were followed by an early September heat wave, and Don came down with pneumonia. Juliet had to take him to the emergency room, then bring him home to her place to recuperate because the elevator at his apartment building went out and he could not climb the stairs in his compromised condition (although he could manage the short climb at Juliet's, with some help). Playing nurse (except on stage) was never Juliet's long suit; she detested the job. Moreover, the roof was still being repaired during Don's stay, adding another stress for both of them. Truth be told, Don was not caring for himself as he should have been; in July he had decided to go off his heart medication. He, like Juliet, sometimes struggled with depression, which may have contributed to this poor decision.

Juliet's problems continued; they seemed to be coming in spades. Since she had had to give up her separate work space, she was seeing clients in her home, and their sometimes heavy energy lingered in her private space. The new answering machine she had chosen was back-ordered; she was missing calls, and business. The Berkeley neighborhood, while a definite improvement over Harrison Street, still had traffic noise, not to mention a few less-than-sterling neighbors.

On September 12th, Juliet sat down and wrote up a list of losses she'd experienced over the past year, from Snuggles to the disappointment over ICOP to the roof leak to Don's and her illnesses. "What next?" she wrote at the bottom of the list.

"What next" happened exactly a week later. On September 19th, as Don was driving over to see her, he suffered a heart attack. He was barely able to pull over and stop the car before he passed out. He died within minutes.

For Juliet it was the last blow. She could not imagine going on without Don. He, more than anything or anyone else, had given her the energy, hope and vision that made her feel she still had a future.

In the end, however, Juliet was still Juliet. She had been hit with devastating blows before. And she had picked herself up and gone on. Now she pulled herself together once again, although she was beginning to wonder how many more times she would be able to do that. She was growing older, and tireder.

To add to her burdens, Don—probably seduced into thinking that her well-organized living space reflected an ability to manage money and carry out mundane clerical tasks—had named her executor of his estate. And of course she was also the most logical person to organize a memorial service for him. She promised everyone she would do so, but as the days dragged into weeks it became apparent that nothing would materialize unless someone else picked it up. Carolyn Elderberry finally scheduled the event at her house. Don's mother—named Dottie, coincidentally, like Juliet's mother—came from Alabama for the occasion, lodging with Carolyn.

It was indeed a wonderful gathering of friends who had loved and appreciated Don, Juliet among them. She had made up a large poster board filled with pictures—some of Don alone but many of herself with Don, and even a fair number of herself alone. When it came time for her to share her memories of Don, they were more about herself than about him. No surprise to anyone present who knew her well.

The months following Don's death dragged for Juliet. It was not until early 1998 that she could summon up the energy to continue work on *Ageless Desire*. Everything about it reminded her of him—

how they would bounce ideas off each other, banter and joke during the long days of filming, and relax together at day's end, relishing their sense of accomplishment or bewailing their frustrations. Without Don she could only go numbly through the motions.

Yet, slowly, the work drew her in. It was, after all, her project, not Don's; she had been dreaming of it even before *Educating Nina*. And the years were slipping away, as the video itself reminded her: it was about sex for older adults. Now was the time for her to put her dreams into action; continuing to put them off would mean abandoning them. *Ageless Desire* was finally released in July 1999, and Juliet dedicated it to Don.

Juliet at a party with her Finnish friend Mirja Kajalo, circa 2000. Photo: Carr/Pettit family collection.

Juliet still dreamed, too, of writing her autobiography, *From School Teacher to Sex Star: Aunt Peg Tells Her Story*, promising it to her fans in her now online newsletter. But, somehow, she simply could not get moving on it. Nor was she able to proceed with the Wild Woman Theatre project; this dream too slipped quietly away.

One other effort that did come to fruition, in December 1998, was to put together a compilation video, *The Best of Aunt Peg*, featuring clips from her movies. Tracking down the copyright holders and getting permissions from them all had been a major project, but she managed to complete it with assistance from a client. Fans even helped out by sending her copies of some of the movies, as many of Juliet's copies had deteriorated to the point of being unusable. She also got the rights to use the movie poster for *Aunt Peg Goes Holly-wood*; she offered an autographed copy of it along with the video, for an extra charge. She added these to her other sex-related mementos—autographed 8 X 10 prints and magazine layouts of some of her sexy photographs;[29] full-color, life-sized molds of her breasts, for use as paper weights, bookends, or just conversation pieces; a mouse pad with Paul Johnson's classic photograph of her in her black merry widow; and a battery-operated pulsating artificial vagina ("Aunt Peg's Passion Pump"). These products, along with *Ageless Desire*, her massage business and workshops, provided her with enough income to live on, at least modestly.

Juliet also ventured into another expansion of her services: hypnotherapy. It was her first webkeeper, Tom Tilton, who turned her on to the idea; he had been training as a hypnotherapist himself. When Tom described the basic idea behind the technique, Juliet exclaimed, "Oh, I've actually been doing that for years with my clients!", for she had always included soothing touch, talk and other verbalizations in her massage work. She signed up for classes in basic hypnotherapy and received her certificate in 1998. She did not, however, continue on to the higher levels that Tom achieved; she never became a full-fledged hypnotherapist. Juliet was always a body-centered person, not really comfortable with or particularly drawn to any type of out-of-body experience.

It was also in 1998 that Juliet started attending some of the regular sex parties at Barry and Shell's Swinger House in Oakland—either the bimonthly women-only ones on Friday evening or the mixed-gender ones held every Saturday night. These parties were a long-standing tradition, having begun in the late 1960s, and they were well attended, averaging thirty to fifty participants a night. The large house was a good venue for such gatherings, with a group room furnished with wall-to-wall mattresses and a mirrored ceiling, and several smaller private rooms. Sort of a straight version of the traditional San Francisco bath house that catered primarily to gay men before the AIDS epidemic.[30] Although Juliet had given up vaginal penetration of any kind—because of the discomfort and even

---

[29] Juliet gave one of these photographs to her friend Greg Franke's father as a birthday present, humorously inscribed: "Dear Al: I hear you're hot! Call me, anytime. Juliet." He loved it.

[30] The San Francisco bath houses were available for rent to private parties after hours, and customers included other groups; they were never exclusively gay-male resorts.

possible tissue damage to her post-menopausal vagina—there were plenty of other sexual acts she could still comfortably engage in.[31]

In the summer of 1999, Juliet got an opportunity to combine her love of performing with helping out her old friend Annie Sprinkle. Annie had moved from New York to the Bay Area shortly after the International Conference on Prostitution. Of course Annie could not do anything so mundane (or expensive) as to rent an apartment and acquire renter's insurance. Instead she anchored out[32] on a houseboat in San Pablo Bay, just off the coast of Sausalito. A friend who was house-

Juliet at a party, circa 2006. Photo: Carr/Pettit family collection.

sitting for Annie when she was away on vacation inadvertently set fire to the place by leaving a candle unattended; the entire boat, along with all of Annie's possessions, including much of her archived material (but fortunately not all of her photographs of Juliet), went up in flames.

The sex-worker community responded in the usual way: as when ICOP appeared to be short of funds, they rallied to raise money for

---

[31] Juliet claimed publicly that her decision to forgo vaginal intercourse was based on the threat of STDs and her dislike of condoms, but the real reason was the physical pain that intercourse caused her. This is evidenced by her refusal to engage in any kind of vaginal penetration.

[32] "Anchoring out" referred to the practice of anchoring a boat just beyond the privately owned shoreline, rather than paying the high price for a slot at one of the private docks. The anchor-outers form a sort of subculture in the Bay Area, although the practice is now much rarer, due to official crackdowns.

Annie, scheduling a *Save the Mermaid: Annie Sprinkle Fire Show* event at the Cowell Theatre in San Francisco. Juliet helped plan the event and performed in it as well. Offerings included the opportunity for couples to have live sex in a private tent and be filmed for an interactive online video for the *Spectator*, or participate in a "Toss the Cock Ring" stunt: try to throw a cock ring onto one of the dildoes strapped onto female volunteers (Juliet was not among these).

Juliet had a great time at this event. She staffed her own booth, sitting on tall stool in front of a tent draped with black peek-a-boo lace, dressed in a black garter belt, hose, panties and heels, with her fabulous breasts exposed. For $20 [$28], fans could "Fondle Aunt Peg's Tits" or get a "Polaroid Photo with Aunt Peg," as in her stage-show days; both activities took place inside the tent. She also helped auction off a designer necklace, parading around on the stage modeling it, and throwing in a bit of sex comedy that had the audience roaring with laughter. The winning bid was $600 [$860].

The fundraiser was a great help to Annie, as well as an opportunity for the two friends to work and play together again. Aside from connecting by telephone once a year on their mutual birthday (July 23), they had drifted apart since the 1980s, when Juliet had stayed with Annie during her live stage-show tours; both of them had become too busy with their lives and livelihoods to spend leisure time together.

Not long after the fundraiser, the two went out to lunch with Tom Tilton, as Annie was looking for some high-tech advice and Juliet thought Tom might be able to help. The conversation soon turned to the 1997 film *Boogie Nights*, loosely based on the life of John Holmes and purporting to depict the real low-down on the American Golden Age of Porn. Juliet and Annie got into a heated discussion over the accuracy of the movie, with Annie defending it and Juliet castigating it for sensationalizing the industry. This public conversation became explicit at times, and the nearby tables were strangely quiet, aside from occasional nervous giggles. Annie and Juliet, however, were nonplused; neither was shy about flaunting her sexuality in public. In fact, as the trio was leaving the restaurant, Annie and Juliet, pretending to be a lesbian couple, pronounced loudly that since Tom was such a good sport, if either of them ever decided to go back to men, Tom would get the first call. This remark was most likely intended to make Tom blush, as it did.

Annie's and Juliet's differing perspectives on *Boogie Nights* may have been partly the result of geography: Annie had been involved in the New York scene, which was in fact more corrupt and degenerate, whereas Juliet had been in California, removed from the influence of organized crime and many of the more dysfunctional activities and participants. Yet Juliet's private journals contradict her protestations, validating much of the content of *Boogie Nights*:

> At the end of a day's work on a film or on stage, I wanted to forget the experience because much of it was horrendous and I couldn't deal with it again; once was enough... I stopped writing [journals] when I got into films because my feelings were so strong that I feared facing them... The 'highs' stayed with me; the rest I buried, for survival.

And Juliet was certainly aware of the seedy side of the porn business, as she had chronicled in her journals in both 1978 and 1991. Many workers had substance abuse problems; Juliet's lesbian friend Lisa had died of a drug overdose. There were sleazy directors, egotistical actors, and filthy or degrading working conditions. Yet she never dwelt on these situations in her public statements, perhaps fearful of exposing her vulnerability or of losing the support she still needed from the sex crowd. She had, after all, left Finland partly because of fall-out from her negative reports on the tourism industry there, and she did not want to repeat that mistake.

Aside from occasional highs like Annie's fundraiser, Juliet's everyday life was beginning to settle down into some predictability. Now over sixty, she was being accepted, both publicly and among her friends and acquaintances, as sort of a grande old dame of the sex business. In May 1998 she was again on the cover of a magazine featuring mature women—*Over Forty*—with a feature article "Aunt Peg: America's Sweetheart Turns 60" and a spread of previously unpublished photographs, this time dating all the way back to 1961, her straight-modeling days, and including current pictures of herself at age fifty-nine. She offered autographed copies of the magazine to fans, for $35 [$50] each.

When Angels Die

Who is this trying to write? Unspoken words hang in the airless space of my cluttered mind. I can't write.. or is that "ripe" – like fruit waiting to burst its skin? Sharp peals of a church tower, its bells deafening coherent thought. I used to be a good writer, or so I thought, but now my brain is cold oatmeal—instant, not steel-cut. Without raisins. Am I depressed, lazy, afraid? There's one of those words to mock me.

Lay-zee... to float in a sea of meaningless words that have their own agenda. To be spewed across the page in a mucked-up mess. Inspired? No, expired. My heart bursting with grief over Angel's death in the street of my worst nightmare. Tears spill from my swollen eyes onto her grave marked with a red satin rose. My loving companion filled the void of Don's absence but one year. Now she is gone too. Will I ever climb out of this sorrow to write again? Patience, patience, patience. For the time being, I will simply listen and wait.

Sorrow held tightly in my clenched jaw. Many long suppressed, painful memories wait to be released. Enough silent suffering. What am I waiting for? Let me shout my anger, wail at my losses. I don't ever again want to deny myself love for fear of loss. To know love is to know sorrow. I kneel and kiss the ground in gratitude. My heart has been set free. I kneel until my knees are stained with the earth to which we all return. I don't know what I'm writing—a jumble of words. I don't know who I am. It doesn't matter. I'm always me.

She stands upright, smiles wickedly and reveals her secret. She is tired of pretending to be other than ALL she is. Weary of avoiding the truth which spills out at inopportune times and terrifies the timid. Your hearts and minds close against the possibility of accepting her in all her guises. Her honesty will force you to face your shallow lives and unfulfilled dreams. Come out of your houses behind locked doors. See her standing tall, proud and beautiful, beckoning you to dance with her in the street, wear garlands in your hair, sing hymns of liberation.

-- *Juliet Carr, December 1999*

Juliet was also inducted into the X-Rated Critics Organization Hall of Fame in 1998, and in 2001 they gave her a Lifetime Achievement Award for Contributions to the Adult Industry. She continued intermittent attendance at Barry and Shell's sex parties, and she was

able to indulge her love of the theater and opera by volunteer usher-
ing or by accepting dates with men friends, many of them clients
turned social acquaintances; they usually paid for dinner out, if not
for tickets to the performances. Another regular social event was a
traditional Day After Thanksgiving get-together of many of the old
crowd of sexual revolutionaries, hosted by photographer Michael
Rosen and his wife Lucile; Juliet's long-time friend Paul Johnson had
been a regular attender for years, and facilitated her entry into the
group. Juliet always spent Thanksgiving itself with her family of
origin, then got to stuff herself again the next day with this second
family.

It was just after Thanksgiving, 1999, that Juliet's cat Angel was
run over by a car and killed. Juliet had acquired Angel just after
losing Lucky in 1997; Angel had also provided some comfort during
her grief over Don. Juliet's capacity for loss was being strained, adding to her stress and most likely to her physical health problems as
well.

For the most part, though, Juliet felt she was settling into a comfortable old age—as comfortable as old age can ever be. She retained
much of her beauty. Her once-blonde hair was silver now, and she
continued to wear it in the short swept-back style that suited her face
and character so well; Greg Franke still took good care of her coif-
fure. While she had developed some middle-aged flab, her breasts
remained, amazingly, as young and perky as a twenty-five-year-
old's. She had her loyal circle of friends, a cultural life, and her quiet
little home in Berkeley, with amazingly cheap rent for the Bay Area—
$750 [$1,070] a month. She still had her car, but often took public
transit, especially on the rare occasions when she traveled into San
Francisco, primarily to attend the opera, plays or concerts.

Juliet also took occasional trips back to the Sierra foothills to visit
her old friends, *Spectator* ex-owners Kat Sunlove and Layne Winklebeck. Kat had taken a job as lobbyist for the Free Speech Coalition in
1998, and spent most of her time in Sacramento. After she and Layne
sold the magazine in 2001, they retired to a small ranch in Pilot Hill,
and Juliet would take the train up to Auburn where they would pick
her up and drive her to their place. She enjoyed this respite from city
life, sometimes even taking a trail ride on one of their horses. Life
seemed to be giving her a much-needed gift of relative peace and

quiet, with just enough stimulation to keep her engaged and fulfill some of her insatiable need for adulation.

Alas, however, the new century was about to deliver another blow.

One day in December 2001, looking out her living room window, she saw her landlady, Susan, leading two men around; they seemed to be inspecting the house. When Juliet went out to inquire, Susan told her that she would be fixing up the property, painting both buildings and making other minor repairs, and then putting it up for sale.

Juliet felt a stab in her gut. Her home, her haven, her affordable housing—and a place that accepted her four cats—was going to be jerked out from under her. She felt like one of those cartoon characters who runs off a cliff, looks down and realizes there is nothing beneath them, and falls.

She went back into her apartment, poured herself a glass of wine, and sat down to think of a plan. Yes! She would buy the property, if sister Chris could be persuaded to do so for her. Juliet could function as property manager, renting out the other spaces to UC Berkeley college students. Surely Chris would see the logic in this plan. "Can you give me an alternative short of selling my soul?" she asked with her usual drama.

The only trouble was the high price of real estate. This was in the midst of the still-ballooning housing bubble. The house eventually sold for over $700,000 [$938,000]—far beyond what any normal middle-class family could afford for a second house, or for income property that would not pay for itself for years to come, as the mortgage payments would easily be triple the amount that college students could be expected to pay in rent. Juliet faced what felt like homelessness again.

24
Tomorrow Is a Long Time

Juliet was sixty-three. She was beginning to experience—in a real and direct way that even her perpetual optimism could not over-come—the limitations and stresses of aging. Over the last seven years, she had lost her father, her house in the Sierra foothills, a beloved and devoted partner, three feline companions, and much of her health. Her memory was going as well—even more than she realized. And now she was bereft of a home again. She moved to the only place she could afford that was not so run-down as to be depressing or completely unlivable—a small apartment in the Fruitvale area of Oak-land. The building itself was not bad—fairly new and well kept—and her first-floor apartment consisted of a large open kitchen/living-room area, a moderate-sized bedroom, and a bath. The yard was no more than a small walkway around two sides of the building.

The surrounding neighborhood, though, was essentially an in-dustrial area, even closer to the freeway than the Richmond Boule-vard house of 1983-85. A concrete jungle, with an abandoned air after business hours. It was in this apartment that this writer first visited her.

Finances were a struggle again. The post-9/11 recession was in full swing, and business of all kinds was down. The novelty of Juliet's return to the porn scene had worn off for many of her fans, her workshops were attracting fewer participants, and her dwindling energy had forced her to reduce the number of massage clients she saw, from thirty to twelve per month, and to confine what limited business she did have to morning and early afternoon hours. She would occasionally accept an evening appointment, but she had always been a morning person, and her internal engine ran down as the day went on. She still sold a few copies of her videos each month, through her website, but these had to be paid for by check or money order, as she could not afford the high cost of taking credit cards as an adult business.[33]

Somewhat reluctantly, Juliet filed for Social Security benefits as soon as she reached age sixty-five, accepting a lower monthly rate in return for earlier retirement. Yet it provided her, as it has so many seniors, a steady, reliable source of income, paying her basic bills, although she still needed to supplement this meager amount in order to have any real quality of life.

Long-term financial stability, if not prosperity, had finally arrived in Juliet's life. Not via any of the routes she had imagined (fame, a well-heeled life partner), but it had arrived nevertheless. Unfortunately, though, financial security did not necessarily translate into emotional equilibrium. For although in some ways Juliet was finally maturing, accepting her own limitations and lowering her expectations of life and other people, she remained ever "young at heart," retaining much of her youthful judgmentalism but also her exuberance and unique "wackiness." She was still given to exaggeration, and often brought her off-beat sense of humor to social gatherings, especially those where she was likely to meet new acquaintances, whom she felt compelled to impress. She often joked about opening a "bed, breakfast and blow job" facility, and at the 2002 sex-worker Christmas party, she related an anecdote about a recent dental appointment: when the hygienist commented on what strong jaws she seemed to have—enabling her to keep her mouth open for longer periods of time than most people—she explained to the unsuspecting woman that this capability was the result of long hours of practice in sucking cock. And Juliet still loved to tell tall tales, recounting some of the old stories about the Christmas she spent in the isolated cottage in Finland, or her travels in Mexico, or even hyping up current incidents; during the double session that she did with me, for example, she informed the client that he had experienced a Tantric orgasm; he looked dubious but did not argue the point.

---

[33] Visa and Mastercard charge an extra $500 to $1,000 per year just to keep such a merchant account open. They claim it is a type of business that suffers a high rate of chargebacks, but they already charge outrageous fees for charge-backs—usually $25 to $30 per incident, even if it is resolved in favor of the business. The real reason for the high charges is the same reason that Atom Home Video was able to abscond with *Educating Nina*: because they can get away with it.

Hope, too—another one of Juliet's signature characteristics—still brightened her days; she had definite plans for the future. She wanted to produce an updated version of *Ageless Desire*, with different actors, addressing more issues in more detail. But she needed investors, and rounding them up took time, energy and connections that she no longer had. She toyed with the idea of a Super Date with Aunt Peg, charging a client $3,000 [$3,850] for a weekend with her; she was even willing to try intercourse again, if she could find an effective lubricant.

In 2003 she and I considered creating some audio fantasy dramas together, similar to the old radio dramas but with explicit sexual content, but it was not clear whether there would be much of a market for these, and Internet marketing and distribution was not well developed at that time. I did help her get set up as an independent phone-sex operator, and she did this for a few months. But it was not really phone sex; she simply talked to callers about her porn career, at $60 [$75] per call. The technology was also a challenge for her; one caller was sure he had been taken for a ride when it took her over half an hour between his giving her his credit-card information and her callback. It had taken her that long to figure out how to put the sale through the credit-card machine. She abandoned this whole venture when she realized that she did not really like talking on the phone—a rather significant disadvantage for a phone-sex operator. The entire experiment actually cost her money, as she did not continue the business long enough to recoup the significant initial layout of $250 [$325] for purchasing the credit-card processing machine, and the more than $1,000 [$1,290] annual fee required to take credit cards for an adult business.[34]

The apartment in Oakland was becoming oppressive, too. As usual she had rushed into something without thinking it through clearly. One evening she was so distressed that she called her cousin Pam, practically in hysterics, telling her that she absolutely could not continue living there; she must find someplace else. She did in fact move back to Berkeley in 2004, to her last apartment. She was able to

---

[34] A year or so after this phone-sex trial, I contacted her about buying the credit-card machine, after mine gave out. She had no recollection of the entire business, vehemently denying that she had ever owned a credit-card machine.

swing it financially by taking on the apartment manager job, giving her a meager 10% discount on the $1,200-a-month [$1,510] rent.

The new property, on Dwight Avenue, consisted of two rows of one-story apartments facing each other across an open, treeless courtyard, with a small building at the base of the U containing a utility room. The entire property was gated and locked, providing a moderate level of security and privacy. Her one-bedroom unit was a quiet, pleasant place, where she could see clients, indulge in her favorite hobbies of cooking, reading, and playing with her four cats, and feel relatively safe and comfortable.

The day-after-Thanksgiving crowd. Paul Johnson seated next to Juliet, Michael Rosen's wife Lucile at the head of the table. Photo by Michael Rosen.

She had her circle of friends; Carolyn Elderberry and Paul Johnson lived within reasonable driving or transit distance; and San Pablo Avenue was nearby, with its shops and restaurants. Greg Franke still styled her hair and remained a good friend as well. Major holidays she usually spent with family at her niece Monica's Marin

County house, and she continued to attend the day-after-Thanksgiving dinners with the old crowd.

On Sundays, she often attended "services" at the Harmony Center for the Joyful Spirit—a sort of New Age church—in Oakland. In fact, she served for a while on the board of directors for the center, and often made up the flower arrangements that were a regular part of the decor. The Sunday programs included a lecture by founder and director Dan Neumeyer, discussions, singing, and—best of all for Juliet—dance music, with a live rock band. Juliet danced as she did everything else that she truly loved and had talent for—with body and soul. At the Harmony Center she usually danced alone, and because the rock music was loud and harsh,

Juliet loved to dance. It is not certain who her partner is here; it might be Paul Johnson. Photo: Carr/Pettit family collection.

she wore ear protectors, with bright red pads. Many of her fellow attenders remember her dancing—sensuously, exuberantly—adorned with her red head-gear, lost in the music.

In 2005 Juliet made one final serious attempt at writing her autobiography. The project had been on her mind for almost thirty years, even before she got into the sex business. She had hung onto her decades of journals, mementos, essays, short stories and partially finished scripts she had written; letters she had sent and received; business proposals; photographs; many of the radio scripts she had written in Finland; even all her expired passports. She had been lugging these treasures around, and accumulating more as she went, from Miami to Greece, to California, to Finland, back to California, up to the mountains and back down again. The paper trail of her life story. With some help from me, she got as far as drafting a book proposal, but even this first step remained unfinished. She could not write, could not get organized, could not stay focused. And in reality, her ability to write was fading; what little she did write during this time was meandering and inarticulate. Although she continued to list writing the autobiography as one of her New Year's resolutions, every year, the truth was that she was no longer capable of the task. It would remain an unfulfilled dream.

The next year, Juliet made plans to team up with a friend from Southern California and produce short videos on a website called fantasycapture.com. Clients would pay to have their favorite sexual fantasy performed in online video format—ironically, the very story line of *Educating Nina*. This idea, however, like many of Juliet's creative endeavors at this point in her life, came to naught. The cost of travel to southern California was prohibitive—an angle she had not considered—and she did not really have the energy to do the marketing, write scripts, perform, edit, etc.

The year 2007, when Juliet turned sixty-nine (an appropriate age for an old porn star), was mixed: traumatic in some ways and gratifying in others. In March she was involved in the first major traffic crash of her entire fifty years of driving, totaling her car right in front of her apartment building, and damaging three other vehicles in the process. Of course, the insurance company treated her like a criminal, as is their wont, adding to her emotional stress and triggering memories of her other encounters with the legal system, especially Bob Watt's trial. She gave up her car, intending to join a car-sharing program but never following through, relying instead on public transit and rides from friends when needed.

A few weeks later, her wallet was stolen as she was leaving the post office. The first trauma was enough to send her to the psychological ward of the hospital for several days, the second, for two weeks.

Crohn's disease flare-ups, and an intense bout of flu, also plagued her during the spring. She was essentially bed-ridden for several weeks. This spell resulted in a final romantic interlude for her, as a devoted client came to tend her frequently. Although he was intellectually challenged and grossly overweight—even more of a mismatch for her than Charles Webb had been—Juliet was always a push-over for attention and adulation, and announced to her family and friends that she would marry him. Fortunately, he drifted off after a few months.

Together, these difficulties put a serious dent in Juliet's finances, especially as her illnesses prevented her from working, reducing her income to Social Security checks and the small amount that trickled in from video sales. Desperate, she asked her webkeeper to help her launch a fundraising campaign, and for a few months the front page of her website featured a lovely non-sexual photo of her holding Snuggles, along with an appeal for donations to offset her medical expenses. Her fans stepped up to the challenge, many of them sending personal notes along with their donations, lauding her talents and expounding on how much her film performances had meant to them. Juliet was deeply touched by these responses; they gave her a much-needed lift, now that she was feeling more and more isolated and useless.

For her sixty-ninth birthday in July, Juliet dreamed of throwing a big birthday bash, and looked into renting her favorite lunch place on San Pablo Avenue for the event. But she could not in fact afford it, and sadly abandoned the idea.

October was a better month. She gave a presentation at the Institute for Advanced Study of Human Sexuality, and, along with several other people, received an honorary doctorate degree from the school. She was also interviewed for a documentary on Alex de Renzy, and was self-possessed enough to complete it in only one take. Yet it was also in this month that she experienced several major health issues: dental surgery and then severe bronchitis, followed by more arthritis flare-ups. She lived on pain pills for long spells at a time.

Illnesses like these came to plague her more and more frequently and more and more intensely. Her Crohn's disease was worsening; she had to subject herself to several colonoscopies—never pleasant or easy. She took medications regularly now, and often turned to Carolyn Elderberry's husband Bruce—a pharmaceutical psychiatrist—for advice when she was unsure about what to take, when, and how much.

The Institute for Advanced Study
of Human Sexuality

By virtue of the authority vested in the Board of Directors,
and on the recommendation of the Faculty,

the degree of

Doctor of Arts

(Honoris Causa)

is conferred upon

Juliet Carr

who has honorably fulfilled all the requirements
prescribed by the Institute for this degree.

Given at San Francisco in the State of California
on this ____11th____ day of ____October, 2007____

For the Board of Directors

Yet it was the deterioration of her mental health that was most troubling. Juliet and objective reality—never fast friends even in the best of times—were beginning to go their separate ways. Her behavior was becoming ever more erratic. She often seemed confused about time and space, not being entirely sure where she was or when she needed to go somewhere.

One of her evening escorts related two incidents that occurred in 2008, when they were attending opera performances in San Francisco. The first took place at the restaurant for their pre-show dinner, when Juliet suddenly became convinced, forty-five minutes before curtain time, that they must abandon their dinner and proceed to the show immediately, although the opera house was only half a block from the restaurant and they had reserved seats. Their food had not even been served. Juliet's companion demurred, determined to have his dinner. Yet Juliet left and proceeded to the theater. When he joined her later—in plenty of time for the show, of course—she made no reference to her earlier panic, seeming to have completely forgotten it.

On another occasion, returning from a performance, her escort was driving her to the BART station but had to take several detours because of street construction. Juliet, apparently feeling hopelessly lost and disoriented, became so distraught that she insisted on getting out of the car and striking out on her own. She did somehow manage to make her way back to the East Bay; who knows how, or at what hour.

And while in her better moods Juliet often joked about her memory loss ("can't remember shit"), her dementia was actually becoming a serious problem. At the end of September 2009, Jill Nelson interviewed Juliet by telephone for her book *Golden Goddesses*, spending a total of three hours, over two sessions, with her. The "true-life" stories Juliet related were over the top even for her, with her tendency to over-dramatize. She claimed that her parents had been very explicit about sexuality when she was growing up, going so far as to inform the children when they were retiring to their bedroom to have sex. She also claimed to have lived, not just in Spain and Italy, as she had been listing (incorrectly) on her website for some time, but also in Portugal, spending two and a half years in each of these countries, and the same amount of time in Greece.

While these recollections may well have been sincere, rather than deliberate fabrications, there was certainly no objective truth to any of them.

Juliet (on right) with her sister Chris (left) and niece Monica (center), 2004. Photo: Carr/Pettit family collection.

Juliet's weakening grasp on reality may also have contributed to her troubles as she tried to fulfill her apartment-manager duties. Some residents found her difficult to deal with, and one tenant actively disliked her to an extreme; for what exact reason is not known, although it is likely that the resident herself was no gem. In November 2009, an even more contentious tenant moved in—a burly biker, who took an instant dislike to Juliet, as she did to him. Juliet, whose judgment was clearly fading by this time, made the mistake of mentioning, in casual conversation, that she was a massage therapist who worked out of her home. The biker tenant promptly reported her to the city; it was not legal in Berkeley to run a massage business (erotic or otherwise) out of one's home.

Juliet was devastated by this blow. She felt at first that her only option was to move again, and she was sure the stress of having to do that would be more than she could handle. Although she settled the issue, at least temporarily, by informing her clients that, if questioned, they had to claim to be personal visitors, not business clients, the feeling of being watched haunted her. She no longer felt safe in her own home.

Juliet's family were also finding her more and more difficult to deal with, much though they still loved her. Juliet suffered frequent bouts of claustrophobia, often overwhelmed by environmental stimulation of various sorts. While she did suffer from some chemical sensitivities, her reactions tended to be overdone. Once when she and her cousin Pam were shopping at a health-food store, Juliet, claiming to be overcome by some kind of toxic fumes, grew almost hysterical, announcing loudly that she absolutely had to get away from whatever it was and rushing out of the store dramatically, pushing other customers out of the way as she ran.

Juliet (on right) with her sister Chris and her mother, 2009. Photo: Carr/Pettit family collection.

It was not only in public that Juliet's behavior was problematic; she was disruptive at family gatherings as well. The last straw for her family came at their Christmas gathering in 2009. The get-together was at Chris's house in Sonoma County, and as Monica and her two small daughters were leaving, Juliet, standing at the doorway with Chris as they bid their visitors good-bye, suddenly declared that she could not tolerate another second of the cold air blowing in, and, rather than walking back into the house herself, slammed the door in the faces of her grandnieces. Stunned by this act of aggression, Chris and Monica concluded that they could no longer tolerate her presence around the children, which meant that she would not be invited to large family gatherings. Chris had the unenviable job of informing Juliet of this decision.

Juliet's life was clearly falling apart. Her health was seriously failing; she was often in pain or misery, a state of mind that still brought up feelings of panic from her childhood hospitalization experiences. She felt under attack in her apartment. She was losing her memories of her own past, and was often confused about the present. Journaling, her emotional outlet, had become impossible because of her arthritis. Her very identity seemed to be slipping away. She was beginning to withdraw, to sink into an almost surreal world of her own making.

Not that she was without some comforts. She had her four cats. She had a few true friends who still valued her and tried to help her as they could. She had reasonable financial security. She still dreamed of leaving a written legacy of her life and work. And her sense of humor still buoyed her up; she had long subscribed to the magazine *Funny Times*, which included a humorous email service, from which she selected her favorites to send on to friends. Her family, too, remained loyal and supportive, and they did love her, despite their need to protect their more vulnerable members from her disruptive behavior. Hopefully she

Juliet in late 2009.
Photo by Paul Johnson.

knew that. "The love I received from my family has sustained me through many difficulties," she had written in 1999.

On Sunday, 10 January 2010, Juliet had to fast in preparation for a colonoscopy the following day. She was in pain, though, from her Crohn's disease and arthritis. She wondered whether it was all right to take pain medication; she had her prescription morphine but was unsure how it might affect her on an empty stomach, or whether it might interfere with the following day's procedure. She called Bruce, Carolyn Elderberry's husband, to set her mind at ease. He assured her that it would be fine to take the meds, and encouraged her to do so.

She called him again a couple of hours later. The pain was still too intense. She wondered if she should go to the hospital. He advised her to take another dose, but to call him again if she felt she needed to go in. She evidently did not feel panicked enough to call 911, and probably lost consciousness soon after this second call to Bruce.

When her friend Aaron came to pick her up the following morning, to drive her to the colonoscopy appointment, he could not get an answer to his knock. After a few tries, he went around to her bedroom window, called out to her and tapped on the glass. No response. Finally, with a mounting sense of trepidation, he used his key to get in.

He found Juliet lying in bed, surrounded by her four cats. She had clearly been gone for some hours.

.   .   .   .

Some people who knew Juliet think she committed suicide, but there is no real evidence for this belief. While she was certainly no stranger to depression, Juliet always pulled herself together again: she was ever hopeful, always making new plans. Suicide did not fit with her personality. It's possible, of course, that she accidentally overdosed on her medication, in her confusion and pain. Her thinking, never too clear even when she was drug-free, was probably compromised by the medication. It is equally likely, though, that she died from some sort of major organ failure, unrelated to the morphine she had taken. Since there was no evidence of foul play in her death, no autopsy was performed.

On January 17th, the Sunday following Juliet's death, a hastily scheduled memorial was held at the Harmony Center for the Joyful Spirit. "What do you think was the theme of Juliet's life?" Dan Neumeyer asked those who had gathered to share memories of their friend. People suggested happiness, beauty, courage, cheerful persistence, vitality, elegant stylishness, youthfulness, overcoming hardship, and being energetic, among others.

"I remember being impressed by her grace in dancing and [her] lovely manner."

"I will actually miss her setting conditions for everything. I expect when I am in my 70's I will be as unwilling to compromise as she was."

"Juliet was so vibrantly alive, still enjoying all of life...still young enough for loving... How beautiful she looked, how she loved doing the flowers for the Sunday ceremony, and of course, her joyous dancing with those big ear protectors."

"I will always remember her smiling face... Juliet was a wonderful person, cheerful and friendly. She loved people and people loved her."

"She blazed a little-trodden trail in the adult film industry, being the first 'older woman' to star in adult films in the ten years between her fortieth and fiftieth birthdays. And for the next twenty-one years of the life that ended this week, she continued to be a cheerleader in the celebration of the vibrant sexuality of older women."

A more formal memorial for Juliet was held on 26 January 2010, at the Center for Sex and Culture in San Francisco—a venue that has, alas, seen many memorials for sex workers and their allies over the years. As many of her friends from the sex business as could attend were there, and they too shared their memories and stories. Juliet, despite often feeling isolated and unappreciated after her withdrawal from the porn film scene, had touched many lives, in many different ways.

Juliet was unique among the porn actresses of the Golden Age. Not only was she older than most of them, but she was also multi-faceted; her life was not defined by her role as a sex goddess. She was an artist, a writer, a poet, a dancer, a comedian, a gourmet cook, a party hostess, and perhaps most of all, an adventurer.

Juliet believed that she had blazed a path from the debilitating restrictions of her childhood illnesses, to become her authentic self: a free spirit who, like the Pied Piper, wanted to lure others onto that path of liberation, too, showing them the limitlessness of life's possibilities. Her own story, she felt, would serve as an inspiration to both women and men: Juliet lived the American Dream of building a life on one's own terms.

While there is certainly a good deal of truth to Juliet's perception of her life as an inspiration, that perspective is only part of the story. The other part included her fears, disappointments and confusions. Yet telling that story would have made her feel too vulnerable, and would have contradicted the glowing picture she wanted to paint. Perhaps that is why she could never write her story herself: it remained incomplete because it would not have been genuine.

Although I initially embarked on this project of writing Juliet's story to honor her memory and to fulfill her dream of inspiring others, I realized as I delved into her private writings that there was another story, different from the one she wished to tell, and in some ways a more inspiring one. For, although she had big dreams and admirable goals, Juliet, like most of us, fell short of achieving many of them. Instead, she acquired other assets: the ability to survive disappointments, to revel in simple everyday joys rather than always chasing after the future, and to feel that life has value even if its purpose is unclear. That Juliet never really figured out what she wanted to do when she grew up is not as uncommon a condition as we are led to believe in this very goal-oriented culture. Living is, ultimately, just living, and Juliet's life demonstrated that well.

To my mind, Juliet fulfilled the three purposes of life: to be and express one's own unique self, to appreciate the amazing universe and all that is in it, and to be of service to others. For Juliet, that service consisted of bringing joy, warmth and genuineness to all who were fortunate enough to know her at her best.

"What I remember most about Judy," her Greek lover Nikolas recalled, "is her warmth and her honesty." (Clearly, he meant "honesty" in the sense of "integrity" rather than "veracity.")

"Juliet had a way of appearing on a scene and taking charge," Carolyn Elderberry observed. "But that was often because no one else was taking charge, and someone needed to. She got things done that needed to be done."

"Juliet was an innate performer. Entering a room and feeling eyes seek her out, she literally lit up like a beacon. She found delight in all aspects of life, from the sublime to the mundane. Silk on skin, a beautiful orchid—or man or woman, a string quartet, walking in nature: all fueled her insatiable lust for life." Greg Franke, Juliet's longtime friend and hairdresser

"Juliet was filled with passion—for life, love and the pursuit of pleasure. She was a great sex goddess pioneer who is sorely missed, but not forgotten. Juliet is of the spirits and she is nearby, showing off her alabaster breasts." Annie Sprinkle, Juliet's friend and collaborator

"Juliet was a Sister Spirit in so many ways: complex, sensitive and committed to her work to elevate sexual consciousness. We only came to know and understand each other later on after I ended my film career, but I grew to love and admire her for her courage and willingness to honor her Soul's journey as I do mine. Her dance continues in the stars." Kay Taylor Parker, friend and co-star, www.kaytaylorparker.com

"Juliet was a force of nature, a feminist pioneer and a remarkable woman. Without her there would be no Nina Hartley, for which I'm very, very grateful. Thank you, Juliet, for being a role model for me." Nina Hartley, colleague

"Juliet Anderson, a.k.a. Aunt Peg, was the first of the red-hot mamas to attain stardom in the blossoming world of adult films in the 1970s. In being a woman working among girls, Juliet brought the real full flame of female sexuality to the screen where so many of the young and pretty ones were only learning how to fake it. Juliet came alive for us. And we were grateful." Howie Gordon, the ghost of Richard Pacheco, Author of *Hindsight: True Love & Mischief in the Golden Age of Porn*

"I knew Juliet as a longtime friend and also as an occasional play partner. Her ability to tune in to the body—to listen to what the body has to say and to respond through her hands and her entire being—was phenomenal. I will miss her spirit, her joy, her sparkling energy,

and her ability to connect deeply and immediately through touch."
David Steinberg, photographer

"[Juliet was] one in a million...uniquely gifted, not a match for many, probably not even a few. [She had a] blend of caring, compassion and intellect." Marc Ceniceros, friend

From her fan letters: "Juliet brought style, elegance and great sensibility to her performances...and to her characters, a quality of knowing enthusiasm and experience that so many of the other actresses lacked. She exuded a sense of self-confidence. No one else has come close to meeting that mark... Juliet seemed to be saying to the viewer: 'Hey, I'm doing what I love, and there just happens to be a camera around.'"

> ### Death script
> #### (written in 1977)
>
> *Greek island, 90 years old, robust, alert. Ride bicycle, go*
> *sailing in small boat. Small comfy cottage with cats;*
> *garden; music; circle of young, intelligent, loving*
> *friends; man; quiet mornings alone with sun, sea and*
> *sound of waking. No fear of death—no illness.*
>
> *Then I know it's time to go—call my closest friends for tea*
> *and tenderness. Then I lie down, holding a friend's*
> *hand, to the strains of some favorite music. I go to*
> *sleep. But no one is sad, there is no funeral... I'll be*
> *cremated and my ashes spread to make flowers grow.*
>
> *Only my body ceases to function. I will go out of my body,*
> *will be able to look down at my earthly home, perhaps*
> *even be able to go back in time and review my former*
> *life. Reincarnation is a possibility.*
>
> *If I do become ill... I hope to Sun that I will have enough*
> *clarity of mind to take an eternal sleep pill.*

I am more than my labels.

To live fully you may have to sacrifice security for
adventure.

In denying our suffering we may never know our
strength or our greatness.

-- Juliet Carr

Afterword:
A Life Lived With Love and Lust

One of Juliet's fantasies, when she reached the stage of being a distinguished-looking silver-haired lady, was to be seated at the table at a formal dinner party and be asked, by her matronly hostess, "So what do you do for a living, dear? Are you retired, or do you still work?"

After a dramatic pause to make sure everyone was listening, she would reply, "I suck cock." Then she would smile and take a sip of her drink, surveying the gathered company for their reactions.

The scene is classic Juliet: adolescent attention-grabbing at its worst. But anyone who knew Juliet could well imagine her playing it out.

Juliet loved attention, yes. She also loved life, and sensuality, and beauty, and adventure, and unconventionality. And... the quiet of solitude, the stimulation of society, the serenity of nature, the excitement of cities. She never could make up her mind about where she belonged, only knowing that wherever she was, she soon wanted to be somewhere else.

She saw herself as a free spirit, yet was totally dependent on other people for attention and approval. In some way, she knew this about herself: "I defined myself in relation to my adventures and how others responded to them. While seeming to have an independent, carefree, pleasure-filled, glamorous life, in fact I was often in extended despair, lonely, angry, sorrowful." And for all of her determination to be unique, iconoclastic, and special, Juliet was in many ways an ordinary person. An ordinary 1950s American woman, to be more precise. This she also knew: "I am: smart, special, talented, loving. Is this just a big ego trip...a clever maneuver to escape facing the fact of my ordinariness?"

While she hung out with Baby Boomers and tried hard to adopt their life style—pot smoking, goddess and New Age spirituality, meditation, bodywork, self examination and fulfillment, the whole shebang—Juliet was never really able to settle into that world. It was not, really, her world.

Her world was the one in which she had grown up—white, middle-class, mid-twentieth-century America. And if she had been able to find a man who could have put up with her narcissism, moodiness and instability, she would have been perfectly content to settle down as a middle-class housewife, financially supported by her husband while pursuing her artistic and sensuous talents in more subtle, less revolutionary ways: being an artist and writer, dressing attractively, taking exotic vacations, hanging out with interesting people. Probably having affairs from time to time, but always coming back to her base, her anchor.

While this may sound shallow, it is actually all most people want. What was different about Juliet was not her goals, but the way she went about pursuing them. And the intensity with which she did so. Ordinary though she may have been, she lived an extraordinary life.

Juliet lived in her body. Not many people do that. It's a vulnerable place to live. It can also be a painful place, as Juliet well knew, from the time she was a child. But if you want to immerse yourself in life, it's the only place to live.

She lived in her emotions, too—another sometimes painful place to be. She never really recovered from the isolation and abandonment she experienced in the hospital as a child. She always felt left out, never quite good enough to be loved for herself, always hanging around on the edge of society, looking in. Never able to see that, in a way, everyone else is out there, too: that the outside is actually the circle itself.

Yet despite her pain, physical and emotional, Juliet knew joy. Joy in her body, joy in experiencing life with all of her senses. And she was able to bring some of that joy to others, in her performances and in her more intimate work.

She was brilliant, creative, perceptive, vibrant, and perhaps most of all, warm. Her self-absorption was never malicious, only thoughtless. At her best, she sparkled, bringing light into dark corners. While she never changed the world as she had hoped to do, she left it the brighter for her being here.

"... Juliet is the sun!"[35]

---

[35] *Romeo and Juliet*

See her standing tall, proud and beautiful, beckoning you to dance with her in the street, wear garlands in your hair, sing hymns of liberation!

Juliet circa 1963, in her mid-twenties.
Photo by Bob Watt.

Juliet (on right) with her cousin Pam Saunders, at her niece Monica's wedding in 2001. Photo by Mirja Kajalo.

❖   ❖   ❖   ❖   ❖   ❖   ❖   ❖   ❖   ❖   ❖

Juliet's video, *Ageless Desire*, is available online, as are many of the movies she performed in during her porn career.

Juliet's mother, Dorothy Carr, died in August, 2015, at the age of one hundred.

Juliet's ex-husband Bob Watt was finally approved for parole in December 2017, at the age of seventy-nine.

❖   ❖   ❖   ❖   ❖   ❖   ❖   ❖   ❖   ❖   ❖

APPENDIX A: Major events in Juliet's life

1938   Born in Palmdale, California, U.S.A.

1947   Family moves to Burbank, California. Juliet diagnosed with childhood arthritis, hospitalized for long periods of time.

1956   Graduates from Burbank High School. Diagnosed with Crohn's disease.

1957-61   Attends Long Beach State College in Long Beach, California.

1958   Loses virginity in typical 1950s scenario.

1961-62   Lives in Japan with first husband, Bob Watt.

1962-66   Lives in Miami, Florida. Divorces Bob. Travels to Portugal in summer of 1966.

1966-68   Lives in Greece and has affair with Nikolas, admiral in Greek navy.

1968-70   Finishes degree at Long Beach State College.

1971-77   Lives in Finland and has career as journalist, primarily in radio. Marries second husband, Velic Pekku, in 1973; divorces him in 1975.

1978   Enters porn film business with bit part in *Pretty Peaches*.

1978-85   Career as porn actress. Lives in San Francisco, Piedmont and Oakland.

1981   Debuts her live stage shows.

1984   Writes, directs and produces *Educating Nina*, starring Nina Hartley.

1985-90   Lives in Placerville, California, works at a bed and breakfast, trains as massage therapist, opens massage business serving both mainstream and erotic clients.

1987   Ex-husband Bob Watt convicted of the 1984 murder of his third wife and sentenced to twenty-five years to life, in New York state.

1990   Buys house in Pollock Pines, California. Moves back to Oakland, continues work as erotic massage therapist.

1994   Loses her beloved father to heart failure.

1995   Inducted into Erotic Legends Hall of Fame. Sells house in Pollock Pines, California.

1996   Meets Don Crane, the last great love of her life. *Women of the Light: The New Sacred Prostitute* is published, containing an essay by Juliet about her life and work. Snuggles, her beloved cat of nineteen years, dies.

1997   Presents talk at International Conference on Prostitution. Writes, directs and produces *Ageless Desire*, a video about sex for heterosexual couples over the age of fifty. Don Crane dies.

1999   Inducted into X-Rated Critics Organization Hall of Fame. *Ageless Desire* released.

2001   Receives Lifetime Achievement Award for Contributions to the Adult Industry.

2007   Awarded honorary doctorate from the Institute for Advanced Study of Human Sexuality in San Francisco.

2010   Dies in Berkeley, California.

APPENDIX B: Juliet's movies

Title	Year released	Director	Juliet's role	Level*	Juliet's rating
All the King's Ladies	1982	Juliet		S	
Aunt Peg	1980	W. Brown		L	**
Aunt Peg Goes Hollywood	1981	P. Vatelli		B	
Aunt Peg's Fulfillment	1981	W. Brown		L	**
Bad Company	1980	Elliot Lewis	Countess Desois	S	
Beyond Your Wildest Dreams	1981	Gerard Damiano	Sharon Morgan	L	*
Body Candy	1980	Dale Martin	Lady Veronica	L	
Bound	1983			B	
Carnal Highways	1980	C. Howard			
Caught in the Act	1981	Lee Young			
Classic Swedish Erotica #3					
Coed Fever	1980	R. McCallum	Dean Speer	S	

* L=lead, S=support, B=bit part

385

Title	Year released	Director	Juliet's role	Level*	Juliet's rating
Coffee Tea or Me	1983	Bob Vosse	Julie Patterson	L	
Cumshot Revue 2	1985	B. Adams		B	
Dixie Ray, Hollywood Star	1983	A. Spinelli		B	
Educating Nina	1984	Juliet	phone sex performer		★★
8 to 4	1982	L. Lewis	boss	S	
Erotic Interludes	1984	J. Winestock		B	
Erotic World of Angel Cash	1982	H.A. Howard	madam	B	
Fantasex Island	1983	Lawrence T. Cole	teacher, madam	B	
Flight Sensations	1983	J. Robertson	(archival)	B	
Foxholes	1982	B. Augustus		S	
Girl's Best Friend	1981	Henri Pachard	Mrs. Leautrec	L	★★

* L=lead, S=support, B=bit part

Title	Year released	Director	Juliet's role	Level*	Juliet's rating
Girls from Charlie Company				B	
Gypsy Ball	1980			B	
Hot Lunch	1980	H. Perkins		S	
Hot Ones	1984			B	
Insatiable II	1984	Stu Segal	Morgan Templeton	S	
Inside Desiree Cousteau	1979	L. Gucci		S	*
It's Called Murder, Baby			(non-sexual)	S	
Kitty Shane's Fantasies	1982			B	
Legends of Porn	1987			B	
Love Goddesses	1981	J. Robertson		B	
Love Notes	1985	J. Robertson		B	
Lusty Ladies	1983		(archival)	B	

* L=lead, S=support, B=bit part

Title	Year released	Director	Juliet's role	Level*	Juliet's rating
Manhattan Mistress	1981	J. Davian	Georgia	B	
Mistress	1982	J. Remy		B	
Object of Desire	1982	J. B. Jime		B	
Outlaw Ladies	1981	Henri Pachard	Abby	L	*
Perfect Gift	1979			S	
Physical	1981	D. Lobo		B	
Physical II	1985			B	
Pretty Peaches	1978	Alex deRenzy	Katie the maid	S	
Purely Physical	1982	B. Thornburg		S	
Randy the Electric Lady	1980	P. Schumann	Dr. Pandrek (non-sexual)	L	
Reel People	1983	A. Spinelli		S	

* L=lead, S=support, B=bit part

Title	Year released	Director	Juliet's role	Level*	Juliet's rating
Rockin' with Seka	1980	Z. Ziggowitz		B	
San Fernando Valley Girls	1983	L. Lewis	Rosie	S	
Shoppe of Temptations	1979	J. Ross	Countess Von Fur Burg	S	
Skin on Skin	1980	A. Spinelli		S	*
Summer Heat	1979	Alex deRenzy	Judy	S	*
Swedish Erotica 2	1981	Bob Vosse		B	
Swedish Erotica 15	1981			B	
Taboo	1980	K. Stevens		S	*
Taboo II	1982	K. Stevens		S	
Talk Dirty to Me	1980	A. Spinelli	Helen	S	*
Tangerine	1979	G. Graver	aunt	S	*
Tender Trap	1978	Kezar	Mistress Monica		

* L=lead, S=support, B=bit part

Title	Year released	Director	Juliet's role	Level*	Juliet's rating
That's Porno	1980	J. Robertson	(documentary)	B	
Undulations	1980	T. Benny		B	
Vista Valley PTA	1981	A. Spinelli	Judy	S	
With Love Annette	1985			B	
Woman in Love	1983	K. Horulu		B	

Sources: Internet Movie Database (imdb.com); Juliet's notes

* L=lead, S=support, B=bit part

Juliet started performing these shows live on stage in late 1981, and continued well into 1987, even after she had ceased her involvement in the film business. She wrote up these descriptions to send to theatre managers, so that they could select which roles they wanted her to perform, and prepare the technical aspects required.

Whenever possible she liked to follow each show with a question-and-answer session with the audience about the X-rated film business.

Character	Scenario
Chris the Carpenter	To the cacophony of construction, traffic and city sounds, I enter dressed in faded jeans, flannel shirt, work boots, hardhat, work gloves and a carpenter's belt laden with tools. I have a 2x4 over my shoulder and a lunch pail in my hand. I measure, hammer nails, etc. until the lunch whistle blows. Out of my lunch pail I take a sandwich, thermos and sex magazine. Looking at a picture of a couple making love turns me on, which prompts a unique strip out of my work clothes to reveal feminine, lacy undies. A provocative and torrid dance follows.
Golden Girl	As Shirley Bassey sings "Take My Love" I enter dressed in a gold lamé gown, gloves, jewels and a boa. I dance, strip, pose and seductively tease the audience.

Character	Scenario
The Executrix	As Dolly Parton belts out "Working Girl" I enter dressed in a stylish suit carrying a briefcase. It is the end of another tough day climbing the corporate ladder. Now at home I start to unwind with the help of a glass of wine (grape juice in a wine bottle). Starting to disrobe, I get a gleam in my eye and my strip gets more provocative. When all my everyday business clothes are off, I get a wicked grin on my face and begin my transformation from the "nice girl" into the strong, sexy dominatrix in black leather and lace, brandishing a riding crop, prowling the stage looking for "boys" to play with.
Helen the Housewife	To the strains of "I'm Nothing But a Housewife" I enter, dressed in frumpy clothes, pushing a mop, carrying a laundry basket. Complaining about the boring life of a housewife, I fantasize about some glamorous jobs including that of an erotic movie star. Confident that I've got what it takes, I perform a slow strip out of bedroom slippers, apron and rubber gloves revealing sexy undergarments. My floor work is slow and sensual and concludes with a dynamic duet with the feather duster.

Character	Scenario
Nurse Naughty	To the sounds of a car crash, sirens and emergency room procedures, I enter, dressed in a nurse's outfit. I go into the audience and take temperatures, heart beats, etc., to locate the "patient." When it is discovered that it is I who have a fever, I suggest undressing to lower my temperature. I perform a slow, sensuous strip, revealing white undergarments. I proceed with floor and chair work and perform with oral expertise on a large syringe.
Suzy the Secretary	To the strains of Leroy Anderson's "Typewriter Song," I enter wearing a conservative suit and horn-rimmed glasses, and carrying a steno pad. I type and take dictation. The phone rings. It is a gentleman friend of mine who recognizes that beneath my prim exterior is a very passionate woman. He invites me over for dinner and tells me to "think sexy." This gets me excited and initiates my steamy strip, erotic dance and creative dalliance with the telephone.
The White Widow (butterfly) Note: This act requires a large stage with good lighting and sound system and no back mirror.	The stage is dark. The music starts its slow, dramatic buildup. A dim spotlight building to full brightness reveals the back of a motionless, black-caped and hooded figure standing center stage. I slowly turn and walk toward the audience. In a well choreographed and scored performance, I incorporate dramatic tension with eroticism to produce an original, powerful and exotic strip and dance of mourning transformed into freedom and joy.

Character	Scenario
Teacher's Pet Note: In this show I have a female partner.	To the strains of "Teacher's Pet" I, the prim school teacher, enter wearing a conservative outfit and horn-rimmed glasses. I go to the blackboard and start to write the day's lesson on it. A young woman student tries to sneak into her seat because she is late. She is wearing a short skirt, knee socks and a tight sweater and is carrying school books. I catch her in the act and start to reprimand her. My sternness melts when she smiles sweetly, apologizes and presents me with an apple. She takes advantage of my dropping my guard to seduce me. At first I resist her advances but soon we are engaged in passionate lovemaking.
Cassie the Cook	To the tune of "Too Many Cooks" I enter in a cute, sexy dress, cook's apron and chef's hat, carrying a big bowl in which I am stirring cake batter. Then I chat with the audience about the relationship between food and sex.. and then with some fruit to prove my point... a humorous demonstration of creative ways to "play with your food." While my cake is baking I proceed with a further demonstration of my culinary skills ... the cookbook strip.

Juliet was notorious, especially among her family—who knew her best—for her enhancements of reality. Her public statements—in interviews and in her own published writings—often clash with the truths she wrote in her private journals, or with others' versions of events. Of course, we all do this to some extent: clean up our public stories to make ourselves look better. But because these doctored versions of her stories became so much a part of Juliet's public persona, perhaps even setting standards that others—especially women—might measure themselves against, an honest account of her life must include their debunking.

Juliet was not, in fact, larger than life, although she was certainly intense, irreverent, and creative. She was as human and fallible, and suffered as much pain and loss of control over people and events in her life, as anyone else.

While details of the true versions of these stories are contained within individual chapters of the book (as referenced below), they are summarized here.

Losing her virginity
Public story: I orchestrated the loss of my virginity in 1958, at the age of twenty, first getting fitted for a diaphragm and carefully choosing the man. I promised him we would have intercourse if we could spend the first summer leisurely exploring each other's bodies. Then, the night before my lover returned to a distant college, we 'went all the way.'
Truth: Juliet's deflowering was a typical 1950s story: boy pressures girl into having sex until she finally gives in. While Juliet was certainly eager and curious, she also held back for many months because of her fear of pregnancy and her lifelong training in "being a good girl"; she had not yet freed herself from that stereotype. As for obtaining contraception before her first intercourse: this would have been very difficult for her. Unmarried underage women (defined at that time, 1958, as under age twenty-one) could not legally obtain contraception of any kind without parental permission, which she did not have. In fact she used no contraception for this encounter, and worried for almost a month about whether she had gotten pregnant; fortunately she had not.

Furthermore, the young man in question was not, by any stretch of the imagination, loving and tender, as Juliet seemed to imply. He was aggressive, had a drinking problem, and was emotionally and verbally abusive. Their encounters leading up to sexual intercourse were crude and hurried. And the "distant college" he returned to was only about fifty miles away—not considered far in southern California. (See Chapter 3, pages 30-31)

Living abroad, international travels

Public story: I lived in Japan, Mexico, Greece and Finland, studying art, teaching English, and exploring those countries and their men. I traveled through Europe alone (unheard of in those days). In 1968 and 1969, I spent a year in Italy and a year in Spain.

Truth: In 1961 Juliet moved to Japan to join her fiancé Bob Watt, who was stationed there in the Navy. They got married, and when he was sent back to the States in 1962 she accompanied him. After her divorce in 1965 she took an extended vacation in Mexico, as consort to two different men. In 1966 she followed another man to Portugal, where they were to have set off on a long sailing voyage in his yacht. Instead, she broke off that relationship and did travel through Spain and Italy, accompanied by a woman friend, ending up in Greece, where she became involved with a high-ranking military officer with whom she had a passionate affair. In early 1968, after a major alter-cation with that lover, she returned to Long Beach, California, stay-ing there until she finished her college degree in 1970. In 1971 she accompanied her then-lover Ed Brown to Finland; they broke up after about a year. She remained in Finland for another five years, partly to stay with her second husband, a native Finn. She returned to the U.S. in 1977, about two years after that marriage ended.

Juliet never lived in either Italy or Spain. Furthermore, while she did pursue some studies in art and worked both formally and infor-mally as an ESL teacher, her primary activities in foreign countries were being a wife or lover. Only in Finland did she have an indepen-dent life and a real career, as a radio journalist. (See Chapters 5 through 8.)

Inability to find sex in San Francisco
Public story: When I returned to San Francisco from Finland in 1977, before I got into the porn business, I couldn't get laid no matter how hard I tried. I hadn't realized how much of the male population there was gay. It was next to impossible for a straight woman to get laid.
Truth: Juliet enjoyed plenty of casual sex in San Francisco in 1977 and early 1978. What she couldn't find was a relationship that was sexually satisfying or long-term—which she was still looking for at that point. (See Chapter 9.)

Relationships with family
Public story: My family is very conservative; I have been a great embarrassment to them, although they secretly envy me.
Truth: Juliet's family was no more conservative than the average mainstream American family, and they were mixed in their reactions to her sex work and lifestyle. While her father, and her sister Chris and Chris's husband Bob were probably the most uncomfortable with Juliet's porn career, they did not go out of their way to castigate her over it; they simply preferred not to discuss it. And even during the height of Juliet's career, Chris and Bob allowed their daughter Monica, then aged eight through fourteen, to visit her, trusting that Juliet would shield Monica from any situations or people who might be inappropriate for a young girl to encounter.

Juliet's cousin Pam was supportive of her career, watching all of her movies and being present at a rehearsal of one of the scenes in *Ageless Desire*, Juliet's video about sex for straight couples over age fifty. Pam's brother Andrew was also supportive; he not only watched all of Juliet's movies, he bought them.

As for her parents, Juliet's father did indeed feel shamed by her career choice, but not because he was conservative, only because he found it embarrassing. Juliet believed that her mother secretly envied her, because she herself had once ambitions of being an actress, but there is no real evidence for this belief. No one else remembers Juliet's mother being an aspiring actress, and in her older age Juliet's mother was suffering from so many mental health and substance abuse issues that it was difficult to determine how she felt about anything. (See Chapters 13, 19 and 20.)

Relationships with men
Public story: I have always sought out men who were not intimidated by my assertiveness, intelligence and lust, and who were
willing to pleasure me the way I liked—and I didn't hesitate to show
them how. We shared adventures and great sex.
Truth: Although Juliet certainly did have and enjoy a lot of casual
sex, she also longed for, but never found, a long-term committed
relationship. The three relationships that came closest to this ideal
were: her marriage to Bob Watt, which lasted from 1961 until 1964;
her affair with the Greek military commander, Nikolas, which lasted
from October 1966 until March 1968; and her relationship with Don
Crane, whom she met in 1996; he died in 1997. Yet she was continually pursuing "true love," and continually being heartbroken.

The man she felt most deeply about was Nikolas, and her emotional dependence on him prevented her from being at all assertive
about her sexual needs. "I can't picture *ever* telling Nikolas how to be
a better lover," she wrote in her journal. Most unfortunate, because
Nikolas was hurried and clumsy. He rarely lasted more than ten
seconds, and Juliet surmised that he "probably doesn't even know
the clit exists." She certainly never told him. (See Chapters 3, 8, 12
and 14.)

Managing a bed and breakfast
Public story: I managed a bed and breakfast in the Sierra foothills.
Truth: Juliet worked as a housekeeper at Blair House, in Placerville,
California, from June 1985 until October 1987, in return for her room,
partial board, and a small hourly wage. Occasionally she served as
hostess and cook when the owners took vacations. She never owned
or managed a bed and breakfast. (See Chapters 17 and 19.)

Overcoming health problems using alternative treatments
Public story: I have several incurable diseases but I keep them under
control using alternative treatments. When I had a hysterectomy in
1989, the medical staff were amazed that I suffered no post-operative
pain. "Are you sure you're not feeling any pain?" they kept asking
me.

<u>Truth:</u> Juliet suffered from arthritis, Crohn's disease (an inflammatory bowel disorder), bipolar syndrome and Attention Deficit Hyperactivity Disorder. She was in physical and emotional pain for much of her life, beginning in childhood. Although alternative treatments and dietary restrictions did help her a great deal, they did not keep the problems at bay, and she also turned to allopathic medicine for help: pain killers, anti-inflammatory and anti-depressant medications. She had taken morphine on the night she died.

And in fact she suffered debilitating pain after her hysterectomy: "The next few hours in the recovery room were dreadful; I was in a lot of pain; locked jaw and weak muscles and trembling violently. I cried out in pain and the nurses massaged my neck and put warm towels on it. And my parched lips and mouth could only be moistened with a damp cloth. I endured this agony it seemed forever... Dr. M, bless his heart, came to recovery several times to comfort me, apologizing for my trauma, that it was an unexpected aftereffect." (See Chapters 19 to 21, and 24.)

All Is Truth
(excerpt)

Meditating among liars and retreating sternly into
myself, I see that there are really no liars or lies after
all,
And that nothing fails its perfect return, and that what
are called lies are perfect returns.
And that each thing exactly represents itself and what
has preceded it,
And that the truth includes all, and is compact just as
much as space is compact,
And that there is no flaw or vacuum in the amount of the
truth—but that all is truth without exception;
And henceforth I will go celebrate any thing I see or am.
And sing and laugh and deny nothing.

— Walt Whitman, another great yarn spinner

David, an intuitive referred to Juliet by her acupuncturist, did this reading at her request. She transcribed it from an audio tape.

I must tell you that you are a very rebellious woman. You like to do everything by yourself and you delay a lot asking for help. You try to do it alone. The same thing happens when you are asked for something. You become rebellious against yourself and you try to do it alone or not do it at all. Before doing it, think! Do I need some advice? Don't do it immediately.

You try to listen to yourself alone and to justify what you are doing. And sometimes it isn't good what you are doing. You need collaboration. Think "I need to consult with my friend or people who could give me clearer ideas." Write down what they say to you. Then think of what you have to do. You have a lot of intellectual capacity, to be able to choose correctly, but you prolong more than is necessary.

The first thing you say when someone proposes something new to you is no, and then you become too easy and you give too much. First ... NO ... and after some time, too much YES. You have never been able to find the medium point. You rush in saying no, and afterwards you rush and say yes.

You need to reflect more and use your intellect more. Don't rush to answer. Think and discuss that within you. Is that convenient? Can I do it? Is it better not to do it? At another time? And following this give your answer, if you have it. If you do not, tell the other person, "Listen, I cannot answer you right now."

What I am telling you, you know perfectly. It is a secret of yours. It is the factor that weakens your whole person because it makes you impulsive without being so. You like to reflect. That gives you tranquility. You don't like immediate answers. You also like it when someone asks for your help. You are content. You feel solid.

You must do the same for yourself. You lack a lot of self-respect with this impulsive attitude. Afterwards even if you have done something well, you are left in a state of uncertainty.

You have always seen your life in parts: this of the body and this of the soul. You make a separation between pleasure, pain, sex, spirit. You forget that you are one person, a unity. All of you is there in each one of those things. When you are into something, you are fully into it. Or if you are interested in studying something or when you are turned on, you are fully there, not just sex, not just heart, but your whole person.

You know very well how to work. But you don't know how to rest. You rest when you feel tired, but you don't rest *before* you get tired. Then you mistreat the body. Distribute your rest throughout the day. You need several activities and several rest periods throughout the day: brief, 5-10 minutes; sit or lie down and forget about everything. And afterwards you will be fresh and content and full of enthusiasm.

Since you are very attentive in all your activities, you don't need to meditate. You are meditating all day long. In those ordinary moments God lives. When you are active and doing all your things, God is with you. You start to meditate and God leaves. You've meditated enough. You tire the brain. You have already meditated enough for several people. You don't need more!

You very much like music. During the time you would be meditating, listen to music instead, then God returns. But when you are meditating, God asks, "What are you doing?"

You need more friendship than physical relations. You could have been a nun—a good, not a repressed, nun. And you would have been praying, truly a nun, active with a lot of friends, but not physical relations. Physical relationships create disorder and make you waste your time.

You understand yourself better with men. You can only relate to women who like to reflect, more intellectual women.

Your body is well, but it is a very delicate machine. It might last for a very long time. If you rest, you can keep it in perfect shape for many, many years. It is like a delicate crystal. Better a delicate crystal than an ordinary crystal. However, it needs more care. It breaks easily.

Juliet's question: *"I am at a crossroads professionally; however, I don't separate my profession from the rest of my life. It is what I do and what I am. Should I put more of my attentions to my continued studies of holistic health and its application, or pursue writing and lecturing about spiritual sexuality?"*

The second is more indicated. Do not confine it only to sexual spirituality. Do it as you think about it, but extend the idea. Free it a little bit from the aspects of sexuality. Lead it more to the aspect of sensibilities: how can one perceive more of nature? how does humanity relate with nature? not how the penis relates to the vagina, not how men relate with women or women with men, or men with men or women with women. But how both sexes can relate with nature, with water, with food, with children; how can one play better? not enclosed in the sexual sphere. Holistic health should occupy only 20% of your activities, a maximum of three days a week.

You are a simple woman, in essence. You are not interested in having a lot of money. You like to have responsibility, but with clarity. And you like to be useful. So work in measure that you can continue to have a simple life. Because very easily you fall into the trap of all the responsibility and so you find yourself doing things you don't want to and you can't stop. This has happened to you many times. You begin one way and you end up in another street and you are forced to knock on the doors of that other street. And you continue; you don't stop. You never finish things. You want to finish them but you only continue them.

And you need to be cultivating yourself all the time. Be more in contact with spirit. You need to read more and pay more attention and reflect on what you are reading. You know very well that you have curiosity, but you are ignorant of many things. And you like to know everything. You like to be well prepared. You are a very good student, and you can always be so. And you need time to study. Ask yourself: "What things at this time am I curious about; do I want to know?" and begin to study them.

Appendix F: Juliet on Sex and the Porn Business

There is no doubt that Juliet loved sex, and sensuality. She loved being in her body; she found her greatest joy there—not only through sex but through other sensuous pleasures: good food, good music, being in the outdoors and experiencing all the sights, sounds, and smells of nature. But her attitude toward sex evolved as she went through various stages of her life, and she often reflected on these shifts in her personal journals.

On first discovering sex as a young adult, Juliet was swept off her feet. It seemed to be, not only a source of extreme pleasure, but also a physical pain-killer, and hence a liberating experience, given her childhood illnesses:

> After the confinement of my childhood I wanted freedom. I went to the other extreme as a young adult. Sex gave me the experience of pleasure, that I had a body that could experience something other than pain. It was a drug of liberation. Nothing ever gave me the high that sex did. I enjoyed it with unabashed joy and abandon, and it was for *me*, for *my* pleasure, not to please "him." Sex was the miracle drug.

Embarking on her career as a porn actress was yet another level of awakening. Now sex was not only a source of pleasure and pain relief, it was a path to self-fulfillment, adventure, glamour, and fame. Sex helped her discover her amazing ability to bring joy to others as well as to herself, to entertain and inform, to support other women in liberating themselves sexually.

> I never thought I'd be a porn star at the age of forty. Nobody could have been more surprised than I to have embraced that dark deep erotic world, at middle age when [most] women are sending their kids off to college and planning with their husbands where to retire in fifteen years. I'm still amazed that I took that road to healing, an invisible hand leading me, direct- ing me thru sex to wholeness and years of unbeliev- able adventures, anguish, power, fame, charisma, wisdom and finally burn-out.

After withdrawing from the business in 1985, though, Juliet developed some distance from her porn career and started reflecting on the negative aspects of it as well—not just the sometimes unsavory people and situations she encountered, but the ways in which porn had fed her ego and her desire to be in control, to have power, especially over straight men. She was also beginning to tire of the intensity and the limitations of making sex, rebellion and glamor the major focus of her life.

> The X biz was a crafty, passionate beast that seduced me with sex, power, fame and riches. It fed on my desire to be loved and admired, and gave me a chance to indulge in exhibitionism and glamor. It almost stole my spirit, but I broke free. With this new insight it'll be fascinating to see how I write my memoirs. I was so 'pro-porno', an eloquent and convincing advocate. What will I say now? I'm certainly having to re-make my map!
>
> I'm bored with it, the flirting, the tease... The truth is I'm tired of sexuality; there are other things in life. I'm tired of being an outlaw, a trail blazer, alienated from society; I don't ever want to be a celebrity again.

She realized that in some ways her porn work was actually negative, anti-male; rather than being loving and giving toward men, she was actually hostile—manipulating and controlling them. It was hard to respect people who were such easy prey.

> I thought I loved men, but actually a deep part of me hated them. Hence my selection in mates and profession—a need to control and get even with men.
>
> Men are so easy, so predictable. Just wiggle, twitch, strike a provocative pose, scratch, adjust a bra strap, lean over—almost anything, consciously or not—men get turned on.

Finally, as she grew older, Juliet achieved a more balanced outlook, learning to appreciate the positive aspects of her work while letting the negative ones go. She was burned out on the hype, the glamour, but could embrace true pleasure, helping others—both men and women—realize their sexual potential, without the need to be a star.

> It is clear that sex plays a very small part in my life. Sexual energy is important, but genital play is not, or at least, release thru genital play is not all that exciting... the touching, kissing and licking etc. all over is the real turn-on for me.

Her new attitude was most apparent in her Tender Loving Touch technique: "a slow, gentle, nurturing touch from head to toe, letting you relax into an altered state...a delightful, sensual/sexual experience." This of course, is basically a feminine approach to sex; the typical male approach tends to be primarily genitally focused, a result of anatomy (including the brain) that has been reinforced by societal expectations. In a way, Juliet was still using sex as a tool for being in control, imposing her own needs and perceptions on her clients. While her clients certainly enjoyed and benefited from her work, it was, as she stated in 1979, her own needs that she was primarily focused on: "I am not selfless; quite the contrary. I give because it pleases me, and it incidentally gives pleasure to others."

Juliet on Oral Sex Techniques

Juliet would love to be remembered as a woman who loved cock, and especially as one who loved to suck cock. Anyone who ever experienced her technique or watched her engage in it can readily attest to her skills.

Many of her clients pronounced her the best oral sex technician they had ever known. "You never knew what she was going to do next," one explained. "Getting a blow job from Juliet was a continual delightful surprise."

While Juliet herself proclaimed that it was not so much technique as style, and that everyone has to develop his or her own unique style—for any sexual activity—she did have a few pointers:

> Use a variety of techniques: licking, sucking, running your tongue up and down the cock, or circling around it. Take it deep in your mouth or throat, or flick your tongue lightly over the head or the shaft. It's also important to make a lot of slobbering noises while you're sucking; bring in sound as well as touch. Visual stimulation can add another dimension, too: a lot of men like it if you look up at their face while you're sucking their cock.

Juliet also claimed that anyone can increase their oral capacity by doing stretching exercises. This has limited efficacy, however; what Juliet did not realize was that she was gifted with the physical capacity for her favorite sexual activity, having a relatively large mouth and small teeth—hereditary traits, not acquired ones.

Ironically, Juliet did not like receiving oral sex, only giving it. Being the recipient put her in a passive position—something she was never really comfortable with. Sex to Juliet always meant being in control, "on top" both literally and figuratively.

BIBLIOGRAPHY

"Bunny Yeager, Pinup Portraitist, Dies at 85." *New York Times*, 26 May 2014: A14.

Carr, Juliet and Kenneth Ray Stubbs, ed. "The Porn Star." *Women of the Light: The New Sacred Prostitute.* Larkspur, Calif.: Secret Garden. 1996. Juliet's description of her life and work. Excellent source for how she saw herself and her work. Beware of the factual errors she promulgated about herself.

Carr, Juliet. *Ageless Desire.* Afterglow Productions, 1999. Juliet's educational video about sex for heterosexual couples over the age of fifty.

Crane, Don. "What Ever Happened to Aunt Peg?" *Spectator Magazine.* Emeryville, Calif. 1996 (exact issue unknown). Don's starry-eyed write-up of his interview with Juliet.

Downer, Lesley. *Women of the Pleasure Quarters: The Secret History of the Geishas,* New York, New York: Broadway Books. 2001. An excellent overview of the history of both the geisha and prostitution in Japan, up to the beginning of the 21st century. (Note: The Geisha are not, and never have been, prostitutes; they are, rather, high-class party hostesses, dancers, musicians, and entertainers.)

Federal Bureau of Labor Statistics, http://www.bls.gov/bls/inflation.htm. For calculating inflation.

Gordon, Howie (Richard Pacheco). *Hindsight: True Love and Mischief in the Golden Age of Porn.* Albany, Georgia: Bear Manor Media, 2013. Some good material in here, including many informative photographs, along with anecdotes about, and descriptions of, some of the major players. But the book is far too long, meandering, and disorganized. Lacks an index—unforgivable in a non-fiction book with so much material. Only two passing references to Juliet, on pp. 200-201 and 392.

Guy, David. *The Red Thread of Passion: Spirituality and the Paradox of Sex.* Boston, Mass.: Shambhala Publications, 1999. Probably the most comprehensive and thoughtful interview ever done with Juliet, although—as usual for her—not completely factual. Very good Paul Johnson photograph of Juliet.

Harron, Mary. *The Notorious Bettie Page.* HBO. 2006. Fictionalized drama of the famous model's life. Well done, heart-wrenching.

Hill, Graham. *Sex Is No Act* and *Sex Is No Act 2.* Graham Hill Productions, 2009. Excellent compilations of sex scenes from Juliet's movies, with appropriately selected popular-song accompaniment. Unfortunately, there is no identification of movies, scenes or actors, within the video itself, only lists of the movies in the liner notes.

Hill, Graham. http://www.cinemaretro.com/index.php?/archives/ 3440-SEX-IS-NO-ACT-A-TRIBUTE-TO-JULIET-ANDERSON- AKA-AUNT-PEG.html. Good critique of Juliet's work, along with some photographs.

Internet Movie Database. http://www.imdb.com

Johnson, Paul. *Juliet and the Bears.* paulsfantasy.com, 2011. (DVD) Mostly still photographs Paul took of Juliet. The title refers to a shoot he did with her and some identical twin brothers, but there is much more on the DVD, albeit difficult to find because of the poor organization. Included are Paul's reminiscences about Juliet and interviews with Nina Hartley and Richard Pacheco, but these are hidden "behind" the still photos, not presented as a separate cut.

Johnson, Paul. http://paulsfantasy.com/Pauls_fantasy_site/ Juliet_memorial.html. Paul's poignant and affectionate remin- iscent photographs of Juliet, along with some early 1960s photos of Juliet from Miami.

Longstreet, Stephen, ed. *Nell Kimball: Her Life as an American Madam.* New York, New York. Macmillan. 1970. Copyright held by Godoff-Longstreet Company. Excellent and entertaining source of inside information on the sex business in general, as well as the social history of prostitution and city politics in 19th-century America. Longstreet's granddaughter believes the book to be entirely fictional. More likely, it is Longstreet's enhancement of incomplete autobiographical material from a 19th-century sex worker, or possibly a composite of several. Irreverent commentary on sex workers, politicians, and other social groups involved with the sex business, and an entertaining and insightful story as well.

McNeil, Legs and Jennifer Osborne. *The Other Hollywood: The Uncensored Oral History of the Porn Film Industry*. New York, New York: Harper Collins, 2005. Good source for overall history of the porn business, but incomplete and biased, consisting entirely of transcribed audio interviews of various participants. No independent research or follow-up, although at least it has an index.

Nelson, Jill C. *Golden Goddesses: Twenty-Five Legendary Women of Classic Erotic Cinema, 1968-1985*. Fort Worth, Texas: BearManor Media. 2012. Very little of value about Juliet, as she was far gone into dementia at the time of the interviews. No independent research or follow-up of any kind, although a small amount of commentary on some of Juliet's films.

Queen, Carol. "The Royal Treatment." *Spectator Magazine*. Emeryville, Calif. April 1997. One-sided report on the 1997 International Conference on Prostitution in Van Nuys, California. Gives all the credit to the sex workers; bashes the academics.

Schlosser, Eric. "The Bill Gates of Porn: How Reuben Sturman Shaped the Sex Industry." *U.S. News and World Report*, 10 February 1997: 51-52.

Spring, Justin. *Secret Historian: The Life and Times of Samuel Steward, Professor, Tattoo Artist, and Sexual Renegade*. New York, New York: Farrar, Straus and Giroux. 2010. Very well-researched biography of someone with a different type of connection to the sex business, from Juliet's.

Steinberg, David. "ICOP '97 and the Movement for Prostitutes' Rights." *Comes Naturally* 56 (Mar 1997). Good background and lead-up story for the 1997 International Conference on Prostitution.

Steinberg, David. "The 1997 International Conference on Prostitution: A Milestone in the Growing Movement for Prostitutes' Rights." *Comes Naturally* 57 (Apr 1997). Very professional, although incomplete, report on the 1997 International Conference on Prostitution.

Vining, Elizabeth Gray. *Windows for the Crown Prince*. Philadelphia, Pennsylvania: J.B. Lippincott & Co.1952. Mrs. Vining's recounting of her experiences tutoring Prince Akihito (now Emperor Akihito) of Japan just after World War II. Some good information about Japanese culture, albeit about ten years prior to the time when Juliet was there.

Woodhouse, C.M., *Modern Greece: A Short History*. 3rd ed. London, UK. Faber and Faber, 1984.

Wikipedia. www.wikipedia.org

INDEX

Page numbers in italics indicate photographs.

Lightning Source UK Ltd.
Milton Keynes UK
UKHW051050120522
402841UK00016B/1507